Advance Praise

for

*DESPERADOS*

"A good case study of an interesting period in the ever-changing West Coast musical landscape. This book brought back wonderful and sometimes sad memories of the last thirty years, as well as recollections of some dearly missed compatriots."
>—**Chris Hillman**, pioneer of country rock music and member of the Byrds, the Flying Burrito Brothers, and the Desert Rose Band

"A skillfully woven story of California's country rock and the people who played a part in the beginning. I learned a lot from reading John's book."
>—**Rusty Young**, of Poco

# Desperados

# Desperados

## The Roots of Country Rock

*John Einarson*

Cooper Square Press

Published by Cooper Square Press
An Imprint of the Rowman & Littlefield Publishing Group
150 Fifth Avenue, Suite 911
New York, New York 10011

**Library of Congress Cataloging-in-Publication Data**

Einarson, John, 1952–
   Desperados : the roots of country rock / John Einarson.—1st Cooper Square
Press ed.
      p. cm.
   Includes discography.
   ISBN 0-8154-1065-4 (pbk.)
      1. Country rock music—History and criticism. I. Title.
   ML3524 .E37 2000
   781.642—dc21

                                                                          00-031752

Printed in the United States of America

∞™ The paper used in this publication meets the minimum requirements
of American National Standard for Information Sciences—Permanence of
Paper for Printed Library Materials, ANSI/NISO Z39.48-1992.
Manufactured in the United States of America.

*Respectfully dedicated to Buck Owens and his Buckaroos—Don Rich, Tom Brumley, Doyle Holly, and Willie Cantu—for inspiring the growth of country rock with their groundbreaking recordings.*

# Contents

# 1

# Sing Me Back Home

*It's a beautiful idiom that's been overlooked so much, and so many people have the wrong idea of it. . . . How little they know.*

—Gram Parsons

Musicians loathe pigeonholes. They go out of their way to avoid categorizing their muse. Journalists, critics, and record companies, on the other hand, love to dream up definitions and labels to lump together music that, while sharing similar attributes, is as diverse as the individuals who create it. Rock & roll itself is less a narrow genre than a melting pot of country & western, gospel, rhythm & blues, folk, jazz, and more. The results are often unique: a product of happenstance and what the cook has brought to the mix. If it tastes good, others attempt their own variation, and before long someone else comes along to identify the spices, count the number of stirs, apply a label, and market it.

Take country rock. In the late sixties, a small faction of young, long-haired musicians sought to inject some country music into their rock & roll. They worked in southern California, but their roots represented a broad spectrum of the North American experience. From a variety of personal perspectives and motivations, these musicians either played country with a rock & roll attitude, or added a country feel to rock, or folk, or bluegrass. There was no formula. They were concocting an entirely new brew.

"I'm not comfortable with the category of country rock," offers Michael Nesmith, one of the genre's early purveyors, whose trilogy of albums in the early seventies with the First National Band are considered fine

1

examples of country-influenced rock. Nesmith's inability (and the inability of others) to come to terms with the label is symptomatic of the difficulty of defining the entire country rock genre itself. "Categorizing music is pretty much a waste of time. There's nothing wrong with it, but it's hard to do. There is an arbitrariness to it. I understand why an ethnomusicologist would say, 'Well, here's a striation. Here's something that's different and distinguishes itself from other types of music, so it should have a name.' I don't go around saying that is this music, and this is that music. It's all just music to me." For Nesmith, the music he created became country rock not by some predetermined plan or grand scheme, but merely the result of drawing on his Texas roots. "I was bringing together those early influences, but not consciously. I didn't wake up one morning and think, 'You know, I've got all these influences, I think I'll bring them all together.' I was like everybody else: those influences were utterly invisible to me. The idea that *this* was country rock—I didn't know from country rock. I wasn't trying to do country rock, I was just trying to do music. I didn't set to stake out any territory, or say 'I'm going to make rock & roll meet country.'"

Existing largely on the fringe of the contemporary music mainstream, playing a brand of music deemed commercially risky by record companies, these same musicians found common interests and pockets of support to sustain their vision of uniting the disparate music idioms of country and rock. Like those notorious outlaws whose oasis was the Hole-In-the-Wall Hideout, these renegade rockers found a creative wellspring in enclaves like the Troubadour and Palomino clubs, where kindred spirits offered an eager if limited audience. Here, bonds were formed and new associations born. From this milieu would emerge a brand of music later termed "country rock," whose identity derives from a variety of country music influences also present in the work of several seminal artists, including the Byrds, Flying Burrito Brothers, Poco, and the Eagles.

Though the name sounds straightforward enough, country rock is, in many respects, a branch of the rock & roll tree that may be one of the most difficult to accurately and inclusively define. Is it country with a rock beat, rock with a country twang, or something else entirely? What comprises country rock is largely in the ear of the beholder, and few of the genre's best-known purveyors agree on its components. Like Justice Potter Stewart who, when asked to define pornography, responded, "I can't, but I know it when I see it," the term "country rock" has come to embrace a varied group of artists whose only common link may be the fact that they all saw the positive qualities in traditional country music and, at some point, crossed each other's paths. For several years country rock operated on the periphery, finding wider acceptance and commercial success in the early seventies with a group of musicians who had served their apprenticeship among the finest early exponents of the genre: the Eagles. Their pedigree was impeccable, as were the sources of their inspiration: Hearts And Flowers, Dillard & Clark, the Flying Burrito Brothers, Gram Parsons, Poco, Rick Nelson's Stone Canyon Band, Longbranch Pennywhistle, and Shiloh, a veritable "Who's Who" of country rock innovators. "We'd watched bands like Poco and the Burrito Brothers lose their initial momentum," notes founding Eagle Glenn Frey on the formation of the group in the early seventies. "We were determined not to make the same mistakes." The four members of the Eagles learned their lessons well and brought a collective experience to bear on the sound of the group, a radio-friendly soft rock with a dash of country flavoring. Today, you are just as likely to hear Eagles music on country radio as on a rock station. What radio has recently dubbed "new country," with artists like Marty Stuart, Travis Tritt, Restless Heart, Clint Black, Diamond Rio, Little Texas, and Confederate Railroad, is the direct descendant of what the pioneering country rock musicians first attempted some three decades earlier.

One need not look very hard to find country influences in the very roots of rock & roll. From the twang of Scotty Moore's guitar on Elvis Presley's earliest Sun recordings, like "That's Alright Mama" and "Blue Moon Of Kentucky," to Carl Perkins' rockabilly "Blue Suede Shoes," country influences permeated rock & roll from its inception. Add to that Jerry Lee Lewis pumping out "Crazy Arms," the Everly Brothers' sweet Kentucky bluegrass harmonies, and Ricky Nelson's recordings backed by James Burton's "chicken pickin' guitar," and you hear the strong country-swing present in their rockabilly. What these and other artists did, consciously or otherwise, was to take the country & western music they grew up with and loved, and give it a bit more of a kick in the ass. "If you really want to go back to the roots of country rock," suggests Chris Hillman (a founding father of sixties' southern California country rock with the Byrds and Flying Burrito Brothers), "it was Elvis. I'm talking Elvis when he was at Sun Records, when he was good, that initial stuff he did for Sam Phillips. That was untouchable. That was country rock, and, of course, rockabilly, it's all the same thing. After Elvis went in the army, forget it, it was over." Adds Nesmith, "I'm not sure rock & roll is that much different than country music. When you look into the origins of these things, you go back to Sun Records and what was going on down in the South. There was a type of amalgamation of sounds and music that was really not self-conscious at all. Nobody was doing anything except playing songs. It only later dawned on everybody that you could call that country rock. But I think when you start doing that, you could sort of keep going back farther and farther to where rock & roll first met country music." That meeting may have taken place in the music of country & western's most revered tunesmith, Hank Williams. Though Hank once declared drums suitable only for parades and not country music, he nonetheless brought a driving rockabilly rhythm to some of his best-known songs, like "Jambalaya" and "Move It On Over," which sounds remarkably like the inspiration for Bill Haley's "Rock Around The Clock." Hank is reputed to have learned his craft as a teenager from an old black blues player in Montgomery, Alabama, named Tee-Tot Payne, and that bluesy rhythm stayed with him throughout his brilliant, albeit brief, career.

"To my mind, the most classically 'country rock' type of music, or what I would refer to as country rock," offers former Burrito Brother Rick Roberts, "is also referred to as rockabilly, stuff like 'Six Days On The Road,' which had that driving beat to it. People who were considered to be at the cutting edge of rock & roll were basically country guys—Elvis, the Everly Brothers, Conway Twitty, Jerry Lee Lewis—some of those guys who made the shift over. Nowadays that stuff sounds pure country." Buddy Woodward, founder of alternative country rockers the Ghost Rockets, answers the question: "What is rock & roll? It's western swing, country music, and the blues. Rockabilly is bluegrass with drums. Take Bill Monroe, take away the banjo and fiddle, put in a big old fat-body Gretsch guitar and a drum kit, and it's rockabilly. It's Carl Perkins and early Elvis Presley."

Divisions between country, pop, and rockabilly were far less significant early on. "The distinction between country music and pop music, especially in Texas, had not been born," Nesmith, who grew up on a steady diet of what would later be categorized as country & western music, remembers. "There was a Top Forty radio show that I used to listen to on Saturday mornings, back in 1952–53, and it was very broadbased and general, not a country music program. It was just the music we listened to. But the guy who would have the Number One record would be Hank Williams, and so forth. So I was influenced by country music, but it wasn't called country music, it was just music."

Even the term "country & western" is an arbitrary phrase dreamed up by the urban-based editors of *Billboard* magazine (the music industry equivalent of *Variety*) in the late forties to lump together two hitherto disparate musical styles: country music (derived from the same Appalachian mountain music that gave birth to bluegrass through the likes of Bill Monroe, filtered through Roy Acuff), and western music (the lonesome wail of the cowboy laments, and ballads of the Old West popularized in postwar America by movie matinee idol Gene Autry and Roy Rogers' Sons of the Pioneers). It seemed to these northern city dwellers a logical union and an opportunity to create a separate country & western chart. The term is anachronistic today, given that western music (the cowboy element at least) has become almost a lost art form, save for the valiant efforts of artists like Michael Murphey and Ian Tyson, two artists who remain dedicated to preserving both the old songs and the tradition of storytelling in newer ballads. The distinctions were obvious to most who had heard both styles. Presley's influences were country, not western.

Country & western music of the forties and fifties has often been termed "white man's blues" for its heartache and lovelorn themes. "It's white man's music, as opposed to the black man's music," claims Chris Hillman. "It's the workingman's song, workingman's music: white man's blues. I mean, we are saying the same thing as a black man. 'My old lady left me,' or 'this happened or that happened,' because we have our way of expressing things and they have theirs."

Country legend Waylon Jennings agrees, "Country music is the same thing as blues, the same man singing the same song about the good and bad times, the woman he's got, the woman he wants." Nesmith sees the similarity in the musical arrangements that country music and blues share. "The blues scale that you hear, from Stevie Ray Vaughn to B. B. King playing on the guitar, really only works against three chords—the three-chord progression. And country music really only works against that same three-chord progression. That's where people are making that connection. Country music, which is played by white men, uses these three chords and they're the same three chords used by blues players, who are mostly black men. So when they say it's white man's blues, it's more a *musical* definition. But there's also the high lonesome quality about it, and the 'she done me wrong' aspect. If you look at how country rock comes together, it really comes together in the blues. It's not so much that rock & roll and country come together, it's more that country and blues are joined at the hip."

But somewhere along the way that country element got left behind as rockabilly evolved into rock & roll music. Migrating across the Mason-Dixon Line from the deep South, where rockabilly originated, and moving into urban areas like New York to mix with black rhythm & blues, doo wop, and hit-parade pop, country music and rock & roll parted company to go their separate ways. Rockabilly lost its innocence as it moved uptown to New York and Los Angeles to become rock & roll, while country (or country & western) music remained the dominion of the rural South. A few performers attempted to bring the two together again with some success, including Ray Charles' series of country-flavored albums, as well as crossover artists like Charlie Rich and Conway Twitty. The American folk music revival of the early sixties drew on the Appalachian acoustic ballad form, country blues, and bluegrass styles, with folk artists regularly delving into traditional country music for their repertoire. Even the folk world's favorite son, Bob Dylan, was not averse to introducing country stylings into his early folk ballads.

At the height of the folk boom in the early sixties, Nesmith came out to Los Angeles from Texas to play his country-influenced folk music in the coffeehouses. "There wasn't much of a distinction between folk music and country music," he notes. "You could get away with doing a lot of different stuff in folk music. When Jim McGuinn started out before the Byrds, he used to come into the Troubadour and bring his twelve-string in, sit down, and play Beatles songs. Then he would switch over and play some old hillbilly song. I never got the feeling there was any attempt on his part to join musical forms, I just thought he was playing music, good music, the music he wanted to play. Which he did well. So when he did *Sweetheart Of The Rodeo* years later, I never thought, 'Oh my gosh, this is groundbreaking.' That was just McGuinn playing his guitar, doing the same thing he's always done." The Lovin' Spoonful's Jerry Yester opines, "Anybody who came from the folk tradition was influenced by country music just by its own nature, because country music came out of folk music."

Ex-Burrito and founding Eagle Bernie Leadon suggests the lineage of country rock can be traced directly from the folk boom. "The folk phenomenon, or folk scare as some people call it, really started in the late fifties after people like Pete Seeger and the Weavers (who had been black-listed) were starting to regain the right to perform live, record, and be on television. There were magazines like *Sing Out*, then came the Kingston Trio, Dylan, and Peter, Paul, and Mary, and that whole wagon. Out of that came many of the late sixties, early seventies folk rockers, and, later, country rockers came directly out of *that* folk movement: the Byrds, Lovin' Spoonful, Buffalo Springfield. The folk boom introduced folk and bluegrass instruments to the middle and upper-middle classes, the college crowd who started playing banjos and acoustic guitars. But some of them realized that the guys in the folk groups were being pretty pedestrian in their technique, and that if you really wanted to see how a banjo could be played you had to check out Earl Scruggs or one of those guys." As a result, the folk music movement rekindled an awareness of traditional country music as a pure and honest form. Young players began to look beyond the Kingston Trio's folk pop to search out the original sources of folk, bluegrass, and country, and in so doing revived interest in American roots music. Notes Herb Pedersen, a member of the Dillards, and later with Chris Hillman in the Desert Rose Band: "There was a real fervent, almost religious thing among the bluegrass community out here in California, guys out here who, like us, weren't around it. Chris Hillman told me he once took a train ride from San Diego all the way up to Berkeley to take a mandolin lesson from a guy named Scott Hambly, who was an early influence. Anything you could find to help you get better, you did. You didn't grow up on your dad's knee playing the banjo, so you had to go where it was. Even when Chris went with the Byrds, he still had a love for traditional music. When I would see him from time to time, he'd still be talking about mandolins and that kind of music. That kind of thing doesn't leave you. It's a part of you."

When the British Invasion hit North American shores like a hurricane in early 1964, several of its leading proponents brought with them an appreciation for rockabilly and country music, notably the Beatles. They covered Carl Perkins' "Everybody's Trying To Be My Baby," "Honey Don't," and "Matchbox," as well as Buck Owens' "Act Naturally," and country-influenced original material like "What Goes On." There were also the Rolling Stones, who took Hank Snow's "I'm Movin' On" into rhythm & blues territory. In so doing, these musicians were bringing country influences to a whole new generation turned off by Nashville's slick country pop.

At the same time, a raucous rumbling from further west was stirring up younger players' interest in the direction of country music. Out in Bakersfield, California, a couple of hours' drive northeast of Los Angeles, a group of country artists were giving their raw, no-holds-barred brand of honky-tonk the electric edge it needed. These were country music's original outlaws, long before Waylon and Willie. Buck Owens, Wynn Stewart, and Merle Haggard were redefining country music, filtered through Fender Telecaster electric guitars and Mexicali rhythms, a vibrant, exciting music that served as a precursor for everyone, from the Flying Burrito Brothers and Poco to Dwight Yoakam. Bakersfield offered a bridge between country music and the Beatles. Owens even incurred the wrath of the country music establishment by openly admitting his fondness for the Beatles, and the "Fab Four" showed their admiration for Buck's recordings when they covered them. "I thought having the Beatles do 'Act Naturally' was the ultimate," enthuses Owens. "I had all the Beatles albums since they first came along. Don Rich and I thought they were wonderful. Could you really like Bill Monroe and the Beatles? 'Course you could."

By the mid-sixties, young players listening to both Buck and the Beatles were beginning to find one another in tiny, out-of-the-way clubs in southern California, and beginning to integrate the two forms. The growing turn back to country music was also a reaction to, and a rejection of, the overblown excesses of the psychedelic, acid rock music scene of 1967's much vaunted "Summer of Love." A change was first signaled by Bob Dylan, whose acoustic-based, stripped-down folk-country album, *John Wesley Harding* (recorded in late 1967 and released early the next year), was a clarion call to others for a return to a simpler, more honest, and wholesome music. There was no meaning, no message, in the aimless guitar meanderings or free-association lyrics of the drug-drenched psychedelic groups. At the height of the Summer of Love, the International Submarine Band, led by Gram Parsons, dared to play straight country (Buck Owens and Merle Haggard) to startled patrons in Sunset Strip clubs alongside acid rock groups like Love and the Doors. For players like Texas-born Al Perkins, the California music scene—both San Francisco's Haight-Ashbury freak scene and L.A.'s hip Sunset Strip—had become too far out to hold any appeal. "When the blues and acid rock and hippie thing became a part of our society, the people who had grown their hair long but who still loved country music wanted to play it, even though long hair might get them beaten up in some of the clubs they were going to. I think that was probably the beginnings of country rock." Alienated by the prevailing music scene, these musicians sought comfort in their roots.

As more musicians drifted westward, bringing with them their affection for country music, a burgeoning country rock scene soon emerged out of southern California. The bond between these like-minded musicians was a strong sense of camaraderie. An almost incestuous fraternity of country music–influenced players supported one another, sitting in at each other's gigs, guesting on each other's albums, and forming new alliances. "There was a real community among some of the bands," acknowledges Douglas Dillard. "I used to go sit in with the Buffalo Springfield, and I played with the Byrds. Chris Hillman and Sneaky Pete played on our albums, and Michael Clarke went on tour with us. Then he went on to join the Burritos. Bernie Leadon went from us to the Burritos. It was pretty interchangeable. We all just had a lot of fun in those days." A glance at the credits and careers of Clarence White or Bernie Leadon, for example, reveals a virtual family tree of the entire country rock field. The atmosphere was less about competition, more about common ground.

Southern California's close-knit music community provided a fertile environment for the cross-pollination of country and rock in the mid- to late sixties, though the musicians involved were almost exclusively non-Angelinos. Although associated with southern California, country rock draws its roots from much farther afield. "L.A. is a cosmopolitan area," postulates Byrds bass player John York, "and a large portion of the people in the music industry here came from somewhere else to make a name for themselves, and they all had a certain amount of baggage. I think that's one of the forces that created that particular style of music, different pieces of that puzzle were brought here. Country rock has a lot to do with the guys who came to L.A . from other places in the country: like Gene Clark coming from Missouri, and Gram Parsons from Georgia, and the Eagles coming from all over—they all grew up on country music. When they came to L.A. they were still carrying that with them, and entering into an existing music scene. Because they had that with them, every chance they got, they breathed that into whatever they were playing. So if you have a bunch of guys playing rock & roll who grew up on country music, it's going to alter the shape of the music."

Larry Murray of Hearts And Flowers waxes nostalgic over the sense of joie de vivre that permeated the early country rock scene in and around Los Angeles. "There was something happening at that time among a number of musicians who knew each other and were interested in what the other fellow was doing. There was so much support from other players. If we weren't working a gig of our own, we were always going to clubs to watch others play. And I don't think that has existed since. It was a moment in time. We were all so close back then.

The best part of my life was that period of time, and hanging out at the Troubadour. It's too bad we don't see one another much anymore. I would venture to say that any of those people, no matter how big they became after that, or how much of a failure after that, would tell you that particular time and place was just magical." Adds the Byrds' Gene Parsons, "There was a certain competitiveness and rivalry too, but there was a real respect and camaraderie among the musicians. It was like an extended family back in those days, and that was what made it so wonderful."

For the Nitty Gritty Dirt Band's John McEuen, the community aspect of the country rock scene was not unlike that of the folkies in New York. "L.A. had its Village, it's just that you had to drive to all its parts, unlike New York, where all the clubs were within four or five blocks and you could walk from one to the other. It was southern California, so you were hearing all these influences. We knew what these other people were doing. There were a lot of influences crossing everyone, but it wasn't intentional, like 'Let's go rip them off.' Orange County, southern California—the Troubadour, Ice House, the Golden Bear, the Ash Grove—never got enough credit, and was equally as important as Greenwich Village, yet never thought of that way."

Clubs like the strictly country & western Palomino on Lankershim in North Hollywood and the folk bastion the Troubadour on Santa Monica in West Hollywood were a beacon for young musicians arriving in Los Angeles seeking a haven for the music they loved. Offers Nesmith, "The Palomino house band, Red Rhodes and the Detours, was this extraordinary collection of players. Leon Russell from Oklahoma was the piano player. You'd go down there, and everybody was hanging out there listening to and playing the music. Bonnie Raitt was there all the time. Wednesday night was open microphone night at the Palomino, and Monday was the hoot night at the Troubadour." The Troubadour became a kind of union hall, where out-of-work pickers could usually find a gig among friends. Three-time national fiddle champion Byron Berline migrated from Oklahoma to L.A. in time to witness the Troubadour fraternity. "It was an amazing time and so much fun. The Troubadour was the focal point, the club everybody went to. I could have gone every night and picked up a session. Every time I went there the place would be jammed, and I'd meet somebody new there every night. 'Oh yeah, man, I want you to play on my record.'"

Linda Ronstadt found the Troubadour a suitable base of operations. "We all used to sit in a corner of the Troubadour and dream. The Troubadour was like a café society. It was where everyone met, where everyone got to hear everyone else's act. It was where I made all my musical contacts, and found people who were sympathetic to the musical styles I wanted to explore." For a young East Texas country rock group with stars in their eyes named Shiloh, the club was their Mecca. "The Troubadour was the first place I went to when I got to L.A.," enthused drummer Don Henley. "I had heard how legendary it was, and all the people who were performing there. The first night I walked in I saw Graham Nash and Neil Young, and Linda Ronstadt was standing there in a little Daisy Mae dress. She was barefoot and scratching her ass. I thought, 'I've made it. I'm in heaven.'" Not long afterward, Henley would meet up with another Troubadour habitué, Glenn Frey, and plans to form the Eagles would be hatched over beers at the bar.

Years later Henley would return to those Troubadour days, drawing inspiration for the Eagles' poignant "The Sad Café," a eulogy to the club. "Those were great times," he recalled to journalist Bill Flanagan, "like when Doug Dillard's girlfriend tried to run him over in front of the club. He was with another woman, and she drove right into the front window of the Troubadour trying to hit him. It had been everyone's favorite hangout. The Dillards, during the revival of bluegrass, would stand up at the front bar and sing a hymn, and everyone would join in. It was the center of the universe as far as I was concerned."

"It wasn't the Troubadour, it was the karate studio next door," protests Suzi Jane Hokom, Douglas Dillard's girlfriend at the time, scotching that myth. "But it was pretty wild in those days."

Shiloh guitarist Al Perkins found the club's convivial social atmosphere conducive to new liaisons. "I think a lot of that was really the social atmosphere in town. I've never been a drinker, so I never was out doing a lot of the clubs in my spare time, but a lot of the guys, particularly those who were single, would hang in the club, socialize and talk. I think people gravitated toward one another, particularly in country rock, because it was new and fun, this fusion of acoustic music, bluegrass, country, and rock being born."

The fraternizing, however, was not strictly confined to darkened nightclubs. According to Nesmith, it spilled out into the canyons above Hollywood and beyond. "We were all part of a group of people who hung out together, knew each other, and were friends. Most everybody lived out in Topanga Canyon, and there'd be these Topanga festivals, players getting together and playing. Linda Ronstadt was living up in the Canyon, and Jackson Browne was living next to her. On the weekend everyone would go down to Will Geer's ranch. Peter Fonda, Brandon De Wilde and J. D. Souther would show up, and Gram Parsons was around then. You divided yourself out according to how hard a drug you took. If you were just a smoker, you were over here, and if you had harder habits, you were over yonder. Everybody was hanging out under their own particular tree."

But it was more than mere drug preference that separated country rockers. There are several strands of the country rock thread that render a simple definition of the genre more difficult. Between 1965 and 1973, at least four unique approaches to country rock can be delineated based on the path each artist chose to take, and the influences they drew upon. There were those who saw country rock as young, longhaired musicians adapting a traditional country music form with a little more emphasis on the rhythm: country music refined through rock sensibilities, attitude, and experience. "It was rock & rollers, or people who had that look, playing Merle Haggard, Buck Owens, and all that stuff," says Al Perkins. "And they played it with a different style, a little more rock. They looked rock & roll but played country." Exponents of this approach included the International Submarine Band, whose leading member, Gram Parsons, would go on to bring a country tone to the Byrds' seminal *Sweetheart Of The Rodeo* before he and founding Byrd Chris Hillman flew the coop to front the much-revered Flying Burrito Brothers. "Country rock," opines Hillman, "involved taking a white blues and adding more back beat, more emphasis on the rhythm section, adding the ingredient of the black emphasis on the rhythm: giving the white man a little more rhythm, which he desperately needed. Gram and I discussed all this thirty years ago. We were listening to r & b, all these Stax artists, and putting more back beat in what we were doing. It just sort of melted into what we were doing. That's country rock." Parsons would later team up with Emmylou Harris to play George Jones to her Tammy Wynette, turning his dream of "Cosmic American Music," a bridge between the redneck and the hippie, into reality. "Gram was the first person I had come across since leaving country music and entering rock & roll," stresses Hillman, "who really *listened*, and understood what country music was, understood how it *felt* to play it." Indeed, the Burritos stage repertoire under Parsons' direction consisted largely of country & western standards drawn from the catalogs of such artists as George Jones, Lefty Frizzell, Buck Owens, and Merle Haggard.

Others who took their country music with a rock & roll chaser included the Great Speckled Bird and Nashville West, a short-lived yet influential quartet featuring future Byrds members Gene Parsons and innovative guitarist Clarence White. The Great Speckled Bird was folk duo Ian and Sylvia Tyson's experiment in country rock, and drew inspiration from both Roy Acuff and Buck Owens' Buckaroos to give their country more oomph. "What we were all doing," states Ian Tyson, "was expressing our love and respect for the real vital country music of the times, represented by artists like Buck Owens and Merle Haggard."

On the other hand, some musicians approached country rock not from the country side but from rock music, adding country music instrumentation to create a wholly original concept: rock with country textures. This approach became the basis for Poco, a group formed from the ashes of the much-loved Buffalo Springfield, when Richie Furay and Jimmy Messina decided to incorporate pedal-steel guitar into a rock lineup. "Some people define country rock from a lyrical standpoint," offers Furay, "but I define it from the musical aspect. It's not so much the sob-in-your-beer lyrics, it was the collection of musical instruments and the way that they were played that gave it a certain sound, like with the steel guitar and banjo. For us, it was introducing steel guitar and Dobro into rock music, and later banjo and mandolin. All these instruments can work together." Rusty Young gave Poco its country edge, though he feels country rock offered a lyrical content that reflected more contemporary themes. "Country rock, to me, is music that has the feel and lyrical content of rock with the instrumentation of country music, such as mandolins, steel guitar, acoustic guitar, and so on. When the country rock craze of the early seventies began, it took the best of country music, but gave it words that a young person could relate to." Poco created a remarkable body of work that brought a youthful country effervescence to rock & roll.

Before Gram Parsons took them, albeit briefly, down a more traditional country road on *Sweetheart Of The Rodeo*, the Byrds had already been experimenting as far back as 1965 with rock tinged with a country feel. "It all begins with the Byrds," asserts Hillman. "And I will argue that point with anybody. Not that we claim all credit." It was Hillman who brought his years of experience in bluegrass and country music to the pioneers of folk rock. "I came into the Byrds as a bluegrass mandolin player, that's what I was comfortable doing. The Byrds recorded a country song on their second album in 1965, 'A Satisfied Mind,' which is a Porter Wagoner hit I brought into the group, and we recorded it. It's an old country song, so we were really making those jabs, but still we had no inkling of what it was we were doing. I had come from a country background. It wasn't really until *Younger Than Yesterday*, in 1966, when I started doing those country things. That's the chronological order of it. From that album and cuts like 'Time Between,' which is probably the first country rock song. What we did in the Burritos came out of the Byrds. The Byrds set the tone, and the Flying Burrito Brothers did it."

Though the *Sweetheart Of The Rodeo* album offered the Byrds' own take on traditional country music, following that album's release, and Gram Parsons' abrupt departure, the group returned to a rock base with country leanings, provided by Clarence White's innovative pullstring bender, a device invented by Gene Parsons to simulate a pedal-steel guitar. "There was a different awareness among the younger musicians who had listened to a lot of rock & roll," suggests the Byrds' John York, "so the back beat and rhythm section was a lot stronger. And the guitar playing was very country, but there was a certain freedom that straight country music didn't have—it may have been the same kind of licks, but there's a whole different awareness and freedom on how to use those licks. It was a lot more open. In most country music, the producers are basically controlling everything, whereas it wasn't like that with the country rock bands. They were free to do what they wanted to do, and that came from their rock & roll experience and attitude."

Ricky Nelson's early teen idol rockabilly success was channeled into a country vein by the late sixties, after he hooked up with a group of seasoned rock players to form the Stone Canyon Band. Together they recorded several albums of pleasant country-flavored rock made all the more appealing by former Buck Owens' Buckaroo Tom Brumley's marvelous pedal-steel work and Randy Meisner's high harmonies. Nelson's single, "Garden Party," became one of the first country rock Top Ten hit records of the early seventies.

Another country-flavored rock group was the First National Band. Following his exit from the Monkees, Mike Nesmith formed the group that owes much of its country flavor to Red Rhodes' innovative pedal-steel work and Nesmith's Texas drawl. "It was impossible to avoid," laughs Nesmith. "I could sing 'Moon River,' and it would sound like a country song. There was no way to avoid it. When I opened my mouth and sang, that's the way it sounded." Others who integrated a country attitude to their rock included The Band, whose use of traditional Appalachian harmony, fiddle, and mandolin lent their music an authentic, down-home, rustic roots quality; Linda Ronstadt, known more as an interpreter than an innovator, who had an uncanny knack for gathering some of the finest country rock players to support her; and, ultimately, the Eagles, who first realized their potential as Ronstadt's backing group.

Still, other artists under the country rock umbrella took their cues from folk and bluegrass and brought to that a country and rock orientation. Among these artists were Hearts And Flowers, the Dillards, and the Dillard & Clark Expedition. Steeped in traditional bluegrass and authentic mountain music from their upbringing in rural Missouri, the Dillards evolved their own bluegrass/country/pop amalgam. "It was controlled by a subconscious urge to do something different," explains Rodney Dillard of the quartet's musical progression toward country rock in the late sixties. "It was part of the creative process. I just thought, 'Wouldn't it be nice if we took Dillard harmonies, that mountain influence, and added other things to it with a little heavier rhythm feel?'" Their groundbreaking 1968 album, *Wheatstraw Suite*, is hailed far and wide for its innovative integration of contemporary country and rock with bluegrass and folk, and served as inspiration for the Eagles' later work. Preferring to stick with the more traditional bluegrass form, Douglas Dillard left the group and joined ex-Byrd Gene Clark to create some of the finest acoustic-based country rock of the genre. "Gene always loved country music, coming from Missouri," claims Dillard. "So he just combined all his knowledge of music, and that's basically what he came up with. My roots are bluegrass, but we didn't have any sound in mind, like rock & roll or country. We were just writing and recording what we did. Basically, we just had a lot of fun." Clark's post-Byrds work revealed that Chris Hillman was not the only member with an appreciation of country music.

Steve Young and John Stewart came to country rock via the folk route. Young was a southern singer/songwriter of note, and an ex-member of the group Stone Country. Stewart had been with the Kingston Trio. Both recorded country-flavored, folk-based albums in the late sixties that would set the direction for other country-influenced solo artists. Young's obscure *Rock, Salt, And Nails* album included what would go on to become a true country rock classic, "Seven Bridges Road," later immortalized by the Eagles on their live album. Stewart's *California Bloodlines*, recorded in Nashville in early 1969, is regarded by many as a country rock classic. The Nitty Gritty Dirt Band began life as an eclectic, acoustic-based, quasi-folk jug band before heading toward bluegrass music with "Mr. Bojangles," "Some Of Shelley's Blues," and the ground-breaking *Will The Circle Be Unbroken*, which did much to mend fences between southern California country rock and Nashville in the early seventies. "My goal was to bring country instruments to as many people as possible," the Dirt Band's John McEuen asserts. "We definitely brought people who didn't listen to country and bluegrass to that music."

And there were those established rock artists who enjoyed a fleeting flirtation with country music, dabbling in the form as a brief diversion in their musical journeys, such as the Lovin' Spoonful's cute take on Music City's guitar pickers, "Nashville Cats," and the steel guitar–flavored "Never Going Back," a song penned by John Stewart. Although starting out as a folk rock group before evolving a highly diverse and eclectic sound, the Buffalo Springfield (featuring Stephen Stills, Neil Young, and Richie Furay) released several tracks with a country feel, including their debut single "Go And Say Goodbye," as well as Furay's "A Child's Claim To Fame," and "Kind Woman," the latter embellished by the pedal-steel work of Rusty Young. Bob Dylan recruited the good old boys in Nashville to apply their sound to his groundbreaking *Nashville Skyline*, which was highlighted by his duet with the reigning king of country, Johnny Cash, on "Girl From The North Country." The two found the experience so rewarding that they recorded a whole album's worth of tracks that remain unreleased. Crosby, Stills, Nash, and Young's anthemic "Teach Your Children" featured pedal-steel guitar from the Grateful Dead's Jerry Garcia, a musician with significant bluegrass credentials. The Grateful Dead are another example of artists who dipped their feet in country music's waters on *Workingman's Dead* and *American Beauty*. Garcia would later form his own country rock group, The New Riders of the Purple Sage. For a time, it seemed that everyone wanted a touch of country in their rock. The Flying Burrito Brothers' Sneaky Pete Kleinow found himself in constant demand to lend his mellifluous pedal-steel tones to a variety of artists, from Fleetwood Mac to Joe Cocker.

Despite the heady atmosphere, healthy diversity, and groundbreaking achievements of the pioneering country rock artists, few enjoyed wider recognition or financial reward for their efforts. The sad fact remains that very little of this seminal country rock music was commercially successful during its time. Though labels like A&M, Epic, RCA, and Elektra weighed in with their best efforts to record and release country rock albums, few sold enough to even chart until the early seventies, when the Eagles' country-influenced rock turned the music world on its ear, selling tens of millions of albums and legitimizing country rock to the masses. But before the success of the Eagles, radio and record executives knew little about marketing this unique and original genre. Upon the release of his *Rock, Salt, And Nails*, Steve Young told *The Journal of Country Music*, "When we finished the album, we took it across town to A&M expecting them to flip out, but they said, 'We don't know what to make of this. What is it? It's country music! What the hell are we going to do with it?' So they sent it to Nashville, and Nashville said, 'No, it's not country. We don't know what to do with it either.' A&M couldn't figure out how to market the album. It never sold, but other musicians liked it." The common response was: too country for rock, too rock for country. "I know the 'country rock' label hurt Poco," offers Richie Furay. "We couldn't get any AM airplay, and we didn't get much FM play."

"We worked hard, and didn't sell a damn record," laments Chris Hillman. "There was no commercial success for any of these bands. It was the pure love of the music, that's why we did it. At that time, we were dealing with a business where you could make three or four records. It was okay. Now we are in this disposable culture, and bands are here and gone in a year. If you're not a two million seller out of the chute, see you later." Promoters, too, found packaging country rock acts problematic, often having no understanding of the genre. Poco opened several shows for hard rock kings The Who, while the Flying Burrito Brothers were paired with retro-rock comedy act Sha Na Na. Near the end of their run, the Burritos were down to playing high school gymnasiums, while Hearts And Flowers found themselves at odds with belligerent audiences opening for The Doors, or Blue Cheer, an early heavy metal prototype.

"All of us wanted to achieve commercial success," responds Mike Nesmith to the notion that country rock retained its integrity by refusing to sell out. "Gram Parsons was working at that as hard as he could, and so was I. The idea that you could sell this music seemed like the perfect thing to do. Every country rock singer that I knew was wanting to have it widely accepted and sell a lot. There was no equivalent between selling records and selling out. The whole country rock movement—how well that music was loved—wasn't a function of somebody holding onto it like some precious little thing. Everybody was working really hard to try to make it popular, and have people make it a part of their lives. And the Eagles brought it all together."

As the second generation of country rockers, each of the Eagles had paid their dues in journeyman country rock groups. They embodied the spirit and integrity of the original visionaries of country rock, combined with exceptional musicianship, astute management, and good timing. "The Eagles were at the right place at the right time," confirms Chris Hillman. "They were well rehearsed, they were tight, and they *worked* at their craft. When we used to play at the Troubadour, Glenn Frey and J. D. Souther would be in the audience studying us." Gram Parsons' death in September 1973 was a turning point for the first generation of country rock pioneers. Some of them, by the seventies, had begun to distance themselves from their country rock roots. Others, like the Nitty Gritty Dirt Band and Emmylou Harris, turned squarely toward Nashville, with their sights firmly set on the country charts. Poco's relocation to Music City in the eighties proved less than satisfying. "Nashville is insecure," maintains Poco guitarist Paul Cotton. "They don't want change. When we moved to Nashville, they wanted to make us the next Alabama."

By the early seventies the Eagles had accepted the mantle handed down by Parsons and others to take the genre to commercial success. "You have to concede that the Eagles are the pre-eminent musical influence in the west over the last two decades," asserts Ian Tyson. "You just have to go into any bar in Alberta, Wyoming, or Montana, and if they're not forced to play Shania Twain covers, the band will be doing 'Peaceful Easy Feeling.' The influence of the Eagles was tremendous. I never thought of them as a shlock band. They're still out there, no question, after Buck and Merle, they're the guys carrying it out in California."

What happened to the vibrant southern California country rock scene? "Country rock was really thriving on the west coast, from the late sixties into the seventies," reflects Byron Berline on the decline of the once fruitful scene, "but by the early eighties, it had dried up. Everybody was gone to Nashville or somewhere else. Even the country places were gone—the Palomino *and* the Troubadour." By the middle of the decade the Eagles began to lean less and less on their country influences, turning toward a more hard rock sound. "When they brought in Joe Walsh and started to be an r & b rock band, I just lost interest," says Chris Hillman. "They became this arena rock band, and it became boring, insipid. I gotta be honest with you, that stuff they did after that just doesn't stand up." Confirms Paul Cotton on Poco's move to a harder sound in the seventies, "The Eagles had gotten rockier, and it was inevitable. They had that pop door open, and we wanted to rock on in with the rest of them. On the *Indian Summer* album, we had the hard rock, orchestra, disco, r & b, but no more or less than the Eagles at the time. We knew there was only so much you can do with country, and it was bound to happen, especially after seven or eight albums."

Although the Eagles have been honored with induction into the Rock and Roll Hall of Fame in Cleveland in 1998, neither the Flying Burrito Brothers, Gram Parsons, Poco, nor the other pioneering country rockers are likely to receive such acknowledgment. The bluegrass fraternity has shunned the Dillards for abandoning their traditional roots for country rock. "Jim and Jesse cut a whole album of Chuck Berry songs in 1966 called *Berry Pickin' In The Country*," notes Ghost Rockets' Buddy Woodward. "It's a great album. And they used drums back then. The Osborne Brothers used drums, pedal steel, and piano. If you listen to 'Rocky Top,' a bluegrass classic of theirs, there are electric instruments on it and drums. The Dillards weren't doing anything more than those guys were. The Osborne Brothers and Jim and Jesse will make it into the Country Music Hall of Fame, but the Dillards won't. Why aren't they getting the respect? I don't know."

Despite Emmylou Harris' admirable efforts to keep Gram Parsons' memory alive, Nashville has only recently come to recognize the significant contributions of the early country rock scene to the evolution of country music. The lines of demarcation remain. "Nashville is still a tight little clique of people," stresses Hillman. "Back in the late eighties, the Desert Rose Band was nominated for the CMA Horizon Award, best vocal band, all this stuff, and we lost. We did everything right and still lost. I just said, 'We're never gonna win this. We don't live here.' It's the same reason why Merle Haggard has never been a member of the Grand Ole Opry, or Buck Owens or Dwight Yoakam. We're outsiders. It's almost like we're Yankee dogs, Northerners." Recognition from other circles has been forthcoming. In a plexiglas case, set among the memorabilia of the likes of Hank Williams and Patsy Cline at the Country Music Hall of Fame, stands Hillman's Nudie bolero jacket from the Desert Rose Band. "It indicates that somebody paid me a wonderful compliment," acknowledges Hillman. "Actually I think one of the best things that ever happened to the Flying Burrito Brothers," he concludes, "was to be included in the Smithsonian Country Music Collection. When I saw that I went, 'Yeah, there we go. Somebody paid attention.'"

"What's funny," smiles Hillman, reflecting on his pivotal role in the evolution of country rock in the sixties, "is that I've fought that country rock label for thirty years. I cut an acoustic album recently, and the tracks just didn't make it, so I went and cut half of it over electrically. And who am I using? Jay Dee Maness, Jerry Scheff, John Jorgenson, Steve Duncan from the Desert Rose Band, and guess what we're gonna call it? It's country rock, I give in. And my wife said, 'That's right, just let it go. That's what you do. It's country rock.' What does it matter to define it?"

# 2

# California Bloodlines: 1963–1966

*We started out in a '55 Cadillac and a one-wheel trailer. We brought a turkey with us that Rodney's mother had cooked for Thanksgiving, because we knew we were going to need it bad.*

—*Mitch Jayne (of the Dillards)*

A healthy country & western scene had been thriving in southern California since the late forties. It continued into the mid-sixties under the shadow of rock & roll and folk rock, allowing budding country rockers the opportunity to hear the real thing. During the thirties, Dust Bowl migrants from Oklahoma and Texas brought the Texas swing music championed by Bob Wills and his Texas Playboys with them. It mixed with the guitar-based music of the Mexican field-workers to become a potent brew that featured mariachi horns, drums, and Texas fiddles on the bandstand. In the postwar years performers like Merle Travis, Gene Autry, Tex Williams, Joe Maphis, and Donnell "Spade" Cooley worked the honky-tonks and ballrooms up and down the coast. By the time Capitol Records began signing artists like Wynn Stewart and Buck Owens, and releasing country records in the late fifties, many had settled in Bakersfield, where a whole new approach to country music emerged, an exciting electric honky-tonk blend. The Bakersfield sound came to typify West Coast country music, a distinctive attitude at odds with the Nashville establishment.

"I grew up a middle-class kid in southern California, in a rural environment around horses," offers Chris Hillman, who was raised in San Diego County. "But we had a television in the mid-fifties, and every

Saturday night I would watch Spade Cooley's show. He was a big act, like a western swing kind of thing—our very own Bob Wills." Though chart success eluded Cooley throughout his career, his weekly variety show, *The Hoffman Hayride*, was one of the most popular programs in southern California. The self-styled "King of Western Swing on the West Coast," Cooley is better remembered for his ignominious end: he died in prison after beating his estranged wife to death. "We had lots of live television shows coming out of L.A., like *Town Hall Party, Spade Cooley*, and *Cal's Corral*, that I could pick up on our grainy little black and white TV. My father hated it, he liked big band and jazz. But he was tolerant of it. 'Okay, if that's what you like.' Then I got into rock & roll when I was in the seventh grade, during the glory years of rock & roll, and really got into Chuck Berry, Little Richard, Elvis Presley, and all that stuff. Then I got into bluegrass and folk music. But when I was a kid, I would listen to Spade Cooley. I don't know why, I just loved that music. The country music scene out here was fabulous, all these wonderful artists, and all these live TV shows offered a vehicle to come out to California. Lefty Frizzell was out here working all the time. I always found that the music out here was so great—not to downgrade Nashville at the time—you couldn't beat it."

Young players heard something compelling in the Bakersfield sound. "We didn't look at it as outlaw music," claims Herb Pedersen, "we looked at it as having a real bite to it. Nashville had a smooth kind of production, it was almost more pop-oriented. Then Buck came along with Don Rich. It was country music, but it had the rawness that we liked about bluegrass. Buck was extremely influential. I can remember going to a show that Buck did in Sunnyvale about 1964 with Jerry Garcia. It was right when 'Together Again' was Number One. And this was like the hippest stuff I'd ever heard. Real raw, but really good. That was wonderful music."

Recalls Hillman, who together with Pedersen recorded a tribute album to the Bakersfield sound entitled *Bakersfield Bound*: "Buck Owens was such a pioneer, and when Merle Haggard got out of prison and started working, there was another contender. Wynn Stewart was a major act who didn't get the recognition that Buck and Merle got, but was the innovator of a whole style they copied. I was playing in this very traditional bluegrass band, the Golden State Boys, and I was buying Buck Owens records. I was nineteen years old. Our banjo player, Don Parmley, asked why I was listening to this stuff, and I said because it was just like what we were doing."

Alvis Edgar "Buck" Owens was born and raised in Texas, but moved to Bakersfield in 1951. He began his music career playing workingmen's clubs with the Orange Blossom Playboys. It has been said that Joe Maphis' honky-tonk classic "Dim Lights, Thick Smoke (And Loud, Loud Music)" was inspired by one of Buck's club gigs with the Playboys. A rebel right from the get-go, Buck's first two records under the pseudonym "Corky Jones" owed as much to Little Richard as Bob Wills. Signed to Capitol Records in the early sixties, he teamed with guitarist Don Rich to form the Buckaroos (Rich, steel guitarist Tom Brumley, Doyle Holly on bass, and drummer Willie Cantu). Owens enjoyed an unbroken string of hits between 1963 and 1967 under producer Ken Nelson, notching fifteen Number One records in a row, and twenty-six Top Ten singles (including "Act Naturally," "Love's Gonna Live Here," "Together Again," "Tiger By The Tail," and "My Heart Skips A Beat").

Buck took the honky-tonk tradition of Hank Williams and Lefty Frizzell and gave it a jolt of electricity, adding a twangier electric guitar sound, courtesy of Don Rich. Rich's role in shaping Bakersfield's guitar-driven sound should not be underestimated. With drums, a strident electric-bass guitar, and the rhythm up front, Buck termed it his "freight train" sound. "Like a locomotive was coming right through the building," laughs Owens. Compared to the Nashville sound of the day, there was a harder edge to Buck's records. His tougher style drew young players raised on traditional country but looking for a bit of that rock attitude. "In Nashville the attitude was 'be a good boy'—you had to play by their rules," notes Owens ruefully. He turned away from Nashville, choosing to remain in Bakersfield. "They made syrupy love songs. I think Nashville thought I would disappear, but I didn't." The recordings of Buck Owens and the Buckaroos contain the first real electric country rock, and provided a blueprint that young country rockers followed.

"Webb Pierce was very rock & roll to me," says pedal-steel guitarist Al Perkins. "He had a rockabilly thing going, but a very definite country direction. Some of that stuff really *rocked*. Buck Owens and his group already had a rock edge to their music. Buck was rocking it out no-holds-barred. I guess the style he came up with was sort of that Tex-Mex style. He was probably the most influential country artist in my development."

When Merle Haggard returned to Bakersfield after being paroled from San Quentin Prison, he entered the thriving music scene, first as a sideman to Wynn Stewart and Buck Owens (he married Buck's ex-wife, Bonnie). He launched his own career with the hit "Someday My Friends Are Gonna Be Strangers" in 1965. Hag's sound was less dynamic than Buck's, more in the honky-tonk tradition. His lyrics featured autobiographical stories in songs like "Sing Me Back Home," "Mama Tried," and "The Fightin' Side Of Me." "Okie From Muskogee" was a tongue-in-cheek poke at the generation gap of the late sixties that brought Haggard far wider attention. Bernie Leadon asserts, "Merle ticked us off *extremely* when he did 'Okie.' But we forgave him for that." Like Owens, Haggard became an early mentor to young country rockers. Gram Parsons sought him out as a producer in 1972. Parsons had gotten himself together to the point he was ready to attempt his first solo album. Unfortunately the sessions fell apart almost immediately, the inebriated Parsons proving too much for even the hard-living Haggard to deal with.

Tom Brumley played pedal-steel guitar in the Buckaroos during Buck's salad days. Tom's father, Albert, had written the gospel classics "I'll Fly Away," "Turn Your Radio On," and "Jesus Hold My Hand." "My brother was recording with Capitol Records in 1961," recalls Brumley on his entry into the California country music scene. "I came out to California, and Buck Owens and Don Rich were there at the session both days. I worked clubs in L.A. for a while (like the Palomino), but I was in Texas, building houses, when Buck called me two years later. 'Act Naturally' was just out at that time, and my first session for Buck was 'Together Again.' Everything I did with Buck was a hit. It was quite a trip." Brumley recalls the genesis of Buck's sound. "What I liked about Buck's music was that it was *fun.* It wasn't supposed to be perfect. We played the way we wanted to play. We didn't use a lot of bottom end, all top end, lots of electric guitars, a real bright sound. We did as many as six masters in a three-hour session, and didn't even know the songs." For Brumley, the Bakersfield sound had a rawness that attracted him. "Nashville put so many restrictions on the music. They've got writers writing songs, and cookie-cutter sessions, all to a formula. It's got to be natural, let musicians play from the heart. That's what country rock was. The sense of adventure was coming from *outside* of Nashville. Guys like Chris Hillman were originals. Buck contributed so much to country, and to rock too. I remember when we started having hippies coming to our shows. I couldn't believe it. I would read write-ups about those guys liking our music, even the Beatles. We did the Fillmore in San Francisco in 1967, and *that* was an experience. There wasn't a chair or seat in the building. Everybody was on the floor smoking pot having a *good* time. We filled that place two nights in a row, and they loved it. It was absolutely amazing."

Recalls Owens of that engagement, "These kids, they know what they like. They wanted stone country. That's why they wanted me." Though he incurred the wrath of his young devotees when he became a regular on the cornpone TV show *Hee Haw*, Owens remains a spiritual godfather to the sixties country rock movement.

Owens wasn't afraid to venture into rock territory, recording Chuck Berry's "Memphis," and "Johnny B. Goode." "'Johnny B. Goode,' that's a country song to me," asserts Owens. "If Chuck Berry had been white, he'd have been a hillbilly, like me." Owens even dared to introduce fuzz-tone guitar into the country charts on his 1969 hit "Who's Gonna Mow Your Lawn?"

"What made Buck and Merle's music different from Nashville was the Hispanic influence," opines Chris Hillman. "These guys came from Oklahoma and Texas, worked in the fields, and would be around other workers who were Hispanic. So when you hear an old Buck Owens record, the way they end a phrase on a song sounds mariachi. It's very interesting, this influence. Nashville has more of a black influence. You listen to Bill Monroe and there's a lot of black music and blues in his music." Adds Tom Brumley, "There may have been a little Mexican influence in Buck's music, but a lot of polka. Buck loved polkas."

Owens' Texas roots played a role in the evolution of his sound. "The Western influence was more Mexican at root," suggests fellow Texan Michael Nesmith. "The cowboys and the western singers of the 1800s, if you want to go back that far, were Mexicans, and the guitar is a Mexican thing when it's put into country & western music. It's not like dulcimers and the stringed instruments of the Appalachians and Smoky Mountains, where a lot of that early Nashville country music comes from. It was much more of the cowboy music. But there's a mistake people make with Western influence, thinking it's Bob Wills and the Texas Playboys. That's certainly a big part of it; Bob Wills and the Texas Playboys have that umh-pa-pa of the German music underpinning it. Down in the San Antonio region where I grew up, you just lived that music. Texas was settled by the Mexicans and the Germans, which is the origin of barbecue—you had Germans smoking meats and Mexicans cooking over wood fires. It also combined in music, with Tejano music having this umh-pa-pa bass, which is German-meets-the-Mexican influences. You cannot grow up in Texas and not be significantly influenced by African Americans and Mexican Americans, because they are the cultural base, along with the cowboys there."

Guitarist Don Rich played a key role in defining the Buck Owens sound, a Telecaster twang that set a pattern for both country and country rock. "Don had his own style," says Brumley, "and it fit Buck's music so well. Nobody played like that before. What a great sidekick to have. They were almost equal. Vince Gill and others were influenced by Don—that Telecaster sound." The Telecaster would become the instrument of choice in the country field. The Telecaster bridge-mounted pickup gives a higher-register sound, and its slender neck makes it easy to pick leads. "The thing about a Telecaster," comments guitarist Bernie Leadon, "is that it's remarkably comfortable for an acoustic player to make the transition to electric guitar. A Les Paul or Stratocaster is more suited for rock. You can play most of the same styles on a Tele that you do on an acoustic, and it just sounds great. It has to do with the tone. Leo Fender designed the Strat to be a country instrument, but over time the Tele caught on more for country music." Don and Buck had a lot to do with that. Indeed, when Chris Hillman and Gram Parsons formed the Flying Burrito Brothers in 1968, they took the twin Telecasters of the Buckaroos as their model.

In late November 1962 the Dillards packed an old trailer with suitcases, instruments, a roast turkey, and bid farewell to Salem, Missouri. Along for the ride were brothers Douglas on banjo, and Rodney on guitar, as well as mandolinist Dean Webb, and standup bass player Mitch Jayne. They headed out for the bright lights of California from the cozy environs of the Ozark Mountains. A demo tape sent out earlier had scratched up interest in their bluegrass sound, and the boys were determined to try their luck in the folk clubs of Los Angeles. After a brief stop in Oklahoma City to pick up some much-needed cash to complete the trek, the Dillards arrived in Los Angeles and immediately made a name for themselves. Bluegrass artists had found a small niche within the folk music revival, which was sparked when the Kingston Trio's "Tom Dooley" topped the pop charts. Though bluegrass groups tended to rely exclusively on traditional Appalachian songs for their repertoire, the Dillards' own blend of traditional bluegrass, original compositions, and Ozark humor set them apart from the pack. "Bluegrass didn't fit completely with the folk scene," offers Jayne, "and it certainly was never really part of the country music scene. Bluegrass was a form of music that seemed to be forever standing in the wings." The Dillards had no intentions of remaining on the sidelines.

Douglas and Rodney grew up on bluegrass music. Their father, Homer, played the fiddle, while mother Lorene picked guitar. With instruments strewn about the house, and a song never far from anybody's lips, the brothers took up banjo and guitar. With childhood friend John Hartford (who would go on to great success as a singer/songwriter on his own), they progressed through a series of local bluegrass outfits that included the Ozark Mountain Boys and the Dixie Ramblers. It wasn't long before Douglas was winning admiration for his facile fingering on the five-string banjo. The Dillards had honed their craft on the back porch of the family house, where they first played with Dean Webb and Mitch Jayne. Jayne was a local teacher and host of a radio program called *Hickory Hollow*. The boys often performed together on that program. Though instrumental virtuosity was their long suit, Mitch and Rodney began writing their own material, blending bluegrass, folk, and country elements, along with Mitch's wonderfully colorful homespun yarns of various local characters, like Ebo Walker and Dooley.

Not strict purists, the Dillards were already stretching the boundaries of the bluegrass form, and were not afraid to break the traditional mold. "Rodney, Dean, and I started writing songs together because we felt it was important we develop and perform our own material instead of copying someone else," states Jayne. "Listening to the songs playing on the radio, we could tell that everybody was already copying each other. What we wanted to accomplish more than anything was to be different."

On arriving in Los Angeles, the Dillards made tracks for the Ash Grove folk club in Hollywood, a bastion of the traditional folk, blues, and bluegrass scene. Unlike the more eclectic Troubadour, the Ash Grove's reputation was built on maintaining a purist stance. At the time, the Grove's bookers resisted scheduling bands that featured electric instruments. For Ash Grove habitués, it had to be the real thing, or nothing at all. On their first visit the group met John Herald and the Greenbriar Boys at the Ash Grove. The Boys invited the Dillards to join them onstage. Jim Dickson, an independent record producer for the Elektra Records label, was in the audience that night. He was impressed enough by the Dillards to approach them. Rodney Dillard notes, "Jim was on the lookout for talent out on the edge of the envelope, looking for new stuff. He happened to be at the club. We just walked in and auditioned. Jim knew Jac Holzman at Elektra, and brought him down to the club. The next thing I knew, we were making a deal. We did the Hoot Night at the Troubadour, and the William Morris Agency people saw us and signed us up." Quickly, the Dillards became the darlings of the West Coast folk *and* bluegrass circuits. They also became "the Darlings" quite literally, on *The Andy Griffith Show*, after Griffith's talent scout hired them for what was originally slated to be a one-shot appearance on the popular show. On March 8, 1963, the Dillards made their television debut, portraying Denver Pyle's backwoods kin, the Darling boys. The appearance led to further guest spots, and the group was on its way.

The Dillards quickly became mentors to other young bluegrass players on the West Coast, who heard and saw something unique in their presentation. "Through the genius of Mitch Jayne's comedy skits and monologues, they had an act," states Herb Pedersen. "Where most bluegrass bands stood up there like five wooden Indians, wanting to sound like Ralph Stanley, these guys had no qualms about doing traditional folk tunes, and they did them very well. So they were able to get into places like the hungry i club in San Francisco, with an opening act named Bill Cosby, and played places bluegrass bands would never *think* of playing, much less be asked to play. That was the cool part of their act. They had already made the crossover." Mandolinist Chris Hillman followed the group as a spectator to observe Dean Webb's playing.

The Dillards' debut Elektra album, *Back Porch Bluegrass*, was produced by Jim Dickson at World Pacific studio in Hollywood, and released in mid-1963. It showcased the group's adroit instrumental abilities on traditional numbers, along with a healthy sampling of their original material. The album also featured the group's tight, three-part mountain harmony singing. But while Dillards fans loved the album, critics were less enamored, asserting that the group's polished recording performance belied the album's title. There was nothing "back porch" about the Dillards to these scribes. "The problem with those critics," groused Rodney to biographer Lee Grant, "was that they were from New York, and their idea of a rural experience was seeing a dead squirrel in a parking lot." As banjo picker Buddy Woodward recalls, "When the Dillards' album came out, and you can go back and read this in old issues of *Muleskinner* or *Bluegrass Unlimited*, critics thought the tapes were sped up. They figured *no* one could play like Doug Dillard. Doug capos up to D, the seventh fret, and banjo players *never* capo up that high, and he plays so fast it kind of sounds like it's sped up. So they were ragging on them back in the early sixties."

Undaunted, the Dillards' second album, *Live . . . Almost*, released in early 1964, presented their live stage show taped at L.A.'s popular Mecca club. The record also contained the group's between-song comedy skits, and Mitch's storytelling. But by the spring of that year, Rodney was beginning to grow restless with the group's material, and was chafing to move on. The Dillards were already incorporating Dylan material into their act, and Rodney was keenly aware of the musical changes in the wind by early 1964.

"The whole folk thing lasted about ten years," recalls Dean Webb. "We felt we couldn't make it anymore wearing our buckskin outfits. We had kind of painted ourselves into a corner, and it got limiting. We never thought of ourselves as hardcore bluegrass anyway. We were influenced by all sorts of things: jazz, folk, classical, or whatever. We touched on the folk thing. We were influenced by whatever we heard." The group owed Elektra one more album. With the atmosphere at the label chilly, the Dillards decided, once and for all, to silence critics who accused them of selling out. *Pickin' And Fiddlin'*, released in early 1965, was a traditional album of instrumentals. "That wasn't a record made for anyone but the traditionals," stresses Rodney. "We got completely hacked to pieces by them. So we said, 'Okay, screw you guys, we'll make an album, and we'll play it right up your ass!,' so we did."

Back in late November 1963, the Dillards had been booked to play a weeklong engagement in Oklahoma City. To promote the gig, the group scheduled an afternoon appearance at the University of Oklahoma. There they met three-time national fiddling champion Byron Berline. "It was the day President Kennedy was killed, November 22, 1963," relates Berline. "I was in school at the University of Oklahoma. I was scheduled to do a show, a thing called *Friday at Four*, a folk music show on campus every Friday at the student union. I had read in the school paper that morning who was listed to perform, and saw the Dillards' name. I just figured they were another folk group I wouldn't be interested in. The school went ahead and scheduled the show despite President Kennedy's death. I was playing in a little group, and once we were finished our part I sat around for a few minutes and caught a few of the other acts. All at once these four guys came walking out of one of the back rooms in their matching buckskin shirts. The manager of the club introduced me to Doug Dillard, who was standing there with his banjo. He said, 'Doug, you should get together with this fiddle player and hear him play.' Doug asked what I played, and I said 'old time stuff.' He said, 'That's what I like too. When we get through with the show, let's pick a tune together.' I went out and watched their show and I couldn't believe it. They were great. I'd never heard a bluegrass band like that. Those guys could *play*. After their show I went back stage, and Doug saw me and said, 'I want to hear this guy play the fiddle.' So he got out his banjo, and I got out my fiddle. I didn't know what to play, so I picked the fastest one I knew, 'Hamilton County Breakdown.' Doug fell right in with it, and in no time the others got their instruments out, and we jammed for two hours right there. It was the most incredible time I'd had."

Recruiting Berline for the *Pickin' And Fiddlin'* sessions, the Dillards laid down an album of straight bluegrass and old-time fiddle material. The recording sessions held in Los Angeles were an introduction to a whole new world for the young fiddler. "When I was out in L.A. in the summer of 1964 to record with the Dillards I had a real good time. I turned twenty in the studio recording the album. *Pickin' And Fiddlin'* was my first recording. We'd hang out at the Troubadour. I met Gene Clark there. I met Chris Hillman too. He was hanging around Dean Webb, watching him play mandolin. Everybody knew everybody and got together to play. If you were a bluegrass player or a folk player, you just got together and played."

One night at the Troub remains particularly memorable for Berline. "Gene Clark didn't have any money, and had to borrow thirty-five cents from me for cigarettes. He came back to the table and said to me, 'You know, by this time next year I think I'm going to be making a lot of money, Byron. I'm thinking about forming another band, and I think we're going to make a lot of money.' And that was the Byrds. He was sure right. Every time I saw him after that I'd tell him he didn't have to pay, I'd rather have him owe me."

Gene Clark had been cooling his heels in L.A. since leaving the New Christy Minstrels. Born in Missouri, but raised in rural Kansas, outside Kansas City, Harold Eugene Clark began playing guitar at age nine. The second oldest of thirteen children, Gene was influenced early on by the country music of Hank Williams, before he turned to rock & roll in the fifties. He joined his first group at age thirteen. With the ascent of folk music in the late fifties, Gene jumped aboard the bandwagon with his group, the Surf Riders. The group came to the attention of folk music impresario Randy Sparks, who happened to catch their act at a club in Kansas City. In June 1963, Sparks tapped Clark to replace a departing member in the New Christy Minstrels. The Kansas boy found himself on the road with the eleven-member outfit, performing across the United States and Canada, and appearing frequently on network television. With their hit "Green Green" riding the top of the charts, it was a whirlwind experience for Clark that culminated in an appearance at the White House for President Lyndon Johnson in January 1964. The group later recorded the title song to the James Garner movie *The Wheeler Dealers*. During sessions for the following albums *Land Of Giants* and *Today*, Clark remained in the background, a member of the ensemble chorus but never a featured voice.

The constant touring soon took a toll on him. He had developed a fear of flying, allegedly after witnessing a plane crash as a child (though his parents argue that he was traumatized by a tornado in 1957 that ploughed through their neighborhood). Realizing that his role in the ensemble would never rise above a subordinate level, and already beginning to compose his own material, Clark began looking for greater opportunities. While traveling through Canada, he heard the Beatles for the first time and a seed was planted. "I knew that this was the future, and that I wanted to be a part of it," noted Clark. Tendering his notice soon after, Clark headed to Los Angeles in search of new prospects, hanging out at the Troubadour while formulating his next move.

Still in his teens, Chris Hillman had earned a reputation on the southern California folk and bluegrass circuit as a talented mandolin player with the Scottsville Squirrel Barkers. Led by Larry Murray, a Georgia-raised guitar player and bluegrass aficionado, the Squirrel Barkers had met each other at the Blue Guitar, a music store cum folk music mecca in San Diego. "The Blue Guitar started out a focal point for anybody interested in folk or bluegrass," remembers Bernie Leadon. Born in Minneapolis, Leadon had relocated to San Diego in 1957 and became immersed in the scene that formed around the Blue Guitar. "You had the two camps, folkies on one side, and bluegrass players on the other. So the Blue Guitar was a really interesting place. I was still very young, but when I met all these guys and started hanging around with them, I realized how much stronger the roots of the traditional folk music were. As a result, I got into bluegrass banjo, listening to and learning from Kenny Wertz. On the weekends, the shop used to hold concerts where the Squirrel Barkers would play. They would do evening gigs all around the city, and play bluegrass festivals up in L.A., so there was a really good little scene happening. Larry

Murray was one of the principals in this Blue Guitar shop in San Diego. He was from Waycross, Georgia, and ten years older than me."

The Squirrel Barkers were local heroes. Comprised of Hillman, Larry Murray on guitar, Kenny Wertz on banjo, Ed Douglas on bass, and Gary Carr on guitar, they recorded one album, released as *Bluegrass Favorites*, on Crown Records. The entire recording session lasted five hours. The album was mixed while the group went out for coffee. Each member was paid a mere fifty dollars for his effort.          ·

Leadon spent a brief period with the Barkers before moving to Florida with his family. "Two of the guys had been drafted," he relates, "and they had a couple of gigs, so I filled in. But I was never a *member* of the Squirrel Barkers. It was wonderful, because I got to step in and play with my heroes." Soon afterwards, Larry Murray moved up to Los Angeles to try his luck on the folk circuit, while Chris Hillman joined the Golden State Boys. Upon Hillman's arrival in late 1962 the Boys changed their name to the Hillmen. The Golden State Boys had been regulars on the music show *Cal's Corral*, one of Hillman's favorites, and his elevation to their ranks at the age of seventeen was an honor. The Hillmen—Chris, banjo player Don Parmley, Vern Gosdin on guitar, and Rex Gosdin on bass played the folk club circuit in the state. Recalls Vern Gosdin, "We decided to change our name, and thought that Chris' name would be good for a bluegrass band. We played every rat-hole in southern California, places where they had twenty-nine people and standing room only. Chris was under age. One time we went down to the Foothills Club, and he had a phony ID. He showed it to the guy, who said, 'Is this your ID?' and he said, 'Hell, no!' We liked to never got him in—his mouth almost got him throwed out."

The Hillmen recorded at World Pacific studio in early 1963 under Jim Dickson. An album simply titled *The Hillmen* appeared several years later on Together Records, put out by Dickson. Besides the usual bluegrass standards, the album also featured Bob Dylan's "When the Ship Comes In." The song's inclusion came about via Dickson, who knew Dylan and had access to his catalog of unreleased material. The Hillmen were clearly straining to move beyond the bluegrass idiom. "We used to play in folk places," recalls Hillman, "but we were modifying our repertoire to include contemporary material—you just couldn't make money playing straight bluegrass. We wanted to play songs that said more than the bluegrass songs—which wasn't much." Released following Chris Hillman's success with the Byrds, *The Hillmen* album has since been resold several times over the course of the years. "Jim

Dickson knew nothing about bluegrass," maintains Vern Gosdin. "What Jim is good at is re-releasing albums." Not long after the album sessions, the Hillmen split up and Chris Hillman headed to Los Angeles to work in the Green Grass Group.

The Kentucky Colonels were one of the most popular bluegrass outfits on the southern California circuit in the early sixties. Unlike the Dillards, the Colonels were diehard purists who rarely strayed from traditional arrangements, though their principal soloist, flat-picking guitarist Clarence White, was highly regarded as an innovator while barely into his teens. The Hillmen, Colonels, and Dillards frequently crossed paths on the club scene. "I grew up with Clarence White," acknowledges Chris Hillman. "I met him about the same time I met Herb Pedersen, in the early sixties. When I was in the Hillmen we were always bumping into each other." The other connection they shared was Jim Dickson and World Pacific studios, where the Colonels recorded two albums.

Born in Maine of French-Canadian heritage and raised in California, Clarence and his brothers (Eric on standup bass and Roland on mandolin) first formed the Three Little Country Boys around 1957. They won a regular spot on a local radio program in Burbank. Taken under the wing of popular country artist Joe Maphis, the trio next appeared on his weekly *Town Hall Party* television show, where Chris Hillman likely first saw them. The following year the group expanded, adding Billy Ray Latham on banjo and renaming themselves the Country Boys. They became regulars at the prestigious Ash Grove club. With the folk revival thriving by the early sixties, the group expanded again, adding Dobro player Leroy "Mack" MacNees and Roger Bush on bass (replacing Eric White, who was drafted). They recorded their first album, *New Sounds Of Bluegrass*, under the name the Kentucky Colonels. It was produced by two of the genre's legends, Ralph and Carter Stanley. Clarence White's flat-picking was already turning heads after he guested on Elektra Records' *New Dimensions In Banjo and Bluegrass*, which later became the soundtrack for the movie *Deliverance*. On the Colonels' second album, *Appalachian Swing* (World Pacific, 1964), the group was still mining the bluegrass idiom, but Clarence was finding the group's traditional approach confining. "It wasn't so much that I was getting bored with acoustic bluegrass," stated Clarence. "I could feel so many new things in the air, and I wanted to get into what I thought was a new kind of music, which combined what you could call a folk and electric rock." The arrival of the British Invasion that year, and the folk rock counteroffensive led by the Byrds a year later, inspired White, who was eager to expand his horizons. "I spent almost every hour with my guitar," he acknowledged. "It was my whole life, but it was all acoustic playing, bluegrass mostly, with some Django Reinhardt too. Then, when I was in my late teens, I began to get interested in electric guitar, which I'd never even played."

In the spring of 1964, Gene Clark was hanging out at the Troubadour, where he met another expatriate folksinger. Jim McGuinn, born and raised in Chicago, had an impressive résumé in the folk community. He had worked as accompanist for Judy Collins, among others, before accepting an offer from Bobby Darin to work his supper club shows. Taken with the Beatles, he relocated to the West Coast. McGuinn began incorporating Beatles numbers into his repertoire, and was playing the Troubadour Hoot nights when Clark first encountered him. Notes McGuinn, "I might have been one of the first people to dig what the Beatles were into musically, aside from the fad. In their chord changes I could see degrees of complexity that folk music had gotten to by that time, and it struck me as being a groovy thing. So I started singing their songs in coffeehouses." Clark heard McGuinn performing the Beatles' "You Can't Do That" on acoustic twelve-string, and he was intrigued enough to suggest they work together. "Jim and I started picking together in the Troubadour bar, which was called The Folk Den at the time," confirmed Clark regarding the first tentative steps toward what would become the Byrds. "We started to write songs, and then one night we went along to the Troubadour and there was this guy named David Crosby who came on stage and played a few songs. I told McGuinn that I thought he was good. We went into the lobby and started picking on the stairway where the echo was good, and David came walking up and just started singing with us, doing the harmony." Crosby had been making demo tapes with Jim Dickson, and he brought the producer into the equation.

"I had the key to World Pacific studios just a few blocks away from the Troubadour," recalled Dickson on the formation of the Byrds in August 1964. "Late at night I would make tapes of folksingers who were on the scene. I was primarily looking for talent for Jac Holzman, and Crosby was one of the many people I recorded. I had also wanted to create a vocal group, and became very interested when David Crosby told me that Gene Clark and Jim McGuinn were writing songs together and that he wanted to sing harmony. We rehearsed all summer at World Pacific, adding first Michael Clarke, and then Chris Hillman,

who had been a mandolin player in a bluegrass group I had been working with." As the Beefeaters, Clark, McGuinn, and Crosby released one
mediocre Beatles-imitation single on Elektra before adding Clarke on
drums and Hillman on electric bass guitar. "I was a mandolin player
and didn't know how to play bass," smiles Hillman, "but they didn't
know how to play their instruments either, so I didn't feel too bad
about it. None of us were rock & rollers, we were all folk musicians,
and, although it was tremendously exciting, it was such an alien thing
to be getting into. So I got hold of a bass and set to it." "The Byrds'
background was primarily in folk music," confirms Dickson, "and
though they seemed to be prepared to abandon this background to follow the Beatles, it was, to me, their strength, and, as their manager, I
felt it should be retained as an element in their music." The results
would inaugurate a whole new branch of the rock music tree: folk rock.

In fall of 1964, Dickson approached Clarence White with the idea
of recording a solo album for Elektra, backed by the other members
of the Kentucky Colonels. One of the tunes he encouraged the young
guitarist to record was from a Bob Dylan demo tape. As Clarence
tells it, "He had 'Mr. Tambourine Man' sung by Dylan, with Ram-
blin' Jack Elliott singing on the choruses. It had apparently been
made for his *Another Side Of Bob Dylan*, but couldn't be used because
Elliott was contracted elsewhere. It was a pretty sloppy recording,
you know, like a drunk might sing it, but the idea interested me, and
I tried to get the other guys to go for it. They turned it down flat, because they thought it was a stupid song, and because they said electric folk was just unacceptable. So I guess Dickson took the song
to McGuinn." Dickson's suggestion initially received the same response from the five Byrds, until he managed to impress upon them
the significance of an electric arrangement of a Dylan number. The
Byrds reluctantly struggled to put together an arrangement, but they
ran into problems with the vocal harmonies. "The Byrds were rehearsing at World Pacific studios where we recorded," recalls the
Dillards' Dean Webb. "I went by there and saw Dickson's old Volkswagen outside, and I stopped by to see what was going on. They
were trying to work out 'Mr. Tambourine Man.' They were fighting,
and couldn't seem to get the right kind of harmony on the thing.
Everybody was uptight about it. I said I had a couple of ideas.
McGuinn stayed in the room, and I sang a tenor part to him, a first
harmony part above what he did. Then they ran the recording back
and I put a baritone part on it. They were trying to be more folky and

modal, which I didn't think fit. I just put a triad harmony on it. So then they learned the parts that I had put on tape and sang it." By June 1965 "Mr. Tambourine Man" was a worldwide hit. "None of us liked the idea of putting 'Mr. Tambourine Man' out as a single," confirms Hillman, "but Jim Dickson was right, it worked."

While his former Squirrel Barker mate rode the top of the charts in the summer of 1965, Larry Murray found a new musical alliance via the Troubadour. "I had just finished a year with Randy Sparks. John Denver was working with Randy at the time. I was kind of burned out on the bluegrass circuit, and just wanted to get into something a little earthier. Then I ran into Rick Cunha and David Dawson, who were just over from Hawaii. Rick and David showed up at the Troubadour, and we just got together and picked." What the trio had discovered became the basis for Hearts And Flowers, a Beatles-influenced folk-rock-country style. "We had a unique sound, a very strange sound, particularly because we found what we did best was old, traditional, country hillbilly music," recalls Murray. "That became the core of what we did, the three of us, and we took it from there." For Hearts And Flowers, "there" meant an eclectic blend of Merle Haggard-meets-*Sgt. Pepper.* "I was influenced by bluegrass groups like the Country Gentlemen, the Louvin Brothers, and the Everlys, of course," adds Murray. "Those were the people I idolized musically. And I liked the Beatles and Dylan."

"Larry Murray was running the Monday night hootenannies in 1965–66," recalls Rick Cunha about the atmosphere around the Troubadour. "There was some interesting stuff going on there. The A & R guys were like sharks feeding on the talent, frothing at the mouth over people like Tim Buckley. There were other people doing what we were doing in varying degrees. There was a duo with Michael Murphey and Boomer Castleman, the Texas Twosome, who came out in sequined suits, and what they were going for was the folk rock market. There were other people looking at country music and wanting it to be popular. That was the key for us. We were real great Buck Owens and Merle Haggard fans. We couldn't understand how that stuff could be going on and people couldn't be jumping all over it."

With Murray and Cunha playing acoustic guitars and writing songs, and Dawson on autoharp, Hearts And Flowers offered a contrast to the folk rock fare that dominated the music scene in 1965–66. Their song selection was widely varied, everything from Merle Haggard to Donovan. "We introduced a lot of people to roots country music, like 'Two

Little Boys' and 'Wreck On The Highway.' We'd do them and people would get turned on to that stuff. The word that always showed up in our reviews was 'eclectic,' and we never knew what that meant," laughs Murray. "We even did that song 'Alfie' on stage, just a verse or so, tongue-in-cheek, and it would bring chills to people because we did it in country harmonies. People would yell, 'Finish it!' And we'd say, 'No, can't you take a joke?'" Offers Cunha, "Had it been up to us, we would have gone way country. We wanted it to be commercial and fit into the pop market, but left to our own devices it would have been even more country. Production changed what we would have done. Our basic repertoire was folk and country, we all sort of came out of that background."

Finding an appropriate venue for their original approach was often difficult for Hearts And Flowers. "We played the pop shows, because that was our audience," recalls Cunha. "If we got into the country side of things, it was our own doing. Basically we worked the folk clubs." For many musicians with country music roots, Hearts And Flowers were proof that you could introduce those influences within a folk and rock framework. Acknowledges Poco's Jimmy Messina, "Those three guys were probably the closest thing to what we were all flowing into. They were the cutting edge of where the rest of us were going. They were the blade that didn't quite have the edge sharpened on it yet. I got my first Telecaster from Rick Cunha."

"We enjoyed playing and singing together," says Murray of their mix of personalities. "That's what held us together; we enjoyed what we could create together. We were always amazed at what we did. When we would learn a song and run through it, everyone would end up smiling. I've never worked with anyone else where that happened continuously. It was always fun."

In 1962, fresh out of the U.S. Air Force, Michael Nesmith headed for Los Angeles. Accompanying him were his future wife, Phyllis, and his musical partner, bass player John Kuehne (or John London, as he would later call himself). Nesmith and London had been working as a duo called the Trinity River Boys. "John London and I came out from Texas together," states Nesmith. "Part of my repertoire was Hank Williams and Jimmy Rodgers songs, 'The Yodeling Brakeman,' traditional country music. But I wasn't doing just country music. Again, there wasn't much of a distinction between folk music and country music. It was more about authors than anything else. You paid a lot of attention to the way certain guys wrote."

The duo, along with a fellow named Bill Sleeper, recorded a folk single as Mike, John, & Bill for the Omnibus label. As The Survivors, they soldiered on to little notice. Nesmith next recorded two folk rock singles for Colpix Records under the name Michael Blessing, including a cover of the Buffy Ste. Marie number "Until It's Time For You To Go" (later an Elvis Presley hit). He also worked the Monday night hoots at the Troubadour, where he met the Greenbriar Boys, led by John Herald. The other "Boys" were Bob Yellin and Ralph Rinzler, who had replaced the legendary banjoist Eric Weissberg. Nesmith taught Herald one of his compositions, "Different Drum," and the Greenbriar Boys included their arrangement of the song on an album. Nesmith's career had stalled by September 1965 when he attended an open casting call in *Variety* for "Folk and Rock Musicians-Singers." It changed his life. In short order, Nesmith was catapulted into the limelight as one of television's Monkees. The Monkees audition drew over four hundred hopefuls, including Stephen Stills, Harry Nilsson, and Paul Williams. Even mass-murderer Charles Manson is said to have tried out. And the entire Lovin' Spoonful were originally considered for the show.

Meanwhile, John London joined two other ex-Texans who were friends of both his and Nesmith's from back home. Michael Murphey and Owens "Boomer" Castleman had formed the Texas Twosome and they were playing folk rock and country music in L.A. clubs. Future Nitty Gritty Dirt Band member John McEuen worked with the Twosome for a time. With the addition of John Raines and Ken Bloom, the group later became the Lewis & Clark Expedition. Despite recording an album and several singles penned by the Murphey/Castleman writing team, the only notoriety they earned was for contributing the country-influenced song "What Am I Doing Hangin' Round?" for the Monkees on their *Pisces, Aquarius, Capricorn & Jones, Ltd.* album. But Nesmith refused to forsake his old friend. Future First National Band member John Ware remembers, "When Mike and John were first in L.A., they were sleeping in the backseat of cars. When Mike joined the Monkees, John London was his stand-in. That's how he made his living. He was in the Texas Twosome and Lewis & Clark, but there wasn't much money in it. He paid his rent from the Monkees. That relationship was very deep, and goes back a long way. They used to fill the bottles full of the chalk paint [liquid paper, invented by Mrs. Nesmith] that Mike's mother was selling. They really loved each other."

During the juggernaut success of the Monkees' bubble-gum pop music, Nesmith continued to write prolifically, accumulating a large list of material turned down by the other Monkees. "I wrote all the time. I wrote a song a day. That was my principal craft. And when I got into the Monkees I started feeding them songs. But most of those songs were rejected. 'Some Of Shelly's Blues,' 'Little Red Rider,' and 'Silver Moon,' I had written while I was in the Monkees. I played them to Don Kirshner, to the producers, and they had been uniformly rejected. A lot of it was rejected not because the songs weren't any good, but because they were country. They'd say, 'Well, that's not Neil Diamond.' And when Mickey Dolenz would sing them, they would take a major left turn so that nobody had any idea what it was. The notion that there was some kind of integrity to the music, and that it had roots and a cultural underpinning, had no currency in the Monkees' environment." Despite the prevailing sentiment, Nesmith did manage to bring a touch of country to the Monkees with "You Told Me" on their *Headquarters* album, where Nesmith dabbled on pedal-steel guitar. Their follow-up album, *Pisces, Aquarius,* included Douglas Dillard guesting on "What Am I Doing Hangin' Round."

The Kentucky Colonels had gone their separate ways by October 1965. The British Invasion, and the advent of folk rock, had all but killed the folk movement. For Clarence White, it was time to move on to newer territory. That meant learning to play electric guitar. "The transition was pretty strange," recalled White years later. "It was almost like starting all over again. I was playing bluegrass, picking along to very fast fiddle tunes. I was achieving a fingerpicking sound, like three-string banjo style, but I was just using one pick, flat-picking real fast, going all over. That way I was able to get a loud, ringing sound, which was clear at the same time. Consequently, when I switched to electric, I found I had far too much strength and power in my right hand. I had to use a more delicate touch. I'd done most of my playing in open tuning using a capo, so I had to learn the whole neck. Because of this, I always maintain that I'm an electric country guitarist working in rock, rather than a rock & roll guitarist, like Clapton or Beck, who came up through blues." Armed with a Fender Telecaster electric guitar, White turned to studio work, his mentor being studio ace James Burton. "I was aiming at the same territory as James."

White's reputation as a country picker par excellence brought him to the attention of several recording artists who sought to grace their tracks with his unique style. His technique was a combination of fast flat-picking, fingerpicking, and string bending. White recorded with many artists, including Ricky Nelson, Pat Boone, the Everly Brothers, and the Monkees. In addition, White backed up Vern and Rex Gosdin on several sessions for Gary Paxton's Bakersfield International label, performing live with them too. It was during these sessions that White first met Gene Parsons in late 1965.

"I was doing a session in Hollywood at a little studio that Darrell Cotton had," recalls Gene Parsons. "He said, 'I want you to meet Clarence White.' The name rang a bell for me, I remembered years back listening to this sixteen-year-old guitar player on an Eric Weissberg record playing all this incredible stuff. I thought, 'It couldn't be the same Clarence White.' But sure enough, Clarence comes in and he had an electric guitar. He had just started playing electric guitar, and was playing it with a capo. He was just getting started with an electric but he was *unbelievably* good on it already."

A native of the California desert town of 29 Palms, Parsons was a versatile musician who had mastered banjo, bass, harmonica, guitar, and drums. His first professional stint was playing bass with the Castaways in 1962. "We were what you might call a country show band," recalls Parsons. "We wore monkey suits. They expected that on the Nevada/Las Vegas circuit, and we had to lace the act with show tunes like 'Pennies From Heaven,' complete with dance steps." The group released several singles to an indifferent public before folding. A former band member, Floyd "Gib" Guilbeau, soon summoned Parsons to play drums. "I'd never played drums in my life," laughs Parsons, "but Gib said any bass player could play drums, and so off I went." Guilbeau lured Parsons with a recording contract with Bakersfield International. Label owner Gary Paxton had been one-half of early sixties duo Skip And Flip. Skip was bass player Skip Battin, who later joined the Byrds. Over the next two years, Guilbeau and Parsons cut several country-influenced singles under the name Cajun Gib and Gene. During these sessions Clarence White began working with them, and the three became the nucleus of the label's house band. "Gary used to record in his garage," Parsons relates. "The garage was the studio, and all the equipment was stacked in a bus parked outside. But some great records came out of that place. We had one local hit with 'Sweet Susannah From Louisiana,' which was a country hit in California. We first played with Clarence on a Gosdin Brothers session, and that tune was a hit too, 'Just Enough To Keep Me Hangin' On.' We saw more and more of Clarence, but it took about a year to get to know him well, because he was so quiet." By then White was performing live with Parsons and Guilbeau.

Besides issuing singles by Cajun Gib and Gene, the Gosdin Brothers, and various former Castaways members, Bakersfield International also released a couple of instrumental singles by Clarence White. One of these, 'Tango For A Sad Mood,' became the theme music for Nashville-based country music DJ Ralph Emery.

The Byrds rode the crest of the folk rock wave throughout 1965, accruing tremendous success, adulation, and financial reward as America's answer to the Beatles, a label pinned on them by the music press. Their debut album boasted five Gene Clark compositions. Two of his songs served as B sides to their biggest hit singles, "Mr. Tambourine Man" and "Turn Turn Turn," so Clark's earnings easily surpassed those of his bandmates. "He was in Ferraris, and we were starving," commented McGuinn. For Clark, stardom was already beginning to take a toll, and the constant air travel was becoming problematic. He turned increasingly to alcohol and drugs. By the time the Byrds' second album, *Turn, Turn, Turn,* was released in late 1965, the other members were beginning to challenge Clark's preeminence as a songwriter. Hillman was among the challengers, suggesting the group cover an old Porter Wagoner country hit, "A Satisfied Mind." Recorded in a folk arrangement during a session in September 1965, the track is indicative of Hillman's abiding interest in country music.

Out on the East Coast, the folk revival had first sprung up in Greenwich Village. For folkies, the Village was Mecca, drawing hundreds of acolytes each year, acoustic guitars slung over their fleece-lined jackets, searching for Bob Dylan's dream. Two such folkies making the pilgrimage in 1964 were Richie Furay and Cecil Ingram "Gram" Parsons. A native of Yellow Springs, Ohio, Furay had grown up listening to country music around the house. "Back then I liked guys like Conway Twitty and Eddy Arnold," recalls Furay. But by the time he enrolled at Otterbein College in 1963, he had become a folk music devotee. A fan of the Kingston Trio, Furay formed the Monks, a folk trio, to play campus get-togethers during his freshman year. In the summer of 1964, the Monks set out for Greenwich Village. Following a brief stint in the basket houses,* the Monks accepted an offer to join a nine-piece folk ensemble, the Au Go-Go Singers, whose members included a brash young southerner named Stephen Stills. After headlining a short-running off-Broadway production titled *America Sings*, the Au Go-Go Singers next took up a residency at the Café Au Go-Go. They recorded a quickly forgotten album of folk standards before imploding following the invasion of the Beatles.

---

*So called because the performers were paid out of a basket through the audience.

Furay, Stills, and the other Au Go-Go Singers lived on Thompson Street in the Village. Gram Parsons had an apartment across the street and became a friend as the shift from folk to folk rock transformed the pop music world in early 1965. Stills had recruited Parsons for an ill-fated attempt at his own folk rock group in the spring of that year. Failing at that, Stills left for California later that summer. Furay and Parsons often crossed paths in the Village, where Parsons' folk quartet, the Shilos, were attempting to eke out an existence in the basket houses. Money was never an issue for Parsons. He was the beneficiary of a family trust that paid out semiannual dividends. The Parsons family owned a thriving orange grove business back in Florida. The rich kid with the haunting eyes was writing poignant songs at an early age. "Gram taught me 'Brass Buttons' when he lived across the street in New York," Furay recalls. "I was just blown away. Sometimes you just hear a song and think, 'Wow, this is *good*.' I stored it away." The two eventually moved to New England, Furay to Wilbraham, Massachusetts, where he worked at Pratt & Whitney Aircraft, and Parsons to Cambridge to attend Harvard University studying theology.

The Shilos, formed by Parsons, were a folk quartet crafted in the Kingston Trio mold. Based in Greenville, South Carolina, the Shilos played folk clubs and proms along the southern East Coast. Moving to New York, they worked in Greenwich Village before splitting up in the summer of 1965. Parsons headed to Harvard in September. Within weeks of commencement, he discovered he wasn't interested in academic pursuits and immersed himself in the social life on and off campus. At one party, Gram met local guitar player John Nuese. Nuese was a true anomaly: a young, longhaired musician with a passion for country & western music. His obsession would ignite a fire in Parsons that set a direction for his musical career.

"Gram had played a little country music back in Florida," remembers Nuese. "But he wasn't really interested in it. At the time I met him in September 1965, he was a folksinger. He wasn't into country music. I introduced him to the music of Merle Haggard and Buck Owens, and the people who were doing great music at that time." Though he had an unusually wide range of musical tastes, Nuese's interest in country music stemmed from an affinity for ethnic mountain music. "I had been listening to country music since 1948. But I listened to blues and rock & roll, like Elvis Presley and the guys on Sun Records. Then around 1957 I started listening to Doc Williams, and his band The Border Riders. He was a fabulous guitar player. I listened to the Wheeling

Jamboree on the radio, and became quite interested in bluegrass too. Ethnic mountain music became popular in the early sixties. Yale used to put on the Indian Neck Folk Festival every spring. They invited people like the New Lost City Ramblers, and Blind Reverend Gary Davis. I remember seeing Bob Dylan when he first performed there. A lot of great music was made at these festivals. By the time I met Gram, I had been listening to country music for years, and I recognized it as a real powerful form of music that needed to be played by young white guys."

Parsons was immediately taken with Nuese. The two jammed together the first night they met. Nuese served as Parsons' mentor. Country was an idiom Parsons would embrace as if born to it. Recalls Nuese, "When I met him I thought he was a talented guy. I said, 'Hey, let me put you onto some country music.' As soon as he heard it he started to get into it. That's how it started." Whether it was the similarity to folk, or the lovelorn stories of its lyrics, Parsons had found his muse. The two decided to form a band. Parsons boasted that he had connections in New York once things got rolling. "Gram was involved with a manager named Marty Erlichman, who handled Barbra Streisand," Nuese, recalls. "Gram had a deal going whereby Marty would look after him, and money would be available for him to record." Parsons had finagled a deal to back former child actor and friend Brandon De Wilde on some demo sessions. All they needed was a band.

Parsons and Nuese recruited bass player Ian Dunlop and drummer Mickey Gauvin, and together they founded a band called The Like. Launched in the fall of 1965, The Like would rename itself the International Submarine Band. Parsons' friend Tom Snow, a Berklee School of Music student, joined the group for a brief time but by November they were back down to a quartet and ready to approach Erlichman. "We got everyone together in Cambridge," related Nuese. "We started to enlarge our repertoire to include country and rock & roll. 'November Nights' was our original song. Gram wrote it. Peter Fonda later recorded it. During the latter part of 1965 we went to New York several times to record."

Nuese and Parsons had a mission with the Submarine Band. "Gram and I felt that country music was the white blues. This is the reason we wanted to get the International Submarine Band started. To get young white people to recognize their roots, and see how significant country music is for young white people who approach it from the rock side of things. Here were a bunch of longhairs playing country music. Kids had never heard it before. They thought it was great. We knew that it was going to work." Playing the rock & roll standards of the day, the group eased into country music, infusing it with rock & roll that was largely the result of Gauvin's strong drumming and Parsons' sympathetic vocals. "We played a lot of black stuff, country stuff, and some regular rock & roll," noted Nuese. "As far as others playing country music, there were none. We were the only guys playing it."

Years later, Parsons reflected on the influence that the International Submarine Band had in his career. "The guys in the ISB were important; they always had their ears open, and they reintroduced me to country music after I'd forgotten about it for ten years. The country singers, like George Jones, Ray Price, and Merle Haggard, they're great performers, but I had to learn to dig them, and that taught me a lot." Ian Dunlop credits Ray Charles as an early, unlikely inspiration for the group. Charles' two country-influenced r & b albums in the early sixties had taken country & western standards and presented them with a tougher rhythm sound, especially on his 1965 album, *Country And Western Meets Rhythm And Blues*. "I think that record is key," Dunlop told writer Ben Fong-Torres. "That was the thing that broke the barriers, getting into this amalgam of a truer country music, but with a rock or a rhythm & blues treatment."

In January 1966, the International Submarine Band moved south to New York to play in the hipper clubs around the city. According to Nuese, "We did a tremendous amount of playing, a lot of clubs, and we did a tour around Florida opening for Freddie Cannon. We played the Night Owl, Trude Heller's, all the New York clubs. We worked a lot. Our biggest show was in the summer of 1966 in Central Park opening for the Young Rascals." Never noted as a country music town, young New York audiences warmed to the Sub Band's sound. "People were surprised we were playing country music. But what we would do was to combine country music with rock. We'd play several rock songs, then a country song. Our repertoire was mostly rock, but we also played Buck Owens and Merle Haggard songs. We played them with that same approach to rhythm that you played rock & roll. Although a little surprised at first, the people got into it. People liked it because the drummer was great." Parsons once described the International Submarine Band as a "rhythm & blues, country & western group."

In New York, the Sub Band dropped Erlichman and signed with managers Monte Kay and Jack Lewis. They secured a one-off record deal with the Ascot label in May for the Sub Band to record an instrumental version of the title track for *The Russians Are Coming, The Russians Are Coming.* The group chose to back the single with a rocking Buck Owens number, "Truck Driving Man," a song well-suited to the band's country-with-a-rock-attitude approach. The sound of this recording proved that young players could play the raucous Bakersfield sound well. Despite the failure of their debut, the group was signed to Columbia Records and issued a second single, "Sum Up Broke," backed by "One-Day Week," the former written by Neuse and Parsons, the latter penned by Parsons. "We went to a great studio in New York with engineer Brooks Arthur and recorded that," Nuese remembers. "'Sum Up Broke' was a song based on a guitar riff of mine, and Gram wrote words to it. That was released as the A side. It was a hard-rock guitar riff." Once again, the single stiffed. Both sides were cut in a definite garage rock vein, rather than the country style the group was beginning to favor. Undaunted, the Sub Band continued to play clubs and share a house in the Bronx, while they waited for the music world to catch up to them.

One visitor to their house was Barry Tashian, the leader of the Boston rock group The Remains, whose claim to fame was touring with The Beatles. Says Tashian, "I saw the Sub Band play in their house up in the attic, with the walls covered in egg crates. I really loved the band. That's what turned me on to country music, hearing Gram and Ian sing Buck Owens' 'Waiting In Your Welfare Line,' and 'My Heart Skips A Beat.' Those were the first two songs I heard and I just thought, 'Wow, cool!' Ian Dunlop was singing harmony. They just sounded great. They had it."

Up in Wilbraham, Richie Furay fretted because his music aspirations were foundering. Working at Pratt & Whitney was not what he had in mind when he left Ohio eighteen months earlier. A visit by Gram Parsons in late 1965 inspired a musical epiphany. "Gram had the Byrds' debut album. He played it for me, and I thought, 'This is *good*, I'd like to be a part of something like this. I gotta find out where Stephen Stills is and get ahold of him.'" Writing to Stills via his parents in El Salvador, he received a phone call from his former bandmate, and an invitation to come out to L.A. to join Stills' group. Furay flew out in early February 1966, only to discover there was no group. It was just Stills writing songs and rehearsing. The two worked up a repertoire of folk rock songs before a legendary serendipitous encounter on Sunset Strip. With Furay and Stills in one vehicle, they spotted Canadians Neil Young and Bruce Palmer driving in the opposite direction in Young's old hearse. It was a star-crossed moment: the four agreed on the spot to form a group. That group would become the Buffalo Springfield. All they needed was a drummer.

After the Dillards had released *Pickin' And Fiddlin'*, their contractual obligations to Elektra were met. They signed with Capitol Records, and entered the growing folk rock field alongside the Byrds. Jim Dickson and Eddie Tickner were handling the business affairs of both groups, so the Dillards plugged in their instruments, grew their hair, and joined the rock circuit. They appeared on rock television showcases like *Shindig, Where The Action Is,* and *Hollywood-A-Go Go.* "Why did I go electric?" laughs Rodney on the group's bid for pop success. "Because it made more noise." With an ear to the current pop charts, their debut Capitol single, produced by David Axelrod, was Tom Paxton's popular folk number "The Last Thing On My Mind." The single was backed by Rodney and friend Bill Martin's "Lemon Chimes," both songs cut in the folk rock style. When it failed to chart it became clear that the Capitol executives weren't sure how to deal with the group. As Dean Webb recalls, "The guy who signed us to Capitol Records was Curly Walters. He seemed to understand perfectly what we did. But we signed and we never saw him again. They started putting us with all these other producers, though we were convinced Curly was going to be our producer—he understood what we wanted to do. After the record failed, nobody down there seemed to understand or know what to do with us. They kept submitting all this material, but they didn't know what they had signed or why. It was really a strange, frustrating situation. The Beatles' version of 'I've Just Seen A Face' had just been released in England, but not yet in the United States. So we cut *that* with the idea of beating them to the punch in the States, but, for whatever reason, it didn't get released. The other track we cut was a Bob Dylan number, 'Lay Down Your Weary Tune,' but it never got released either."

In early 1966, the Dillards joined the Byrds for a major American tour. "We had a common bond with Chris Hillman; he played bluegrass too," states Rodney. "It was an interesting tour. It also brought us the Byrds' audience." The Dillards added drummer Dewey Martin for the tour. A Canadian-born veteran of several Nashville-based country artists including Faron Young and Patsy Cline, Martin had been working on the West Coast for the last few years. He had recently led his own pop group, Sir Raleigh and the Coupons. "We opened for the Byrds, and we'd leave it up to the promoter in each town to decide what he wanted," recalls Dean Webb. "We'd tell them we had three ways we could do it: we could do a total acoustic set, or we could play a total electric set, or we could play half-and-half. We could lay down the acoustic instruments half way through and pick up the electric ones and do the rest of the show that way. It would differ from place to place. The Byrds did total electric, and they were *loud*. Sometimes, after our part of the show, those who came specifically to hear us, not a whole lot of the show, would get up and leave. They couldn't take the loud music."

The tour proved to be a turning point for Gene Clark. His fear of flying had reached the crisis point, and his flying anxiety was increasing as the time for each flight approached. Attempts at sedating him with alcohol and drugs proved unsuccessful, and only intensified his hysteria. On one occasion, his shrieking premonitions of impending doom resulted in several members of the entourage refusing to board as well. It was clear Clark would have to come to terms with his growing fear if he wanted to continue to tour.

The Dillards returned to an acoustic format and jettisoned the amplifiers following the tour. This meant cutting drummer Martin loose. As Martin recalls, "Rodney and Doug Dillard were at odds at that time. They were searching for something new, but they weren't cutting it. Rodney was pissed off because they weren't going over like they had when they did bluegrass. After the tour I was sitting with Doug Dillard out at The Ice House in Pasadena. He said to me, 'We're going back to bluegrass, and we don't need you anymore. Call Jim Dickson, he's got a gig.' I called Dickson. He gave me Stephen Stills' number, and I called him. Stills said he'd heard of me and asked 'When can you bring your drums over and audition?' Audition? I'd never auditioned for anybody! Who'd these guys think they were?" The next day, with drums in hand, Martin arrived to audition for the cocky young group. "When I walked into the room the first time and heard Richie and Steve singing 'Go and Say Goodbye,' I knew I had never ever heard a vocal sound like that." When Martin asked for the group's name, lead guitarist Neil Young simply pointed to a metal nameplate hanging on the wall that he had torn from a steamroller parked outside: Buffalo Springfield. With amplifiers and guitars cast aside by the Dillards, the new group set about forging their own unique folk-country-rock sound.

Less than a week later, on April 11, 1966, the Buffalo Springfield made its public debut at the Troubadour. Four days later the group opened for the Byrds and the Dillards at the Swing Auditorium, Orange Showgrounds, in San Bernardino. Gloats Martin, "The Byrds could hardly follow us. We had so much energy because we had a high-powered set right through, and the audience was *digging* it." The short six-date tour in southern California marked a turning point for the Byrds. It was their first official appearances without Gene Clark. In March, following the Dillards tour, Clark had announced his departure. According to Jim McGuinn, "He got uptight on airplanes. He reached the point of crisis, the mounting pressure of the whole gig, and at that point it was pretty intense. He's a country boy from Missouri, a farm boy who got into this high-intensity city thing, and the airplanes got to him." Commented Clark years later, "It wasn't that I was afraid of flying, but that I was tired of flying. Basically, the group had a nervous breakdown. That's the only way to describe it."

Although Clark's fear of flying was cited as the reason for his exit, there were other issues festering below the surface. A power struggle between McGuinn and Crosby on one side, and Clark on the other, had resulted in his role in the group diminishing. His contributions were being pushed aside. With the release of the ambitious single "Eight Miles High," which had been co-written by Clark, America's premier group was already distancing itself from folk rock to explore what would become, albeit briefly, raga rock, a precursor to psychedelic acid rock. Throughout the tour the group was met with shouts of "Where's Gene?!" By leaving the Byrds, Clark became the first member of a top echelon group to go out on his own and attempt a solo career.

# 3

# Nashville West: 1966–1967

*They assigned us a big-time country producer, Ken Nelson, but we just didn't connect. Then they tried to throw us to a guy who produced Wayne Newton. I remember they had a big meeting with us, and they were coming up with songs written by somebody's brother-in-law, and we just looked at each other and said, "screw you" and walked out.*

—Rodney Dillard

In July 1966, following a lengthy engagement at Hollywood's Whisky-A-Go Go, the newly formed Buffalo Springfield released their country-influenced debut single, "Go And Say Goodbye." Written by Stephen Stills, it was a sprightly country-flavored number featuring Stills' and Richie Furay's tight harmonic vocals over country licks from guitarists Stills and Neil Young. The unique opening guitar signature, picked country-style by Stills, was inspired by a friend's suggestion. "That intro lick was from 'Salt Creek,' a bluegrass instrumental," confirms Chris Hillman. "Stephen and I were screwing around, and I played it for him and he liked it and used it." Attests Furay, "I thought 'Go And Say Goodbye' was a really good song. I later re-recorded it with Poco. I liked that song a lot; I liked singing it and playing it." During recording sessions, another acquaintance was solicited to contribute a uniquely country flavor. "We tried to get Doug Dillard to play jug on 'Go And Say Goodbye,'" continues Furay, "but we could never get it in tune. So he kept drinking it to get the right pitch. He'd go, 'Whoo' and we'd say, 'No, still not right.' By the time we got the right key he was too drunk to play it." Unfortunately, due to some behind-the-scenes politics at

49

Atco Records, "Go And Say Goodbye" was relegated to the B side at the last minute, replaced by Neil Young's moody "Nowadays Clancy Can't Even Sing." The flip-flop failed, and the single didn't chart well. Springfield manager and producer Charlie Greene feels he knows why. "'Go And Say Goodbye' was a bit too much of a shit-kicker for that time. Too country & western."

The Springfield continued to introduce country textures into their original blend of folk rock. "When it comes to integrating country in-fluences in rock," opines Hearts And Flowers' Rick Cunha, who shared billing on several shows with the Buffalo Springfield, "for my thinking, the Byrds were close, but the Springfield were even closer because in their live shows they did some country-style picking. It didn't always get to the albums, but they could play it."

Meanwhile, the Dillards had entered Capitol's studios again in 1966 to record another single. This time Rodney was determined to exert more influence in the selection and production. "Jim Dickson and I had differences of opinion on what it should sound like," says Rodney. "At one point he said, 'Okay, you go ahead and mix it.' So I did. I had started out early wanting it to sound a certain way." The result was one of the first bluegrass/country rock singles ever released, incorporating the Dillards' harmonies with electric instruments and a country beat. "The Dillards had one of the first country rock singles ever made, called 'Nobody Knows,'" maintains the Lovin' Spoonful's Jerry Yester, "which ended up later on their *Wheatstraw Suite* album, and 'Ebo Walker,' with Douglas Dillard fingerpicking an electric twelve-string to great effect. It was just an amazing sounding record, I loved it to pieces, but nobody heard it. I don't remember hearing a country rock thing be-fore that time. Those songs were bluegrass put to electric bass and drums, kind of a folk rock approach, but the Dillards' natural extension into folk rock would be bluegrass rock anyway, which is country about as much as you can get." Confirms Rodney, "On that song, Douglas fin-gerpicked the twelve-string and doubled the part on electric banjo. No-body had ever done anything like that before." "Ebo Walker" may be the first electric bluegrass recording.

Once again, the record-buying public ignored the single and the Dil-lards were forced to reassess their relationship with Capitol. They had updated their sound and approach to a more contemporary style, with folk rock, country, and pop influences. They had cut six sides for the label, four of which had been released only to disappear almost imme-diately. The music the group was writing and recording was far more adventurous than their previous work, yet the label seemed unable to market it. "We had left Elektra because we felt we weren't getting a fair deal," Rodney Dillard recalls, "and the guy who signed us at Capitol disappeared, so no one knew what to do with us."

After enjoying enormous success in the late fifties to early sixties with a pop/rockabilly style that harkened back to Elvis's early recordings, and selling in excess of twenty million records, including "Hello Mary Lou," "Travelin' Man," and "Poor Little Fool," Ricky Nelson's career had bottomed out by the mid-sixties. The British Invasion had made him seem tame and rendered Nelson and other squeaky-clean American teen idols obsolete. Though he continued to record, few of Nelson's singles and albums managed to chart. It was time to pause and reassess his direction. Signed to an unprecedented twenty-year contract with Decca, a deal secured by his manager at the time, his father Ozzie, Nelson was keen to shed his boy-next-door persona. After all, he was a married man in his mid-twenties with children, not the toothy kid on his parents' weekly television show. He dropped the "y" to become Rick Nelson, and sought a more adult image and sound. He had always worked with the cream of the L.A. studio session players, and his ace-in-the-hole had been guitar hero James Burton. But by 1966, Burton and the other band members had tired of the road grind, and turned to more lucrative and secure session work. Although a hysteria-filled tour of the Far East in April of that year had been an ego boost, Nelson's record sales in America remained sluggish.

In a move calculated to appeal to an entirely new market, but one that could still relate to his name and rockabilly credentials, Nelson took James Burton's suggestion to release a straight country & western album, *Bright Lights And Country Music*, in May 1966. Backed by Elvis' vocalists the Jordanaires, and driven by the stellar work of gifted session players like Burton, Glen D. Hardin (both of whom would graduate later that year to Elvis' touring band), Joe Osborn, Glen Campbell, and the prodigy Clarence White, Nelson found himself comfortable with the softer country sound. A single he wrote, "You Just Can't Quit," was an autobiographical medium-tempo country number. It drew some interest, but failed to chart. The album finds the former teen idol at home with country but at odds with his image. It had several country standards: Terry Fell's honky-tonk "Truck Drivin' Man," (popularized by Buck Owens and the Buckaroos, Fell's original recording had featured Buck on guitar), Doug Kershaw's Cajun-flavored "Louisiana Man," Willie Nelson's "Congratulations," and the evergreen "Hello Walls." Nevertheless, Nelson's foray into country music led other rockers to the genre.

"I've liked country music as long as I can remember," Nelson told an interviewer at the time. "I've always been a big fan of guys like Johnny Cash and Jim Reeves. Most of my early recordings were at least part country." He introduced his new sound at an all-country music show at L.A.'s Shrine Auditorium the following month. Backed by Burton, Hardin, White, and Bob Warford (an acolyte of White's), Nelson's performance drew critical praise. *Los Angeles Times* critic Robert Hilburn wrote that Nelson could have a promising career in country music.

Like the Blue Guitar in San Diego, McCabe's music store out in Long Beach was a gathering place for novice folk musicians seeking to work on their craft and spend time with each other. Detroit-born guitarist Jeff Hanna was attending high school in the South Bay area when he started giving guitar lessons at McCabe's. A chance encounter with two local players, Jimmie Fadden and Ralph Barr, led to the formation of the Illegitimate Jug Band. The three recruited Hanna's friends Bruce Kunkel and Les Thompson and named themselves so because they were a jug band without a jug. For a brief few weeks the group included a very young Jackson Browne before he moved on and another Long Beach native, John McEuen, signed on. "The group that I joined had backed me up at a banjo contest which I ended up winning," recalls McEuen. "That was in the summer of 1966. Prior to that the band had only had one job. I was the guy who played acoustic instruments: banjo, fiddle, mandolin." With McEuen on board and his brother William, a popular local DJ, ensconced behind the scenes as manager, the group became the Nitty Gritty Dirt Band. They were an acoustic-based folk and jug band and vaudeville act that performed in Los Angeles/South Bay folk clubs, including a semiregular spot at the Paradox. Their colorful act drew a loyal following at the spot. Dressed in pin-striped suits and sporting handlebar mustaches, the Dirt Band's presentation reminded listeners of England's New Vaudeville Band (of "Winchester Cathedral" fame). They had a repertoire heavy with ragtime numbers like "I'm Gonna Sit Right Down And Write Myself A Letter," "Hard Hearted Hannah," and "Candy Man." Signed to Liberty Records in late 1966, the Nitty Gritty Dirt Band's early albums offer an eclectic blend of styles, and the group enjoyed a surprise hit single in early 1967 with the evocative folk tune "Buy For Me The Rain." "We had a lot of confusion for a year or so about electric versus acoustic," states manager

William McEuen, "and we often found ourselves playing to only a handful of persons at the Ash Grove."

Following bluegrass loyalist John McEuen's lead, the Dirt Band soon ventured into country and bluegrass territory. "My personal mentors," offers McEuen, "were Jesse McReynolds from Jim and Jesse on mandolin. I liked his cross picking sound. That's why you hear the mandolin the way it is on 'Mr. Bojangles.' And Earl Scruggs and Doug Dillard for banjo—Doug Dillard first because I saw him first. The Dillards influenced thousands of people toward bluegrass music, yet the bluegrass world has never given them one bit of notice, one hall of honor or anything." McEuen was smitten with Douglas Dillard's facile banjo picking after witnessing a Dillards performance at the Paradox in 1964 and, like Chris Hillman, took to following his hero from gig to gig. "When Doug Dillard came out and kicked off with 'Hickory Hollow,' I don't think I took a breath for awhile. I had never heard music that excited me like the Dillards' music did." Seated in the front row at Dillards engagements, McEuen would bring along his banjo nestled in his lap to copy Douglas' fingering technique. "The first time I spotted him in the audience with his banjo," Mitch Jayne told writer Lee Grant, "I thought 'That yokel is going to play along with us!' but he had enough sense not to do that."

In the late summer of 1966, Denver's Soul Survivors left their home for the bright lights of Los Angeles. Local favorites for several years, the group members thought the time was ripe to take their shot at the big time. "We were top dog in Denver because a guy named Hal More at KIMN radio played the hell out of our record," recalls drummer Pat Shanahan. "You couldn't get it off the air for about six or eight weeks. We were working at a place called the Galaxy which was what they called a 3/2 club because they would serve 3/2 beer* to anyone eighteen or over. We had a steady gig at this club. We were so popular in town and were rivals to a band called the Moonrakers and it was kind of 'Who's going to be first to actually put out a record?' The guy who owned the Galaxy decided to take us out to California, he arranged a deal with Dot Records to record a tune. I wrote a song called 'Can't Stand To Be In Love With You,' and we recorded it. We came back with an actual record on the Dot label and got lots of play in town."

The Soul Survivors were a quintet: Shanahan, John Day on vocals, Gene Chalk on keyboards, guitarist Allen Kemp, and Bob Raymond on bass. "We decided to go to California after our hit record here in

*Beer generally has an alcoholic content of 5% or more. In some more conservative areas of the nation beer is produced and sold with a reduced rate of alcohol, 3.2%.

Denver," continues Shanahan. "We thought we were big shots. But our bass player, Bob Raymond, didn't want to go. We figured we had to get a bass player if we were going to go to California so we went to what was called a battle of the bands, which was kind of a big deal where bands from around the region got together and played. Gene Chalk and I went specifically to find a bass player because all the bass players in the region would be there. We came up to this group with the singer who was playing bass and he had a great voice. It was Randy Meisner. I said to Gene, 'This is what we need. This guy's got a great voice and he can play the bass.' They were called the Dynamics and were from Scottsbluff, Nebraska." Born and raised on a farm in Scottsbluff, Meisner began playing out at age fourteen in bands called the Thunderbirds and the Dynamics. "I heard country music growing up but I wasn't influenced by it," says Meisner. "My influences were Elvis and Conway Twitty. The first song I ever performed in public was 'Honeycomb' at a PTA meeting. I had my first guitar by then and knew a few chords. I later changed to the bass when I started going to school in town." Meisner's talent was distinguished by his amazing high-register vocals as well as his fine playing. A trip to Denver got him noticed by the Soul Survivors. "We went up to Randy afterward," continues Shanahan, "and told him we were the hot shots in town and we were going to California to try and make it. 'Do you want to go with us?' And he said, 'Yeah, I'll go.' That was it. That's how we ended up with Randy. He left his wife Jennifer and kid behind in Nebraska and went off with us."

Gene Clark returned to Los Angeles from his family home in Kansas rested and recuperated from his whirlwind year with the Byrds and formed Gene Clark and The Group. This time he took it slow, playing small clubs around L.A. and no flying involved. Recruiting several friends from the local scene, Clark's Group debuted June 22, 1966, at the Whisky-A-Go Go, following the Buffalo Springfield's legendary stint, for an extended stand into early July. He continued to gig in L.A. clubs throughout the summer. "We had a good idea of what we wanted to do," recalled Clark on the genesis of The Group. "Chip Douglas was in the group playing bass. He later went on to produce records for the Monkees. A man named Bill Rhinehart on guitar, who was a very good friend and a good musician. Joel Larson, he was the Grass Roots drummer, the original Grass Roots. We all got together; but what it really amounted to was it was too soon for me to try and put something together. It wasn't that the musicians in the group weren't good enough or anything like that. It just wasn't formed under the right circumstances." Gene Clark and The Group had disbanded by September. "It was frustrating," said Clark, "excellent as the musicians were, they were all qualified people. But it was confusing because, once again, we were trying to do something and nobody could quite see what." Perhaps because of his frustration, Clark resumed his fast-lane lifestyle, indulging in the latest recreational drugs and enjoying a brief fling with Michelle Phillips, the Mamas and Papas' beauty.

Clark entered Columbia studios to record his debut solo album in the fall of 1966 with a wealth of material. He was still signed to Columbia Records, and the label wanted to capitalize on his notoriety as an ex-Byrd by putting out a solo record. "It was time to make an album of my own," noted Clark. "I wanted to write all the material and do more with my own musical ideas. With the Byrds, most of the ideas had been developed more or less cooperatively. What I had in mind was closely related but more personal. My inspirations, as I remember, were the Beatles' *Rubber Soul*, and early Mamas and Papas." Calling on fellow Byrds Chris Hillman and Michael Clarke to back him in the sessions, Gene also enlisted arranger Leon Russell, Van Dyke Parks, and country pickers Douglas Dillard, Glen Campbell, and Clarence White. Clark also recruited Larry Marks and Gary Usher, who were working with the Byrds at that time, to produce the tracks. Jim Dickson came in near the end of the project to finish up after Usher became too busy with the Byrds' sessions. For vocal support, Clark called on two friends from the Dickson stable of bluegrass/country artists, Vern and Rex Gosdin. "The Byrds and the Gosdins had the same management," stated Clark, "so we had been doing a lot of concerts together, especially in California. Clarence White was playing guitar for them, and their act was kind of country, just country enough for what I wanted to do, and Clarence came along with them. We worked out the basic arrangements for most of the songs, along with Bill Rhinehart and Chris and Michael from the Byrds. The Gosdins and I did the vocals."

"I met Gene through Gib Guilbeau," recalled Vern Gosdin. Gosdin had been recording for Bakersfield International around that time. "Eddie Tickner, the Byrds' co-manager, was looking after us at the time. We had a wonderful time doing Gene's album. Leon Russell was playing on it, and Glen Campbell too. I did all the vocal arrangements for the songs. In fact, I did them while I was painting the inside of a house. I thought that album was way before its time. Gene was nervous about doing his first album. He was a good fella but he was into drugs too much."

With the Gosdins, Hillman, Dillard, and White involved in the project, a country flavor was inevitable. Two numbers, "Tried So Hard" and "Keep On Pushin'," are early examples of country with a rock beat. "Pushin'" featured Douglas Dillard's Rickenbacker electric banjo, a holdover from his electric period in the Dillards. Clark's introspective folk ballads were cloaked in elaborate arrangements with complex backing vocal harmonies. Leon Russell's beautiful orchestration on "Echoes," released as a single in December, highlights the work offering an intriguing example of what has since been labeled "baroque" folk rock. The sessions served notice that Clark wasn't ready to be counted out, and the album reinforced the widely held belief that he had been the most gifted Byrds songwriter.

Following the Clark sessions, the four remaining Byrds entered Columbia studios to record their fourth album, *Younger Than Yesterday*, produced by Gary Usher. While David Crosby had emerged in Clark's absence as a songwriting contributor on their previous album *Fifth Dimension*, he and Roger McGuinn* now vied for creative control of the Byrds. In the power vacuum that resulted, Hillman used the tension between the two to exert his own influence and placed four of his compositions and one co-credit on the new album. Two of these tracks, "Time Between" and "The Girl With No Name," are early examples of country rock. Maintains Hillman, "It's bluegrass with more back beat, with drums. 'Time Between' is probably the first country rock song." To achieve the country feel, he enlisted Clarence White and Vern Gosdin. "When I joined the Byrds I lost track of Clarence for a couple of years," notes Hillman. "Then, around the end of 1966, I found him again living way out of L.A. and playing in country groups in bars and things, playing electric guitar now. So we got him to help us on a couple of tracks. We had never ever used other players, other than on the first single, which had studio players on it. Clarence had just started playing electric guitar but he didn't have that stringbender attachment on yet. It worked out great. Clarence was wonderful, and he grew with the electric music. Bluegrass is a wonderful style of music but it's very limited and confining. It got to a point where I felt restricted by it and had to jump out of it and go somewhere else. And I think Clarence felt that too."

Vern Gosdin contributed backing vocals and rhythm guitar to the initial tracks. "We did 'Time Between' and 'The Girl With No Name' with the Byrds," maintains Vern. "The Byrds were fighting, and wouldn't go into the studio together, so my brother and I went

---

*McGuinn had changed his name from Jim to Roger following his conversion to the eastern religion Subud.

in and did it for them." Hillman points out, "Originally it was Vern Gosdin singing harmony on 'Time Between,' then David came in and replaced it." These tracks mark the earliest attempts at creating an original new musical form: rock music with a country edge.

In December 1966, Hearts And Flowers signed to Capitol Records' new subsidiary label Folk World, and entered the label's studio to record their debut album. Produced by Nick Venet, who had worked previously with the Beach Boys, the record signaled a new direction. Folk World was set up specifically to produce and market less mainstream pop and rock albums. They also signed Fred Neil and the Stone Poneys (featuring Linda Ronstadt). "We were all set to sign with Elektra," remembered Rick Cunha, "but at the last minute Nick Venet came over and told us we would make a mistake signing with them. He told us Capitol was a happening place, and we were going to make a lot of money. His saying was 'Order your new cars now, boys.' When we started recording at Capitol we'd see Buck Owens and others there all the time and that was just heaven on earth for us. They'd be recording in the studio next door and that was really a trip." Cunha asserted that the eclectic nature of the group's folk-country-pop sound was an attractive feature to record companies back then. "It was a time when record companies were going through a transition. Five years before, if you look at the rosters of the labels, it was still a carryover from the forties postwar big bands, Frank Sinatra and stuff. When they started getting into rock & roll it really wasn't a broad base, and they did it reluctantly. What happened was once they started getting successful with these offshoot things that they had no idea what they were doing, the real staid industry people basically found liaison guys to go out and find this crazy stuff and bring it to the label. And the executives would just shake their heads and say 'Okay, give it a try.' Back then you could do it. Album costs were ten to twenty thousand dollars, and they could write it off. And Los Angeles was a very fertile place."

For the sessions, Venet augmented the trio's sparse accompaniment with studio players, though by then the group was working with a regular bass player. Mayne Smith played Dobro, and The Modern Folk Quartet's Cyrus Faryar contributed balalaika. Venet also attempted to moderate the group's overt country influences into a more commercially palatable folk context while retaining their unique bluegrass vocal blend. "The band was even more country before that first album," claims Larry Murray. "On stage, when we were working small clubs, we really got into country. Buck Owens and real roots country, like old Louvin Brothers." Venet had his own agenda regarding the group. "I think Nick felt that was his job to soften the country influences," suggests Cunha, "to take what he perceived as a very raw element, the country three-part harmony, and put it in a modern context. The singing, the harmony, was something we made sure we got the way we wanted." The members battled Venet over the inclusion of Merle Haggard's "I'm A Lonesome Fugitive." "We had to fight for that one," recalls Cunha. "We wanted to do something specifically like that, and I don't think our producer cared too much for it. Our own bass player, Terry Paul, played on it. Nick Venet didn't let him play on anything. He was one to bring in studio musicians. So that sort of showed me this was kind of a throwaway tune for him."

Nineteen sixty-six ended with the release of a tasty bit of country picking from the Lovin' Spoonful entitled "Nashville Cats," an affectionate ode to the hot studio players down in Music City. The single was pure country, and by early 1967 was a surprise Top Ten entry. With that single the Spoonful made country music hip, and it probably introduced the idiom to many younger players. "It was unique in that we were really targeting that country sound as the sound we were trying to get," said Spoonful bass player Steve Boone. "In previous recordings we would touch on country, and that's what came out naturally. But in this particular song, because it was a tip of the hat to the guitar pickers from Nashville, we consciously tried to make it sound country, like we were really Nashville cats. Nobody thought it was going to be enough of a hit on the pop charts because it was so country, and as a result was given no chance to be a crossover hit. In 1966 that was very rare, to have a pop record cross over to the Nashville charts. So the record company loaded it up on the B side with 'Full Measure,' which became a Number One hit in L.A. and other West Coast markets where 'Nashville Cats' hadn't done particularly well. It turned out it did cross over to country where it did pretty well."

Boone claims the Spoonful always had country leanings. "There was a hint of that direction right from our first album. I was a huge fan of Buck Owens. In my opinion, he was the first person deserving of crossover status from country to rock. I was always fascinated by the country sound, and was influenced by it from 1965 on. We loved Floyd Cramer. All of us were major fans of somebody or other in country music. I think the Lovin' Spoonful were one of the front runners in bringing country influences into rock." Adds guitarist Jerry Yester, who replaced original guitarist Zal Yanovsky the following year, "There was a lot of country influence right from the beginning of the Spoonful. A lot of Zally's guitar playing was based on Floyd Cramer piano licks, that little raised third he used to play a lot. He was a big fan of George Jones as well. A lot of the folk musicians were influenced by country music because country music came from folk."

The Summer of Love, 1967, is perhaps best remembered for the Beatles' *Sgt. Pepper* album, the emergence of the San Francisco freak scene, Monterey Pop, and psychedelic music. But it was also during this period that country rock was beginning to evolve. Taking their cue from the Beatles, many artists began experimenting, and stretching the boundaries of the rock form, sometimes to extremes. *Sgt. Pepper* changed things because it was an epochal moment in contemporary music and popular culture. Rock became an art form. The studio wizardry and musical savvy involved in creating the various tracks on *Sgt. Pepper* launched a whole new era in record production. Where the Jefferson Airplane had taken a matter of weeks to record their best-selling *Surrealistic Pillow* album, its follow-up, *After Bathing At Baxters*, took more than six months to complete. Most of the extra time was spent in a drug-induced haze, with Airplane members experimenting with the knobs on the studio console. The Grateful Dead instructed a bewildered studio engineer they wanted him to record the sound of heavy air on their latest effort. Folk rock–turned-psychedelic group Love devoted the entire second side of their *Da Capo* album to a monotonously meandering studio jam, while the Electric Prunes' *Requiem In F Minor* was an overblown concept piece that stretched the limited capabilities of the individual musicians far beyond their range. Drug-fueled San Francisco bands took onstage jamming to the limits of creativity and often into the realm of tedium for those who weren't as high as they were. Excess became the norm. Jumping on the bandwagon a little late, the Rolling Stones weighed in with their own drug-drenched drivel on *Their Satanic Majesties Request*, an album that ushered out the year with suitable pomposity and false-note "flower power" rhetoric.

But not everyone wallowed in these excesses. For many listeners, the acid rock scene and Fillmore freakouts offered nothing of value musically or spiritually. The hippies deemed country music unhip. It was the music of their opponents: the redneck, pro–Vietnam War, "Okie from Muskokie" establishment. But the original hippie ethos was already dying out. In San Francisco's Haight-Ashbury, the storefronts became commercialized head shops and tour buses lined the streets. The "back to the land" movement emerged from the ashes, vaunting a

return to simpler values and lifestyle: granola instead of LSD. Music
followed suit. Fans weary of psychedelic excess turned the sound
down. Once again, Bob Dylan would be at the forefront of this return
to roots and honesty in music.

In January 1967, the king of country music, Johnny Cash, crossed
over to the pop charts with his live recording of "Folsom Prison Blues,"
a remake of an earlier Sun label song, earning a surprise pop hit. His
album *Live At Folsom Prison* also drew the attention of the youth market. Among the artists who took notice was Bob Dylan, still in seclusion
after what was alleged to be a serious motorcycle accident the previous
autumn. Dylan was recording in upstate New York that summer in the
now famous pink house in Saugerties amid the Catskill Mountains.
Turning his back on psychedelic music, Dylan instead drew creative inspiration from Cash and returned to the work of his first folk hero,
Woody Guthrie.

With two Byrds-related albums set for release (Clark's masterful
debut solo and the Byrds' *Younger Than Yesterday*), Columbia Records
made the bewildering decision to release both albums simultaneously.
Both discs made their way into record stores on the week of February
20, 1967, competing for essentially the same fan base. Clark's Byrds
pedigree was hyped, but given the choice between the real thing and
an ex-member's solo record, *Younger Than Yesterday* eclipsed *Gene Clark
with The Gosdin Brothers*. It is a shame that two such innovative albums
should have been forced to go head-to-head in the marketplace. Had
Columbia seen fit to release Clark's record earlier, or hold it back until
the hoopla surrounding the Byrds' release faded, Clark may have fared
better, but his album was buried. Despite critics' support, the album
disappeared quickly, leaving Clark disillusioned.

*Gene Clark with The Gosdin Brothers* still stands as an accomplished
solo effort by an artist taking folk and folk rock into more complex
arrangements and orchestration without sacrificing the integrity of the
music. Heavily influenced by Dylan's work, Clark's folk numbers are
given greater sophistication by arranger Leon Russell's astute ear.
Russell's presence on several tracks defines the album's style. "If I'd
had my way," reflected Clark in the seventies, "Leon Russell would
have produced the whole album, because he is one of the few producers I've worked with who had an excellent empathy for my material."
There is a country feel to some of the tracks, most notably "Tried So
Hard" and "Keep On Pushin'." Driven by Doug Dillard's banjo and
Clarence White's electric guitar work, the album has been errantly

credited with launching country rock. It is, rather, a folk rock pop album with undertones of country music, a path Clark would soon follow more directly

*Younger Than Yesterday* marks a return to former strengths for the Byrds. Their previous album, *Fifth Dimension*, had offered nothing new with the group in a holding pattern while it processed the absence of Clark from the mix. So reviews for *Younger* were generally positive, critics noting a renewed spirit and progressive tone in the music and praising Hillman's emergence from the shadows of McGuinn and Crosby as a creative boost. Choosing to include Dylan's "My Back Pages" was criticized as playing it safe and cashing in on the stature they enjoyed for their "Mr. Tambourine Man" cover. And Crosby's egocentric dalliance, the pseudo-intellectual "Mind Garden," was unanimously panned. Nonetheless, loaded with so many exceptional tracks like the dreamy "Renaissance Fair" and the jazz-flavored "Everybody's Been Burned," *Younger*'s artistic success obscured Hillman's valuable contributions to the album. His two country rock numbers, featuring Clarence White's innovative electric country flat-picking, were all but ignored by all but the most savvy country-influenced musicians. "Anybody who wants to can go back and listen to 'The Girl With No Name' or 'Time Between,' where I utilized Clarence White's skill on guitar," argues Hillman in retrospect. "That was the first jabs at country rock right there."

While the Byrds toured in support of *Younger Than Yesterday*, Clark played small venues like L.A.'s Ash Grove folk club, accompanied by White and the Gosdin Brothers. "We performed with Gene at the Hollywood Palladium on the *Hullabaloo* show," recalled Vern Gosdin. "I believe Clarence White played with us too." With the Gosdin Brothers soon off on their own, Clark retained White to form another Gene Clark Group, drafting ace studio drummer Eddie Hoh and a young bass player named John York. A New Yorker born and raised, John had moved to L.A. in the mid-sixties, working at various times with the Sir Douglas Quintet, Johnny Rivers, and the Mamas and Papas. "When I played with Gene Clark," recalls York, "Gene was playing acoustic guitar with a pickup and Clarence had his Telecaster so we could make any song sound country rock because of the way Clarence played and the way we sang." Though the group gigged in and around L.A. that spring, Clark's profile in the music world had slipped considerably. Plagued by personal and professional problems the group folded without recording. Clark returned to the studio in May to lay down two tracks, his "Only Colombe" and a cover of Ian and Sylvia Tyson's "The French Girl," both of which remained unreleased until many years later.

"Gene was the most prolific writer in the Byrds, earned more money, and owned two Ferraris," opines York. "His stature had grown so there was a lot of animosity toward him from the other Byrds. When Gene left the Byrds, a lot of it was that a certain group of people were telling him, 'You don't need those guys. You can do better on your own.' But he didn't have very good guidance, nor was he the kind of guy who could accept guidance. He wasn't the kind to say, 'I need help here.' He believed that there wasn't anybody there to help him. He needed someone who understood that part of the business." But he could be very vulnerable to offense. "Gene had the kind of personality that was very smooth and gentlemanly," York continues, "but he was also a very emotional guy. One time we played the Whisky, and there were a bunch of record executives there to see the act we were opening for and not listening to Gene. We did about three songs and he got so upset that they were ignoring him and talking through the music. He turned to us and said, 'Let's just jam,' and the rest of the set we just played a blues in E. He was so emotionally upset that he didn't even want to sing to them. He felt the music very deeply. Later in life that kind of mood swing got more extreme. You had to be prepared for either side of his personality."

Clark retreated for a time to lick his wounds following the failure of the album and the group's implosion. Further sessions yielded nothing of substance, and the disappointed singer/songwriter showed up at Byrds' concerts drunk, attempting to get up on stage. The Gosdin Brothers, following their brief moment in the pop spotlight, returned to their roots. "We had a couple of records out on our own that hit the charts," recalls Vern. "Didn't do anything but they did chart. Then we left southern California and went back to Atlanta, and then I went up to Nashville."

Out on the East Coast, the International Submarine Band was preparing to go to California, inspired by Gram Parsons' recent vacation in L.A. "Thanksgiving time 1966, our dear friend, actor Brandon De Wilde, went to Los Angeles to do some television and movie stuff," remembers guitarist John Nuese. "Gram went to visit him and met a girl who was with David Crosby. Their eyes met and it was instant love. So Gram took this girl away from Dave. He called and told us he was in love, and of course we guffawed mightily over the phone. Gram returned, and in December 1966, Nancy Lee Ross came out and stayed at our house in the Bronx for a couple of weeks. Gram was tired of New York and pushing us to move to L.A. Things were jumping for us in New York; we had done some television and had work but New York was getting pricey. We didn't own a van and had to rent those whenever we did gigs. So we started formulating plans to move to L.A. Gram went out first and got connected with a manager named Larry Spector who handled people like Peter Fonda and eventually handled the Byrds. He arranged a large place for us to live in Laurel Canyon and in the early part of March we got one of those drive-a-cars and drove out."

The International Submarine Band quickly found work in the clubs, supporting Iron Butterfly and Love, and with De Wilde's help, signed to contribute to the soundtrack of a Peter Fonda movie, *The Trip.* "There was a session we had done in May or June," confirms Nuese. "We did a movie with Peter Fonda, went into Gold Star studio, and recorded six or seven tunes, rock and some country. That tape has disappeared. Nobody knows where it is. There's some great stuff on it. One song is called 'Hooked,' an r & b redo of the Bobby Marchand tune that we played. There were a few original songs too." The sessions also included another attempt to record Parsons' "November Nights." Their efforts were futile: despite a brief appearance on screen, the International Submarine Band's tracks were replaced on the soundtrack by the Electric Flag. Prior to those sessions, the group had recorded Parsons' rocking "Lazy Days" produced by South African trumpet player Hugh Masekela, who had recently contributed to the Byrds' "So You Want To Be A Rock & Roll Star." The song was never released, but three years later the Flying Burrito Brothers played it on their second album.

Though the epicenter of the psychedelic flower power music scene was up in San Francisco, Los Angeles felt its influence, and the Sub Band found themselves fish out of water. "It was love-ins and acid, flower power, girls taking off their clothes," smiles Nuese. "It was a wonderful time to be in L.A. but they were receptive to hearing country music too. Our approach to country music was from a rock end of things. We weren't like a bunch of rednecks from Dixie, straight arrows with a quarter of an inch of hair. It was longhairs playing country music. So from that angle it was new to them and took a little bit of acclimating to but once they heard it they got into it and liked it. To our knowledge, we were the only people playing hard-core country around L.A. at that time."

Despite their success, the Sub Band was beginning to splinter into two camps. Gauvin and Dunlop started heading toward their first love,

rhythm and blues, abandoning what they considered an ill-fated country experiment. Parsons and Nuese, on the other hand, remained
wholly committed to country music. "Shortly after moving into Burrito
Manor," recalls Nuese, "we were joined by two friends who had played
in the Remains, Bill Briggs and Barry Tashian. Barry was just starting
to get into country music, but at the time he was one hell of a rock
singer. Gram and I talked, and we both felt that the medium for us was
country music. The two other guys in the band decided that they
would form a band with Barry and Briggs, and were joined by a fellow
named Junior Markham from Tulsa who played trumpet and harmonica, and a saxophone player from Lubbock, Texas, named Bobby Keys.
That was the original Flying Burrito Brothers. That would have been in
June 1967. Gram and I were peripheral members and they would do little gigs in the San Fernando Valley and around Hollywood."

"The International Submarine Band split in two," confirmed Parsons
in a 1972 interview. "The bass player and drummer began using the
name Flying Burrito Brothers, or sometimes The Remains of the International Main Street Flying Burrito Brothers Blues Band, depending on
who played. They jammed a lot in clubs with people who wound up
becoming strongly identified with Delaney and Bonnie, Barry Tashian
from the Remains, and, occasionally, myself. They played at the Pre-
lude and all those clubs up and down Lankershim, like the Hobo and
the Red Valour." Recalls Tashian, "Gram was involved with the first
Flying Burrito Brothers when we played in clubs. But the Submarine
Band was breaking up anyway. In hindsight, it's kind of clear to me
that Gram wanted to move off and go on his own, but here he had
moved all these guys out to California. There must have been pressure
on him. When Ian and Mickey left California they were pretty disillusioned. It was a pretty interesting year or so out there. We had a lot of
fun together even if we didn't make any money or history-making
music at that time. I've got some tapes of some crazy nights at Burrito
Manor where we had the tape running. A lot of silliness going on."

Parsons and Nuese went in search of country players and a record
deal. "Gram and I kept the International Submarine Band name," recalls Nuese. "Our plan was that we were going to put together our
own full-fledged country band. So we started by going way out of
L.A. to a place called City Of Industry to hear a steel player named Jay
Dee Maness. We recruited him to do some recording with us, and also
recruited a piano player named Earl Ball." Maness was a regular
player at the Aces club in El Monte, a popular country music venue

east of Los Angeles. "It was the place to hang for country musicians," states Maness. "All I was really interested in was country music. That was my regular job: playing in the house band with Earl P. Ball and Eddie Drake. Everybody went there. I remember Chris Hillman coming out a few times."

The group next signed with a tiny record label, LHI. "Our manager was Steve Alsburg, who had a friend named Suzi Jane Hokom," Nuese continues. "She was involved with this rich record company owner named Lee Hazlewood who owned the LHI record label. One time, Steve brought Suzi Jane over to Burrito Manor and we played, this was the original Submarine Band, live in the living room. She was really impressed and told us we had a deal. Within the following ten days we had a meeting with Lee Hazlewood, and Gram and I told him of our plan to do a full-fledged country band, get studio players and do a country album. Lee was really enthusiastic about that. So at that time the first Submarine Band came to an end and the second Submarine Band was born. The last gigs the original International Submarine Band played were in June 1967. The second Submarine Band was basically a studio band. We never performed. I wish we had." Comments Tashian, "John had a problem performing in public. It was hard for him to loosen up. He could play some fantastic Telecaster stuff in private, but to carry that out to the public was difficult for him."

That spring the Everly Brothers emerged from a long hiatus to release a lush country-flavored single, "Bowling Green," written by their British bass player Terry Slater. Following their induction into the Marines and the changes in pop music ushered in by the British Invasion, the brothers had fallen into obscurity. But they had always loved country music, learning their vocal craft from a tender age on the knee of their musician father Ike Everly. The whole Everly family was featured on Ike's radio show. At the start of their career in 1958, Don and Phil had recorded an album of traditional country and folk material titled *Songs Our Daddy Taught Us*. From the late fifties up to their entry into the U.S. Marine Corps, the Everly Brothers had enjoyed a long string of hit records. But following their military service, the well had run dry. The immortal "Crying In The Rain" was their last chart hit. In 1963 they released *The Everly Brothers Sing Great Country Hits*, recorded in Nashville, where they had cut all their early hits, supported by the cream of the studio players. "Bowling Green" was an attempt by the boys to reconcile their country roots and rock & roll sensibility. It was a superbly full, rich country rock sound that owed much to the pop harmony work of folk rockers like the Mamas and Papas. Though barely entering the Top 40 (despite being a hit in Canada), the single was a magnificent achievement. The brothers would follow it up later in the year with the country album *Roots*, a tribute to their family's musical heritage.

Despite *Bright Lights And Country Music*'s lack of commercial success, Rick Nelson persevered. He released a follow-up, *Country Fever*, featuring the same session players, Burton, Hardin, Campbell, and White. Like *Bright Lights* it was a soft Nashville country sound. Recorded in August 1966 and released the following April, the album features more covers of country standards, like sympathetic versions of Hank Williams' "You Win Again" and "I Heard That Lonesome Whistle Blow," and a smooth version of Willie Nelson's "Funny How Time Slips Away." Other tracks include Dylan's "Walkin' Down The Line," which reflected the Dillards' version of the song more than the original, Gib Guilbeau's Cajun-flavored "Take A City Bride," and the traditional bluegrass number "Salty Dog." While *Country Fever* offered sanitized, "countrypolitan" Nashville country music, once again critics lauded Nelson's country move. The record-buying public, however, continued to ignore him. Stints in musical theater kept his face in the footlights while he formulated his next move. Nelson's follow-up albums, *Perspective* and *Another Side of Rick*, embraced both folk and pop, with covers of Eric Andersen, Nilsson, Paul Simon, and Randy Newman. The eclectic choices reveal an artist still searching for a style that would reconcile his past and give him a future. His friend Andersen was also an admirer of his songwriting and encouraged Rick to write his own material.

In July *Now Is The Time For Hearts And Flowers* was released on Capitol Records' Folk World label. The innovative trio's debut was country influenced, like the single "Rock And Roll Gypsies." Written by Roger Tillison, it had sparked interest around the group's Los Angeles base but failed to set the world on fire. An unfortunate circumstance torpedoed efforts to promote the single. "'Rock And Roll Gypsies' was on the radio and we were really excited, and all our fans were really excited," laments Larry Murray. "It hit on the West Coast and was getting played on the Top Forty stations. We did *Hullabaloo* and those corny television shows with the go-go girls. Capitol came up with some bucks and hired a real heavy-duty disk jockey, Humble Harv Miller from KHJ, and had him do our promos on the air. Back then he was the guy. It was great. '"Rock And Roll Gypsies" by Hearts And Flowers, get it at Wallach's Music City' and so on. They were saturating the air with it and made us feel like stars. The next day in the newspapers the headline read, 'Harvey Miller, famous disc jockey, slaughters his wife.' He'd killed his old lady. Capitol Records yelled, 'Get those ads off the air right now!' We couldn't believe it."

Mixing bluegrass and country harmonies with folk, pop, and country material, *Now Is The Time For Hearts And Flowers* offered a fresh sound at the height of the Summer of Love. The group's take on Tim Hardin's folk chestnut "Reason To Believe" sounds like what the Louvin Brothers might have become had they been recording in 1967. Filing down Merle Haggard's rough edges, the group transforms his hit "I'm A Lonesome Fugitive" into a bluegrass masterpiece without losing the song's country feel. The folk-country singing on "Save Some Time" is simply gorgeous. Larry Murray's folk pop "Rain, Rain" and Cunha's lone contribution "1-2-3 In Carnivour Thyme" reveal the group's commercial pop side. Nick Venet's production work is impressive throughout, highlighting the group's vocal strength with arrangements that integrate acoustic instruments with Dobro, cellos, and understated orchestration. "Hearts And Flowers were doing this weird acoustic music mixing different styles," comments the Dirt Band's John McEuen. "I never thought of it as country music."

Through Capitol's promotional efforts, Hearts And Flowers' profile was raised beyond the folk clubs and Palomino. "We played with The Doors a lot," laughs Murray, recalling the often mismatched bills the group found itself on. "We opened shows for Simon and Garfunkel, The Doors, Chad and Jeremy, Buffalo Springfield. We played some strange gigs. The strangest was at the Whisky with Blue Cheer. There was hardly room for the three of us on stage, they had all these Marshall amps. The music was so loud up in our dressing room we had to walk down the street to talk over our next set. We played a few gigs for them. Why they had us as opening act for their crowd I don't know. Their audience threw firecrackers at us at this big outdoor gig. We sort of knew at the time that we didn't have any competition. Nobody was doing what we were doing. When we got booked it was because people definitely knew what we did. And we had a bit of prestige too, because we had played the Ash Grove with Bill Monroe when there were bluegrass groups who would have done it for nothing."

For larger venues, the group found it necessary to augment their trio with sidemen. "If we were playing a gig where we were being paid enough to afford it," states Murray, "we'd have a bass player and a drummer come in and play with us. We had various people who would do that, everyone from Jim Gordon to Karen Carpenter. She was a damn good drummer; I didn't even know she could sing until years later. David Jackson played bass for us, Terry Paul who later played with Kris Kristofferson, Pete Carr the bass player from Hourglass, which became the Allman Brothers."

With the International Submarine Band's status on hold while the two factions negotiated musical turf, Gram Parsons returned to his family's estate in Florida. While there he bumped into drummer Jon Corneal, an old friend from one of his earliest teenage rock & roll outfits, the Legends. "When I ran into Gram in the spring of 1967," remembers Corneal, "I was just down for my yearly visit home to see the orange blossoms. I had already moved to Nashville in July 1964, and had been playing country music around Nashville. In 1965 Gram had a folk group called the Shilos, and when I ran into him back home then he kind of made fun of me for playing country. When I ran into him in the spring of 1967 he said, 'Man, I've got some music I want to play you, some stuff I've discovered.' And he had a reel-to-reel tape full of George Jones, Merle Haggard, Buck Owens, and Loretta Lynn like *he* had discovered them. I had just come off some Grand Ole Opry–style jobs. I had worked for the Wilburn Brothers for a year, Roy Drusky, Kitty Wells, Connie Smith. I was just leaving Connie Smith when I ran into Gram." Already a veteran on the Nashville scene, Corneal was experimenting with a more contemporary country sound, and drawing on rock influences. "I cut a country rock session in 1966 before I ran into Gram," says Corneal. "It was with the Carpenter Brothers, they sang Everly Brothers–style. I'd come in off the road with the Wilburn Brothers and we'd get together and sing our songs. So I booked a session at Bradley's Barn for us. We cut five tunes of mine. When I played Gram that tape he acted like he didn't like it. He thought it was *too* country."

Now Parsons was intent on following a country aesthetic. With a new Submarine Band lineup in mind, Parsons approached the Nashville-based Corneal with an offer to join him out in California. "He told me about this deal happening with LHI Records and he asked if I wanted to come out and do this thing. So I came out and did the first session, but things weren't happening and were moving slowly and I was used to working as a player."

On July 17, Parsons gathered Nuese, Corneal, pedal-steel player Jay Dee Maness, and pianist Earl Ball at Studio B at Western Recorders in Hollywood to record a single that Suzi Jane Hokom would produce. They added session ace Joe Osborn on bass and cut two tracks, "Luxury Liner" and "Blue Eyes," both Parsons' originals. The singles reflected Parsons' affection for the rollicking Bakersfield honky-tonk tradition and were further authenticated by Parsons' double-tracked southern drawl. The single remained in the can until after the release of the International Submarine Band's one and only album the following year. It would have made a terrific country single, even though it probably would have failed to chart in either the rock market (too country for rock) or the country market (young, longhairs playing country? No way!).

The Submarine Band expanded again that summer when they enlisted two more members. Rather than play out they worked on writing and rehearsing their music at Burrito Manor. "Gram met Bob Buchanan at a music festival in Topanga Canyon," notes Nuese. "He had played in the New Christy Minstrels, real nice guy, good singer, good guitar player. He became a peripheral member and played a minor role in the Submarine Band. We met bass player Chris Ethridge through some friends. He was such an easygoing, affable guy, and loved the sound and concept and was really enthusiastic about it." No gigs meant no income, so Corneal returned to Nashville. "Not everybody was in the same situation as Gram was in," asserts Corneal. "Money was really not a problem to him, he had plenty of it. But I had to work for a living. We needed to be gigging but we didn't. Gram and I would go out and play places. We actually could have performed, but John didn't want to so Gram and I would go and sit in at the Palomino. It was kind of a strange situation. But I knew I could go back to Nashville and get work." With Corneal gone, the group remained on hold until sessions resumed in November.

Of the three singer/songwriters in the Buffalo Springfield, Stephen Stills had the fewest country credentials. He had come out of the folk revival, but Richie Furay had grown up around country music at home. Stills' first passion was blues. Neil Young had played some country numbers in his early Canadian group the Squires. Despite these facts, in the spring of 1967 Stills recorded what many regard as his Springfield-period masterpiece, "Bluebird." Released in June as the follow-up to their Top Ten hit "For What It's Worth," "Bluebird" was a tour de force. Originally titled "Ballad of the Bluebird," the song was, according to Stills, an attempt to emulate "an Appalachian ballad feeling in the lyrics. I wanted it to start as a rock & roll song and slowly develop into what it really is, which it does in the third verse when the banjo comes in. That's the kind of music I started out doing in the Village in little coffeehouses, passing the hat." Incorporating crystal clear country-style acoustic guitar flat-picking and banjo and arranged in a rock style, "Bluebird" draws on Stills' roots in acoustic folk and blues music and his growing sophistication as an arranger and producer. "I was sure that we had *the* follow-up with 'Bluebird,'" muses Furay. "This one was going to put us on the map. I thought 'Bluebird' was the song that was going to make our mark and take us to the top."

With its juxtaposition of acoustic and electric guitar, underpinned by a strident bass line and topped by a traditional clawhammer banjo reprise, "Bluebird" is not necessarily country rock. What it *is* is country-flavored rock. Chris Hillman was awestruck on first hearing the record. "That song was so derivative of an old mountain song with the banjo and that melody. It was something you didn't hear. I loved it." Expectations ran high, but the single stalled at Number 58 in *Billboard*, a disappointment for the band.

Richie Furay's own country inclinations found expression that summer as well. During the Springfield's set at the Monterey Pop Festival in late June, the group, joined onstage by the Byrds' David Crosby, debuted several numbers, including Furay's countrified "A Child's Claim To Fame." It was a bold move for a top-ranked rock group at a major showcase to present such a blatantly country number to the ultra-hip West Coast music cognoscenti. "It was daring to do country then," Furay concedes, "but for me, I never thought about that. That's just what the song sounded like. It was all-natural to me because of my background. My Dad was a big country music listener. I didn't think in terms of categories. I didn't isolate this instrument from that instrument, like 'This is a country instrument and this is an orchestra instrument.' It just all kind of fit together for me." Recorded in August, the Springfield managed to convince James Burton to grace the track with his Dobro playing, adding an authentic country feel. "It was a real thrill to have James Burton play on the track," enthuses Furay. "Boy, I was excited about that. I had been a huge Ricky Nelson fan as a kid. We were sure glad to have him come over and play Dobro with us. He's an excellent player. It was somebody's idea to get James, maybe Steve or Neil or Jimmy Messina, who was working at the studio then. James had a big influence on Jimmy personally, he really liked his style." Employed as a staff engineer at Sunset Sound studios, Messina became a confidant of the Springfield, working with them on tracks for their second album. Only nineteen, he was already an accomplished guitar player who had learned Chet Atkins' style of country picking from his father. Furay further reveals the song's inspiration. "'A Child's Claim To Fame' was a cynical look at Neil's in-and-out of the group, leaving and coming back. I was just tired of that game he was playing." Young's wavering commitment to the Springfield (he deserted the band three times) was a major frustration for Furay.

The track ended up on the B side of their next single, "Rock And Roll Woman," as well as appearing on their second album *Buffalo Springfield Again* that November. To Furay, country-influenced rock seemed like an appealing route to follow. "I think I brought a lot of the country elements to the band, but Neil did, too. Even though Dewey played with some country artists, I don't think his influence as far as the way a song would eventually sound had as much effect as the way a song was written and recorded. I think we all had some country influences, though Steve was more folk and blues maybe, and Bruce [bass player Bruce Palmer] had rock influences. 'A Child's Claim To Fame' was very country. But it had a context on that album because there was a lot of variety. From James Burton's Dobro to Jack Nitzsche's strings, there's a lot of space between those songs. But that's who we were at that time individually." The album shows the internal tensions of the band; despite flashes of brilliance, it lacks cohesiveness. The group had suffered personnel crises that had derailed its momentum at critical junctures in its career.

By early 1967, the Soul Survivors had come to the conclusion that cracking the big time was far more difficult than they had anticipated when they left Denver the year before. They rented a run-down house in East Hollywood and were signed by fast-talking Buffalo Springfield managers Charlie Greene and Brian Stone but the group barely eked out an existence opening for the Springfield and other established L.A. groups at clubs like the Whisky-A-Go Go. "I think maybe we tried to be too original," postulates Meisner, "and we ended up the same way we arrived, with nothing. We lost all our money and the house, then briefly struggled under the name of The North Serrano Blues Band. Then we got to thinking, 'What would be a good name for the band?' Well, we were poor so we decided, okay, The Poor." Two singles on the independent Loma label, produced by ex-Springfield manager Barry Friedman, sank without a trace and the group struggled on through

1967. Laments Meisner, "I had to sell my car, because I was basically down to nothing." By this time Chalk had left, and Randy Naylor came out from Colorado to replace him. The group briefly expanded with the addition of a sixth member, Veedor Vandorn.

Back in Denver, the new kingpins of the local rock scene were a group with the unusual name Boenzee Cryque. Formed in 1965, the group had endured several personnel changes, including the defection of Randy Naylor to the Soul Survivors, to settle by late 1966 on a lineup of six: Joe Neddo (on sax and vocals), Sam Bush (on bass), guitarists Dan Nash and Malcolm Mitchell, drummer George Grantham, and the last addition, steel guitarist Norman Russell "Rusty" Young. "Rusty Young and I went to the same school, Lincoln High in Denver," recalled the Soul Survivors' Pat Shanahan. "My first professional job was playing with Rusty at a place called the Stag Bar on North Federal in Denver with a standup bass player. I was so young I couldn't even drive, so my Dad took me and sat in the audience until I had finished. Rusty and I played a bunch of country & western stuff. At the time I didn't like that music. Rusty was playing all this whining Hawaiian stuff."

"I started playing guitar in 1952," recalls Young, who was only six years old at the time. "In Colorado back then, if you wanted to play guitar they started everyone on lap steel. I started playing in bars in Colorado when I was twelve. In the fifties and sixties that meant playing country music, although we'd try to sneak in Santo and Johnny every once in a while. But I loved Buddy Holly and Chuck Berry, and I listened to rock just like every other teenager. I'd play on Sunday afternoons. They would pass the hat, and that's how we got paid." Young rapidly advanced to pedal steel once he was old enough to reach the pedals with his feet. "When I got to be a teenager of sixteen or seventeen, I started getting professionally serious. I worked in a guitar studio in the afternoons giving lessons from four to seven, and then I would pack up and play country music at 8:30. I'd play until 1:30 when they would close the bar down. I did this for years."

Despite the presence of definite country & western elements, Boenzee Cryque were a rock band. Young doubled on guitar when not playing fuzz-tone steel guitar solos. "Boenzee Cryque's music was pretty similar to Poco, actually," offers Young, who, with drummer George Grantham, would later be a founding member of that band. "We had the steel guitar and were playing Buffalo Springfield, Moby Grape, basic rock songs and some originals. We were one of the two big local acts. We had had a record out that had been number one in Colorado for week after week." Recalls Grantham, "Rusty comes from a big country background. That's all he played before Boenzee Cryque. That was his first time stepping into rock music. But he used to tell us stories about Buck Owens and the Buckaroos being the first country rock band, and I can see what he meant. We thought it would be a great idea to bring Rusty into our band, something new. He started experimenting with different sounds on the steel, and incorporating it into rock music. It just sounded like a good idea. Rusty didn't play steel guitar all the time in Boenzee Cryque, he played both steel and regular guitar. Anything we had the steel guitar on though, was going to take the flavor of country. The style we started really liking was that country rock mesh kind of sound. Rusty played at least as much steel as he did guitar in the band." At the time, Young was content to play in a popular Denver group by night, supplementing his income by day working in a local music store.

In early June 1967, the Buffalo Springfield appeared in Denver at Hal Baby's Teen Club, a converted supermarket. Opening for them was Boenzee Cryque. "Rusty and I just thought the world of the Buffalo Springfield," enthuses Grantham, "so that was like the biggest show of that year for us. I just stood right by the stage with my mouth open watching the whole show. They were our favorite band. We played a lot of their songs, we did a lot of originals too but we did a lot of covers and some of that was Buffalo Springfield." Though the Denver musicians failed to meet their idols, Young managed to get backstage when Stephen Stills asked to borrow a thumb pick. "I remember really well Richie Furay sitting in a corner in a chair wearing his little round John Lennon wire-rimmed glasses, strumming his twelve-string guitar and singing," notes Young. "I thought that he was a real interesting character because he was so anti-rock star. He looked more like a school kid than a rock star."

By the fall of 1967, Rick Cunha had grown restless in Hearts And Flowers and wanted to pursue songwriting in a straight country form. Personality conflicts had also clouded the initial bonhomie. "There was something we had in the group that needed to be nurtured more, but by then everybody sort of went off in different directions. It's hard to get along in a trio because somebody's always at odds," recalls Cunha. "The other member besides Larry was David Dawson, who was an old friend. We had started playing as a duet back in Hawaii, where we had first started playing music. There was a lot of friction between him and Larry, and I just didn't want to be a part of it. So I was looking to move on and do some things on my own, including some production." Cunha served notice, and the others turned to a familiar face. "Larry had known Bernie Leadon, because Bernie had grown up down in San Diego," continues Cunha. "When he was a kid he had been hanging out with the Scottsville Squirrel Barkers. So Larry called him and got him to come out. Bernie stayed with me and I showed him the guitar parts I played. He was twice the guitar player I was."

Leadon had remained active in a variety of musical fronts and had followed the changes through the mid-sixties. "In 1964, when I was sixteen, my Dad moved to Florida so I went there for a couple of years. The American folk era was mimicked in England by skiffle. That was followed by the rock music of the British Invasion, which was British working-class kids echoing black American music. When that happened those of us who could play and were younger just went, 'Wow!' I could already play, so we all ended up in bands, grew our hair out, got Beatle boots, Vox amps, and were off. I did that with Don Felder in my high school band. I had this dichotomy going: I had the folk thing, the bluegrass thing with old-time bluegrassers in north Florida during the week, and I had a British Invasion pop band. When I went back to L.A. in 1967 I had *all* these influences. The thing I didn't have was the Buck Owens' Telecaster thing yet. By 1967, when I came back, Larry Murray and many of the San Diego folk guys had moved to L.A. I remember earlier going to a record store and looking at a Byrds album and thinking, 'Holy Toledo, Chris Hillman's made it.' They were big heroes, bigger than the Beatles for awhile. So I started paying attention to what was happening in L.A. Larry knew my ability to play various instruments, and sing harmony from the bluegrass days in San Diego. In the middle of 1967 I got an offer to move to L.A. and join a group with a major record deal. I showed up, lived with Larry, and we were in the studio within two weeks."

"Bernie was exactly what we needed," claims Murray. Leadon was a gifted multi-instrumentalist with a keen sense of harmony from years in church choirs as a youth. "He was a great player. He was head and shoulders above David and me. We needed more musical dynamics, and Bernie added that. He had been a child prodigy. When he was fifteen years old he could play circles around everybody."

With Leadon in the mix Hearts And Flowers carried on performing their bluegrass-country-folk music in clubs around Los Angeles. "Mainly, Hearts And Flowers played the folk clubs, like the Ash Grove and Troubadour," notes Leadon, "mostly opening up for others. Doug

Weston had top-rank headliners at the Troubadour, and we opened there for people like Gordon Lightfoot, Arlo Guthrie, Judy Collins. We played a lot. Our sets were acoustic then." Larry Murray laughs as he recalls one of the group's notices. "The best review we got was from Robert Hilburn. We were opening shows for Arlo Guthrie, and Arlo got a half a page review, which he warranted. At the end of the article it said, 'Opening the show for Arlo Guthrie at the Troubadour were Capitol recording artists Hearts And Flowers. There were three of them.' That was it. Is that great?"

Meanwhile, the Dillards felt it was time to move on. The failure of their two singles had soured their relationship with Capitol Records. Jim Dickson got them some time in Columbia studios to try out some new material to pitch to other labels. Two tracks appeared several years later, repackaged by Dickson's Together Records label: an old bluegrass number by Ruth Talley titled "Each Season Changes You," and Rodney and songwriter partner Bill Martin's "Don't You Cry." These two cuts reveal the band still stuck somewhere between folk rock, bluegrass, and country rock. "Jim, Eddie Tickner, and Derek Taylor were all trying to do something with us," states Rodney on the period following the Capitol contract. "They funded us to go into the studios, so we cut some Dylan tunes and other things; we had guys from The Leaves and others playing on our sessions. It was very experimental. We were fielding for a new deal at that time. Douglas was still in the band. We weren't with any label then."

Rodney soon fell out with Dickson, insisting that the Dillards needed a new direction. Sensing that the new breed of record managers were more receptive to the group than they had been two years earlier Rodney brought the Dillards back to Elektra Records. "Douglas and I weren't happy with Jim's concept," recalls Rodney. "He was putting in tympanis. It was getting further from what I wanted. It was sounding like the Byrds, and I didn't want to be the Byrds. So we stopped the project and parted ways." Adds Dean Webb, "Circumstances had changed at Elektra, there was a guy in charge we really liked, and we felt we could get better results from him." The contract finalized, Rodney began forming his vision of the Dillards' sound and wrote appropriate material he felt would bridge the various genres the group covered. "I felt extremely limited by bluegrass," comments Rodney about his need to progress and grow, "and I was ready for a radical change."

By autumn of 1967 David Crosby had worn out his welcome with the Byrds, and in October he was ousted rather unceremoniously.

Tensions came to a head after his unannounced appearance on stage with the Buffalo Springfield at Monterey Pop, bickering in the studio over song selection, and Crosby's blunt refusal to participate in the group's new single, Goffin and King's "Goin' Back." When Crosby insisted that the Byrds include his paean to a ménage à trois, "Triad," on their next album, the others confronted him with a fait accompli: a cash settlement and termination of his services. As several tracks had already been laid down in various states of completion for *The Notorious Byrd Brothers*, McGuinn and Hillman soldiered on. Drummer Michael Clarke was also growing increasingly disenchanted with life as a Byrd, and planning his own exit from the group. Jim Gordon replaced him on some tracks. But while session players could easily be recruited, live performances remained another matter. Crosby had to be replaced soon. To everyone's surprise, Gene Clark stepped up to offer his services.

Claiming to have come to terms with flying, Clark appeared ready, willing, and able to return. With his solo career in limbo following the abrupt halt of sessions with producer Curt Boetcher, he needed money. He was the proud owner of two Ferraris, his career had hit bottom, and bills had to be paid. Larry Spector handled Clark's affairs, those of the Byrds, the International Submarine Band, *and* Peter Fonda, so the timing seemed right. The Byrds needed Clark, and he needed them. Besides, friends felt that Clark regretted quitting the group. As he was their most prolific songwriter and a popular performer, the others welcomed him back, though not without reservations. McGuinn and Hillman worried about his mental state, and were keenly aware of the group's declining fortunes. The move was viewed as a potential shot in the arm, but it proved brief.

Clark appeared with the group on the Smothers Brothers show looking petrified. The group headed out on the road soon after. As road manager Jim Seiter told Byrds' biographer Johnny Rogan, "We were booked for three days in Minneapolis and then New York. The first night was weird. Gene was so scared. He kept asking everybody, 'Did I play good? Was I OK?' He was so insecure. I turned his rhythm guitar off. We weren't using it. He was singing flat. I turned his mike off. His own songs weren't that bad, except that he'd get paranoid halfway through them. They couldn't believe what they'd got themselves in for." The group went on to New York as a trio after Clark bailed out on them at the Minneapolis airport, hightailing it home and disappeared into the L.A. night. Clark's return as a Byrd lasted three weeks and involved no recording, though he did co-write "Get To You" on *The Notorious Byrd Brothers*. Unfortunately his credit was omitted upon the album's release. "Gene's credit got lost in the bureaucratic shuffle," claims McGuinn. "It was given to Chris Hillman by mistake. Gene later said that he didn't remember writing it with me, so I guess the authorship will stand as it is."

Undaunted, McGuinn and Hillman resumed sessions for *The Notorious Byrd Brothers*. The name apparently was based on a passing comment from a visitor to the sessions, Gram Parsons. When asked what his current musical endeavors might be, Parsons replied "The Flying Burrito Brothers." The Byrds liked it and adapted it for their needs. Clarence White was enlisted for several tracks, notably "Change Is Now," a McGuinn and Hillman composition, and "Wasn't Born To Follow," another Goffin and King number. The latter ended up on the soundtrack to the Peter Fonda–Dennis Hopper film *Easy Rider*. West Coast pedal-steel guitar ace Red Rhodes was also brought in to lend a country feel to several tracks. Once again, Hillman came through with a number of excellent contributions and brought his country leanings to tracks like "Old John Robertson," on which he plays a country-style lead guitar.

By the fall of 1967, Clarence White and Gene Parsons were drawing the curious to the outskirts of Los Angeles to hear their new group playing country standards with a rock & roll twist. "We had a little band at the Jack of Diamonds called The Reasons," recalls Gene Parsons on the country rock scene east of L.A. "The Jack of Diamonds in Antelope Valley was a major spot. We were their house band. Clarence joined that band, and Sneaky Pete, Lloyd Green, and Bud Isaacs used to sit in. Isaacs was one of the grandfathers of pedal-steel guitar. He played with Hank Williams and was the first man to have an instrumental hit with the pedal steel. A lot of people played with us. Around the time Clarence joined us, we got this gig at the Nashville West, so we called the band Nashville West. It sounded good anyway. The club was a huge barn and could hold fifteen hundred people. There was a big audience for country music—not a young audience or a longhair audience—mostly truck drivers, farmers, and ranchers. We played there seven nights a week with a double session on Sunday, then we'd go to the after-hours sessions at the Aces club in El Monte and play there. Clarence, Gib, and I were also doing sessions for Gary Paxton, so we were playing a lot. There was country and rock at these clubs; some of it was hard-core country, some had a bit of rock in it. We were playing both. I suppose we were crossing the two. There were so many influences back then. We were listening to the Beatles and the radio, and trying to advance from straight country into other genres using more complicated rhythms and chord patterns. Gib Guilbeau, Wayne Moore, Clarence White, and I played these clubs as well as a club in Bakersfield called Greg's High Life where Merle Haggard and Bonnie Owens used to come in to hear us."

Chris Hillman, Roger McGuinn, and Gram Parsons also visited Nashville West. "When we were working there, the Byrds would sit in with us," claims Gene Parsons. "They were studying country music and we were one of the hottest country rock bands in southern California. Clarence knew Chris because of their bluegrass connections. Chris and McGuinn came out when Lloyd Green was playing to check him out. Gram Parsons came out to see us, too."

Playing country music with more rock & roll rhythm, Nashville West's repertoire covered a wide range, from Merle Haggard's "Sing Me Back Home" and Mel Tillis' "Mental Revenge" to the country pop of "Ode To Billy Joe" and "Green Green Grass Of Home." White's unique guitar picking established Nashville West as the all-important link between Buck Owens' music and the Byrds' *Sweetheart Of The Rodeo*. "I feel that Nashville West was more influential than was obvious at the time," postulates Parsons. "A lot of people came and listened. It was influential to the Byrds around the time of *Sweetheart*. It wasn't the *sole* influence, but it was part of it because Clarence and Chris were hanging out together. There were quite a few bands playing country music with electric guitars, bass, and drums, but we were the most advanced. A lot of bands came to listen to us and ask questions about how we did this and that. We had a real advantage because we had Clarence. No one else came anywhere near what Clarence was doing." Indeed, budding country rockers beat a path to Nashville West gigs to marvel at his virtuosity.

While the Byrds finished up *The Notorious Byrd Brothers*, the International Submarine Band was recording its only album for Lee Hazlewood's LHI label. Hazlewood had some credentials in the country market. He was a producer, and an artist (having had a crossover hit with Nancy Sinatra with the song "Jackson"). His girlfriend, Suzi Jane Hokom, was entrusted with production chores for the Submarine Band while Hazlewood looked over her shoulder. Raised in Hollywood, Hokom began her career singing backup on studio sessions before hooking up with Hazlewood and taking on the role of record producer.

Gram's personal problems and a lack of players caused the long delay between the July session for *Luxury Liner* and the November album sessions. In the interim, his girlfriend Nancy had become pregnant and Gram was having difficulty coming to terms with it. Speaking about the delay, John Nuese remains coy: "I'm not really sure. A number of reasons. Gram was involved with this gal; he had emotional problems. There were logistical problems with the record company." Nevertheless, led by their vision of playing pure country music, the Submarine Band resumed recording their album.

"The sessions were pretty straightforward," notes Corneal, who had returned from Nashville. "We weren't a big act, didn't have hits, so you've gotta get as much done as quickly as you can. We'd have rehearsals up at Burrito Manor. We all kind of hung out there that summer. We had done a session in July, and it was a different lineup than the one that did the album. By the time we went back into the studio in November, Chris Ethridge was in the picture." There was no question in the minds of the participants that this was a country album, not rock or even country rock. States Corneal, "It was straight-out, hard-edge country, but contemporary for the time." Adds Maness, "All Gram wanted to do was be a country singer. He just picked these country songs, and we played them. He wanted to be George Jones, but he didn't have what it took to be a George Jones. But what he did have turned into something pretty special."

In a 1972 interview, Parsons boasted: "It's probably the best country album I've done, because it had a lot of really quick country shuffle, brilliant sounding country."

"We had some real difficult times making that album," recalls Hokom. "We had to do it in about two weeks because Lee didn't want to spend a lot of money." As one of the only female record producers in the business at that time, Hokom found it tough earning the respect of the male musicians. She and Gram, however, got along just fine. "I had big problems with John Nuese. He hated me. There was nothing I could do to make him like or accept me. It was a battle with him every day." For his part, Nuese characterized Hokom as "bossy." "Although she could sing some and had some knowledge of being a producer, she was by no means a great producer."

The manner of recording became a contentious issue between Hokom and Nuese. While Hokom recalls Nuese insisting the album be recorded track by track using overdubs, he claims it was Hokom who preferred that approach. "I remember Gram and I fighting with the other guys," she maintains. "I wanted to capture that live, spontaneous country feel sitting in a circle and just playing. To me, the group dictated that kind of sound, the feel of every country band I'd ever seen. Gram loved that style. John looked at himself as a very high artiste and wanted to overdub all his guitar parts. He walked out several times during the sessions. He was a good player but he took himself far too seriously. I didn't want to lose the spontaneity. Gram and I and Jon Corneal were all in agreement on that."

Nuese challenges Hokom's claim that he resisted the recording-in-the-round approach. "*She* wanted us to record piecemeal, building it section by section. We told her that's not the way to do it. We had been used to sitting in a circle and playing. You get the pickers together, and you flat play it. That's the way it had been done for years." Nevertheless, Nuese suggests his problems with Hokom ultimately tainted the final results. "I personally had a beef with her, so consequently a lot of my guitar playing was removed from the final mix." According to Nuese, the original master tapes of the album, with his original guitar playing intact, are now in the possession of John Delgatto of Sierra Records who plans to release the album someday as it should be heard.

Bob Dylan's problems during this period have been the basis of a great deal of speculation. Some people assert it was drugs, and not the storied motorcyle accident, that sent him into seclusion. Following his controversial world tour backed by The Hawks in 1966, Dylan retreated from the world, returning to the recording studio in November of 1967 healthy and focused. Though he had recorded *Blonde On Blonde* in Nashville the year before, the city's sound had little influence on his music, which at the time consisted of stream-of-consciousness lyrics backed by an electric folk rock. This time out, Dylan let the city's influence seep into the sessions, producing a laid-back album of original, bare-bones, country-tinged acoustic folk. Released in March 1968, *John Wesley Harding* was Dylan's return to roots. A back-to-basics album, its starkness was a pleasant diversion from the psychedelic excesses that had dominated 1967. Backed by Dylan's spare acoustic guitar, with Nashville veterans like Charlie McCoy on bass and Kenny Buttrey on drums, the record served notice that it was time for a return to a simpler American music. Songs like the title track, "I Pity The Poor Immigrant," "I Am A Lonesome Hobo," and "I'll Be Your Baby Tonight" (which featured Nashville studio ace Pete Drake on pedal steel) let the listening public know that, as before, Dylan was setting the course and bringing it all back home.

# 4

# Pickin' Up the Pieces: 1968

*I grew up listening to Johnny Cash, Chet Atkins, Spade Cooley, and Bob Wills and the Texas Playboys. So when I got to those sessions in 1965 I was inspired, because I was hearing all the music I had grown up on.*

—Jim Messina

In 1968 several seminal country rock groups formed from the seeds planted during the previous two years, a half dozen groundbreaking records were produced, and a number of key players emerged, notably Chris Hillman, Gram Parsons, Gene Clark, and Richie Furay.

Hillman's influence exerted itself immediately. *The Notorious Byrd Brothers*, released in January, garnered rave reviews from critics, who cited the album's progressive approach as testament to the band's ability to carry on in the face of what could have been crippling personnel changes. The critics praised McGuinn and Hillman for imbuing the Byrds with a new sense of purpose: in the face of a crisis, the two had gotten the record finished on time, with no loss of quality. Perhaps more than any previous Byrds release, *Notorious* offers a greater diversity of sounds, with scant reliance on the jingle-jangle sound that had characterized previous efforts. Crosby's influence is present on the record, despite the absence of his name in the credits. Hillman's country inclinations continue to inform the music, and were obviously encouraged by McGuinn, given the increasing use of pedal-steel guitar and Clarence White's flat-picking. "Wasn't Born To Follow" illustrates the group's ability to fuse genres: it uses a standard country approach mixed with a distorted psychedelic guitar in the middle break. The same idea is repeated in Hillman's "Old John Robertson" with the use of a phased-fugue interlude. Hillman stands tall on the album, his rising presence during this period a continuing source of strength for the Byrds.

Nevertheless the Byrds continued to have personnel problems. During the group's set at the Winterland Ballroom in San Francisco the previous December, drummer Michael Clarke erupted, throwing down his sticks at the end of the final number and walking out on the group. Hillman drafted his cousin Kevin Kelley, formerly of the folk blues group The Rising Sons, to fill in for Clarke, though as only a salaried employee. Although he was a solid player, Kelley's understated style left a bit of a hole in the Byrds' rhythm. But there was a new album to promote, so the group hit the boards as a trio. McGuinn and Hillman assumed all the vocal duties.

Personnel shuffles also plagued the Buffalo Springfield, whose lineup had been in a state of flux throughout 1967. Both Bruce Palmer and Neil Young had left and returned, with a revolving door of temps filling the gaps. In mid-January 1968, following a gig in L.A., Palmer was arrested for drug possession. It was not his first offense, and he was soon deported to Canada. The group, working on their third album with engagements pending, turned to Jimmy Messina. An engineer on several of their recent recordings, Jimmy knew the band members, and stepped forward to offer his services. Richie Furay recalls, "We were recording at Sunset Sound, and, during one of those periods when Bruce was gone, somebody asked 'Who can play bass?' Jimmy wanted the job." An accomplished guitarist with experience leading his own group, Messina got a bass and practiced diligently before his audition. "I asked Neil if I could play a few gigs for some extra money," recounts Messina. "I wanted the money to start a recording studio. He told me to come to a rehearsal. When we started playing, it felt right, and I knew I wanted to do it." Messina became the last in a line of Springfield bass players.

Raised in Texas and southern California, Messina learned guitar at an early age. "I started playing guitar when I was about five," he recalls. "My father was a guitarist in the style of Chet Atkins. I wanted to learn how to do that, too." Following an infatuation with the progressive surf-guitar stylings of Dick Dale, Messina had fallen under the sway of Buck Owens and Don Rich. "I moved to Hollywood when I was sixteen, and built this studio for Al and Sonny Jones. When I started working there were guys like James Burton, Joe Osborn, and Jerry Allison of the Crickets. I was cutting sessions that were really rockabilly, and that was country rock to me. That rockabilly music was Ricky Nelson, Elvis Presley, and all that stuff I had grown up on."

For Furay, Messina offered more than musical competence. "I saw in Jimmy a friend, and I saw stability. There was a connection there when we were talking and playing. We all sort of knew the band was falling apart. Neil quit on us not long after Jimmy joined." Barely nineteen, Messina was unaware he was joining a sinking ship. "I wasn't really privy to a lot of what was going on. I was pretty naive. I was more interested in the music and producing. I had no idea what their economic situation was."

The group was battling by February. Each member preferred recording without the others. Stills and Young could barely stand to be in the same studio. Young had quietly withdrawn, and Furay and Messina were given the unenviable task of flying to New York to finish tracks for an album release coinciding with an April tour. "Everyone was doing his own thing," recalls Furay. "What we did was take what everybody did individually and put it together." Having found himself as a songwriter, Furay was bursting with new material, and drawing inspiration from the group's current drama. Several compositions he wrote at the time, though, were more suited to his next musical venture.

Furay and Messina laid down the basic track for a country number recently penned by Furay. "Kind Woman," inspired by his wife Nancy, evinced his growing interest in country music, following in the wake of "A Child's Claim To Fame." Wanting a true country sound, the two decided to add pedal-steel guitar to the track. "'Kind Woman' was more country than 'A Child's Claim To Fame,' which was more bluegrass," says Furay. "It had the pedal steel, one of the first rock songs to feature steel guitar. It was an indication of the direction Jimmy and I wanted to go if the band broke up." Springfield roadie Miles Thomas had suggested Rusty Young as a steel player.

For Young, California was hard to resist. "Miles had gone to Los Angeles with Randy Meisner's group, The Poor. They opened for the Springfield at the Whisky, and that's how Miles got hooked up with the Springfield. He was always trying to get me to come out to Los Angeles. I was doing really well in Colorado, working in a guitar store and playing in a local band. Miles called and said, 'I've got this thing set up for you. The Springfield need a steel player, and I've got an audition for you with this guy named Gram Parsons.' For a chance to play on a Springfield album, it was worth going."

Young never made it to the Parsons' audition, instead joining Furay and Messina. "When I went into the studio with Richie and Jimmy, we really hit it off. They knew the Springfield was ending, but they wanted to keep playing music." Confirms Messina, "Richie and I, in the process of folding the Springfield, were trying to figure out where we were going, defining country rock as we were looking for players. Rusty was important because his instrument bridged the gap between rock & roll and country. It was already in the melody and lyrics Richie was writing. So it was a natural, bringing those things together." By the time Young made it to Los Angeles that March, Parsons had already left the International Submarine Band for the Byrds.

The Submarine's Band's existence had been tenuous since its split into two factions in June 1967. Dunlop and Gauvin went on to form the more r & b-oriented Flying Burrito Brothers, while Parsons and Nuese pursued straight country. Following sessions for their album, Parsons and Nuese prepared to gig by assembling a performing group. Ethridge and Corneal were on board, but Maness was not willing to abandon a studio career or his regular gig at the Aces club. The word was sent out for a steel player, but before any auditions could be held Parsons jumped ship. Nuese avers that his compatriot was going through a particularly difficult time personally, and no longer wanted to work with Jon Corneal. "Jon was a good drummer, but at the time a total redneck. He eventually became hip and is a nice enough guy, but when he came to L.A. he was a real straight arrow. Gram and Nancy were falling apart. This was after their child Polly was born. Gram wanted to play with stars, wanted to *be* a star, and he had some type of offer from the Byrds."

Chris Hillman remembers meeting Parsons in a most unlikely place. "We met up in a bank. We shared the same manager. The Byrds were scattered at that point so we grabbed Gram. He was hired for six months as a side guy, with my cousin Kevin Kelley on drums. We were just trying to keep the thing going." Parsons was recruited to flesh out the group for live performances, but he soon began to exert his influence, befriending Hillman and playing his trump card: country music. "It wasn't until Chris Hillman and I got together and sang a bunch of country songs that we convinced McGuinn that it would be best to take a country excursion," stated Parsons. "Chris had just been aching to get back into country music, and when I came along, that was it." Parsons knew that rock audiences were resistant to country, but since the Byrds had a loyal following he figured half the battle was won. With the Submarine Band a failure in his eyes, he viewed the Byrds as his chance to realize his vision of "Cosmic American Music." Not everyone was thrilled by Parsons' ambitions. Notes McGuinn ruefully, "We set out to hire a piano player and good God! It's George Jones in a sequin suit."

Parsons wasted little time in promoting his own agenda, insinuating himself between McGuinn and Hillman and steering the Byrds toward country. Within weeks of his arrival, the band was working on country numbers and edging away from McGuinn's concept: a double album tracing the evolution of contemporary American music, from its roots in Appalachian hillbilly songs to space music. McGuinn wanted to bring a Moog synthesizer into the sound. That was not in Parsons' plans. "We had talked of doing a country record before we got Gram," notes Hillman, who viewed Parsons' arrival as an affirmation of his own country direction, "and we discussed a double album that Roger wanted to do with some kind of space thing with the Moog. Thank God we didn't do that. I found an ally in Gram and I thought, 'This guy knows how to do all this country music. He knows Buck Owens.'" Acknowledges McGuinn: "Hillman and Parsons talked me into doing the country album. I don't regret that. Gram thought we could win over the country audience. He figured, once they dig you, they never let go."

With rehearsals underway, Parsons delved into his country catalog. Drawing from sources like the Louvin Brothers and Merle Haggard, the band set to work. Eschewing the Hillman-White country rock experiments of two years earlier, the Byrds pursued a more traditional approach under Parsons' leadership. It was quite a risk for an established group to make such a drastic change. The new Byrds made their debut at Derek Taylor's "Farewell to L.A." party in early March, held at Ciro's. There was a history with the club: the Byrds had debuted at Ciro's three years earlier. Taylor had worked as publicist for various L.A.-based pop artists, including the Byrds. He was leaving America to work for the Beatles at Apple Corp in London. Parsons suggested that Jay Dee Maness join the band to enhance its country sound. Maness was not impressed with his fellow players that night. "I do remember that it was terribly loud and thinking, 'Man, this is nuts.' I had no visions of going on the road with them. I wanted to be a session player. I was pretty square at the time." Another guest proved unwelcome. Gene Clark arrived in rough shape, and managed to reach the stage, where he made a fool of himself, falling backwards into an amplifier before making a hasty exit.

Parsons and Hillman continued to look for a steel player for the group. At various times Maness, Lloyd Green, and Sneaky Pete Kleinow were short-listed. But in the end McGuinn's reluctance, as well as financial considerations, killed the idea, much to Parsons' consternation.

Within days of the Taylor party, the Byrds flew off to Nashville to begin sessions on their country album. Skeptical, McGuinn became a participant. "Roger never did like country music," offers Hillman. "He's in a different place musically." Recruiting several Nashville players, including John Hartford, Lloyd Green, and Roy Huskey, the group began recording straight country numbers for *Sweetheart Of The Rodeo*. For the first time there would be no McGuinn or Hillman originals on the record. "We were trying to do a *traditional* country album," emphasizes Hillman. "I think we were sort of playing at it. We were trying to imitate country, but not very well." Hillman, however, defends their direction. "We just did something we wanted to do. It really came from doing stuff like 'Eight Miles High.' We went all the way across the spectrum into this other direction. Maybe Roger wasn't a big country music fan, but he did it, and he later went on and did other country stuff with Clarence White."

On March 15, in the middle of recording, the group took time off to perform at the Grand Ole Opry, the shrine of country music. The original Opry was located in a converted church in downtown Nashville. At that time it was a radio broadcast, and its rules had the weight of the word of God. Columbia Records had pulled some strings to have the Byrds scheduled on the broadcast, the first rock & roll group ever to grace the Opry stage. It was a memorable night. Neatly attired in shirts and jeans, hair trimmed shorter, the Byrds took the stage to muted applause. It's likely that no more than a handful recognized their name. "It was a little chilly on stage that night," offers McGuinn on the momentous moment when a rock group met the country crowd.

"As far as I can remember everything was fine," Hillman recalls. "Everybody was nice and polite. We were on the Tompall Glaser segment of the show. I think everyone was a little leery of us, but nobody was saying anything. What happened was one of my better recollections of Gram Parsons. He decided, out of nowhere, to do 'Hickory Wind,' which I thought was interesting. But that really incensed Tompall and he screamed at Gram afterward. They were taking themselves way too seriously, and they still do. But I've got to hand it to Lloyd Green for having the guts to get up and play with us. He was the top steel player in Nashville then. Skeeter Davis was great, really open to us. She came up to us afterward and said, 'Don't worry about these people. They don't understand.' It was interesting. We played and sang good, and Gram was right there, dedicating a song to his grandmother, which was right on the money for the Opry."

The Byrds went back to L.A. to resume recording sessions, employing, at various times, Maness, Clarence White, piano player Earl Ball, and even Jon Corneal on drums. "Gram was the boss of that whole thing," notes Maness. "Chris was only the bass player. I think Chris got a little attitude from that, because he wanted to be more than just the bass player. The Byrds at that point *were* Roger and Gram. Gram was calling the shots. He wasn't nasty about it. He was just a strong personality. But he never told me what to play. He just told me to play whatever I wanted to play." And Maness did, on tracks like "You're Still On My Mind," and "One Hundred Years From Now." "Lloyd Green played *way* better than I did. I was a very busy player, playing over the top of the lyrics and everything. I remember doing 'You're Still On My Mind,' and we did sixty takes," laughs Maness. "They just wanted to do it over and over again. I think it's take forty on the CD." The steel player *did* find his employers' habits rather odd. "Those guys were *always* late. I'm a real punctual guy, and I'd show up on time ready to do my job because I wanted to be a session player. And nobody would be around. So I would wait and then here they'd come in a Volkswagen bus. It was a weird kind of thing, but I figured I was there to play so I just went with it."

On April 2, with the Byrds interrupting sessions to fulfill several college engagements in the east, Columbia released "You Ain't Goin' Nowhere" as a single. The song came from Dylan's *The Basement Tapes*. The single was the first indication to the record-buying public that the Byrds were trying something new. Recorded in Nashville, "You Ain't Goin' Nowhere" was a stone-country number dominated by Lloyd Green's virtuoso steel work and McGuinn's vocals. Parsons plays a minor role on the track. With McGuinn recognized as the voice of the Byrds, the choice of single was a safe bet. But it should have been no surprise when the record failed to make much of a dent on the charts, peaking at Number 74. The months-old "Artificial Energy," from *The Notorious Byrd Brothers*, was added as the B side. In interviews around the time of the single's release, McGuinn waxed philosophical about the shift to country. "If you want to get into the psychological reasoning behind it, it's sort of a backlash from the psychedelic scene, which

I'm tired of. We were influential in starting that stuff before it was really appreciated, and a year later other groups made a great success
with it. I think that we can offer country music what we know from
other fields. It's basically a very simple music but will accept a little
change every once in awhile." He further outlined Parsons' role in the
Byrds. "Gram is caught between the International Submarine Band and
us. It depends on how their record does. Gram worked with us on this
last tour, and he was great. The audience loved him. He likes to work
with us and we like to tour with him." Despite the failure of the single,
there was no going back. The Byrds stayed the course with their country experiment.

Prior to the release of the Byrds' "You Ain't Goin' Nowhere," Bob
Dylan's spare *John Wesley Harding* had been released to resounding
kudos, and took the top spot on the chart, holding it for several weeks.
The album marks the return of Dylan the balladeer, the Guthrie influence once again apparent. And it served as a wake-up call to the psychedelic crowd that their day had passed.

In April, LHI finally released the International Submarine Band's
*Safe At Home* album. With Parsons' profile elevated as a Byrd, Lee Hazlewood wanted to capitalize on his prominence. Hazlewood had already served papers on Parsons during the *Sweetheart* sessions, to re-
mind the singer he had contractual obligations to LHI. He threatened
Columbia with a lawsuit to stop Gram from singing on the Byrds'
records. Columbia's lawyers panicked, ordering several of Parsons'
lead vocals erased and replaced by McGuinn. Back in February, Parsons had simply marched into Hazlewood's office and naively announced that he was now a Byrd and would no longer be recording for
LHI. Reminded of the album in the can and the contract in the files,
Parsons agreed to relinquish all claims to royalties on *Safe At Home*, as
well as any right to the Sub Band name. With "You Ain't Goin'
Nowhere" out and Columbia's publicity machine gearing up for an
imminent Byrds album, Hazlewood beat them to the punch with *Safe
At Home*.

Choosing country favorites like the old Bobby Bare hit "Miller's
Cave," Porter Wagoner's "A Satisfied Mind," Johnny Cash's "Folsom
Prison Blues," and Merle Haggard's "I Must Be Someone Else I've
Known," *Safe At Home* illustrated the Sub Band's keen understanding
of the country idiom, both lyrically and musically. Several of Parsons'
own compositions grace the record, including the plaintive "Do You
Know How It Feels To Be Lonesome?" (re-recorded a year later on the

Flying Burrito Brothers' debut album). Much of the material is played in a comfortable country shuffle beat, Parsons' favorite tempo. When sticking to the straight country route, Parsons is a natural: his voice, a southern drawl with a delivery well suited to country, is a pure pleasure. But when he strays into rock territory with Elvis Presley's "That's All Right Mama," his limitations show. According to Jay Dee Maness, "Gram wasn't a great singer, but the way he *interpreted* country music made him special. He wasn't a great country or rock singer. I think he could have contributed a lot more and he didn't know it. He thought he had done it all already."

*Safe At Home* is an interesting album, not for innovation or vision, but because these were young, hip musicians, tackling pure country—both in covers and originals—and playing it well. A vitality, as well as a sense of purpose, infuses the album from start to finish. There is nothing hokey or derivative about the Sub Band's approach, just an honest appreciation of country music, with a strong bias toward the twang of the Bakersfield sound of Buck Owens. Often hailed as the first country rock album, *Safe At Home* is definitely country—if it's rock, it's only because the players approach country from rock & roll experience. It has a stronger rhythm and beat than contemporary Nashville recordings. "I look at that record as being fluff now, lightweight," opines Chris Hillman. "Gram had not quite developed into the soulful guy he was going to be."

With no group to promote the album, Hazlewood simply put it out and let it founder. Even the cover is cut-rate: a black-and-white pencil sketch of the group, with comments solicited from Glen Campbell, who played on the album, and Duane Eddy and Don Everly, friends of Hazlewood. Contrary to a popular belief, Everly did *not* contribute to the album. He had heard the tape and was impressed enough to contribute a liner note. "Because Gram had already started to perform with the Byrds," notes Nuese, "Hazlewood told us he wasn't putting a cent into promotion. But our single, 'Blue Eyes,' got a lot of air play around L.A." Backed with "Luxury Liner," a song later made famous by Emmylou Harris, "Blue Eyes" was an up-tempo honky-tonk number that could have been a hit in Bakersfield had it received a push from LHI. The New York–based *Hit Parader* magazine gave the album an encouraging review, citing the group's "bravery" in tackling the country genre. "The band is dealing with country & western music honestly. No gimmicks. Although the Buckaroos are much more exciting, the Submarine Band is at least exploring an area that most groups wouldn't touch." The rest of the media ignored the record and it disappeared quickly, resurfacing to become a cult classic following Parsons' untimely death.

"It was really a great crossover opportunity had it not been for the problems between Gram and Lee," laments Suzi Jane Hokom. "It came down to an ego thing. Lee had a difficult time with this bright and very articulate young man. Lee just didn't like him. Gram was too smart and too talented. We threw a couple of huge parties and everybody was hot for the band, but it never got *promoted*. Lee didn't know the finer points of marketing and promotion."

"It's a great album," asserts Nuese. "It's a record that never got a chance. The problems were not musical, they were personal problems of Gram's, especially when it came to women. I don't think it was the group's fault that the Submarine Band didn't make it." Nuese pulls no punches in assessing the Submarine Band's importance in the development of country rock. "We were *the* founders. We predated *Sweetheart Of The Rodeo*. Let me make a definitive statement: Gram turned the Byrds on to country music, and I turned Gram on to country music."

Parsons' departure didn't quite kill the group. Attempts were made to recruit a replacement and carry on. "We tried to sustain it until June," laments Nuese. "We had one guy from Nashville come out to audition as a singer/bass player. His name was Larry Fulham. He sang great and played great, but it just didn't gel. Chris Ethridge wanted to continue. But we just couldn't find anybody who could replace Gram." Adds Corneal, "The way I heard it then, Gram was originally only supposed to go out with the Byrds for a few jobs. We had commitments to fill, a gig with the Turtles. When Gram pulled out I ended up selling my trailer and supporting the band until I ran out of money. I was still thinking that maybe we could make it work." Corneal recalls further replacements being considered. "We auditioned some people, one was Cass Elliot's sister Leah, another was Brandon De Wilde. Brandon almost joined the group, but his agency thought it would harm his career." Thus the International Submarine Band passed into legend just as Parsons' star was rising. In the end, none of the Sub Band members saw a profit from *Safe At Home*. One can only wonder what the course of country music might have been had Parsons and the Submarine Band remained together.

After singing in the folk clubs in Tucson, Arizona-born Linda Ronstadt moved on to the University of Arizona, where she met up with another folk enthusiast, Bob Kimmel. With her brother and sister on board, Ronstadt and Kimmel worked the clubs around campus before they split for Los Angeles, without her siblings, in 1965. Though primarily known as an interpreter of other folk's material, Ronstadt grew up in an environment filled with country and Mexicali music, influences that would emerge later in her career. One night at the Ash Grove, she and Kimmel met Kenny Edwards, a folksinger plying his trade in the coffeehouses, and the three decided to form a group. They chose a name from an old Charlie Patton song: Stone Poney Blues. Rejecting an offer to record surf music, the Stone Poneys signed with manager Herbie Cohen. Cohen was interested in Ronstadt as a solo artist, but at her insistence signed the trio. Cohen managed to gain the ear of Capitol Records producer Nick Venet, who was launching that label's Folk World subsidiary. Venet liked what he heard, and signed the group to a three-album deal, resulting in the release of the Stone Poneys' eponymous debut in March 1967. Linda was featured on three numbers. The album was folk pop. The release that followed, *Evergreen, Volume 2*, was made in the same style. The second album spawned a hit record, a cover of Michael Nesmith's "Different Drum."

Recalls Nesmith, "I was hangin' out with John Herald, a member of the Greenbriar Boys. He taught it to his bluegrass band, and they sang it. Linda was really a country freak, an ethnic purist. She heard it on their record and used their arrangement." In the hands of producer Nick Venet, the arrangement differs completely from the Greenbriar Boys' rendition. Venet added oboes, a harpsichord, and orchestration. Recalls Ronstadt, "I wanted to cut it as a bluegrass song. The producer liked the way I sang it. And so he decided to just turn it over to an arranger. I remember coming into the studio at ten o'clock in the morning, and there was this whole session that had been going on, with strings and everything, for a couple of hours—without us even *being* there. I still don't know what to think of that piece of music."

By autumn of 1967 Ronstadt had a hit but no band, the Stone Poneys having split up after the second album. With tour commitments pending, a call was put out for musicians. One player responding was Oklahoman John Ware, who was loosely associated with Leon Russell and other Oklahomans in L.A. Notes Ware, "I was living in Claremont, and Chris Darrow was my next-door neighbor. Chris told me, 'There's a girl who is about to have a hit record, and she's gonna need a band.' I went to her house in Santa Monica to audition, and we recognized each other. I had been in this bizarre band

with Jesse Ed Davis while I was in college. Those guys went on to become Derek and the Dominoes. We used to rehearse where the harmonica player lived. And the little girl that cooked was Linda. I got
the gig in Linda's band. John London was in it too. Herbie Cohen,
Frank Zappa's manager, was managing her then."

The reconstituted Stone Poneys put a set together, and by the new
year headed out on the road riding the success of the single, though it
was a low-budget tour. "There was no money," recalls Ware, who
stayed with Ronstadt from 1968 to 1970. "It was a pitifully small income, so there was a turnover of musicians. I stayed with her because
I thought she was so good. We did shows sometimes for fifty people,
with a Number One record. At times Linda had to sing through a mike
attached to a lectern, no PA system. When we went out on the road, we
did John Herald's arrangement from the Greenbriar Boys, not Nick
Venet's. It's a swing arrangement, a great version."

Ware recalls seeing a familiar face at the Ronstadt rehearsals.
"There was this guy with a beard who sat in the corner watching. He
knew John London. I asked John who he was, and he said, 'That's
Mike Nesmith.' 'You mean the *Monkee* guy? Why is he hanging out
here?' John said, 'He wrote this song we're doing.' I met Mike and we
got to be friends. Mike was pretty uninterested in the Monkees by
then. As the Monkees started to disintegrate, Mike suggested that we
should become a band. That was when Chris Darrow, who was in the
Nitty Gritty Dirt Band, said that the Dirt Band was falling apart. Jeff
Hanna, Chris, John London, and I got together and played a few
times and it sounded good. So we backed Linda as the Corvettes.
Bernie Leadon was in it for awhile later when we toured." With revolving personnel, the Corvettes supported Ronstadt through the
year, Leadon joining in 1969 to replace Jeff Hanna upon his return to
the Dirt Band. Meanwhile, Ronstadt continued to go farther into
country music and established contacts among the young country
rockers at the Troubadour bar.

The Dillards were about to record a long-overdue fourth album that
spring when a conflict arose. Rodney Dillard wanted to create a more
contemporary sound and expand the group's range. His older brother
Douglas had other ideas. Recalls Rodney, "I was discouraged, and felt
this was going to be my last album. I had been approached by a group
with three hit records, and I figured I'd do one last Dillard album and
go with them. I wanted to do this one the way I heard it in my head.
Chip Douglas, producer of 'Daydream Believer,' and albums by the

Monkees and the Turtles, was working with us. When Chip got involved, the communication really started breaking down. Douglas wanted us to play more traditional. He wanted to do his thing, what was in his heart. And I wanted to do what was in mine. It was an amicable split." As Rodney told biographer Lee Grant, "There is no banjo player in the world better than Douglas. The problem was that I simply could not live, breathe, and sleep bluegrass music—it's just not in me. I wanted to explore other musical styles. When you are afraid of breaking tradition, you are creating your own limitations."

Dean Webb recalls: "Douglas wasn't happy, and decided to part company and try it his way. We were working on *Wheatstraw Suite*, and Douglas got upset about the material, and what it represented. I feel the split was good because we all wound up cutting more music, and it gave us more possibilities. It had gotten like it was taking a family vacation—each family member wants to go somewhere different. But it can't be a democracy in a group. There has to be a leader. Douglas wasn't too happy, but he was the one to quit. The elements weren't working and the problems kept getting bigger."

In May, Douglas Dillard joined the Byrds for a series of European dates. When the band was unable to recruit pedal-steel player Sneaky Pete Kleinow, Dillard was invited to add electric banjo to their mix of new country material and old Byrds hits. The band was slated for two engagements in London at the Middle Earth ballroom in Covent Garden, with two club dates in Rome sandwiched inbetween. By all accounts, Douglas' presence on the tour was a bonus. "It was a blast! We had a wonderful tour!" enthuses McGuinn. Their live set in mid-1968 illustrated the dilemma the Byrds faced: their best-known material, the early favorites, were played as usual—loud, with guitar and bass-heavy arrangements that completely overwhelmed Parsons, who was relegated to strumming an acoustic guitar and adding the occasional harmony. Then the group would present its new material, reverting to acoustic guitars with Parsons front and center. He crooned country numbers like "Hickory Wind" and "The Christian Life," to the bewilderment of fans. Dillard's banjo offered a whole new flavor to songs like "Turn, Turn, Turn" and "Mr. Spaceman," presenting them as neo-bluegrass numbers, though his vain attempt to keep up in the hyperactive "I'll Feel A Whole Lot Better" was less than successful. The new sounds did signal to fans that the times were changing for their beloved group. The Byrds experience offered Dillard an insight into the possibilities of an electric country format. "The country stuff went down okay in most of the places we played," notes Hillman. "Roger is really the consummate professional, and he always made sure we did 'Eight Miles High,' 'Tambourine Man,' and the best-loved stuff. But we'd throw in the new stuff too." Parsons and Dillard roomed together on the tour, and the pickin' parties often went long into the night.

Replacing Douglas Dillard, arguably the finest banjo player in the business, was difficult. But the Dillards struck gold when they turned to Herb Pedersen. He would prove to be the missing piece to Rodney Dillard's puzzle, allowing him the means to realize his musical vision.

Pedersen had been a member of the close-knit folk and bluegrass community in Berkeley during the early sixties that included David Grisman and Jerry Garcia. "We had a bluegrass band, at the same time Garcia had another bluegrass band," recalls Pedersen. "David Nelson, who was later with the New Riders of the Purple Sage was with us. Jerry grew up in the Bay, so we would see each other a lot. He was into the real traditional stuff, Ralph Stanley and all that, and played banjo."

Pedersen left California for Nashville in the mid-sixties. "It was just before the San Francisco boom, and the area was getting into that whole freak-out trip. I wanted to get into music where I could listen to everything that was happening. I had just come off the road with Flatt & Scruggs. I took Earl Scruggs' place, playing five-string banjo for a brief period. I had known the Dillards from 1963 when I lived in L.A., before I moved to Nashville. Dean Webb asked if I would be interested in auditioning for the Dillards. I was working in Nashville with a duo, Vern and Ray, and we were coming out to Los Angeles to play the Ash Grove. I told Dean I'd come out a day early and we could talk and see if it'd work. My banjo playing was different from Douglas'. I was more influenced by Earl Scruggs; Doug was more influenced by Don Reno and Ralph Stanley."

Earning Earl Scruggs' stamp of approval as a player gave Pedersen credibility, but his strongest asset was his voice, and that immediately became evident to Rodney at the audition. "I knew some of their material," continues Pedersen, "so when it came to the choruses, I just jumped an octave higher than what Douglas had sung. I'm a tenor singer. That changed the whole color of the vocals. Rodney thought it sounded great, so he suggested we try some of their original tunes. So we worked and it seemed to gel real nice. That's kind of how that whole thing came to be."

"Herb had vocal abilities that added a new dimension to our singing," offers Webb. "Before, we relied more on instrumental stuff, but we could lean more on our singing with Herb." Adds Rodney, "I finally had the opportunity to make the band a vocal band. That's what I wanted to concentrate on. When Herb joined, it just started happening." The Dillards would go on to work on a collection of songs that would cross genres and break all the bluegrass rules.

On May 5, 1968, the Buffalo Springfield gave their farewell performance at the Long Beach Sports Arena. A much publicized drug bust was the death knell. Neil Young was departing again. The others decided to disband following the completion of engagement commitments. For two years internal conflicts and their inability to come together during crises had plagued the group. "We had gone back and started over *so* many times," sighs Furay. "How many times can you break up and get back together again?" But the band's output never suffered: they created some of the finest folk/country rock of the latter sixties.

The Long Beach concert was a charged event, with emotional fans rushing the stage, halting the show until order could be restored. The group gave a brilliant performance, capped off by an incendiary rendition of "Bluebird," with Young and Stills dueling fiercely on lead guitars. "Backstage at Long Beach was fairly positive," recalls Furay. "I felt a sadness that we never really accomplished what we should have. But I saw stability in being able to put together another band with Jimmy." Confirms Messina, "Richie had put so much of himself into the Springfield. I saw the demise of that band as an opportunity for me to pull country music out of him. Richie loved country music."

In attendance at the Springfield's finale was Rusty Young. "We were already talking about who was going to be in Poco by then," confirms Young. But one obstacle still remained: they owed the label a final album. Tracks submitted to Atco in March were deemed unacceptable. The group's reputation for quality heightened the company's expectation, and, unhappy with the masters, it sent the group back to the studio. With Stills, Young, and drummer Dewey Martin already involved in their own projects, it was left to Messina and Furay to piece together a final product. "It was a difficult album to finish," admits Messina. "Neil had expressed no interest in the sessions, and I was having a real hard time getting Stephen into the studio, and Dewey was out of control. When he showed up to do 'Carefree Country Day,' he was so inebriated he couldn't sing it. Richie said to me, 'It's your song, you do it. It's gotta be better than what we've got.' I was not prepared to sing it, but I put it down on tape."

In July, the Lovin' Spoonful's final single, "Never Goin' Back," edged up the Hot 100. The group had fallen apart over the previous twelve months. A controversial drug bust, in which Zal Yanovsky and Steve Boone were coerced into naming their source, had scuttled one of America's most beloved mid-sixties groups. John Sebastian was looking elsewhere, but the group still owed one single on their contract. They turned to an old friend for help. Recalls Jerry Yester, Yanovsky's replacement in the Spoonful, "John Sebastian wasn't involved. A friend of mine in the Modern Folk Quartet, Chip Douglas, was doing well producing. I said, 'Why don't we call Chip?' Chip hired Red Rhodes to play steel guitar. He had a big influence on us going in that country direction."

Despite "Never's" failure to recapture the Spoonful's old glory, it was a marvelous recording, turning the John Stewart ballad into a tour de force. It was propelled by Rhodes' steel playing, and percussion by Milt Holland. Drummer Joe Butler handled the lead vocal, and rendered a lovely reading of the song. "It was a very strong song going in," offers bass guitarist Steve Boone. "I was very impressed with Red Rhodes because I had never worked with a steel guitar player before. We had a Moog on it which was new to me, too. It was one of the most memorable sessions I can recall." Though it fared no better than Number 78 on the charts, "Never Goin' Back" would ultimately have an interesting history. It was recorded by its composer, ex–Kingston Trio member Stewart, in Nashville a year later, as well as being covered by a most unlikely artist. "Zally and I produced that song again just a little over a year later, with Pat Boone singing, and did a great version of it," laughs Yester. "Red Rhodes played, as well as Clarence White, Jerry Scheff, Larry Knechtel, and James Burton. But it was never released because the record label folded."

That same month the Byrds returned to London, England, for a July 7 performance at the Royal Albert Hall before they flew off for a controversial and probably ill-considered tour of South Africa. With a musician's union ban in place, and world trade sanctions aimed at that country's discriminatory apartheid policy, few international artists were performing in South Africa. Miriam Makeba, a South African folk artist and McGuinn's friend, had convinced him that the Byrds should witness apartheid for themselves. She suggested that by playing there before mixed audiences, they could draw attention to the issue. It was odd that McGuinn agreed to do so; he was not outspoken on political issues. Yet that July the Byrds played before South African audiences.

Parsons balked at leaving for South Africa. Citing his personal op-
position to segregation borne from growing up in the southern United
States, he stayed in his hotel room, refusing all entreaties to go to the
airport. With little choice, the remaining three Byrds—McGuinn, Hillman, and Kelley—left him behind and fulfilled their commitments
amid a flurry of bad press and *segregated* audiences. Road manager
Carlos Bernal was forced to impersonate Parsons, both in interviews
and onstage, throughout the ten-day, sixteen-concert tour. Hillman and
McGuinn didn't share Parsons' feelings toward the hot-button issue,
and his refusal to go outraged them. They threw Parsons out of the
band. For Hillman, his desertion was a personal blow.

"Gram was inconsistent," stresses Hillman, who doesn't really ad-
dress the greater political issue involved. "It was his lack of discipline.
Gram was seduced by the trappings of the business. When we went
over to Europe, Mick Jagger and Keith Richards invited Roger and me
to go out to Stonehenge in the middle of the night, and we took Gram
with us. That was his downfall. Gram started following them around.
It was embarrassing." Parsons was seduced by the Glimmer Twins.
Given the choice between a questionable tour of South Africa or hanging out in London with the Rolling Stones, he chose the latter.

It's possible that the politics of apartheid may have offered a con-
venient excuse for Parsons' mutiny. His demands on the group had
been met with resistance. Claims Bernal, who saw something other
than political righteousness in Parsons' attitude, "The bags had been
collected by the porters, and Gram wasn't going to go on the tour because he couldn't have things just *exactly* how he wanted them in the
group. He wanted a steel guitar and things that the band wasn't prepared to jump into overnight. So Gram didn't make it to the airport."
While Parsons stayed on in London enjoying the rarified air of the
Stones, the Byrds returned to Los Angeles following their South Africa
debacle and, as they had done so often before, regrouped.

On July 22, the Byrds' *Sweetheart Of The Rodeo* was released to a startled public. Aiming for both the pop and country markets, the album
failed to garner a response from either. Gone was their trademark
Rickenbacker twelve-string guitar, and for the first time there were no
McGuinn or Hillman originals. With the exception of two Parsons'
numbers, the entire album consisted of covers. Writing of the album
in *ZigZag* magazine years later, musicologist Brian Hogg voiced what
many felt at the time, "Much as they may now love *Sweetheart Of The
Rodeo*, I know of no Byrds aficionado who was not, at best, uneasy

when they first finished listening to it." That's being diplomatic. Most fans hated the album. The album hit the shelves with a thud, and stayed there. "*Sweetheart* was shunned by both rock and country audiences," admits McGuinn. If rock fans were less than enthusiastic, Nashville was outraged. Influential Nashville DJ Ralph Emery took shots at them for being longhaired hippies desecrating the sanctity of country music. Parsons and McGuinn later responded by penning "Drug Store Truck Drivin' Man" as a vitriolic ode to Emery and his ilk. *Sweetheart Of The Rodeo* remains the group's least-selling album, but its influence cannot be measured by sales. The album marked a major turning point for country rock, a watershed for the development of the genre despite the fact that it wasn't rock-oriented.

Critics were guarded in their response. *Rolling Stone* magazine termed it "affectedly straight C&W," suggesting the album was a perfect candidate for the easy-listening charts. In response, writer and *Stone* editor Jon Landau defended the Byrds' move, asserting that "the Byrds have approached country music as an entity in itself and have aimed at a greater degree of fidelity to the rules of the style."

"I look at the *Sweetheart* album," muses Hillman, "and it's an interesting record, but I don't like it that much. I thought we were in a better place with 'Time Between'—without having to emulate something. On *Sweetheart* we were emulating country music. You listen to a song like 'Life In Prison' and it's ludicrous. Gram Parsons singing 'I'll do life in prison'? It just doesn't work. There were some good ideas on the album. It opened a lot of doors, but it's not my favorite Byrds album."

What the Byrds were attempting on *Sweetheart* was to recreate the sound of traditional country music rather than taking country further into the realm of rock. The only thing remotely rock-flavored is Parsons' "One Hundred Years From Now." *Sweetheart*, it may be argued, is a step backwards. Instead of country rock, what we get is old-time country music played by young rock & rollers. There is a reverence, almost a solemnity, permeating the tracks, as if the Byrds were dealing in something so sacred that to tamper with it would be sacrilegious. "We were trying to record an authentic country album," McGuinn confirms. "I'm very proud of *Sweetheart* now." All the tried-and-true country & western themes were present: broken hearts, lost love, Christian living, romantic outlaws, liquor and saloons. The dominant instrument throughout is steel guitar, though banjo and mandolin are prevalent as well.

Contractual entanglements with Lee Hazlewood necessitated what some musicologists and Byrds-watchers claim was a gutting of the record. What resulted, they feel, is a pale recreation of what the Byrds did in the studio. Parsons handled lead vocals on several tracks that were edited due to the legal issues. According to Parsons, "Columbia thought they were going to get sued, because my release from Lee Hazlewood looked shaky. A few songs they overdubbed completely, and my voice was used *way* in the background. It didn't work. It gave too much of that old Byrds sound, which we were fighting at that time. Things really came out well until the lawsuit. They were about to scratch 'Hickory Wind' when somebody ran in with a piece of paper. That's the last one they had saved." Under pressure from the label, McGuinn went back into the studio and overdubbed lead vocals on the Louvin Brothers' "The Christian Life," and the r & b number "You Don't Miss Your Water," with unsatisfying results.

"Roger is definitely putting on an affected southern accent on that album," notes Hillman. "I think he approached it like an acting job, although not a good acting job. But I couldn't sing at the time because I didn't have the chops developed as a singer. So Roger was the guy to sing them. It's funny, it's silly. The original vocals Gram did are on that Byrds boxed set, and it's not that much different. It's not that Gram captured it any more than Roger, as far as I can see." Producer Gary Usher offers another twist to the story. "Yes, it is true that some of Parsons' leads were overdubbed, but those legal problems were resolved once we were in Nashville. Whoever sang lead on the songs on *Sweetheart Of The Rodeo* did so because that's how we wanted to slice the album up. McGuinn was edgy because Parsons was getting a little bit *too* much out of this whole thing. You just don't take a hit group and interject a new singer for no reason. The album had just the exact amount of Gram Parsons that McGuinn, Hillman, and I wanted." Recalls McGuinn, "Gram was under contract to another label who threatened to sue us if the vocals were not removed. They changed their minds, but some of my vocals stayed."

The album starts and finishes with two excellent Dylan covers, featuring McGuinn on lead vocals. What falls in between runs the gamut of country music, from traditional bluegrass to the honky-tonk of George Jones and Merle Haggard. Included were Merle Travis' "I Am A Pilgrim," featuring Hillman on vocals; "The Christian Life"; "The Blue Canadian Rockies" (another Hillman vocal); the old George Jones hit "You're Still On My Mind"; and Merle Haggard's "Life In Prison."

William Bell's Stax ballad "You Don't Miss Your Water" rounded out the eclectic mix. But in spite of all the well-chosen covers, the standout track is Parsons' own "Hickory Wind," a minor masterpiece awash in steel guitar and honky-tonk piano he would later reprise during his *Grievous Angel* sessions five years later.

The Byrds' *Sweetheart* is important to the evolution of country rock because it introduced country music to young audiences, as well as other rock players. The album is a flawed diamond representing the first time a contemporary rock group of stature embraced country music wholeheartedly, though other artists known to the Byrds' circle were already blending country and rock. The Byrds themselves had strong country connections: Hillman's previous bluegrass work; Gene Clark's work with the Gosdin Brothers; the Dillards' music; and Parsons' pioneering work with the International Submarine Band. Seen in that light, *Sweetheart* is not some aberration. With the passage of time *Sweetheart* has been assigned legendary status, which it deserves to an extent. As innovative country rock, it falls short. Several outtakes from the sessions, such as McGuinn's Rickenbacker-dominated "Pretty Polly," "Reputation," and Parsons' "Lazy Days" lean far more toward country rock. Perhaps for that reason they were omitted from the album. However, as a bold step by a daringly innovative group to bring rock back to its true roots, *Sweetheart Of The Rodeo* succeeds.

Released a week earlier, the Buffalo Springfield's *Last Time Around* was invariably compared to the Byrds' effort. Given the close relationship between the two groups, comparisons were difficult to avoid. Hardly a country album, *Last Time Around* did include some country flavor, and one pure country track, Furay's wonderful "Kind Woman." Cobbled together from a mountain of unfinished tapes, *Last Time Around* maintains the Springfield's high standards, but it lacks a focus. "The third album, to me, was really disjointed," muses Furay. "It was left to Jimmy and me to collect bits and pieces from everybody and do the best we could. Everybody else was off doing their own thing by then."

Critics fell over themselves with praise for the Springfield's final effort. "The best folk-rooted group to emerge since the Byrds . . . brilliant and original," commented the *Los Angeles Times'* Pete Johnson. *Rolling Stone* dubbed *Last Time Around* "sweet-country flavored," saving its most glowing accolades for Messina's loping country textures on "Carefree Country Day." Minneapolis critic Ray Olson lined up the Byrds and Buffalo together and concluded, "In *Sweetheart Of The*

*Rodeo*, the Byrds took an imitative approach to country music. By contrast, in their last album, *Last Time Around*, Buffalo Springfield have mixed country with other styles to produce the only completely perfect record I've ever heard. *Last Time Around* is possibly the best rock album ever made." Closing out the album with "Kind Woman," a track featuring Furay, Messina, and Rusty Young, marks not only the last gasp of the Springfield but the first breath of the trio's next venture, the country rock Poco.

"I remember a conversation with Stephen Stills near the end of the Springfield," recalls Messina. "He urged me to listen to 'Kind Woman.' Even though Stephen was concerned about himself at that point, he was also very much aware of what Richie was writing. He was saying, 'I know we're all doing our own thing but don't forget this one song.'"

Hearts And Flowers saw their second effort, *Of Horses, Kids And Forgotten Women*, released by Capitol that same month. Produced by Nick Venet, the album has Bernie Leadon, a new band member, taking a largely supportive role. "That second album was Larry Murray's record," confirms Leadon. "The material was stuff he picked. Hearts And Flowers really demonstrated the dichotomy or blend of influences everybody had at that time." Offering more original material than their debut release, *Of Horses, Kids And Forgotten Women* finds the trio exploring the traditional country and bluegrass in songs like "When I Was A Cowboy," "Two Little Boys" (first covered by progressive bluegrass outfit The Country Gentlemen and later a hit for Rolf Harris), and "Legend Of Ol' Tenbrookes," adapted from an old Carter Family number. "'When I Was A Cowboy' we got from a Leadbelly album," claims Murray. "'Legend Of Ol' Tenbrookes' I put together as a compilation of all the songs I'd ever heard like that. There were so many songs about the Molly and Tenbrookes story. We didn't do that much original material. We didn't want to get that ego thing going. We were having too much fun, and it was just as easy to do songs we wished we had written." Once again, the style was eclectic, a diverse mix of bluegrass harmonies, acoustic simplicity, and heavy-handed string arrangements. "Larry was really into the later-era Beatles," opines Leadon, referring to the *Sgt. Pepper* influence. The album also boasts a reprise of "Now is the Time," with added vocals, as well as a brief snippet of "Rock And Roll Gypsies."

One of the highlights of a record full of brilliant turns was the group's rendition of Jesse Lee Kincaid's whimsical "She Sang Hymns

Out Of Tune," from Nilsson's debut, *Pandemonium Shadow Show*, released earlier that spring. Kincaid had been a member of the Rising
Sons, along with Taj Mahal and drummer Kevin Kelley. In the hands of
Hearts And Flowers, the song is transformed, with playground sounds
and lush harmonies revealing the group's more progressive attitudes.
Despite the stellar effort, the album was ignored by record buyers.
Only those in the know marveled at it. "We always thought our albums
were ahead of their time," muses Murray, "but we figured being ahead
of our time was wrong."

Hearts And Flowers petered out after the release of their second
album, due to a lack of interest. "Nothing was happening," acknowledges Murray. "We were in a rut. Bernie was playing with some other
players and so was I. I'd hooked up with Jesse Ed Davis, Carl Radle,
and Jim Keltner, and I gravitated toward that southern music. Leon
Russell was involved with them. Bernie started to gravitate toward the
Dillards. But for a simple twist of fate, we could have been huge. We
had what it took, we had a lot of charisma, the personality of the group
was amazing. But I don't think we were focused business-wise. We
tended to go with losers, because they were less high-pressure, and we
dodged the real pressure people whose asses we should have been
kissing. But you do what you do. Everything we did seemed like a
good idea at the time."

Murray remains circumspect about the group's impact. "As far as in-
fluencing other people, I'm not sure. I didn't see a lot of Hearts And
Flowers clones out there, but I saw a lot of people who respected us. I
think maybe our influence was more like, 'Well, those guys wear their
hearts on their sleeves and aren't afraid to go out and play a Louvin
Brothers song.' We got up and did what we felt, and the audience
would get behind us. Our music wasn't for mass appeal. We left just
before the miracle, before the Byrds' *Sweetheart Of The Rodeo* and the
Burritos." Murray, like Rick Cunha, went the solo route for a time, contributing songs to a number of artists' albums before turning to television as one of the head writers on Johnny Cash's popular television
show. Dawson left the music business.

Prior to his brief stint with the Byrds in Europe, Douglas Dillard had
recorded an album of banjo music for Jim Dickson. Dillard enlisted his
friends, including Gene Clark, Bernie Leadon, Don Beck, and John
Hartford. Hartford was by then a successful L.A.-based songwriter.
Glen Campbell had taken Hartford's breezy "Gentle On My Mind" to
the top of the pop charts. "Gene had helped me with a banjo album I

did for Together Records," recalls Dillard. "He played harmonica, and helped with different things. Right after that I went with the Byrds, and when I returned Gene and I got together again. He said he was going to do an album for A&M, and he wanted me to join up with him. That's how we came together. We just always had a lot of fun playing and writing songs."

Clark had signed to A&M Records that spring. After cutting only a few tracks on a new effort (including Dylan's "I Pity The Poor Immigrant"), he abandoned sessions begun in June with producer Laramy Smith to pursue a more country sound. He and Dillard pooled their resources to make a record built on an ongoing jam session at Dillard's house. Various musicians passed through, but Bernie Leadon stayed on. "I was living with Douglas and doing this mentor thing," states Leadon. "I was keeping him up all night playing banjo. At the same time, Gene had a deal with A&M and wasn't very comfortable doing a solo record. He had done a previous solo album with the Gosdin Brothers, and I think he enjoyed collaborators. So while I was living with Douglas, Gene and Douglas decided to work together. Gene invited Douglas to do an album with him at A&M." Joining them were Leadon, ex–Hearts And Flowers sideman David Jackson (on upright bass) and Don Beck (on Dobro and mandolin). Thus was born the Fantastic Expedition of Dillard & Clark.

One early observer at those jam sessions was Rusty Young, who maintains that Dillard & Clark offered the closest thing to a true country rock blend at that time. "The best I heard was Doug Dillard, Gene Clark, Bernie Leadon, and a bass player, the four of these guys. They were making tapes of their music; they were further along than we were. They were going to be real bluegrass. There was acoustic bass. Doug played some fiddle, banjo, and mandolin. Bernie played banjo, mandolin, and guitar, and Gene Clark played guitar and sang. They were making four-track tapes at their house, and I was blown out! If you took that early Byrds stuff that was real good and made it bluegrass, a lot of that singing and everything had real bluegrass roots, and the twelve-string guitar that McGuinn used to play in that fingerpicking style. That was all played on the banjo instead of the twelve-string, so it sounded like bluegrass Byrds. Gene wrote great songs. There were Gene Clark's tunes, and some of Bernie's tunes—all played by three really fine bluegrass players, and sung with that Byrds harmony. I thought they were great. That was the closest thing to what I would consider country rock that I have heard ever."

Although he parted from the Dillards over musical differences, and professed to be heading in a more traditional direction, Douglas Dillard began exploring a whole new direction with Clark. In the end he created a unique folk-bluegrass-country blend. "Douglas went off and did some very interesting things with Gene Clark," acknowledges Rodney. Confirms Dean Webb, "Douglas was opposed to taking it out of original bluegrass. Then he turned around and went that way with Gene Clark, farther in some cases than we did. He did a different music altogether." Clark had already proven he wasn't afraid to cross the musical boundaries dividing folk, country, and rock, and he found an unlikely ally in Dillard. "Gene always loved country music," claims Dillard. "So he just combined all his knowledge of music and that's basically what he came up with." Clark was buoyed by the collaboration with Dillard, and felt rejuvenated by the experience. "He was going back to his Missouri roots," suggests Leadon.

For Leadon, the attraction was, surprisingly, more Clark than Dillard. Though a dedicated disciple of Dillard's banjo virtuosity, Leadon saw an opportunity to hone his budding songwriting skills around Clark. "I've always liked bluegrass, but nobody's ever made money off bluegrass except people who could take the folk idiom and make it popular. So when I came out to L.A., I made it my business to find out how the business worked; how does one put oneself in a position to get the booster rocket strapped on? I studied it." Leadon and Clark quickly found kinship, and began a loose collaboration. "It was really easy to write with Gene," confirms Leadon, at the time a neophyte songwriter. "He would come in with a piece, he might have the chorus or something, and we'd just play it over and over. Then maybe the next morning he'd come back with lyrics for that part. The lyrics were never written collaboratively. We were creating the music and Gene was bouncing off of that, reacting to what we were playing, coming back with lyrics, and we'd put harmonies in and a new section if someone had ideas. 'Let's do a new section, here's a new chord progression.' That's the reason I got a writing credit for 'Train Leaves Here This Morning.' I didn't do that much writing on the song, but I threw a couple of chords in that Gene thought were significant enough to merit a credit."

"Gene Clark was a very creative person," reflects Dillard. "One of the best writers I've ever seen, very prolific. I could watch him write a whole song without ever lifting his pencil from the paper. It just seemed like it came through him all of a sudden. It was really amazing." Leadon agrees, "Gene is a very underappreciated writer. Seriously, people talk about Gram Parsons and others, but Gene was a very deep and mystical guy. He would write these lyrics that had very deep meaning. He was Dylan-influenced, and very much an artist. He was just as talented and tragic as Gram—just as tortured—and as susceptible to having his appetites harm him."

In August, the Dillard & Clark Expedition entered the recording studio to commit the creative energy of their jamming to vinyl. Chris Hillman played mandolin, and Andy Belling harpsichord, and the results, released in November, were astounding.

At that same time, Richie Furay, Jimmy Messina, and Rusty Young were recruiting musicians for their country rock venture. Following the breakup of the Springfield and completion of *Last Time Around*, the three forged ahead with plans of their own. "We wanted to take what was to become Poco into the country vein," confirms Furay. "Steel guitar seemed like an obvious instrument, especially after we heard Rusty play. Rusty is one of the best. He's an innovator. We definitely wanted to cross it over between country and rock. What we wanted to do had a more visionary goal than the Springfield ever had. But we were never given the privilege of playing the Grand Ole Opry, like the Byrds were." Furay acknowledges Messina's role in helping to chart their direction. "Jimmy made the group more country than I had ever envisaged it. I wanted it more rock & roll right at the beginning." Messina remembers, "Richie was already exploring country with 'A Child's Claim To Fame' and 'Kind Woman,' and I was into Buck Owens, Don Rich, and the Bakersfield sound. So those seeds had already been planted in terms of my enjoyment of it. The question was whether Richie was there. And Richie was definitely there."

With Rusty Young on board, the country element was in place. "I was a huge Springfield fan. When we talked about a new band, taking it more toward country was a natural. There were no synthesizers at the time, so if you wanted new sounds you had to go to real instruments that hadn't been widely exposed. The Beatles had opened the doors to new sounds and experimenting, and that's what everyone wanted—new sounds. We didn't really consider the commerciality of it all. We were just interested in making great music. At that time radio was very different than it is now. Underground or non-mainstream radio was very popular and could reach a great number of listeners."

Auditions were held at Furay's Laurel Canyon abode in July. "I thought that Jimmy and Richie would bring some big time stars into the group," laughs Young, "but it took a long time to get Poco together. We tried Gregg Allman, and Gram Parsons before he took off to do the Burritos thing, and various bass players and drummers. At the time the Allman Brothers were called the Allman Joys. Their whole band was staying in a little apartment. Gregg was going to play piano and sing in our band. He had a great voice. But we were more into country, and he was into a blues-based music." Messina recalls Allman's arrival with amusement. "The one audition I remember was Gregg Allman's. Gregg showed up at my house on his motorcycle. He'd had a few drinks. We started, and before we knew it he was playing away and having a good time, but it didn't have much to do with what we were doing. Then he needed to get some air so he went out, got on his motorcycle, started it up, and sped down the street in this quiet neighborhood. He came back and said, 'I feel a lot better now. Let's go back in.' And we kind of looked at each other and said, 'Whoa, this guy's different!'"

"There were a lot of guys from the L.A. music scene that we tried," mentions Young, "but it never was right. That's when I told them about George Grantham and Randy Meisner, who I had always wanted to work with." Grantham was recruited after attempts to find a local drummer failed. Those trying out included Jimmy Ibbotson, of the Nitty Gritty Dirt Band, and Jon Corneal, of the International Submarine Band. Young suggested Grantham, who got the nod. An excellent drummer, Grantham also added another high-register voice to the group's incredible harmonic blend. "When Rusty left, we had all gone our separate ways," remembers Grantham of Boenzee Cryque's breakup. He also went out to L.A. to audition for Young's new group. "I was in an r & b band then. After Rusty came into the picture with Richie and Jimmy, they looked for a drummer who sang. There were a lot of really good drummers in L.A., but they couldn't find one that sang the parts they wanted. And Rusty knew that I had sung high harmony stuff, so he convinced them to give me a try. We were just four pieces then, so we auditioned bass players and Randy was the final piece. Rusty and I knew Randy, because he used to come to Denver to play in a band and we thought he was phenomenal." Grantham moved into Miles Thomas' house for several months as the new group rehearsed.

By the summer of 1968, prospects looked pretty bleak for The Poor, who seemed to be making every effort to live up to their name. "We lived in a dive in East Hollywood," recalls drummer Pat Shanahan. "We had no food. The clothes we had brought from Colorado wouldn't even fit us. We were living on rice. There was no money." Shanahan remains philosophical about their predicament. "Everybody else was broke too. You just do these things. A lot of people around us were doing great things but nobody was making money. When you're nineteen or twenty you don't think about money, you just wanted to be there doing it. Randy was the first to leave." Meisner got wind of the auditions for Furay's new band from Miles Thomas. Meisner recalls, "Miles Thomas was the guy who got me the tryout with Jimmy and Richie. I played about three songs with them, and it was my voice—which was real high and strong, and meshed with Richie's—that worked. We didn't use any falsetto in those days, just full out blasting. Funnily enough, Tim Schmit was just leaving when I arrived for the audition." While the other members of The Poor drifted back to Denver, Shanahan and guitarist Allen Kemp took on studio work to sustain themselves for the time being.

Since the demise of the Springfield, Furay had written more than a dozen songs—all in a country vein—suited to the new group's approach. Notes Meisner, "Richie's songs were a lot different and a lot better than what I'd heard to that point." Comments Furay, "I was given the freedom to develop my writing after the Springfield folded. Even though I'd written several songs during my time with them, they didn't get released because they weren't quality songs. But it was certainly an opportunity to develop my songwriting. I wasn't the kind of writer who wrote a straight verse into a straight chorus. There were musical adventures that I would go off on, that I have to thank the guys in the band for allowing me to go off with them. They allowed me to experiment and were willing to try different things, musical bumps in the road."

Messina's arranging talent and Furay's creative energy got the new group off to a strong start. With Young, Meisner, and Grantham, they appeared to have a winning combination. "It's easy to look to Richie and Jimmy as the guiding force in early Poco," suggests Young, "and there's no way you can overlook their importance. Those guys had *been* there, had done it, and without them we'd have never even been able to get a record contract. But I've always been a fan of Randy Meisner, ever since I first heard him sing and play back in Colorado. I don't think Poco or the Eagles were the same without him. I'd also like to think I played a part in what Poco was. The band really gave me the chance to show off what I did best." The interplay between Messina's Telecaster lead playing and Young's amazing pedal-steel work became Poco's signatures. The two developed twin leads in the Buck Owens–Don Rich mold that were innovative for a rock outfit at that time. "People weren't doing twin-guitar lines in rock back then," confirms Young. "It was common in country music, but not rock & roll. And Richie's songwriting was not country, it was rock, with contemporary lyrics and country instruments behind it. I was a big Buck Owens fan, and I thought what Buck was playing *was* country rock. The lyrics were corny, but the sound he had, and the approach with the instruments—that Jimmy Messina/James Burton sound on Telecasters—I really thought that would work in rock & roll."

Following his sojourn in London with the rock & roll elite, Gram Parsons returned to L.A. in August determined to pursue "Cosmic American Music." One of the first people he crossed paths with was his East Coast buddy Richie Furay. The two hadn't seen much of each other since the Springfield played New York in January 1967, when Parsons had dropped by to see the group at Ondine's club. Experimenting with LSD by then, Parsons gave some to the Springfield members. "I remember when we were in New York, Gram Parsons wanted to give me a cube of acid and I said, 'Uh-uh, no way. I know better than this. I'll smoke some dope and I'll sit with you guys, but I'm not taking that.' Those guys were *out there* for the rest of the night."

Nosing around for musicians to form a band of his own, Parsons learned of Furay's attempts to launch a rock band with steel guitar and country leanings. He approached his friend with a proposition: why not join forces? Parsons already had pedal-steel player Sneaky Pete Kleinow in mind for his fledgling group but briefly entertained the possibilities of joining forces with Furay. "We both knew that we were putting bands together," recalls Furay. "It's not that Gram and I talked about putting one band together, at least that's not what I remember. Gram and I had the same love for country music, and we certainly wanted to incorporate that into a more acceptable thing on the rock & roll side of it. We wanted people to see this kind of thing work together. I don't know if that was real adventurous at that time, because country music certainly had its influence, but there were definitely dividing lines at that point in time with rock & roll and long hair as the rebel side. Both of us wanted to see if that acceptance could be there between the two. Both of us had bands together that had steel guitar players, and we dressed the part. And one time we both talked about, 'What if there was just one band?' But I certainly wasn't going to make changes to the lineup I had because I knew what I had and

Gram was comfortable with the lineup he had going. I think any conflict revolved around Sneaky Pete and Rusty Young, and I wasn't
about to give up Rusty. He fit for what we were doing and Pete was
more suitable for what Gram was doing. Rusty complemented my
music. Rusty was so innovative, and could change with the music. It
would have been a huge mistake and it just wasn't meant to be. Rusty
and I just seemed to fit together. Jimmy and I were pretty much set in
our direction and Gram was in his."

The idea, though, reached the rehearsal stage. "I saw Gram Parsons
as a very talented young man," offers Messina, "but there was an edge
about him, even back then, that was very destructive. It came across
when we were auditioning him. I didn't feel good about it. As much as
Richie wanted him in the band, I think he felt a little of that too. I felt
he would have been a disruptive element and I think Richie just naturally sensed that. So much of any kind of art is the people. Richie was
a good human being, he was raised to be a good person. Rusty was
raised that way, as were George and I. Probably if we had any fault collectively, it was that we weren't into any indolence or degenerate kind
of decadence. We had hope. We wanted to instill positive feelings
through our music, a positive note into society. None of us wanted to
be the Jim Morrisons of country rock music. Each one of those guys,
Rusty, George, and Randy, was just perfect for what we wanted to accomplish. It just felt right."

Though the joint venture foundered, Parsons had left a mark on
Furay's sound. "Gram turned me onto George Jones, and I thought,
'Man, this guy is absolutely phenomenal.' But we were more into the
Bakersfield influence, the Buck Owens kind of thing." Regarding
Furay's country credentials, Parsons later commented, "I like Richie
Furay's singing a lot, but I don't see that the two of us have anything
in common more than a steel guitar. The Burritos started off playing
country music where Poco was playing Buffalo Springfield music.
That's about all I can say about that." Muses Grantham, "I thought
Gram would have fit into Poco real well. But it didn't happen. He
would have made us more country than it was though."

Rusty Young saw Parsons' presence in the band as divisive. "Gram
was trying to surround himself with the best country band he could.
There was us trying to get our trip together. There were all sorts of
country rock scenes going on—Doug Dillard and Gene Clark, Hearts
And Flowers, the Byrds—everybody knew what everybody else was
doing. I think everybody was trying to beat everyone else to the punch,

more or less. There was a lot of changing around of the musicians in the different situations and this, that, and the other. Gram decided *he* was going to be in Poco then, instead of having his own separate thing. It didn't work out because he didn't like Jimmy Messina. He had a confrontation with Jimmy and told him that he couldn't be in a band with Jimmy. Jimmy was our friend and Gram was a little strange, so we told Gram we thought we'd stick with Jimmy. Then he went off and got the Flying Burrito Brothers thing rolling."

Young recalls a humorous incident at that time involving himself, Furay, Parsons, and Buck Owens. "I told Richie, who wasn't that familiar with Buck Owens, that he had to go see Buck. 'You'll really dig it.' Gram Parsons was in town, and Richie talked to Gram and he wanted to go along. Gram said, 'Buck's a friend of mine. I'll take you backstage.' Buck was playing at Disneyland and we agreed to meet Gram at the gates. It was 1968, and the world was quite different then. We're standing around at the gate waiting for Gram, and we hear this *big* commotion over where they're letting people in. So we walked over and there's Gram wearing what looks like a ladies' dress. He had long hair and a pretty face so he looked like a guy in drag. Back then if you were blatantly gay they wouldn't let you into Disneyland. And he's there with his wife and a baby in a stroller and he's yelling and screaming and causing a fuss. Finally they went and got Buck Owens' manager, and he says, 'It's okay, I know him, let him in.' So there we are walking down main street in Disneyland with Gram, and he's *such* a sight. Everyone's staring at him. And he says in his slow southern drawl, 'You wait, next year everyone's going to be wearing these.' Years later we played at one of Buck's radio stations in Bakersfield and Buck came down to hear us and talk to us. So I said, 'Buck, I've gotta ask you if you remember . . . ,' and I told him that story and he said, 'Boy, I sure do remember. I had to send my manager Jack down to get him out and all that yelling and screaming.'"

# 5

# Hot Burrito #1: 1968

*Gram was very charismatic and very influential. It was mostly Gram and Chris Hillman who were pushing the group toward country very hard. McGuinn kind of let it go. I think—later on—he started getting into it some, but he was never really into country music all that much. But when Clarence and I joined, we were pushing hard to take it into rock.*

*—Gene Parsons, on the direction the Byrds took*

Clarence White needed no persuading to accept the offer from McGuinn and Hillman to join the Byrds in late July 1968, stepping in for the wayward Gram Parsons. With the *Sweetheart Of The Rodeo* album just in the stores and a tour pending, White was a natural to jump aboard. Having guested on the previous three albums, he was held in high regard by the two remaining Byrds. It was a dream come true for the former bluegrass-picking child prodigy and studio ace. In fact, White's name had come up in discussions back in February after Gene Clark had departed yet again, but Parsons had insinuated himself into the Byrds' ranks, with unfortunate results. When Gram left the group in the lurch, they turned to White. He made his debut as a Byrd at the Newport Pop Festival on July 28.

With the release of *Sweetheart Of The Rodeo*, the Byrds needed to recreate its country sounds on stage. "The Byrds wanted to be able to do that steel guitar stuff but they were hurting for dough at the time," claims Gene Parsons. "They couldn't even pay their airline bill. They couldn't afford to take a steel player, and they wanted a real good guitar player who could do all the steel parts, like in 'You Ain't Goin' Nowhere.' With his stringbender Clarence was able to reproduce that sound." Having integrated the stringbender, a device attached to his Fender Telecaster guitar that allowed him to bend or pull the B string to create a pedal-steel effect, White gave the Byrds a flexibility they had been lacking, and shared the burden of playing lead with McGuinn. "Clarence was a very gifted guitar player," acknowledges McGuinn, wryly contrasting White's contributions with Gram Parsons'. "He was one of the best musicians I ever worked with. As for Gram, he had some good ideas, but the Byrds had been doing country before he came around." White's touch brought new life to many well-worn Byrds numbers, adding a Telecaster twang to songs like "Mr. Tambourine Man" and "Mr. Space-man." "Clarence was a *real* country player, but also a country rock player, who put country licks into rock & roll *and* folk rock with the Byrds," offers guitarist Al Perkins.

White popularized the stringbender, invented by his friend Gene Parsons, by incorporating it into his own innovative flat-picking style, so that the sound became his signature. He and Parsons first conceived the device that spring while working in their own country rock group, Nashville West.

Gene Parsons recounts the invention of the gadget that helped define the country rock sound. "We were doing sessions at Gary Paxton's studios. Clarence was one the innovators of chiming the harmonic at the B string or E string, and pulling it over the nut. He wanted to be able to do it not only at the open position, but also the fourth and fifth. We were recording for someone, I forget who, and Clarence said, 'I need a third hand.' I said I'd be the third hand, and pulled the string over the nut for him as he played. Clarence said, 'There must be a way we can do this without having someone else do it.' And I said, 'We can use pedals and cables, and hook it onto your guitar with a pedal-steel guitar bridge on it.' And Clarence said, 'Nah, I don't want to do that. If I want to play a pedal-steel guitar, I'll get a pedal steel. I want a regular guitar that fits in a case and doesn't have a lot of things hanging off of it.' It came to my mind to incorporate the shoulder strap for pulling the lever. I got some pedal-steel parts from Sneaky Pete and made up some drawings. I worked on Clarence's 1954 Telecaster, carving it up. The first thing I had to do was cut a two-inch square hole behind the bridge to slip the mechanism in. I took it over to him the next morning and he looked at it and said, 'Oh my god!' But we were past the point of no return, so I carried on. Clarence invented a need for the device, and a way to play it. I invented it.

Eddie Tickner put up the money for the patent. The three of us shared the patent. Clarence started using the stringbender near the end of Nashville West when the Byrds were already eyeing him."

Did the stringbender influence what became known as the country rock sound? "Absolutely. No question about it," emphasizes Parsons. "Guys who don't use one had to play like they did. James Burton admitted he had to learn how to do stringbender though he didn't have one because he'd go to sessions and they'd want *that* sound. He'd imitate it, come close, but no cigar. I think the stringbender was and remains very influential. Between Clarence and I, we probably made a dent there in country rock."

The Byrds remained an unsettled band. Once White joined, he began lobbying for his friend Gene Parsons to replace Kevin Kelley on drums, feeling Kelley's jazzy style was badly suited to country rock. An audition was held behind Kelley's back, and Parsons got the job. "Clarence was my advocate in the Byrds," notes Parsons, who folded Nashville West following White's move to the Byrds. "Within a month of him joining they needed a drummer, and so Clarence said they had to get me. They auditioned me and it was basically Chris' decision. He said, 'Yeah, I like him, let's do it,' and then Chris left." It was down to Hillman to dismiss his cousin, though he too departed not long after. "I'd got Clarence into the group," states Hillman, "but it wasn't really happening the way it should have been. Kevin was a good drummer, but sometimes you need to cool out and have a rest. It got a little too much for Kevin for one reason or another, and so we got Gene in. He'd been playing with Clarence for a year or two, and Clarence reckoned that he was the man for the job. I always wanted to be in a group with Clarence, but as it happened I only did three or four gigs with him and then I left. It was very sad in a way, but that's the way it came down."

Financial woes, not musical conflicts, brought matters to head for Hillman, who quit in a fit of pique following a gig in early September. Frustrated over what he perceived as Larry Spector's mismanagement of his funds, Hillman engaged in a shouting match with Spector before smashing his bass guitar against a wall and walking out. Hillman later lamented the lost opportunity to work with White. Had the two been able to stay together, the chemistry might have produced some truly innovative country rock. "It would have been interesting," he muses. "I regret that move. I should have worked a little longer with Clarence; he was such a brilliant player. We had Clarence in and out of the Burritos for awhile, but he did the right thing at the time. He went and got a taste of that other thing with the Byrds." Indeed, Hillman attempted to lure both White and Gene Parsons from the Byrds soon after, to no avail. "We did some gigs with Chris still in the group," Parsons recalls, "and even did one with Gram at the Hollywood Bowl I think. We were a four-piece, but Gram sat in for the gig. He was hanging out with Chris again, and they were talking seriously about putting the Burrito Brothers together at that point. They tried to encourage Clarence and me to join the Burrito Brothers, but we decided to stay with the Byrds. We liked what was going on there, and saw we could really key into that. One of the reasons we didn't go with the Burrito Brothers was that we came from country and were looking to go to rock. We discussed it, and figured we could go with the Burritos, but we'd be going right back into country, and we wanted to go the other way."

With the Byrds' fortunes at their lowest ebb, White and Parsons decided to stick it out. They saw a chance to build the group back up into something respectable again. "There was no money in working for the Byrds," comments Parsons. "We were hitting the bottom of the barrel, working some pretty bad gigs, playing down the bill to all kinds of other groups, and it was hard." Nevertheless, the two pulled the group up by its bootstraps. The first order of business was a replacement for Hillman. Recalls Parsons: "Roger didn't seem too perturbed. He reckoned that Chris was always quitting, and always came back. But this time he didn't, and we were in a spot, because we had a gig to play in Salt Lake City later that week." White again advocated for a former bandmate, John York.

"I had worked with Gene Clark and Clarence, and the chemistry between Clarence and myself was good," notes York, who had first shared a stage with White in the Gene Clark Group back in 1967. "And I knew Lawrence Spector. I had met Roger before, when I was with the Sir Douglas Quintet. So when Chris left they approached me. People knew me from other bands in L.A." York feels Hillman was burned out on the bass and wanted to return to his first love. "Chris Hillman was a brilliant mandolin player before he took up the bass, and at a certain point he wanted to get out from behind the bass and do other things. What did he do in the Burritos? He didn't play bass." A capable bass player and harmony singer, York was enlisted as an employee of McGuinn, a status he shared with both White and Parsons. The three new Byrds set out to rebuild the once-mighty franchise. "I remember seeing the Byrds when I first came out to California," recalls York. "They had tremendous charisma and their sound was so unique that it was great. But there was no performance ethic; there was no awareness of the audience. They'd play a song and tune for twenty minutes, play another song and tune for twenty minutes. You'd watch them and they looked like amateurs. Yet when they played, something magic happened. There was so much conflict that those guys couldn't keep it off the stage. Clarence, Gene, and I had been sidemen for years, so we were used to coming into a situation, and knew how to pump up the band with energy."

Getting the Byrds afloat would be no mean feat. The new lineup was entrusted with the unenviable task of going out and selling the least popular album in the Byrds' catalog, playing country music to audiences not familiar with the Louvin Brothers or Buck Owens. Putting out a country music record meant you had to face the critics' brickbats. Standing before an audience of thousands clamoring to hear that jingle-jangle Rickenbacker and performing "The Christian Life" instead was no easy gig. "Initially, Byrds fans were alienated by it," Parsons concedes. "We didn't have anybody booing us—we played too well. And if you heard Clarence play you didn't boo. But we had people saying, 'What are you doing?!' We did get a lot of fans talking with us about it, but they were generally polite, maybe one or two were belligerent about it. That lasted a few months—at the most a year—then we started getting our own fans following us and it started picking up. In spite of managers ripping us off, and this incredible debt the Byrds had incurred, we became one of the top road bands in the United States. For a couple of years it was pretty magical." Despite his initial ambivalence toward the genre, McGuinn carried on, nudging the Byrds' music more toward country rock, and carrying the torch first lit by Hillman back in 1966 with "Time Between."

The popular folk duo Ian and Sylvia had taken the bold step of releasing a country album entitled *Nashville* in early 1968, which they recorded there, using the cream of that city's session players. They followed that with *Full Circle*, also cut in Nashville and released in August 1968. Their music blended traditional folk with country backing. With the folk boom deflated by the British Invasion, Ian and Sylvia Tyson had managed to survive by playing folk rock after the We Five took Sylvia's "You Were on My Mind" to the top of the pop charts, but following that they had suffered through lean years. Formed in 1961 in Toronto's Yorkville coffeehouse district, an area similar in spirit to Greenwich Village, the duo had come to the attention of Dylan's brusque and burly manager, Albert Grossman. He had nurtured their songwriting abilities and put them on the college folk circuit, where they were soon the darlings of the folk crowd. With folk classics like "Four Strong Winds," "Someday Soon," and the covers of early Gordon Lightfoot and Joni Mitchell songs like "Early Morning Rain" and "Circle Game," Ian and Sylvia enjoyed tremendous success in the early sixties, routinely selling out the Troubadour and Village Gate. But by the mid-sixties the duo found work harder to come by. "The Beatles shut us down," admits Ian Tyson. "It was over. It came and went pretty fast. We were the hottest ticket in California for about a year and a half, but then I remember standing in the Troubadour, and the announcer was publicizing upcoming acts, and when he mentioned Ian and Sylvia some of the people booed. We had gone from the hippest people around to being booed. I knew there was something wrong with that audience." For Tyson, the transition to the new pop reality was a hard one. "We didn't know how to play with electric instruments. We didn't know how to use drums. All of us folkies were just standing there with egg on our faces. The only one who had the guts to challenge the rock & roll guys on their own terms was Dylan. He just jumped in." Attempts to update their sound with folk rock fell on deaf ears, and by 1968 Ian and Sylvia were rethinking their direction.

Raised in western Canada, Ian Tyson had strong country & western roots. As a teenager he had worked on a ranch and enjoyed rodeo riding, until an accident put him in the hospital. He learned to play guitar while convalescing. His earliest musical memories are of cowboy songs and country & western music he heard on the radio. "Roy Acuff will always be my original turn-on and influence—I was eight years old," attests Tyson. It was those early country influences that Tyson brought to the duo after meeting young Sylvia Fricker, fresh from Chatham in rural southern Ontario, in a Yorkville coffeehouse. Sylvia's traditional English and Appalachian folk sensibilities blended with Ian's country roots, and that combination gave rise to their unique sound. "If a song had a western theme, it held my interest," maintains Tyson. "I started getting into the great western writers during the early days, but I had no ambitions about anything. I liked the songs more if they had some bluegrass picking in them, or if they were western-flavored, like 'Texas Rangers' or 'Molly and Tenbrooks.'" At least one or two songs on every Ian and Sylvia album featured Tyson's country or bluegrass stylings, including their cover of Johnny Cash's "Come In Stranger" and "Big River." Married in 1964, the Tysons maintained residences in New York and Toronto, and a ranch in rural Ontario, where Ian pursued his love of horses.

Ahead of the country rock pack, given their previous body of work, and judging themselves eminently qualified to pursue the country path, Ian and Sylvia recorded the *Nashville* and *Full Circle* albums before taking time off to consider their options. "We took almost a year off," recalls Sylvia. "I had a small child at the time. What we decided was we did not want to go on the road again as just an acoustic duo, we wanted to be able to reproduce the music we had done on that album. If we went back on the road, that was the kind of music we wanted to make, country. We didn't want to go back to the old status quo. We felt alienated from the acid rock thing. That wasn't our lifestyle. It seemed—for the most part, except for the occasional bit of blues—to be pretty rootless music." The *Nashville* venture, featuring Ian's production and offering Dylan's "The Mighty Quinn" and "This Wheel's On Fire" (as well as Tyson's original country material) is a revelation. Played by studio stalwarts Fred Carter, Pete Drake, Norbert Putnam, and Jerry Reed, the disc was a high-energy entry into the country market, despite its limited commercial success. Tracks like "Taking Care of Business" and "Ballad of the Ugly Man" showcased the duo's high level of comfort in the country genre.

Produced by Eliot Mazer, who would go on to work with Linda Ronstadt and Neil Young, *Full Circle* repeated the formula, blending folk, rock, and country with orchestral arrangements. One of Ian's finest songwriting efforts, "Stories He'd Tell," graces the record: it is a heartfelt tribute to his father. There is also a moving cover of Dylan's "Tears of Rage," which predates The Band's better-known version. "Grossman was pushing Dylan's songs," Sylvia later told writer Nicholas Jennings. "He owned a piece of the publishing, so we were always getting early demos of that stuff, including *The Basement Tapes*." Following their hiatus, the two pursued a country direction. "The *Nashville* album was an experiment, and basically a trade-off deal with Vanguard," notes Sylvia. "They had a very ambiguous contract, and everybody on Vanguard's roster suffered as a result. Either you had given them one album too many, or you owed them one, depending on how they interpreted it. So they basically released us to do an album for another label, MGM. What they were hoping was that we'd have a huge hit album on this other label and have to come back and do another album for them. Which of course didn't happen. But the *Nashville* album experience gave us a very good handle on that scene. It took us out of the New York scene, where we had always recorded, and put us into a whole field of players who we didn't know, and who didn't know us."

That same month saw the release of one of the most influential albums of the latter sixties, The Band's legendary *Music From Big Pink*. A seminal statement on how country music had influenced rock and contemporary music in general, the record took the idea of "bringing it all back home" to a new level with laid-back, roots-influenced rock. Dylan's former backing group—four Canadians and one American who had previously played with Ronnie Hawkins up in Toronto—were led by guitarist/songwriter Robbie Robertson and Arkansan Levon Helm. Incorporating Appalachian harmonies and bluegrass instrumentation blended in a rock context, the ex-Hawks were now called The Band for lack of a better handle.* These gifted players drew on the Bible Belt landscape to paint evocative portraits of bygone days. The inclusion of Lefty Frizzell's "Long Black Veil" is a wake-up call announcing that country music *is* cool. "The Band had a major influence on the country rock scene, bringing in mandolins, fiddles, and country-harmony singing with Hammond B3s and saxophones," notes the Dirt Band's John McEuen. "They also brought back a lyrical style of writing that was similar to country, telling a story, and they painted their pictures very well. They're the most underrated group in the country." *Music From Big Pink* remains a significant turning point in popular music, despite the fact that the album barely made it to Number 30 on the album charts. It was a disappointing showing for one of the most important albums of the 1960s, and perhaps was more a failure of the listening audience, who just didn't get it. Musicians far and wide knew how groundbreaking the music was.

If Chris Hillman was angry with Gram Parsons for leaving the Byrds high and dry in London, his fury was short-lived. "I was ready to murder him," concedes Hillman, recalling the animus he harbored. Yet by late September the two had reconciled, and began charting a course for a pure country band. "Chris Hillman wouldn't speak to me because of the rough time they had on tour after I quit," noted Parsons in a 1972 interview. "But later, when he left the band, we eventually got back together and began jamming at country bars. We picked up Sneaky Pete Kleinow and Chris Ethridge, and resurrected the Flying Burrito Brothers. We stole the name." The two country rock renegades rented a house in Reseda that they dubbed Burrito Manor, and they began crafting original material for their country music vision: bridging the gulf between hippie and redneck. "We were still trying to do my deluxe number, a dream of soul-country-cosmic, what I called in my earlier college days 'Cosmic American Music,'" continued Parsons. "Chris

*A horrified Capitol Records rejected their early choices: The Honkies and The Crackers.

had been wanting to do that kind of thing for a long time. Maybe even longer than me, because he was playing in a real authentic bluegrass band a long time ago where I was playing rock and roll a long time ago and had sort of forgotten about country music." With Ian Dunlop and Mickey Gauvin back on the East Coast fronting a version of their loose jam band, Parsons and Hillman revived the Flying Burrito Brothers moniker and went in search of kindred players and a sympathetic record label.

With all past transgressions forgiven, the two enjoyed a close camaraderie frequenting the country music clubs and bars. Parsons either heckled or joined whoever was playing onstage. "At that time," notes Hillman, "we'd go out and watch Bonnie and Delaney, they just were starting and that's how it was originally billed. That band had J. J. Cale on guitar, and Bobby Keys on sax. It was a really good bar band. Then we'd go down to the Aces club in City of Industry, which had an all-night jam session. That's where I met up with Jay Dee Maness again after using him on *Sweetheart*. He'd be there for, like, forty hours—playing steel. It was *unbelievable*. So we'd go back and forth from one end to the other. That was a lot of fun back then." As Maness remembers, "Gram would come in and be at the bar, just out of his mind, yelling, 'Hey, I wanna *sing*.' And sometimes we'd get him up, and sometimes not—depending on the condition he was in. Sometimes we'd say, 'Not tonight, Gram.'"

What Gene Parsons terms a "prototype Burrito Brothers" had already been test run that fall. "Clarence, Gib Guilbeau, Gram, and I did some sessions for Eddie Tickner before the Flying Burrito Brothers," relates Gene Parsons. "We did two or three tunes, and Eddie Tickner still has the tapes." With Gene Parsons and White choosing to stick with the Byrds, Gram Parsons and Hillman continued to look for players. He picked up ex–International Submarine Band member Chris Ethridge along the way. Parsons had been eyeing pedal-steel player Sneaky Pete since his Byrds days, and approached the guitar wizard with an offer to become a Burrito Brother. "Gram and Chris came into the Palomino while they were still with the Byrds," recalls Pete on first meeting Parsons and Hillman. "Everybody kind of knew each other. I actually played a show with the Byrds, with Gram and Chris. It was shortly after that when Gram and Chris came into the Palomino and asked if I'd like to be in a new band. I didn't say no to anything back then. It sounded really interesting to me because they already had a deal with A&M Records, and I thought I could finally make a living with music. It was very exciting."

Peter Kleinow was raised in South Bend, Indiana. He had taken up the pedal steel as a teenager, before moving west to California in the fifties to work in the film industry. He worked as an animator by day and a country musician by night. "When I first came out to California in the early fifties," he remembers, "I got a job at the Bostonia Ballroom, which was the showcase for Smokey Rogers and the Western Caravan. Everybody in the group had a silly hillbilly or cowboy nickname. I was obviously Sneaky Pete. And I hated the name for *years*, until I got into the recording business and discovered it was an asset. People could remember it." By the mid-sixties, Pete had moved on to play in various Los Angeles bar bands. "I played at a bar in North Hollywood, and places like the Palomino. Our drummer, Mel Taylor, played with the Ventures and would moonlight with us when not recording or touring with them. The Ventures wanted to put steel guitar on a song called 'Blue Star,' which was a television theme song. That was my first professional recording." Though best known as a musician, Pete is also renowned as an animator. "During my career in the film business, I was working on the *Gumby* series, where I was the head of animation, as well as the *Davy & Goliath* show. I wrote the Gumby song."

Parsons and Hillman shared their vision with Pete, who was initially skeptical. "Gram and Chris had a direction," avers Pete. "There were elements of that direction in *all* of the songs, I thought. It was social commentary. I was a little disappointed when I heard some of their material. To be very frank, I thought it was kind of a poor imitation of the Everly Brothers, and I *loved* the Everly Brothers. The songs were not as straightforward. It was tongue and cheek, and innuendo, almost a lampoon—things which, at the time, I didn't see the value of. Stuff like 'Hippie Boy' I really hated." Nevertheless, the pedal-steel player, a family man ten years older with children to support, tied his fortunes to the two cosmic cowboys, unaware of what kind of ride he might be in for. "It was undeniably supposed to be country rock, which was just beginning to be accepted as a name for the music then," he maintains. "I don't think people were using that appellation until then. We were at the cutting edge of that."

Fueled by copious quantities of marijuana mixed with other illicit substances, and infused with a missionary zeal to redefine country music for the young masses, Parsons and Hillman found creativity in their partnership. Within a few weeks they had conceived most of the material for their debut album. "We sat up in Topanga Canyon, smoked a lot of dope, and sang a lot of country songs," recalled Parsons. "'Gee that sounds good,' you know?" Hillman sees that time as one of the most productive periods of his career. "I think some of the best stuff I've been associated with came out those days. It still stands up. It was fun writing that stuff. Probably the most grounded time in Parsons' life was that period. I was getting a divorce, and so was he, and we shared a house and were putting the Burritos together. We woke up in the morning and wrote every morning, as opposed to partying all night, which we were inclined to do. Gram woke up one morning, got the mail, and found his draft notice. We wrote 'My Uncle' because of that. 'Sin City' was about our manager, who had robbed us. He lived on the thirty-first floor, and had a gold-plated door. It was a give-and-take thing. We would sit down and do it with give-and-take on each line, and that's what was neat. It was a great time."

The duo secured a recording deal with A&M Records, owned by former Tijuana Brass leader Herb Alpert and partner Jerry Moss. Alpert and Moss had already shown their interest in country rock, having signed the Dillard & Clark Expedition. As Parsons remembered it, "Mo Ostin (Warner Brothers) called me and said, 'I sure like some of the stuff you've been writing. Joan Baez has just recorded "Hickory Wind"—wouldn't you like to do something for us?' Herb and Jerry came in real fast—'you can start right away here, and we'll give you the equipment.'"

The quartet—Parsons and Hillman on guitars and vocals, Ethridge on bass, and Sneaky Pete on pedal steel—began recording their debut album in November with producer Larry Marks, a veteran of the *Gene Clark With The Gosdin Brothers* sessions and the debut of the Dillard & Clark Expedition. Jon Corneal was brought in on several tracks after studio player Eddie Hoh, plagued by his own drug-related demons, bailed out on the project. "I had come back east and wound up back in Florida," recalls Corneal. "Steve Alsburg, manager of the Submarine Band, was working with the Burritos, and asked me to come out and play on the first record. We did some gigging around town, the Golden Bear, the Topanga Corral. I was supposed to be the permanent drummer, but at the time I was suffering from a culture shock. There was a little too much cocaine around, and I was scared of that kind of thing. That was the elixir of the moment. We were at a party at Alan Pariser's house and Gram whipped out a little spoon and a vial. I wanted to be in the band, but I didn't want that type of scene." Drummers Popeye Phillips and Sam Goldstein also sat in during those sessions.

Without a permanent drummer, rehearsals proved problematic: material had to be learned *and* played in the studio. "There was no rehearsal time," remarks Pete. "I just showed up at the studio. I had already been doing sessions here and there—you had to be very spontaneous, so it was no big deal. Everything I played on that album was off the cuff. They gave me total freedom to do what I wanted. What the whole thing lacked, though, was a bit of finesse." With Pete's steel guitar as the lead instrument, his unique sound was a major coup for the new band. "My steel playing was innovative for that time—nobody was doing anything *remotely* like it," Pete claims. "Gram and Chris thought it was spectacular and wonderful. This kind of stuff had never been done." Hillman's memory is a bit different, "We didn't have a lead guitar player, so Sneaky would just try doing Telecaster stuff on his steel guitar. It was pretty crude. It was very weird. Sneaky's quite an interesting musician. He can be just brilliant sometimes—and other times he can sound like he's playing for Lawrence Welk. He never played the steel like anybody else."

For this excursion Parsons departed from form, eschewing country & western standards and going instead with the new material he and Hillman had composed. They did cover "Do You Know How It Feels?" from the Sub Band's *Safe At Home* album, which only a handful were likely to have heard, and opted to cover two rhythm & blues classics, "Do Right (Woman)" and "Dark End Of The Street." "On the very first Flying Burrito Brothers album we took rhythm & blues songs, and we did them *country*," stresses Hillman. "We did 'Sin City' then 'Dark End Of The Street.' You couldn't get any deeper south, any more Memphis Stax, than 'Dark End of the Street' or even 'Do Right (Woman).'" For the latter, David Crosby dropped in on the session, adding his golden throat to the chorus.

Sessions were held in a convivial atmosphere on the A&M lot, located on the site of the former Charlie Chaplin film studio, at 1416 North La Brea in Hollywood. Various friends and contemporaries came and went. "All these people knew each other," marvels Pete. "It was like hanging around a movie studio lot, where all the stars knew each other. I started getting requests from all the people at A&M to come and play on their records. It was almost overwhelming." Adds Bernie Leadon, recording with Doug Dillard and Gene Clark at the same time, "The A&M lot was a real neat artist-oriented enclave. Very like a little village. We would run into each other all the time and then socialize in the evening as well." One surprise mentor popped in to observe: "Don Rich, Buck Owens' old guitar player, came to a lot of Burrito sessions," remembers Hillman. The sessions proceeded through early December, though few realized that groundbreaking music was being laid down.

Another patron of the A&M lot who crossed paths with various Dillard & Clark and Burrito members was Steve Young, recording his solo debut for the label. Formerly a member of the much touted Stone Country band, Young had gone solo, signing with A&M. Stone Country's lone album, released on RCA in 1967, was notable only for Young's two country-influenced contributions, "Magnolia" and "Woman Don't You Weep." When Young split for greener pastures, the group folded. Don Beck, another Stone Country member, eventually surfaced in the *Fantastic Expedition Of Dillard & Clark*.

"Some producers in L.A. heard my voice and liked it," notes Young. "A couple of them became interested, and I wound up doing my first solo album for A&M with Tommy LiPuma that came out in 1969. But it was just because he heard me sing on the Stone Country record and figured I could sing and approached me. This wasn't really a legitimate group, it was all these guys going in different directions, and nobody knew what was going on. One element within Stone Country wanted to be the next big pop group, like the Association, and I was real opposed to that. So I left the group and went and did my first solo album, *Rock, Salt, And Nails*." Young managed to enlist the aid of several musicians signed to A&M at the time. "Gram was just finishing up his *The Gilded Palace Of Sin*, and Dillard & Clark were about to finish theirs," Young remembers. "Tommy played Gram some of my stuff. He loved it. He lent his moral support *and* played on some of it. Only a bit wound up on the record, but there were some outtakes where he played a lot. Bernie Leadon played on one session, Gene Clark, too. And James Burton. I think some of James Burton's finest playing is on that album." Other session guests included the Burritos' Chris Ethridge, David Jackson, Don Beck, top session drummer Hal Blaine, and the young bluegrass fiddler Richard Greene (later a member of Seatrain).

"Gram Parsons was very supportive," acknowledges Young. "We had an unspoken bond, because we were both from Georgia. We loved the music of the south, and we were both experimenting with music in the strange land of L.A. The drug issue, though, prevented me from hanging out much with Gram."

Recorded that November, *Rock, Salt, And Nails* managed to include what would become a much covered and widely respected country rock classic, "Seven Bridges Road." "Tommy didn't want me to record original songs," claims Young. "He wanted me to be strictly a singer and interpreter of folk songs and country standards. One day, while we were in the studio recording material for *Rock, Salt, And Nails,* I started playing 'Seven Bridges Road.' LiPuma interjected, 'You *know* I don't want to hear original stuff.' But James Burton said, 'Hey, this song sounds good, and it is ready, let's put it down.'" Inspired by a road Young traveled near Montgomery, Alabama, the song was later covered by several artists. Ian Matthews, on his *Valley Hi* record (produced by Mike Nesmith) did a rendition, but the most acclaimed version was done by the Eagles. "I was amazed that that song was so successful," reveals Young. "I sure never thought it would be, or that anyone would even *like* it. But my greatest success in the business was due to the Eagles' version. The Eagles began to sing it at the end of a long night and the crowd wanted *more.* When the Eagles' live album came out, 'Seven Bridges Road' was the only new song on it, so it got a lot of attention and airplay." New country band Ricochet recently recorded the song, borrowing the Eagles' arrangement.

Like most country rock albums out in the late sixties, *Rock, Salt, And Nails* disappeared soon after its release. It gained cult status due more to the storied players who guested on it than for the excellent music it contained.

Having done a traditional country album with *Sweetheart Of The Rodeo,* McGuinn and his new Byrds began recording sessions that ran through the autumn of 1968 for their follow-up. They were intent on merging country with rock, in essence carrying on the experiments Hillman had begun with "Time Between." White and McGuinn were keen to pursue a more rock-oriented direction, using country as a texturing agent within their concept. In this sense, they were working within a country rock frame of reference. John York feels, once Gram Parsons was out of the picture, McGuinn was freed to stretch the envelope. "The *Sweetheart* album was traditional country music because of Gram's influence. Gram knew that style. He wasn't an innovator, so he was trying to make a record like his heroes. The force of Chris and Gram pushed Roger against the wall. But once Gram was gone, there existed a greater possibility of a bridge between the two forms of music. There was no attempt to be the Louvin Brothers anymore."

From this environment the album *Dr. Byrds And Mr. Hyde* emerged. It's an appropriately double-edged title: the tension within the Byrds was based on the disparity between hard rock and country. Having gone out on a long slender limb with *Sweetheart Of The Rodeo*, McGuinn was not inclined to abandon country influences, especially after recruiting the finest country guitar picker on the West Coast. Clarence White did not want to be limited by the country form, he wanted to rock. But his distinctive sound was so much a part of his essence that even when he plugged into a fuzz-tone and attempted to emulate Clapton-style blues rock—as he did on this album—it sounded country. White's stringbender made its recording debut on this outing. The sessions marked the heaviest sound the Byrds had ever attempted, juxtaposed with some of their softest and most subtle country stylings. It was indeed a Jekyll–Hyde situation. "If you look at *Dr. Byrds And Mr. Hyde*," notes York, "there are these different pieces. There are songs that are really like L.A. hard rock—like 'Bad Night at the Whisky,' where Roger was saying, 'This is the state of things.' There was no attempt to make a record where all the songs had a cohesive theme. It was Roger saying, 'Okay, I'm going to take everything out of my pockets, and you're going to take a picture of what you see.' It was a very honest record for its time. But it was not a big seller." Had McGuinn, chastened by the negative response to *Sweetheart Of The Rodeo*, hedged his bets with the follow-up? "I don't think we gave any thought to that when we recorded *Dr. Byrds*," he responds. "We were just playing whatever came to mind at the time."

"A lot of what was going on in the band was a breath of fresh air," says York of the atmosphere around the band. "Everybody was breaking away from the previous situations they had been in. And that included Roger. When you look at Clarence—coming out of bluegrass, where there were certain parameters you had to adhere to—once he got an electric guitar with a stringbender he could do whatever he wanted. There was nobody saying to him, 'You can't *do* that on that song.' Gene and I could play whatever we wanted. Suddenly Roger was relaxed enough to say, 'What do you think of this song? Do you want to play this song?' And we were free to try things out."

Gene Parsons concurs with York on that looseness: "We were in an experimental mode on that album, but we were kind of over our heads and letting it fall where it wanted. I was there during the *Sweetheart Of The Rodeo* album sessions, and it was very regimented. 'We'll get Lloyd Green in here to do this part, and Jay Dee Maness to do that part, and John Hartford to do the other part.' Gram and Chris were calling the shots. It was a very carefully produced record. *Dr. Byrds and Mr. Hyde* was just pandemonium." The album's poor fidelity was a result of producer Bob Johnston's inexperience. He all but buried McGuinn's Rickenbacker, and turned in a muddy final mix.

York claims some of the finest country-flavored music of those sessions never made it onto the album. "Clarence and Gene had a background in playing that kind of music. They were the authentic guys, the real thing. The public never heard some of the best stuff they made. Clarence and Gene would be working on some bluegrass harmony in a stairwell, for the sound, and would teach me a lead part to sing, so they could do these *incredible* harmonies. God, it was beautiful."

By late October, Richie Furay's new group was ready for its debut. Rehearsals had moved from his house to the Troubadour through summer and into autumn. It was time to repay club owner Doug Weston with several free sets. The as-yet-unnamed group breezed in for an unannounced guest spot at the weekly Monday night hoot on October 28, billing themselves as RFD. "Dickie Davis, our first manager, came up with the name RFD, which was supposed to stand for Rural Free Delivery," chuckles Furay. "But somebody said it meant Richard F. Davis. I don't know if his middle name was Frederick or what, but all of a sudden it was, 'This isn't Dickie Davis' group. He's not going to sneak his initials in here!' We were struggling for names at that point." With handles like White Lightning, Fool's Gold, Pop Corn, Buttermilk, and Pepper Box bandied about, the group ultimately settled on Pogo, the title character from Walt Kelly's popular cartoon strip.

Reporter Michael Etchison happened to be present that first night and described the new group as "something between country and rock, authentically both, with leanings one way and another." He went on to note that "the group goes in for the high, rich harmonies that the Springfield loved, except that in the Springfield, Furay was usually the highest voice, and in RFD the bass player, Randy Meisner, sings above him. The sound is much like the Springfield's."

"We knew there was something fresh and creatively unique about what we were doing," enthuses Furay on Pogo's sound. "There was no denying that. We knew we were on the edge of something unique. I think that's what really gave it the thrust. We were hungry and wanted to do it. And to have the talent and ability in the band to be able to do the things we wanted, like Rusty and Jimmy playing their duets like Buck Owens, was exciting. Nobody in rock was doing that back then." Adds Rusty Young: "We were different and we knew it. But the time was right for something new and different. I think a great part of our originality was Richie's amazing songs. They weren't like anything else I'd heard before, and I loved them."

On November 19 Pogo made its official Troubadour debut, backing Biff Rose through to December 1. It was truly a magical event. "It was like the Whisky-A-Go Go with the Springfield, with more focus and sincere excitement," says Furay. "When the Springfield played the Whisky, there wasn't the family connection that George, Rusty, Jimmy, Randy, and I had, and we were excited about that. Though the music was never any better for the Springfield than at the Whisky, the energy level and the excitement of where we were going with the new group was expressed more openly."

One witness to that excitement was Paul Cotton, guitarist and singer with the Illinois Speed Press, who later wrote about that evening in the song *Livin' In The Band*. "The Speed Press moved to Hollywood in March 1967, and we recorded two albums for Columbia with Jim Guercio producing. I don't know where I heard about Poco, but I'd been a big fan of the Springfield through the Speed Press years. I had no idea what to expect from Poco that night, not a clue. It was really quite an up evening. The audience was blown away. I know I was. They were really well rehearsed. Most of the songs that night ended up on that first album. You could just feel the excitement. George was amazing, a singing drummer. I was really intrigued with George and Randy's voices. I was already familiar with Richie's voice from the Springfield, and here were these absolutely heavenly voices surrounding him. You had solos by Jimmy and Rusty, which were so tasteful and energetic. It was the freshest music I'd heard since the Byrds' debut album— impeccable harmonies, Richie's voice, and Rusty's steel. Nobody plays like Rusty, then or now. The marriage of country and rock was there."

Like Furay, Meisner feels the presence of pedal-steel guitar in a rock context created the first country rock. "Having a steel guitar in the band was something that set us apart from other groups. Nobody else had one. And Rusty was a real showman. Everybody just loved watching him. Rusty didn't play it a lot like a steel. He made a whole different instrument out of it by playing it through a Leslie speaker. *That* was really unique. He could get a B-3 organ sound so we could get that r & b feel, and when we did strictly country stuff he could go back to that. George was a really strong drummer, and between him and me, we clicked as a rhythm section. George was a big strength, too, in the middle of the harmonies. Richie and I would sing up really high and George could get right under there and probably go just as high if he wanted to." Critics frequently cited Meisner's vocal contributions as one of the group's high points, noting that his singing on Furay's "Anyway Bye Bye" sparked cheers from audiences. "'Anyway Bye Bye' was a killer song for us at the Troubadour," acknowledges Meisner. "It was one of those really high songs that Richie and I did. I was just grateful somebody was writing good songs." Meisner also handled lead vocals on "Calico Lady" and "First Love."

The new group held court at the Troubadour off and on to the end of the year, drawing considerable interest from record labels and large crowds eager to hear their sound. "We had so much fun together," Meisner asserts. "Every time we played the Troubadour it was packed, people hanging out of the rafters. We'd go up to Doug Weston's office, have a shot of tequila and some beer, then hooting and hollering we'd run out, which is really great for a group just before you go on stage, like a football team psyching-up. By the time we'd hit the stage the whole audience would be yelling. We'd have 'em cranked before we even started playing. When you know the audience is with you, it gives you that extra boost of natural energy. It was just so much fun. Some nights Jimmy would have his dog Jasper with him, and he actually came on stage with us a few times." Notes Young, "Once we played the Troubadour everyone was on the bandwagon. Robert Hilburn of the *Los Angeles Times* called us the next big thing, so all of a sudden there were lots of others working similar territory." How does Young compare Poco's country rock to other early exponents of the genre? "I think we were a little different. The Burritos were more traditional country, the Byrds had the obvious rock edge, and later the Eagles were more geared toward commercial radio."

The Nitty Gritty Dirt Band's John McEuen remembers Poco's early excitement. "Poco was one of the most underrated groups. What they did for country rock was to take it to the max. There was one night Poco opened for the Dirt Band, and boy did we feel tiny going on after them." Young feels that Poco had a hand in the Dirt Band folding shortly thereafter. "We opened for the Nitty Gritty Dirt Band, who were so blown away they dissolved the band, only to reform in a Poco-like form later. Ha!" Poco had plenty of critical accolades and fan adulation but little money. "We were so broke," smiles Young, "that I used to steal ham sandwiches from the kitchen at the Troubadour when we'd play there."

One person was not a fan. Walt Kelly, the cartoonist who created Pogo, served papers on them for copyright infringement, necessitating a quick name change. "After playing in the Los Angeles area for a few months as Pogo," recalls Furay somewhat bitterly, "Walt sent us a stack of papers about two inches thick that said, 'Get out of my tree.' So after establishing the name and getting a following, we really didn't want to do anything too radical. I don't know whose idea it was but we liked to say we just took the little line off the "g" and called ourselves Poco."

While Poco were setting the Troubadour stage ablaze, Dillard & Clark's debut album, the *Fantastic Expedition Of Dillard & Clark*, was released in November. Rooted in acoustic folk and bluegrass, and expanding those forms into country and rock, Clark and Dillard drew energy from their partnership, creating a wholly original sound. The album offers a stunning example of where traditional country and bluegrass music could be taken in a contemporary context. With support from Bernie Leadon, who co-wrote six of the eleven tracks, Clark is in fine form. He sounds relaxed and confident, and his laid-back acoustic approach is underpinned by Michael Clarke's drumming on a couple of tracks, although he is not credited. The harmonies of Leadon and Dillard are beautiful bluegrass renditions, and the picking from Leadon, Chris Hillman, and Don Beck is understated and supportive. Clark brings his folk rock sensibilities to bear on several of his tracks, notably on "Out On The Side," released as the lead single. With its organ, drums, and electric guitar, it sounds like it could have been an outtake from The Band's *Music From Big Pink*. The evocative "Something's Wrong" is an introspective musing on coming of age. Dillard lends an authentic bluegrass touch to two numbers, "Don't Come Rollin'," and the band's cover of Flatt and Scruggs' "Get In Line, Brother" (which they retitled "Get It On, Brother"). Although the moody rock arrangement "Out On The Side" sounds slightly out of place among the acoustic bluegrass here, Dillard insists it came from the same sessions. It was the only song Clark brought with him to the new group. All other tracks were recent collaborations. Highlights on the album include Clark and Leadon's marvelous "Train Leaves Here This Morning," later recorded by the Eagles on their debut album. Also praiseworthy were "She Darked The Sun," written in the style of a traditional mountain song, and "With Care From Someone," a minor-key bluegrass number on which the three collaborated.

"Doug and Gene did some really good records that nobody paid attention to," laments Chris Hillman, an unabashed Clark supporter. "That first album was fabulous, way better than anything the rest of us were doing when you measure it song-per-song. Better than Poco and the Burritos—consistent and lyrically brilliant." Said Clark at the time of the album's release, "I'd written a lot of songs since the Byrds. I have two or three albums I made for myself in a closet somewhere. But when we decided to do this record Doug and I wrote all new songs." Leadon describes the group's creative process: "A lot of these songs—like 'Don't Come Rollin',' and the ones that the three of us wrote—were banjo instrumentals that Douglas and I had worked up, or Douglas had written that I played with him, where he was kind enough to consider me a co-writer. To be honest, in most cases, Douglas had written a banjo piece that I would put chords behind. Then Gene showed up and would say, 'I love that piece of music,' because Douglas would be playing that stuff ad nauseam. We never stopped. Gene would come back the next day with a set of lyrics and a melody and we'd start singing that. Douglas loved to sing, so we'd just sit around and sing this stuff in three-part harmony. Then Don Beck and David Jackson came over and that was it, we just played. So when we went into the studio it was a piece of cake, we knew the songs very well."

Besides the marvelously fresh music inside, the album cover drew some attention: the two friends astride a Harley-Davidson motorcycle with a sidecar, looking like outlaws. "They had a bad-boy image on the motorcycles," laughs Rodney Dillard, "passing that cigarette that everyone thought was a joint. I got a big kick out of that."

Reviews of the album were solid, though the record failed to chart. Michael Etchison wrote, "Dillard & Clark are taking the chance that the great country music boom, predicted ever since Guy Mitchell's 'Singin' The Blues' brought on rockabilly ten years ago, is about to happen." In an accompanying interview, Dillard and Clark enunciated their feelings about the current music scene and where country music fit in. "There's something else happening," commented Clark. "Country music is changing a lot. The Grand Ole Opry people, the Red Foleys, Lefty Frizzells, and Roy Acuffs, will be around a long time. But the young people, especially the ones who don't come from Nashville, are trying to change. Buck Owens, Merle Haggard, Waylon Jennings, all these guys are making those Nashville cats very nervous 'cause they're bringing in a whole new kind of fan." Added Dillard, "Things just have to settle down. There has to be something besides loud music, and a lot of people are finding out they can listen to country music. We're going to be playing out pretty soon and if the audiences want it, we can always do electric things."

Between the album sessions in August and their debut performances in December, the Dillard & Clark Expedition plugged in and amplified their sound. David Jackson exchanged his upright bass for an electric Fender, Leadon picked up an electric guitar, and ex-Byrds' drummer Michael Clarke joined the mix as the Expedition headed into less familiar electric territory. Dobro player Don Beck opted out soon after, uncomfortable with the change in direction. Again, reviews were encouraging. "They have the best country sound of any ex-rock group around," exclaimed Etchison, who went on to describe the group's Troubadour shows. "Dillard really does pick and grin, and Clark sort of hunkers over as he sings and strums. Clark sings lead on everything. If anything, his voice is even more lonesome than it was with the Byrds. Dillard and Leadon join him in a mix of high hill and flatland harmonies. They do only one or two songs from their album. Instead, they do songs like Merle Haggard's 'Mama Tried' and 'Folsom Prison Blues.' Fortunately they also do some bluegrass, giving Dillard a chance to showcase his picking prowess, especially on the feisty 'Uncle Penn.' Dillard even played some cautiously idiomatic fiddle on Clark's 'She Darked The Sun.'"

According to Leadon, the group found it difficult to recreate their studio sound on stage. "Gene and Doug made this record, then there was the pressure to go out and play. So all of us who played on the record did a few gigs. I got a Telecaster, and we sort of transformed into a country band. We got Michael Clarke to play drums briefly. We played the Ash Grove, the Golden Bear, places like that rather than the Whisky, which was a heavy club where you had to be loud." He feels the group suffered as a result of poor organization and a lack of discipline. "The Dillard & Clark Expedition was not a very good live band because, like the Burrito Brothers, they hadn't any ability to rehearse and be focused and organized about anything. With absolutely zero organization, we walked onstage—without any prepared set list, without having properly figured out how we would begin and end songs, without having really rehearsed the harmonies on microphone, and be in some kind of balance. The result was complete noise and confusion. We would come out looking quite cool, and proceed to make absolute idiots of ourselves. Some of us, like me and Don Beck, approach it very intellectually, the complete opposite to what I just described. To competently play bluegrass banjo, it's about organization and methodical thinking, analytical stuff. You want to play it with feeling but it's very intricate and needs structure. Douglas had bluegrass training and instincts, but he would go completely over to playing on the vibe and the flow. And the others thought they could too. When it absolutely all came together the thing would *soar*, but it was so complicated it didn't come together on stage. They would become self-conscious. Sometimes in the studio you might have one of those magical evenings sustained for hours, amazing fluidity of creation. But bringing all that virtuosity to the stage is difficult. There's a rather large audience, sitting there expectantly, waiting to be entertained on cue. Neither of these bands, Dillard & Clark or the Burritos, had a clue how to do that."

With a limited number of venues suitable for their music, and Clark's aversion to flying, the group was stymied. "We were playing places like the Troubadour and the Golden Bear in Huntington Beach, mostly folk clubs, because there weren't really any other country rock clubs then," recalls Dillard. "We also played the Palomino. We played a show with the Jefferson Airplane once. *That* was a unique night." With record sales sluggish, the Expedition members needed to work in order to eat. "We made the first album for around twenty thousand dollars," remembers Leadon, "but though the record company made their bread back, the sales weren't high enough to bring the group any money. So we had to support ourselves entirely on gigs, which weren't too wonderful. I can't recall us having any formal management. Eddie Tickner was nominally involved, but not really working with Dillard. He might have been advising Gene loosely, but the upshot was there was a record company but no management, no plan, and so no money. It was Gene's deal, Douglas maybe got a taste, nobody else got anything. After all this jamming, we did the record and maybe turned in six or ten sessions apiece at union scale, and that's what we got for doing the record. 'Train Leaves Here This Morning' only made me money when the Eagles did it."

In January 1969, following a notoriously disastrous stand at the Troubadour, the Expedition went on hiatus. "We had one horrible show at the Troubadour, one of the worst experiences I've ever had," remarks Leadon, still smarting thirty years later. "Douglas and Gene became completely unglued. It just stopped working. Gene was terribly shy and spent all of the shows with his back to the audience. Douglas was playing the fiddle, which he didn't play as well as the banjo. It all came to a screeching halt and they just stared at each other. Douglas threw his fiddle down, and stomped and broke it. And the two of them just stood there stunned before they exited the stage, leaving the rest of us up there feeling like our pants were down at our ankles. I think I played a bit of 'Buckaroo' and left the stage soon after."

Prior to the fiasco, Michael Clarke had abruptly left the group to join the Burrito Brothers. Moments before their set was to begin, Jon Corneal, who was in the audience, was enlisted to join the group on-stage. "I was hanging out at the Troubadour and Gene Clark approached me at the bar. He came and asked if I had any drums with me. I told him I had a snare and a set of brushes. He said, 'That'll work. Do you want to sit in with us tonight?' I said sure. It was kind of strange because they all got up and started running through a medley of their tunes, it wasn't their regular set. Gene and Doug had eaten psilocybin and they went from one song to the next in a matter of seconds. After they left the stage I was just sitting there wondering what in the world was going on. I had never seen anything like it. Doug Weston came in and told them that if they ever wanted to play there again they had better clean up their act. They were playing the following night but they didn't ingest any substances. I played with them the next night. That's how I ended up in the band. It was easy. We all liked each other. Doug and Gene liked me because I drank as much as they did."

Laments John McEuen, "If they hadn't been doing so many drugs and had been hungrier, Dillard & Clark would have been a major contender." Despite critical praise for their sound, with their album failing to sell and their live engagements chaotic the Expedition circled the wagons to reassess their situation.

Douglas Dillard and Gene Clark were busy that autumn redefining bluegrass and country rock, but Rodney Dillard was far from idle. Freed from his brother's tradition-based constraints, Rodney set about blending Appalachian harmony and bluegrass picking with a contemporary sound, utilizing drums, electric bass, pedal-steel guitar, and strings. The end result would become the standard against which all other contemporary bluegrass-influenced music would be judged. "*Wheatstraw Suite* represented a turning point for me and the band," acknowledges Rodney. "I was finally able to express myself musically. It was a very exciting, creative period. That album is my favorite, the one I'm proudest of."

The Dillards spent much of the summer with Herb Pedersen, working on the numbers intended for the album. They concentrated on their harmony singing and honing their writing and arranging skills rather than relying on their instrumental prowess. "It was a very experimental time," notes Pedersen. "Jac Holzman at Elektra Records was trying different things. On the label at the time were the Doors, Judy Collins, Bread, and us, so it was a very eclectic label. They didn't really know what to do with us, and our budget was very small. So we tried mixing the traditional with the new, writing things that were a little more contemporary and adding things like strings and pedal steel. It was a pretty bold step adding strings to bluegrass instrumentation."

Enlisting the talents of steel guitarist Buddy Emmons, Joe Osborn on bass, and drummers Jim Gordon and Toxey French, the sound was more rhythm-heavy than previous recordings. Rodney and engineer Jimmie Hilton produced, and Al Capps was brought in to score the orchestration. "I sat down with Al and explained what I wanted," relates Dillard, "the strings and cellos—all that—from my head. He went away and wrote the arrangements. I didn't hear them until the day I came into the studio, and he had this twenty-five-piece orchestra. Man, when it cranked up on 'Don't You Cry' and he started bringing in the strings on this fast banjo part, I just fell apart. It was *wonderful*." Dillard was quite content to stretch the envelope of acoustic bluegrass music to, as he puts it, "change the texture and rhythm."

"It was so different from what we had done," admits Dean Webb. "I liked the way it sounded, and I guess a *lot* of other people did too. And I felt we were capable of more sophisticated music than we'd been making. It's hard to gauge the end result during the recording process, but I thought it was really interesting the way it was coming together." Resurrecting three songs from his Capitol period, "Don't You Cry," "Nobody Knows," and "Lemon Chimes," as well as Tim Hardin's "Reason To Believe," Albert Brumley's "I'll Fly Away," and the Beatles' "I've Just Seen A Face," Rodney rounded off the album with original tunes from Mitch Jayne and Herb Pedersen. "You can't have too much variety," chirps Webb. "If you can mix it up and play something that isn't hard-core bluegrass, it just makes all the rest of it sound better when you come back to it. You don't want to play seven banjo tunes in a row, everybody'd go to sleep."

Released in December, *Wheatstraw Suite* set the country rock community on its ear. "When *Wheatstraw* first came out I listened to it two or three times before I made up my mind," says fiddler Byron Berline, "because it was so much different from what the rest of them were." Notes Bernie Leadon, "*Wheatstraw Suite* was a beautiful album; the three-part harmonies were meticulous. That influenced the sound of

Buck Owens and his Buckaroos, 1963. Left to right: Doyle Holly, Willie Cantu, Tom Brumley, Don Rich, Buck Owens (courtesy of Tom Brumley).

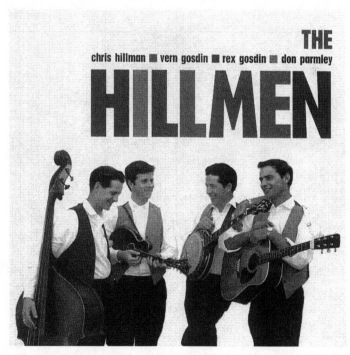

The Hillmen, featuring the Gosdin Brothers and a teenage Chris Hillman (second from the left), 1964 (courtesy of Sugar Hill Records).

Pickin' and Fiddlin': The Dillards with fiddler Byron Berline, 1964. Left to right: Dean Webb, Byron Berline, Doug Dillard, Rodney Dillard, Mitch Jayne (courtesy of Dean Webb and the Dillards).

The Dillards go electric on Hollywood-A-Go Go, 1965. Left to right: Mitch Jayne, Rodney Dillard, Doug Dillard, Dean Webb (courtesy of Dean Webb and the Dillards).

The legendary Troubadour Club, 9081 Santa Monica Boulevard, West Hollywood, circa 1968, the meeting place for the folk and country rock fraternity (courtesy of Morgan Cavett).

Rick Nelson's first country foray, 1966 (courtesy of Into The Music).

Hearts And Flowers, 1966.
Left to Right: David Dawson,
Larry Murray, Rick Cunha
(courtesy of Rick Cunha).

The final lineup of the Buffalo Springfield, March 1968. Left to right: Dewey
Martin, Jimmy Messina, Neil Young, Richie Furay, Stephen Stills (courtesy of
Richie Furay).

The original lineup of the International Submarine Band, 1966. Left to right: John Nuese, Gram Parsons, Ian Dunlop, Mickey Gauvin (courtesy of John Nuese).

Hearts And Flowers, 1968. Bernie Leadon, far right, replaces Rick Cunha (courtesy of Capitol Records).

The Sweetheart Of The Rodeo lineup of the Byrds at Rome's Piper Club, May 1968. Left to right: Chris Hillman, Roger McGuinn, Gram Parsons (courtesy of Raffaele Galli).

Doug Dillard guesting with the Byrds at Rome's Piper Club, May 1968 (courtesy of Raffaele Galli).

The Fantastic Expedition of Dillard And Clark, 1968. Left to right: Doug Dillard and Gene Clark (courtesy of Homer Dillard and Doug Dillard).

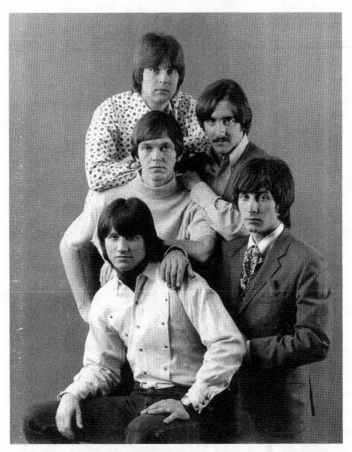

Pogo (later Poco), December 1968. Clockwise from top: Randy Meisner, George Grantham, Jimmy Messina, Richie Furay, Rusty Young (center) (courtesy of Gene Trindl).

Ad for Pogo's debut at the Troubadour, November 1968 (courtesy of Jerry Fuentes).

The revamped Byrds, September 1968. Left to right: Clarence White, John York, Gene Parsons, Roger McGuinn (courtesy of Jim Bickhart and Columbia Records).

Bob Dylan's groundbreaking *Nashville Skyline* album (courtesy of Columbia Records).

The original Flying Burrito Brothers at Joshua Tree, California, 1968. Left to right: Sneaky Pete Kleinow, Chris Ethridge, unidentified models, Gram Parsons, Chris Hillman (courtesy of Archive Photos).

The Wheatstraw Suite era Dillards, 1968. Left to right: Dean Webb, Herb Pederson, Rodney Dillard, Mitch Jayne (courtesy of Dean Webb and the Dillards).

Rick Nelson and the Stone Canyon Band at the Troubadour recording their live *In Concert* album, October 1969. Left to right: Randy Meisner, Rick Nelson, Allen Kemp, Tom Brumley (Pat Shanahan on drums behind) (courtesy of Tom Brumley).

Folksinger turned country rock artist John Stewart (courtesy of John Stewart and Michelle Stevens).

Linda Ronstadt, 1970, a Troubadour favorite with a talent for assembling exceptional backing bands (courtesy of Henry Diltz).

The roadmaster: Gene Clark, 1972 (courtesy of Jim Bickhart and Columbia Records).

The original cosmic cowboy: ex Monkee Michael Nesmith, decked out in his finest Nudie outfit, circa 1973 (courtesy of RCA-BMG Records).

Last of the red hot Burrito Brothers, 1972. Left to right: Rick Roberts, Al Perkins (seated at his pedal-steel guitar), Bernie Leadon (courtesy of Rick and Mary Roberts).

*Longbranch Pennywhistle*, 1970. Left to right: John David Souther, Glenn Frey (courtesy of Carny Corbett).

The pride of Linden, Texas: Shiloh, 1971. Back row, left to right: Al Perkins, Jim Ed Norman; front row, left to right: Don Henley, Richard Bowden, Mike Bowden (courtesy of Carny Corbett).

Ian and Sylvia's Great Speckled Bird, 1970. Left to right: N. D. Smart II, Buddy Cage, Ian Tyson, Sylvia Tyson, David Wilcox, Jim Colegrove (courtesy of Sylvia Tyson).

The Nitty Gritty Dirt Band's groundbreaking 1972 album *Will The Circle Be Unbroken*.

Poco, 1973. Left to right: Paul Cotton, George Grantham, Richie Furay, Timothy B. Schmit, Rusty Young (seated in front) (courtesy of Epic Records).

The original Eagles, 1972. Left to right: Don Henley, Bernie Leadon, Randy Meisner, Glenn Frey (courtesy of Archive Photos).

the Eagles. Henley and Frey were big Dillards fans." Rock critics gushed over the album, though the traditional bluegrass community snarled. *Rolling Stone* termed *Wheatstraw Suite* "a treat," going on to describe it in their Record Guide as "a brilliant rush of fierce playing and beautifully precise vocal harmonies with several excellent originals." Laughs Pedersen, "Oh, we thought we were very hip back then, doing very different things. We were all just drawing from a lot of different influences and throwing them into this stew to see what would come out. The fact that we had the opportunity to try different things was great. We didn't have an A & R guy breathing down our necks saying, 'No, we need hits,' which is what it's like today."

Opening with an a cappella version of the traditional bluegrass gospel number "I'll Fly Away," the album soars until the final fade of the strings on "She Sang Hymns Out Of Tune." "You listen to that album and it left you with a good feeling," Dillard says with pride. "It wasn't negative. 'I'll Fly Away' comes from our roots. I grew up in a country church where this kind of music was sung, and I wanted that to be a part of the sound. 'Nobody Knows' was our sad love song. Mitch and I got into this thing of writing bummer love songs because we were both in the middle of divorces. It had more of a contemporary feel, with the minor changes, the shuffle feel and the strings. I knew Tim Hardin and loved 'Reason To Believe' so I wanted to do it. Doing 'I've Just Seen A Face' was a bold endeavor, but I liked the tune—I felt it was the Beatles trying to find what bluegrass was all about. I got 'She Sang Hymns Out Of Tune' from Harry Nilsson. Harry and I had a mutual friend, Bill Martin, who was a writer who wrote things with me like 'The Biggest Whatever.'" Tackling a Beatles number in bluegrass form was not out of context, given the range on the album. "That was pretty much Rodney's idea," confirms Pedersen. "They had already worked up a version of 'I've Just Seen A Face' for *Wheatstraw* when I joined." The group carried the Beatles' idea to their next album. "On *Copperfields* we did 'Yesterday,' which we wanted to treat like an old gospel tune."

Jesse Lee Kincaid's "She Sang Hymns Out Of Tune" made its third appearance on vinyl that year on *Wheatstraw Suite*. "We were aware that Hearts And Flowers had done it already," acknowledges Pedersen, who sang the closing number, capturing the whimsy of the lyrics perfectly. "But ours was different. It was an interesting tune to do. We had never done a waltz tune, so that was kind of a nice thing to have on there. I'm sure we pissed off a lot of people with that, using strings on bluegrass. Forget *Bluegrass Unlimited*. I'm sure they threw up their hands, 'Oh God, what's this guy done to this great band?' I had already alienated the traditional Dillards audiences by replacing Doug. I was the new guy, and got comments like, 'Oh, you're not really from Missouri?'"

"When *Wheatstraw Suite* came out, another career started for us," emphasizes Rodney. "We started playing other venues and places we hadn't played before. It was really a career boost for us. We didn't have to rely on the comedy as heavily as we used to, once we had the vocals sounding so good. In the very beginning we were a comedy act with bluegrass. Now the music could stand on its own, and we didn't have to feed it to them through humor. It was so new. No one had done anything like that up to then. And it was an accident. When you are right in the middle of things you don't get that sense of perspective. It was a time of creative inspiration and exploration. There was still room for originality without having to worry about marketing or adhering to radio play lists. You could take risks. But I'd still feel a sense of accomplishment if it never sold a single record. *Wheatstraw Suite* influenced a lot of people—from the guys in Blood, Sweat & Tears to the Eagles."

"When drums were added on *Wheatstraw Suite*," concludes Rodney, "we were asked, 'How does changing the chord patterns in bluegrass music fit? How does changing acoustic to electric fit?' All those questions were asked, and you can only tell by time. How does an orchestra fit behind banjos? Well, we did that."

# 6

# *Country Honk: 1969*

*Getting the acceptance of the Nashville crowd was tough, but we earned that.*
*They got to like us. They were taking us out to dinner. They were surprised that*
*we could play. "These longhaired assholes can really play!"*

—N. D. Smart, drummer, the Great Speckled Bird

Michael Clarke left the erratic Dillard & Clark Expedition in January 1969 to join the Flying Burrito Brothers. With Clarke on board, the Burritos set out for engagements intended to raise their profile in anticipation of their soon-to-be-released debut album. But as Sneaky Pete recalls, the group's reputation for sloppy performances was earned early in its history. "I cannot recall one performance where I wasn't embarrassed to tears. Our first showcase after recording the first album was at the Whisky-A-Go Go. Jerry Moss and Herb Alpert were sitting downstairs waiting. We went up and started playing. Gram was so stoned he couldn't play the piano. Chris Hillman, of course, was right up there plugging, but Chris Ethridge had smoked a little too much of something. As we started to play, after about three or four songs, Chris Ethridge got to the point where he wasn't able to stand up anymore. As he continued to play he got more and more stoned and finally passed out, dropping his bass. One of our roadies picked it up to play. The suits got up from their table in midconcert and walked out. We thought we were finished. It was typical."

Undaunted, the record label launched the Burritos by organizing a barn dance on the A&M lot. Invitations sent out to the media came accompanied by a bundle of hay. Singer/songwriter Tom Russell recalls: "It was probably early 1969. The invitation came in the mail with hay or alfalfa in the envelope, which caused a *lot* of problems—the postal service thought it was marijuana. The band took the stage in their Nudie suits.* The music was real interesting, though the sound was *really* loud. It sounded like Buck Owens turned *way* up. The audience was a mix of rednecks and hippies. Gram was famous for trying to bring these two elements together. The music was loud and Sneaky Pete was playing extremely bizarre steel guitar; nobody'd ever heard fuzz-tone on a pedal steel, with this rock edge. And the songs were about pills and drinking. The whole thing really set the stage for what came after, that southern California country rock." As for Parsons himself, Russell notes, "He had this sort of 'wasted boy in Hollywood' charisma about him. He had a real soulful voice, and he'd done his homework. He could do Louvin Brothers songs, or Hank Williams and Little Jimmy Dickens all day long. Gram used to go out to cowboy country bars in Encino in his cape and long hair and almost get killed until he'd sing a George Jones song. And he'd do the same in hippie bars and try to sing George Jones."

Sneaky Pete recalls the event unhappily. "I remember trying to turn my instrument up to the point where I could rise above the din, but it was contributing to it so I just turned down and sat there like an idiot. When music gets that bad I don't even want to play."

Despite the dubious debut, the group set out on a notorious train trip through the American Midwest en route to gigs in Chicago, Detroit, Boston, New York, and Philadelphia. With A&M Records footing the bills, the excursion is fondly recalled by band members more for the nonstop gambling and conspicuous drug consumption than for the chaotic performances at each whistle stop. Parsons, however, drew strength from the response the Burritos received. "When we went on the tour that A&M set up across the country, people really dug us. Man, they were *really* excited about us. They had no reason to be, nobody had ever heard of the Flying Burrito Brothers. We were playing with groups like Savoy Brown and people loved us. I was used to people being very cold to country music." The bottomless supply of cocaine and pills no doubt had much to do with his positive spin on the tour. Expenses became so overwhelming that the group remained in hock to A&M for the next few years, although the label virtually washed its hands of the group soon after.

In the midst of the tour, Parsons telephoned A&M's Jerry Moss to arrange studio time for the group to lay down a new single conceived and inspired by the train trip. The group ended up recording "The

*So called because they were designed by Hank Williams' tailor, Nudie Cohen.

Train Song" following the conclusion of the tour. Produced by rhythm & blues musicians Larry Williams (of "Bonie Maronie" fame) and Johnny "Guitar" Watson, the single was a crude jumble of gospel, country, and rock that, to no one's surprise, failed miserably. "'The Train Song' was just horrible," winces Hillman.

In February, while the Burritos were bringing Parsons' "Cosmic American Music" to the masses, the Byrds' latest album, *Dr. Byrds And Mr. Hyde,* was released. Reviews were mixed, though McGuinn's attempt at merging country with rock was applauded. The inconsistency of the musicianship and the muddy production quality hamstrung what could have been a strong debut for the new lineup. Unlike the traditional country of *Sweetheart Of The Rodeo,* the *Dr. Byrds* album was more a pastiche of straight-ahead rock mixed with country rock. "The album seemed to be the result of poor planning," suggests drummer Gene Parsons. "It was just a bunch of tapes thrown together in one package. The sound was bad, the mixing was bad. We weren't too pleased with what we did, frankly." Adds John York, "I wish we could go back and remix that album again. Even the reissued CD has the same poor quality."

Opening with a Dylan number from *The Basement Tapes,* "This Wheel's on Fire" attempts to posit Clarence White's stringbender playing into the realm of heavy blues-based guitar a la Clapton. "That's the most embarrassing thing I've ever done," admitted White. "It's horrible. I wasn't ready for it." Yet what follows is an interesting album, and White's unique country rock guitar sets the mood for the Byrds' new sound. Tracks like "Old Blue" are given a new country rock twist. "'Old Blue' was an acknowledgment of where Roger was coming from—the basic lack of pretension," offers York. "'Your Gentle Ways Of Loving Me' by Gary Paxton and Gib Guilbeau was brought to the group by Gene." McGuinn and Gram Parsons' "Drug Store Truck Drivin' Man" is the only track to hark back to the traditional country sound, where Lloyd Green plays pedal-steel guitar. Like his efforts on *Sweetheart,* McGuinn affects a contrived southern accent for the number. The rock tracks are less satisfying; the group was still growing into its new identity. "Bad Night At The Whisky," "King Apathy," and an oddly chosen jam on "Baby, What You Want Me To Do?" show the Byrds attempting to stretch their limitations, without much success. *Dr. Byrds* is a transitional album, with the group searching for its voice.

With a new album out, the Byrds hit the road to promote it. On a weekend in late February at the Boston Tea Party, the group shared a stage with the Flying Burrito Brothers where the inevitable jam took place. "We all knew each other, played a lot of the same venues often on the same bills, and were friends," notes York. "At one point we all just said, 'Why don't we all play together?' So at the end of our set we just started calling them up. The gig that stands out was at the Boston Tea Party, when Jon Landau wrote about it in *Rolling Stone*." Pulling out numbers from their *Sweetheart* period, Gram Parsons played "Hickory Wind," "You Don't Miss Your Water," and "The Christian Life." He also played with McGuinn while the latter performed "Pretty Boy Floyd." Hillman dug deep into his treasure chest for "Time Between," with White recreating his unique guitar lines from the recording. The assembled ex-Byrds and associates closed out the evening with Lefty Frizzell's "Long Black Veil" and a number of Byrds favorites, closing appropriately enough with "Goin' Back." A few months later, back in L.A., Clarence White would sit in with the Burritos at the Palomino Club for another legendary session that was widely bootlegged. White and Gene Parsons also kept busy that spring guesting on the Everly Brothers' "I'm On My Way Home Again" (backed by "The Cuckoo Bird").

By the time the Burritos reached New York, A&M had released their debut album, *The Gilded Palace Of Sin*, one of the most important albums of the country rock genre. The album consists mainly of original material composed by Parsons and Hillman during the intense writing period the previous autumn. Blending country with rock and rhythm & blues influences, Parsons and Hillman create a uniquely original contemporary country sound. *The Gilded Palace Of Sin* is a remarkable achievement, and a testimony to the duo's love of country. "Basically, I love the first album, although it is crudely recorded," offers Hillman. Adds Sneaky Pete, "It was a significant album for that time." On *Gilded Palace*, Hillman and Parsons virtually redefine country music in a contemporary context, using the traditional music form as a base, and adding contemporary lyrics and themes in order to appeal to younger audiences.

Opening with "Christine's Tune (Devil In Disguise)," inspired by a member of the female group the GTOs,* the tone of the album is set by Hillman and Parsons' Everly Brothers–style harmony and Sneaky Pete's virtuoso pedal-steel guitar work. As Hillman told musician Sid Griffin, "They were harmonies, first and thirds. Like 'Devil In Disguise,' Gram would sing the harmony to me, and we'd switch on the chorus, where I would sing the harmony and he would sing the lead."

*"Girls Together Outrageously," a band of *extremely* adventurous young women well known in the rock world for their excesses.

Pete's innovative use of fuzz-tone pedal steel on the track is amazing. "I had used a fuzz-tone for a long time before that album," he notes. "I had been piling up gadgets I could use with the steel guitar. I started hanging outboard equipment on my steel way before then even when I was playing the clubs. I tried to be as innovative as possible. I always felt the steel guitar was an instrument that could be boring, so I wanted to get as much variety into the sound as possible. I think the fuzz-tone was a bit heavy handed on that first album though." Noted Parsons years later, "[Producer] Larry Marks let Sneaky go with some of the weirdest ideas. I mean, there were times during the first album when I wanted to quit because I couldn't understand this guy doing eight steel overdubs over himself. But I liked it."

Perhaps the ultimate Burritos number is "Sin City," Hillman and Parsons' take on Hollywood, and a shot at their former manager. "I think 'Sin City' is the song that personifies the Flying Burrito Brothers," Hillman maintains. Combining their penchant for tongue-in-cheek lyrics with traditional country arrangement and backing, "Sin City" is a stunning example of hip country music. Chris Ethridge deserves singling out on "Sin City." His solid bass playing lays a strong foundation, lending a rhythm & blues flavor to the mix, though Parsons would later opine that Ethridge was not the right bass player for *his* country vision.

The two tracks that follow represent Parsons' vision of country rhythm & blues inspired by listening to Ray Charles' early attempts to merge the two genres. "On the very first Flying Burrito Brothers album we took r & b songs and we did them country," recalls Hillman. "You couldn't get any more Memphis Stax than 'Dark End of the Street' or even 'Do Right (Woman).' We were more than aware of Percy Sledge and Robert Carr and things like that, those kinds of singers and those kinds of songs like 'Dark End.' We were consciously welding the two. That was the merging of the black and white blues. The crying out, taking those R&B songs and putting a light country & western arrangement to them. Gram listened to a lot of r & b (Bobby "Blue" Bland, Percy Sledge, James Carr). And he listened to straight country like George Jones and Hank Williams. He didn't listen to any contemporary rock as far as I can remember." "Dark End" had been a hit for soul singer James Carr, and was also covered by Aretha Franklin and Percy Sledge, while "Do Right (Woman)" had been a hit for Aretha. "Spooner Oldham and Dan Penn were influences on Gram," acknowledges Pete. "He did bring that R&B element to the Burritos."

Hillman and Parsons' satire was put to good use on "My Uncle," a song inspired by Parsons' draft notice, and the closing track, "Hippie Boy," done in a Red Foley talking–style by Hillman. In between are a couple of Parsons' numbers that are cited as his most heartfelt vocal performances, "Hot Burrito #1" and "Hot Burrito #2," written with Chris Ethridge. "There are a few things that Gram got on record that are magnificent," muses Hillman in retrospect. "One is 'Hot Burrito #1,' and the other is 'Hot Burrito #2.' It's the most beautiful singing I've ever heard." Parsons' vocals, while revealing his limitations, absolutely drip with emotion, cracking at times but conveying a feeling akin to soul and blues.

*The Gilded Palace* was like nothing released to that point, a sound that would influence many other country rock artists. Regrettably, it would also be the Burrito Brothers' high water mark. They would never again be so good. The public's response was limited, the record charting at Number 164. Hillman, on the commercial dilemma of country rock, noted: "The rock & roll stations said we were too country, and the country stations said we were too rock & roll because we had more emphasis on the bass and drums, more rhythm." In spite of its poor showing, the album remains an important turning point for Hillman, and testament to his highly creative collaboration with Parsons. Reflecting on A&M's quandary over marketing issues in a 1972 interview, Parsons opined: "They knew we were a country group and knew what would make a country group, it's just that we didn't really have it together on the first album. They hoped we would on the second."

The idea for the Nudie suits was exclusively Parsons', though the others bought into it willingly. "We loved the Nudie thing," laughs Hillman. "It was very tongue-in-cheek, from Sneaky's pterodactyl suit to Gram's drug suit, Ethridge had flowers, and I went for this weird stuff with peacocks. Mike had to get his off-the-rack because he joined late." Concurs Pete, "I liked those Nudie suits. I designed my own. I was a motion picture special effects guy so I figured 'Dinosaurs, wow, that'd be great.' Gram's influences were obvious." Parsons' outfit was festooned with marijuana leaves, poppy plants, pills, nude women, and—ever the good southern Baptist,— a cross stitched on the back.

In New York the Burritos were booked into Steve Paul's The Scene club for several nights, giving Parsons the opportunity to renew old friendships with his folk-era cronies. Ian and Sylvia happened to be in town. Hearing the sound of new country noises coming from the club they stopped in. What they heard would have a profound impact on their musical direction. "We went to hear the Burrito Brothers in New York," notes Ian Tyson. "They were tremendously loud and you couldn't hear what they were doing over this huge gigantic wall of drawl and twang, but Gram was a real charismatic kid. I really liked what they were doing." Energized, the Tysons returned to Canada determined to create their own country rock group from musicians they knew around Toronto's Yorkville music community.

For the duo, the new direction was not out of character. "Country music wasn't new to me because I had listened to it for a long time," emphasizes Ian. "The folk music thing had lost its energy with the onslaught of the British Invasion. We were all plugged into Buck Owens—us, the Byrds, Gram Parsons and the Burrito Brothers—that Bakersfield thing. I had my ideas of how this new thing should go." Through to the early summer, the two tried a number of different line-ups to create the Great Speckled Bird, a country rock band featuring steel as well as lead guitar, driven by a heavier drum sound. "I think the transition from Ian and Sylvia to the Great Speckled Bird was logical," offers Sylvia. "The roots of the Great Speckled Bird were always visible in the earlier stuff. We knew about the Byrds and Burrito Brothers. We knew all of them. We had met Roger McGuinn when he was playing with the Chad Mitchell Trio. We got the name for the band from an old Roy Acuff song. I remember that there was a particularly potent amphetamine that was popular in Nashville at the time of the same name." The group's distinctive speckled-bird logo was designed by cartoonist Walt Kelly, by this time over his anger with Pogo/Poco.

The Bird's lineup was a mix of Canadians and an American: pedal-steel guitarist Bill Keith (a banjo legend formerly with Bill Monroe), drummer Rick Marcus, bass player Ken Kalmusky, and lead guitarist Amos Garrett. Keith and Marcus were soon replaced by Buddy Cage on steel and American Norman "N. D." Smart II on drums. "There was a lot of talent in that band," acknowledges Ian. "I'd known Amos for a long time. He had been in the Dirty Shames in Yorkville. I'd heard about Buddy Cage through the local musical grapevine. He used to play at the Matador and Horseshoe Tavern. Waylon [Jennings] used to play at the Matador when he'd come through. So I knew about Buddy and Amos and somehow I heard about N. D."

In a time of guitar imitators, Amos Garrett remains an innovator with a style so distinctive it can be recognized by other players from the opening notes. "My original roots were in rock & roll," reflects Garrett. "It wasn't until my late teens that I started to hear some acoustic music, especially acoustic blues, and got interested in that. I started studying and playing acoustic guitar and got a lot of work around the folk scene. I was watching what was going down on Yonge Street. There were a lot of great bands playing—I saw Robbie Robertson among others." Familiar with Garrett's reputation, Ian Tyson recruited him for his new group. "Ian told me about his idea to do a country band with a heavier-sounding rhythm section," he recalls. "People weren't even using the phrase 'country rock' at the time. He asked me to be the guitar player, and to help him find musicians to fill out the band."

Garrett's unique two- and three-stringbending technique, heard on Maria Muldaur's hit "Midnight At The Oasis" a few years later, was developed during his time with the Speckled Bird. "A lot of it came from playing with a steel guitar player. I envied the fact that a pedal-steel guitarist could glissando more than one note simultaneously, and I thought it would be great if I could do the same. Don Rich and Roy Nichols of Merle Haggard's Strangers were two of my favorite Telecaster players, along with James Burton." The interplay that developed between Garrett and Buddy Cage became one of several signatures of the Bird's sound.

Ohio-born Smart had served his apprenticeship with rock groups The Remains and Mountain before catching Ian Tyson's ear. "I was playing in Mountain at the time and living in New York," states Smart. "But I got tired of playing so loud; the volume was getting to me. Felix Pappalardi and I had an agreement that he would find another drummer, and he knew of a band up in Canada that Amos Garrett was playing with. Felix knew Ian and Sylvia and he gave them a call. Me and Buddy Cage joined the band at the same time." Smart's rock experience brought a stronger drum sound to the Bird. "That's what made it country rock," chuckles Smart. "That's probably one of the positive influences Mountain exerted." Smart found his new boss a taskmaster though. "Ian was pretty authoritarian. It wasn't easy working for him. He hated me. But I did my job. And that's all he cared about. That band was up for *anything*. We could have gone anywhere."

Combining Ian and Sylvia's folk-based harmony and songwriting plus the dazzling Buckaroo-style interplay between Garrett and Cage, the Bird set out to bring country rock to audiences on the East Coast. "We knew we were unique," states Garrett. "I don't think it had a name yet, we weren't even calling it country rock. With the Burrito Brothers and Byrds we were one of the earliest bands."

In March, following her success with the Stone Poneys' "Different Drum," Linda Ronstadt's debut solo album *Hand Sown . . . Home Grown* was issued by Capitol Records. Recorded the previous October, and produced by Chip Douglas (who had produced for the Monkees, Turtles, the Dillards, and the Lovin' Spoonful), the album presents a pleasant blend of folk, pop, and country in mainstream arrangements. *Hand Sown . . . Home Grown* is more a product of Douglas' direction than Ronstadt's personal tastes. Years later she publicly declared that her first two solo albums were worthless. She reveals her country roots on tracks like "Silver Threads And Golden Needles," backed by Red Rhodes' fuzz-tone pedal-steel guitar, and John D. Loudermilk's "Break My Mind." Clarence White contributes his characteristic stringbender guitar to several tracks. The album finds Ronstadt searching for a direction yet wearing her country influences on her sleeve. Her backing band, The Corvettes, was in a state of flux as well: Chris Darrow and Jeff Hanna left that spring, and Dillard & Clark alumnus Bernie Leadon joined John Ware and John London to round out their sound.

Signed to Epic, a Columbia Records subsidiary, Poco had entered Columbia's Hollywood studios in mid-January to lay down tracks for their highly anticipated debut. The deal followed a musician trade between labels: Graham Nash went over to Atlantic Records in exchange for Richie Furay. "The first album was mostly what we were doing live," offers Rusty Young. "It was such a new world for me. I'd never been in a professional studio before except for the Buffalo Springfield session for 'Kind Woman.' We recorded at CBS studios. It was interesting: we would be in one studio and in another room we would see Dean Martin, Johnny Mathis, or Dan Hicks and the Hot Licks recording. I was just awestruck."

During mixing sessions in March, Randy Meisner abruptly quit the group, necessitating a hasty change of both the album tracks and cover art. "When we recorded the first album," recalls Meisner, "I thought we were five people, a group. The day came when we were going to mix it so I called the studio and said, 'Hey, man, I want to come down and listen to the mixes.' I was always interested in recording and learning things from Jimmy. Richie said, 'No, Jimmy and I don't allow anybody in the studio when we're mixing.' I said to Richie, 'If this is a group, why shouldn't I be able to come down and listen to *our* mixes?' And Richie said, 'I just can't do that, Randy.' He wasn't mean about it or anything. So I said that if that's the case then I was just going to have to leave the group. Richie said something like he couldn't do anything about that. So that was it. It made me feel like it really wasn't a group. Nobody tried to talk me out of it, that was the funny part. All I needed was for someone to explain it all to me but at that point I just felt like I wasn't a member, just a sideman." Comments Messina, "As time went on we learned that Randy was very sensitive. Sometimes things were said that weren't intended to be hurtful, but were interpreted as such. He's just a very sensitive man."

Because Meisner's bass playing and high-harmony singing were key components of Poco's sound, Messina was forced to overdub several tracks, relying on George Grantham to cover Meisner's singing parts. "I never really understood what happened to this day," acknowledges Grantham, who found himself thrown into the fray. "I heard about five different stories. Part of it was a personality problem with management. Randy and Dickie Davis weren't getting along, and he wasn't allowed to come to some mixing sessions. Randy sang 'Calico Lady' in the live show, but when he left I sang that one and sang some of Randy's harmony parts, though some of them were left on. You can still hear Randy on some of the backgrounds on that first album. I sang some stuff with Richie on 'Pickin' Up the Pieces.' But I never really wanted to be a lead singer. Even though Richie kind of tried to push me to do more of it I tried *not* to. Richie is an *incredible* singer and Randy?—my gosh all these *great* singers around. The real concern was that we were right in the middle of mixing our first album and Randy was all over it. We had to take it from there as a four-piece for a while. We had auditioned Tim Schmit, but he had to stay in school or get drafted. It delayed the album a little bit."

"There wasn't really much money at the time, so it wasn't like I was throwing anything big away," offers Meisner on his impetuosity. On the other hand, Epic Records *did* have money invested, and panicked. "From management and the record company," Messina recalls, "there was this hue and cry: 'How can you guys make an album and break up *before* it's even out?' There was a great deal of fear that if the record came out with Randy on it and was a success it would be difficult for us to perform and have people say, 'Where's Randy?' We thought it best to correct that problem. The cover had Randy on it and suddenly a dog was put in his place."

The group carried on throughout the spring and summer as a four-piece, with Messina back on bass, Young playing all the solo guitar spots on his steel guitar, and Grantham filling in on harmony. "When Randy was in the band I sang low harmony," states Grantham, "and I had always been a high harmony singer. So I went back up to high harmony and Jimmy had to cover low harmonies. And Jimmy wasn't singing that much so we had to do a lot of shuffling around to cover the vocals. All the leads were on steel because Jimmy was on bass. There was a feeling that I needed to play a bit more on drums to fill gaps there. But it gelled after a couple of shows. But we wanted to be a five-piece band, Jimmy wanted to get back to guitar. His love was guitar, even though he was a great bass player." For Young, relying on the steel guitar alone for Poco's country rock was risky. "I thought we were crazy," he asserts. "I hated that. 'How can we *do* this, guys? We *gotta* have rock & roll instruments. I can only stretch the steel so far and then it's gonna get old.' But we did it for several months."

As a member of the Kingston Trio, John Stewart had considerable cachet when he launched his solo career in 1967. A songwriter of note, he had sold his well-crafted tunes to a variety of artists, including the We Five and the Monkees, for whom his "Daydream Believer" was a million seller. His 1968 debut release *Signals Through The Glass* was a worthy effort but failed to spark much interest. The following year Stewart teamed up with Capitol Records' staff producer Nick Venet. The two went to Nashville in February 1969 to record an album employing session stalwarts. The resulting disc, *California Bloodlines*, offers a remarkable blend of Stewart's original folk and Nashville's finesse. While Venet's deft hand is important to the project, it's Stewart's exquisite songwriting that stands out consistently from start to finish, with the "Music City Mafia" gracing each track with subtle country textures. Critics applauded Stewart's efforts. Despite his later success under the aegis of Fleetwood Mac's Lindsay Buckingham, *Bloodlines* remains his most celebrated work, featuring several of his most treasured songs.

Despite his extensive folk background, Stewart asserts that he grew up around country music. "I worked with my Dad at the race track, and country & western was very big there," he recalled in a later interview. "Folk music was very much like it." It was Venet who suggested Nashville as the place to record the album. "John had never worked in Nashville before," recalls the producer, "and to tell the truth he wasn't very enthusiastic. I just thought the combination of John's songs and the session players' skills could be a winner, and it was. Dylan was recording *Nashville Skyline* across the street at Columbia Studios, and I was calling in favors from guys I'd known for ten years, saying things like, '*Forget* Dylan, if you don't play on these dates for me, our friendship is over.' I wanted the best people for the album. Johnny Cash was there too, and Kris Kristofferson. There was so much electricity in that little one block area that week."

Much of the album was laid down live in the studio, by Stewart and the backing musicians, including Nashville luminaries like drummer Kenny Buttrey, bass player Norbert Putnam, pianist Hargus "Pig" Robbins, and steel player Lloyd Green. "There was magic in that studio," offers Stewart, "a magic that can't be duplicated. The only noncountry people to record there before I did were Bob Dylan and Joan Baez. That was the peak energy time in Nashville. Those cats were at their zenith, masters of their craft." Stewart forgot to include the Byrds, who had already broken that ground. Nevertheless, the sessions were extraordinary, including such songs as "Mother Country" and an elongated workout of "Never Going Back," which had been previously covered by the Lovin' Spoonful, featuring Stewart singing the praises of his sidemen, all suitably nicknamed, through the coda.

Venet recalls a ploy he used to bring out the best in the studio players for the stirring, historically motivated "Mother Country." "John had told me about this song he had, and the lyric just sounded like one that everyone in the studio could relate to. I told John to hold off on that song until the end, until all the other tracks were finished. And I'll never forget that moment. The musicians and I were all huddled in the control booth, drinking Jack Daniels and beer, when we heard John sing 'Mother Country' for the first time. Well, everybody was just *moved*. There were goose bumps, some red faces, and even tears. And when John had finished, they just went straight out into the studio and cut it, first take, perfectly. Absolutely no rehearsal, no arrangement, nothing." Stewart finishes the tale, "I finished the song and they came into the studio for the first take and some of them had tears in their eyes! Jesus, I thought, I must have really moved these guys! Afterward I was talking to Nick about how the song had moved them and he looked at me, lowered his voice, and said, 'Actually, John, I told them that you had written the song about your dad who's just died of cancer.'" Although untrue, the ruse worked, bringing out the best in the pickers.

Released at the same time as *Bloodlines* and using many of the same studio cats, Bob Dylan's *Nashville Skyline* album turned far more ears toward country music than Stewart's record, and was a major seller that year. Featuring Dylan's new adenoidal voice, and straightforward up-tempo numbers, *Skyline* was the logical extension of his back-to-the-roots foray that started with *John Wesley Harding*. Featuring Johnny Cash on a duet of "Girl From The North Country," Dylan seems at ease in the country setting. Cash and Dylan clicked in the studio, dueting on chestnuts from both their catalogs, including "One Too Many Mornings," "Big River," and "I Walk The Line." Dylan even taped a guest spot on Cash's popular weekly television show, backed by his cadre of Nashville session players. Dylan and his host performed their duet among an odd mix of Grand Ole Opry buzz cuts, bouffants, and longhaired musicians. Cash and Dylan enjoyed each other's company in the cross-cultural mutual admiration society.

*Nashville Skyline's* lyrics are uncharacteristically simple and upbeat. "The new songs are easy to sing and there aren't too many words to remember," remarked Dylan at the time of the album's release. Three singles ("I Threw It All Away," "Lay Lady Lay," and "Tonight I'll Be Staying Here With You") did well on the charts. Though hardly country rock, Dylan did offer a solid endorsement for country music, a genre he would soon abandon in subsequent releases.

Poco's Epic debut, *Pickin' Up The Pieces*, was released that spring. A wholly unique, fresh, and effervescent collection of original country rock songs, the record was written largely by Richie Furay, but driven by Young and Messina's guitar interplay and elevated by the group's astounding harmony singing. To Furay and Messina's credit, it remains a major statement of the genre. "A lot of the songs on that first album are my reflections on what had just happened and what was about to happen," offers Furay. "These songs are my recollections of the Springfield. It might even have been from an egotistical, pride thing, 'Hey, I can do this too, guys. I can write some songs.' Deep down in my heart, I felt I'd been left out of the creative mix with all the other stuff that was going on with the Springfield, and with Stephen and Neil's incredible contributions. These are the songs that released that frustration in me. The album is optimistic but there is some sadness in it. I felt shortchanged in the Springfield."

Opening with a poem from Kathy Johnson set to music by Furay, the band segues easily into "What A Day," the perfect song to set a positive tone for the album. Explains Furay, "'What A Day' had been saved from the Springfield but fit Poco more. After all that we had gone through in the Springfield, we looked at Poco to be the kind of band that had that positive outlook, and that's what that song is all about. It was a beginning, a new day, a happy time for us. Kathy Johnson was a fan who had heard us playing at the Troubadour and sent us this little poem. I thought the poem really summed up what we wanted to do, so I put it to music. She also made the wooden collage that is on the cover of *From The Inside* and gave it to us."

Working in a rock format, it is Messina's James Burton–influenced guitar picking and Young's versatile pedal-steel work throughout the album that bring the country textures to Poco's music. Buck Owens' influence can be heard on "Just In Case It Happens" and "Consequently So Long." Whether filtered through a Leslie speaker cabinet, plugged into a wah-wah pedal, or picking it to sound like both a banjo and piano, Young takes his instrument to new heights. "I did some stuff on steel on that album that I haven't done since," marvels Young. "I listened to that album recently and thought to myself, 'That sounds cool.' All of us were doing stuff no one had done before. I was so proud of that first album. I can't believe we did that work thirty years ago." Young shines on his instrumental "Grand Junction," switching from steel to Dobro with incredible agility. "Calico Lady" showcases drummer George Grantham's lone lead vocal, replacing Meisner's original lead. The lyrics came courtesy of Skip Goodwin, who also contributed to two other numbers. "'Calico Lady' was Skip's song," Furay acknowledges. "He wrote the lyrics to that, along with 'Consequently So Long' and 'Tomorrow.'" Goodwin was a friend from Furay's days at Pratt & Whitney back in 1965, who hooked up with him again near the end of the Springfield's run.

Though absent from the cover, Meisner didn't disappear from the record entirely. "Randy's on a couple of cuts on bass," confirms Young, "and a few oohs and aahs where they couldn't remove him without losing all the harmony blends that had been mixed down. He only plays on two songs, 'Calico Lady' and one other." Counters Meisner, "As far as I know I think I played bass on all of it and sang backup on a lot of it. But they pretty much replaced my lead voice on all the tracks."

Furay's poignant "First Love" is his statement on the implosion of the Buffalo Springfield. "I'm sure if you look into the songs I wrote on the first Poco album," he ponders, "I was still trying to figure out what had happened and express my feelings on those last two years in the Springfield. To be able to do what the Springfield had done and yet to have it so short lived. But it was time to move on and there was probably something in the lyrics I was writing struggling to express myself on how I really did feel about what had gone on." The title track "Pickin' Up The Pieces" further reflects his desire to carry the Springfield torch to his new group.

"I think Poco started country rock," suggests Meisner, "and the Eagles legitimized it." Chris Hillman disagrees. "Poco had some nice songs, maybe you could call it country rock, but that song they did with 'pickin' and a grinnin',' that kind of lyric makes me retch. That was so vanilla. That was like the *Beverly Hillbillies* to me. That wasn't like 'This whole town's filled with sin, it'll swallow you in if you've got some money to burn.' Which one's gonna mean something?"

Production problems with CBS President Clive Davis in the wake of Meisner's defection soured the group's relationship with the label, and may have blunted the company's promotional efforts. Marketing remained a dilemma. "There was a lot of political stuff going on with the record company," acknowledges Furay. "Radio never really picked up on us and the record company had some hard feelings. They didn't hear the commercial aspect of any of the music we were doing, and kind of backed away from us."

After a hiatus, the Fantastic Expedition of Dillard & Clark reemerged in the spring, adding Jon Corneal on drums and Donna Washburn on lead and harmony vocals. "Donna was a folk musician; she played guitar and sang folk songs when I met her," states Doug Dillard. "She became my girlfriend at that time. Her Dad was president of 7-Up." Though a capable singer, Washburn soon became the spanner in the works for Bernie Leadon. "The band basically broke up after that Troubadour disaster," Leadon recalls. "There was a hiatus but then they were going to do another record so they got everyone back together. Donna was dating Douglas by then and she wanted to be a part of it. So she came in and was singing my harmony parts. We tried it for one day and I just figured it wasn't working so I left. We had a three-part harmony vocal thing but when Donna came in she took over my part, leaving me with nothing to sing and nothing to play except just rhythm guitar. When Michael came into the band, Doug electrified his banjo, David Jackson switched from upright bass to Fender bass, I swapped my Martin acoustic for an electric, and we started doing more country & western stuff, which is when I started getting into lead guitar. But when we went back to ethnic bluegrass and acoustic music, I just couldn't get any satisfaction from what little I was doing so I left. I joined Linda Ronstadt, picking up where I'd left off playing electric lead and rhythm guitar."

The group recorded three sides that spring, one session including a revved-up cover of Elvis Presley's "Don't Be Cruel." Gene Clark delivers the vocal with surprising power, revealing a heretofore hidden side of his talent. Chris Hillman acknowledges that Elvis was an important early influence of Clark's. The track was paired with Clark's honky-tonk shuffle "Lyin' Down The Middle," but was a single that failed to chart. The sides reveal the group moving away from its acoustic format into more country rock territory. Another single, "Why Not Your Baby," (backed by "The Radio Song") was a more radio-friendly country offering bathed in a lush string arrangement and silky harmonies that should have been a hit but, alas, sank without a trace.

Undaunted, the band persevered with sessions convened in June for a follow-up Dillard & Clark album. Seeking to add instrumental muscle to replace Leadon's lead guitar, the group called on fiddler Byron Berline. "Quite a few years passed before I got involved with all those guys again," acknowledges Berline, who returned to Oklahoma after recording *Pickin' And Fiddlin'* with the Dillards. "I went back to finish college. In 1965 I was invited to play the Newport Folk Festival as a result of the album I did with the Dillards. That was the festival where Dylan got booed for playing electric." Berline subsequently joined bluegrass pioneer Bill Monroe in Nashville before serving a stint in the army. Upon his discharge in June 1969 Berline received an invitation from Douglas Dillard. "He said, 'I want you to come out to California and record an album with me and Gene.' And I said, 'Man, I'll be there.'"

With Leadon's folk and rock sensibilities gone and traditional and bluegrass fiddler Berline on board, the Expedition veered in a decidedly more bluegrass direction. Clark soon found himself out on the side. "Donna had come in and was singing Bernie's parts," states Berline, "but we'd lost our other guitar. I liked Donna but she couldn't play rhythm all that well. I became the lead instrument after Bernie left. And poor old Gene felt like he was being pushed out more and more. He'd bring a song or two to the band and it just kind of didn't fit what we were trying to do. I wanted to play bluegrass and Doug did too, and Gene realized that." Nevertheless, the sessions proceeded with Chris Hillman, Sneaky Pete, and even Bernie Leadon guesting on various tracks.

Two outtakes recently surfaced from that period on the Clark compilation *Flying High*: a cover of Reno and Smiley's "Wall Around Your Heart," and "Dark Hollow," previously a hit on the country charts for Jimmie Skinner. Evidently the group had no interest in mining Clark's store of originals, choosing instead to lean on cover versions of well-worn country and bluegrass material.

Once the sessions were done, the group hit the road on July 4 for their debut tour. Clark's aversion to flight kept the group grounded, going out in a convoy of cars that necessitated traveling light. All Corneal took with him was a snare drum and brushes. First stop was Chicago where, despite a change of locale, old habits soon threatened the tour. "It was a big eye opener for me," chuckles Berline. "The owner was giving us free drinks at the bar. Donna came up and said, 'You better go get Doug and Gene away from that bar, they're drinking too much.' And I said, 'Oh, they're not either. They're alright.' So she said, 'I know they are. You just wait and see.' Sure enough, we got up on stage and they all but fell off of it. I thought, 'Good God, what is *this*?' I was really disappointed and told them. I said if this was the way it was going to be, I was going back home. It was a little better the rest of the tour. But seems like every time we played the Troubadour they did the same thing. Their bar bill was more than they made in a week, that's a fact. It's funny now, but they didn't care then."

Jon Corneal recalls an insight into Gene Clark's rural upbringing. "On our way back from our tour through the Midwest, Gene called his folks when we were about fifty miles out of Bonner, Kansas, and by the time we got there they had a picnic for us, ham, potato salad, two washtubs full of beer. Just real down-to-earth people."

The country-flavored rock being played in and around L.A. that spring energized Rick Nelson. So much so that he decided to form a band. "I wanted to grow, to create and to perform on my own without big studio arrangements," recalled Nelson, "and for that I needed my own group again. We started to rehearse four or five days a week at a building my dad owns in Burbank. We improvised and experimented and listened to other people's work, people like Randy Newman and Tim Hardin. Then one day I heard *Nashville Skyline* and I knew where I wanted to go. I listened to that album for days, the songs were so simple, yet cryptic. I wanted to sing songs like that, and, if possible, also write like that." Nelson set out in search of players and found the key ingredient at the Troubadour. Hearing about Poco, Nelson, by then a club regular, ventured into the Troubadour to witness firsthand the country rock fever. The combination of pedal steel and high harmonies was an instant attraction, as was bass player Randy Meisner, who in the early days played a prominent up-front role in the group. By March 1969 Meisner was at loose ends, and Nelson gave him a call. As ex-Poco roadie Miles Thomas remembers it, Nelson happened to mention in passing that he'd love to work with Meisner. "I can get him for you," was Thomas' reply. "Having left Poco, I was ready to give up," acknowledges Meisner, "but then Rick called and asked me to join his band, so I went with him. I loved Rick Nelson. He'd seen Poco playing the Troubadour. He'd got real buzzed by hearing us play that kind of music." Within days, Nelson and Meisner were scouting for suitable musicians for their new venture, a Poco-style country rock band.

"After Randy left The Poor and went with Poco," states drummer Pat Shanahan, "we were doing whatever studio work we could get. We had a house in Van Nuys with a room we rehearsed in that we had soundproofed with egg cartons. Then one night someone said Rick Nelson was coming over to play. We rehearsed with Rick the first time in that little room. Ricky Nelson was somebody we watched every week on television growing up. We were pretty excited when we heard he was coming down."

Initially plans had drummer Toxey French and pedal-steel ace Buddy Emmons joining, but neither could commit full time to the group. Shanahan got the nod instead, joining ex-Poor guitarist Allen Kemp. The steel guitar position remained unsettled until fall. "We didn't have a name for the band," notes Shanahan, "and Rick had a horse farm out in Stone Canyon someplace in Malibu. So he just said, 'Why don't we call it the Stone Canyon Band?'" The new group rehearsed in earnest, preparing for a six-night stand at the Troubadour in April. Nelson's appreciation of Dylan inspired him to include several songs from his catalog in the group's repertoire. There were also a number of new compositions inspired by his reincarnation as a country rocker.

The Troubadour debut was a resounding success. "Everyone was hypnotized," Kemp told Nelson biographer Joel Selvin. "They couldn't believe Rick Nelson was playing right there." There was a definite buzz surrounding the event, which was Rick's coming-out party in the burgeoning country rock field. "We had a great time playing the Troubadour," enthuses drummer Pat Shanahan. "It was an event; all the players in town were there to see what Rick was up to. But we were just excited to be working. This was new for us, playing the Troubadour with *Rick Nelson*! Wow! For a time, if you weren't a British band you couldn't sell any records. That's why Rick kind of disappeared for awhile. But he came back and said, 'I've got some stuff, I can write some stuff.' It was pretty daring of him to come back out." For the debut, the lineup was Nelson, Shanahan, Meisner, Kemp, and Emmons on steel guitar. "Our first major appearance was at the Troubadour and the audience was very enthusiastic," recalled Nelson. "That was very encouraging. I'd never tried a steel guitar before that date, and I only had three or four days to rehearse using one, although I had a feeling it would be okay because many of my songs had been country influenced." The overwhelming success of the date prompted Troubadour owner Doug Weston to book Nelson for a four-night stand in early October.

With hip young producer John Boylan involved, Nelson set out to convince Decca Records to let him record his vision of country rock. The group (with Emmons) cut a gorgeous country folk cover of Dylan's "She Belongs To Me" prior to the gig, which managed to reach the lower register of the pop charts, a promising start considering Nelson's long dry spell. Decca agreed to record several nights of their October run for a live album, to be released in January. By then Boylan had been eased out in favor of Nelson's manager Joe Sutton.

Having failed to chart a follow-up hit after the successful single "Buy For Me The Rain," the Nitty Gritty Dirt Band accepted an offer to appear in the feature film *Paint Your Wagon*, starring Clint Eastwood and Lee Marvin, spending months in the Oregon forest while the film was made. The experience proved to be too much for the group, which broke up soon after their return from the wilds. John McEuen found an unlikely employer in Andy Williams, performing in his Caesar's Palace nightclub act while guitarists Jeff Hanna and Chris Darrow joined Linda Ronstadt's Corvettes. The split would prove to be short lived. As John McEuen recalls, "We had just spent four months on the set of *Paint Your Wagon*, and we got back at the end of October. We were so bored with each other and there was no new music. We had no record contract, and had a couple of people we wanted to get rid of. We broke up in 1968, and for six months there was no band. Jeff and I ended up at the Golden Bear one night watching Poco and we looked at each other and said, 'We can do that.' Because they were doing country rock and people were going nuts. So Poco was an influence on us. Before *Wagon*, the group had been like an eclectic jug band."

In June 1969, the Nitty Gritty Dirt Band re-formed without Ralph Barr and Chris Darrow, but with a renewed sense of purpose. "That's when we really started to sort ourselves out," maintains McEuen. "We'd used drums before, but this was the first time we began to use them properly and we spent several months rehearsing six days a week, at least seven hours a day. We determined to start again with a vengeance and do everything properly, including recording, the results of which we'd never really been pleased with in the past." Recruiting drummer Jimmy Ibbotson, late of Evergreen Blueshoes, the Dirt Band set about integrating country and bluegrass textures into their blend. "We started rehearsing and looking for material," recalls Hanna, "and realized that there was really no style we couldn't do—jug music, country, pure acoustic mountain music, Cajun, folk rock—just anything. On the *Uncle Charlie* album we tried everything from bluegrass to hard rock, and for once the FM stations appreciated it." Recorded later that year, the band's seminal *Uncle Charlie And His Dog Teddy* would define the Nitty Gritty Dirt Band's sound for more than a decade, a mix of various roots genres in an appealingly straightforward presentation, dominated by Hanna's voice and McEuen's multi-instrumental abilities. Adds McEuen, "With the Nitty Gritty Dirt Band I recorded acoustic guitar, banjo, mandolin, fiddle, lap steel, and dulcimer well before it became popular to do so, and I feel that I may have had a small part in spreading the word. I think we were among the pioneers of country rock." The album includes two perennial Dirt Band favorites, the hit single "Mr. Bojangles" and Mike Nesmith's "Some Of Shelly's Blues." The group followed a variety of paths, from traditional bluegrass (tracks like "Clinch Mountain Back Step" and Earl Scruggs' "Randy Lynn Rag") through folk pop (Kenny Loggins' "House at Pooh Corner") to rockabilly (Buddy Holly's "Rave On").

As McEuen describes it, "Jeff brought the folk music side, I brought the country bluegrass side, Jimmy Fadden brought the blues, and Jim Ibbotson had the craziness of rock & roll. I don't feel the Dirt Band really became a unit until 1969 with the addition of Ibbotson and the *Uncle Charlie* album. We were an experimental group of people trying to learn music. That album had the best conglomeration of all those mixes. We had learned how to record and how to pick material better. We'd chosen the music carefully from a whole load of stuff we liked, and had plenty of time to rehearse. 'Mr. Bojangles' gave us credibility, and raised our profile immensely—it showed we were in the game." The Jerry Jeff Walker number, done in waltz time, was a hit single for the group the following year.

As the sessions evolved, producer William McEuen came up with the notion of tying the album to a concept, and, once it was completed, set about realizing that idea. "Mr. Bojangles" evoked the image of an aging, itinerant tap dancer whose best years have come and gone. McEuen incorporated tapes he had made years before of a similar character. "It was his wife's great uncle Charlie," recalls Hanna. "Bill had been documenting the lives of these old musicians on tape, so he had this amazing recording of Charlie and his dog Teddy, who would howl along with Charlie's harmonica." An authentic touch was added with the addition, at the record's end, of an actual recording of Charlie playing "Spanish Fandango."

Still honing their songwriting skills, the Dirt Band relied on outside material. Mike Nesmith wrote two songs on the album. "Mike was working for $15 a night at the Troubadour, back in the early days before the Monkees," states McEuen. "That's where we heard 'Shelly's Blues.' Jeff and I went up to his house to get the demo to learn it. We kind of knew him but the Monkees thing was starting by then. Jeff had heard Linda Ronstadt doing 'Shelly's Blues,' and we asked Mike if we could hear it. So he gave us a tape of that song and another called 'Propinquity,' both of which we recorded on *Uncle Charlie*." The Troubadour provided a gold mine of material. "We were at the Troub one night and this guy came up offering us his songs. We'd had the idea of writing our own stuff but we would always listen to other people's material. This guy played us some of his songs and we ended up recording them. That was Kenny Loggins." Loggins would later find fame teamed with Poco's Jimmy Messina, and greater fame as a solo act.

The album had a far-reaching impact on both country rock and the direction of the Dirt Band. "After Earl Scruggs heard *Uncle Charlie* he sought us out backstage in Nashville one night," states Hanna to *Mojo's* Johnny Black. "That inspired doing an album that would bring together the traditional and contemporary sides of country music." That record, recorded the following year, would become an epochal moment in country rock. Adds Hanna, "It's not an exaggeration to say that *Uncle Charlie* set the tone for everything we've done since."

Several personnel shuffles in some of the leading country rock groups happened in the summer and fall of 1969. In August, Randy Meisner's place in Poco's lineup was filled by Timothy B. Schmit, formerly of The New Breed and Glad. The son of a violin and bass player, Schmit grew up around music, and began playing in bands at an early age. He had recorded an album with Glad in 1968, but had also answered the casting call for bass players for Furay and Messina that summer. As Meisner was going out, Schmit was coming in. Like his predecessor, Schmit's strength was less in his playing than in his voice, which blended naturally with Furay's. Schmit was not officially announced as a member until February 1970. Nonetheless, he entered the studio with the group that fall to record their second album. "I was never satisfied with Poco as a four-piece band," confirms Furay. "We were lacking in our vocal ability. We had given Tim a try earlier and I liked him. As it turned out I probably was closer to Tim than I was to anyone in the band. I don't think everyone appreciated his talents. But I felt he was a good choice." Adds Messina, "Richie really needed a singer who could stand up there and harmonize, hit the notes, and make his arrangements sound as beautiful as he heard them."

"Tim wrote, so we had another writer," states George Grantham. "Randy didn't write at the time. I think the biggest thing, though, was that I stayed on top in harmony, and he took over the lows that Jimmy had been doing. But he sang so close to Richie as far as blend. They sounded so great together. And his writing style was a lot closer to Poco writing. Richie liked his writing. Tim added a lot." That August, the group recorded one of Schmit's compositions, "Hard Luck," for the B side of their next single, Furay's "My Kind Of Love," a song dating back to the early Springfield. The single failed to dent the charts.

Schmit's youthful good looks drew a strong contingent of female fans to Poco's shows, a point not lost on Rusty Young. "In the old days there used to be two lines outside the dressing room when we finished a concert," laughs Young. "One long line of really pretty girls and another long line of hairy-legged old boys. And the girls would all be waiting to meet Tim and the guys would all be waiting to ask me how I tuned my steel guitar." Still, Young was less than enthusiastic with the choice of Schmit, and he disagrees with the version of events that had Randy walking out on his own. "They fired Randy without even talking to me, and Randy was my friend. They hired Tim without even asking me, and I was not thrilled about it. I just didn't think the whole thing was right. Jimmy and Richie were asserting their authority. They'd do that every once in awhile."

The Flying Burrito Brothers lost bass player Chris Ethridge that August. The group had spent much of the year revisiting the same musical terrain without making any significant headway into newer territory. The Burrito's reliance on country standards for much of their stage repertoire left Ethridge's more rhythm & blues style out in the cold. "I had never realized he wasn't a country-bass player," Gram Parsons told Chuck Casell in a 1972 interview. "What we needed was someone who could play country shuffle, du-du-du-du, and it wasn't happening and I never heard that. I don't know why. I just dug watching old Chris play the bass. But Chris understood that. So he split. I suppose from the time he split I got sort of disillusioned. He was the person who convinced me to come back from England when I split with the Byrds. And I liked writing with him an awful lot. And it just blew my mind that he wasn't the right bass player." The group's tendency toward overindulgence had taken its toll on the bass player. "I do remember playing in New York at this club called The Scene," recalls Chris Hillman. "Someone had baby powder on the amps—they used it to keep their hands from getting sweaty—it got knocked over and Ethridge thought it was cocaine and stopped playing. I would carry him out of gigs usually, he'd get so drunk, God bless him." With Hillman reverting to his more familiar role as bass player, the group carried on into early September as a quartet.

The gap in the lineup was filled by Bernie Leadon, who became a Burrito Brother in September following his stint with Linda Ronstadt's Corvettes that summer. "Michael Clarke had already left Dillard & Clark and joined the Burrito Brothers, who were also on A&M," explains Leadon about the incestuous nature of the country rock fraternity. "Jeff Hanna had the guitar slot in Linda's band following the Dirt Band's split. When they got back together Hanna went back, so I went to Linda's band. I spent that whole summer with her, playing country rock on electric guitar, recording with her and doing other sessions around town. At that time Chris Hillman became more aware of me. When Ethridge left the Burritos, Hillman went back to bass and they asked me to join on guitar."

Leadon sheds further light on the musical chairs of the country rock genre. "Linda was a solo artist, Gene and Douglas were essentially solo artists, and they all needed a band. But band members got nothing for playing, so you had to hustle for whatever gigs you could get. And it was the same pool of musicians. It's the same thing in Nashville today. Most of the country artists are solo artists and can't afford to keep a band together when they're off the road. Only the big ones pay a retainer to keep the players committed for the next tour. So when the tour or album is over the musicians aren't being paid, and they're looking for the next gig. And you always looked for better opportunities."

John York was dismissed from the Byrds in September after complaining to McGuinn about the direction of the group. "At the time," notes York, "it seemed to me that Roger was treading water, and that we could give audiences much more than the old hits. I got really unhappy with the way things worked, but I didn't have a way of working them out. I would go to Roger with everyone's grievances and it appeared like it was just me who was unhappy. The others were smart enough to not jeopardize their position. The other guys had a friend, Skip Battin, who wanted to be in the band. So they saw it as an opportunity to go to Roger and say, 'John's not happy in this situation and Skip would love to be in the group and will do whatever you want.' I remember saying to Gene and Clarence after a gig in Texas that I was going to give it another six months, save some money, because it wasn't working for me. I imagine I would have felt better about it the next day but in the meantime they went to Roger and said, 'John's going to quit. We've got this friend of ours who'd be perfect.' And that's how it went down." Battin, formerly of duo Skip and Flip and Evergreen Blueshoes, had known Parsons and White for several years and came aboard the Byrds' ship with definite ideas for the direction of the group. "Skip came in and was a force to be reckoned with," notes York. "The Byrds had always been like a pond that reflected whatever was in the sky above it, you get a real honest representation of what was going on with the members of the band."

Released in late October after York's departure, the Byrds' next album, *The Ballad Of Easy Rider*, showed the group to be much more comfortable in the country rock genre. A more consistent and satisfying effort from start to finish, the record is missing the heavy sounds attempted on *Dr. Byrds*, presenting a laid-back sound that would have a great impact on the Eagles. McGuinn judiciously allowed room for York, Parsons, and White to step forward with their own suggestions for inclusion, and the results proved successful. "I liked that album," maintains Gene Parsons. "It had a lot of good stuff on it, and I had more fun recording it because I had more input." Recorded in June and July, the new lineup had gelled after several months on the road, earning back the Byrds' following with superb live performances. Notes York: "On *Easy Rider* the band was more on its feet. I always thought there was a greater sense of honesty on that record. We played that stuff because it had meaning for us. The presence of Terry Melcher had something to do with that. He wasn't really heavy-handed like other producers, and I think it helped having a producer who had been on other Byrds' records and knew the sound. We had been touring heavily, and as a result were much tighter by then." The son of Doris Day, Melcher had produced the Byrds' first two albums back in 1965. He was a reassuring presence in the studio for both McGuinn and the newcomers, and the selection of material reveals his steadier hand. For many Byrds *aficionados*, the *Easy Rider* album is the group's most gratifying effort of the post-*Sweetheart* period.

One of the standout tracks on the album is Pam Polland's "Tulsa County Blue," a song suggested by York, who first heard it on Polland's album with the Gentle Soul, produced by Melcher. Previously a country hit for June Carter, White's superb stringbender picking leads the way. The Byrds' "Blue" provides a blueprint for the later Eagles' songs, like "Peaceful Easy Feeling" and "Lyin' Eyes." "I think some of that stuff on that album *was* influential to the Eagles," asserts Gene Parsons. "A lot of artists have talked to me about some of those tunes as their favorites. I think the role of the Byrds in the growth of country rock was pivotal." Clarence White makes his Byrds vocal debut singing the traditional gospel tune "Oil In My Lamp," while Parsons handles Vern Gosdin's ballad "There Must Be Someone" and his own excellent "Gunga Din," which the multitalented musician acknowledges as one of his finest compositions. York contributes "Fido," a rocker that, despite its lack of country textures, fits comfortably into the laid-back attitude of the album. McGuinn resurrects Dylan's "It's All Over Now, Baby Blue" in a subdued arrangement complemented by White's guitar. He also pays further homage to his mentor in the title track, the opening lines of which were donated by Dylan to the film *Easy Rider*. McGuinn's sympathetic rendering of Woody Guthrie's "Deportee" is another understated delight. Earlier, Parsons had brought "Jesus Is Just Alright" to the group from an Art Reynolds gospel album, and it quickly become a concert favorite. Melcher transforms the song for the album, turning it into a tour de force. McGuinn's fascination for space and sea shanties was evinced by the cuts "Armstrong, Aldrin And Collins" and "Jack Tarr The Sailor."

Clearly, with *The Ballad Of Easy Rider* the Byrds' country rock had matured. Now it was time to move on. McGuinn would spend much of the following year composing for the ill-fated musical *Gene Tryp*. The Byrds would follow *Easy Rider* with the uneven *Untitled*, a double disk featuring one record containing the new lineup with Battin on bass, recorded live, and with a studio album of songs intended for the musical. The live disk boasts some fierce playing by White, on "Lover Of The Bayou" and Dylan's biting "Positively 4th Street," plus a side-long "Eight Miles High" that is as tedious as it is long. The studio disk offers some nice country-flavored moments: the storytelling "Chestnut Mare" and Lowell George's "Truck Stop Girl," but it is uneven. The album was popular, and helped reestablish the Byrds name. It also marks a turning point for the group, as it began to distance itself from country rock on the subsequent albums *Byrdmaniax* and *Farther Along*.

Where some country rock pioneers made the transition toward a more rock-oriented style with greater success and satisfaction, the last Byrds lineup wouldn't fare as well.

A&M released the second Dillard & Clark album, *Through The Morning, Through The Night* in September, to a muted response. Unlike the group's first effort, *Through The Morning* was far less adventurous, more in a bluegrass mold, with several standards by the likes of bluegrass pioneers Reno and Smiley, Bill Monroe, the Everly Brothers, and others. Though Gene Clark contributes four songs, they are overshadowed by the banjo and fiddle playing that dominate the record. Where Clark had set the tone for the debut album, now it was Dillard who seemed to be calling the shots. With Clark's ally Leadon out of the picture and fiddler Byron Berline in the lineup, Clark had less clout. "I was on every track," commented Clark a few years later on the second album. "Nothing was really happening between Doug and me as friends; it's just that he had things he wanted to do and I had things I wanted to do, so we tried to find the best medium to do them in. But we didn't have enough time to rehearse. We did that second album very quickly. It was a fun album to record. It was schizophrenic, but it was something we wanted to do but didn't have the time like we'd had on the first album."

Clark turns in an impressive performance with "Kansas City Southern," a staple of his solo shows well into the next decade. His penchant for melancholy folk & country emerges in the title track as well. The harmonizing between Clark and Washburn is a surprising plus on several tracks, and presaged Gram Parsons' work with Emmylou Harris. Perhaps the least appealing cuts are Washburn's awkward take on the bluegrass "Rocky Top," where the singer tries just a bit too hard to recreate an authentic Appalachian style. Of Clark's vaudevillian "Corner Street Bar": the less said, the better. One cover that stands out as both an intriguing choice and well suited to Clark's somber mood is the Beatles' "Don't Let Me Down." In Clark's capable voice the minor key ballad becomes a mournful country wail of angst and heartache only he could deliver. "That was kind of a studio whim," recalls Berline on the genesis of the unusual choice. "Gene had it in the back of his mind to do that one. Sneaky Pete was there, and Doug and I put double fiddles on it, and David Jackson played the cello. Chris Hillman can be heard on mandolin." On the track, Sneaky Pete surrounds Clark with superbly smooth pedal-steel accompaniment, while Washburn's harmony supports his lead vocal admirably.

*Through The Morning* boasts several strong performances from Clark, yet reveals the group in search of a direction but stumbling. The band's chemistry is lacking. It is more Dillard and less Clark, with Gene ceding the captain's seat to his old pickin' buddy. Gone is the unique acoustic interplay that made the debut so much fun. In its place is a more formulaic country bluegrass approach. "I like the first album the best," concedes Dillard. "We threw that second one together quickly, and it was a little heavier on the steel guitar and drums. It was intermingled with a lot of different ideas."

In October Rick Nelson and the Stone Canyon Band returned to the Troubadour to record a live album before an enthusiastic sellout crowd (the then unknown comic Steve Martin opened). Sneaky Pete was originally scheduled to play pedal steel but bowed out at the last minute due to Burrito commitments. Nelson then turned to country music veteran and ex-Buckaroo Tom Brumley. After six years of success backing Buck Owens, Brumley tired of the road grind and left the Buckaroos in March 1969 to pursue a less-traveled vocation: building steel guitars for Zane Beck's ZB pedal steel guitar company. His replacement in the Buckaroos was none other than Jay Dee Maness. But Nelson managed to coax Brumley out of retirement. "I had known James Burton since 1961 or '62," recalls Brumley, "I told him to urge Rick to get a steel player because I always thought Rick had a country flavor to his music. Rick had always liked country, you could tell that from his early records. He had 'She Belongs To Me' out, and Buddy Emmons had played on that. I was just knocked out by that song. I sat in at the Troubadour gig and it was just such a kick to play that stuff. It was so different from what Buck had done. We did four nights at the Troubadour, two shows a night."

In the audience for Nelson's Troubadour performances were two young men whose impressive debut album had been released that fall to little fanfare. As Longbranch Pennywhistle, Glenn Frey and John David Souther had become regulars at the club, opening for acts that included the Flying Burrito Brothers and Poco. After their set the duo would take a front-row table and watch the headliners, taking notes for the future. "We were the rebel band," asserts Chris Hillman of the Burritos' impact on impressionable young musicians. "We were *the* original outlaw band. The Eagles really developed out of that. I'll never forget Glenn Frey and J. D. Souther opening for us as Longbranch Pennywhistle. Glenn Frey was just in awe of Gram. He learned from Gram. He learned about stage presence and how to deliver a vocal, and don't think Glenn Frey wasn't *studying* Gram. He was."

Both Frey and Souther migrated to L.A.: Frey from Detroit and Souther from Texas. Frey had played with Bob Seger back in the Motor City. He met Souther in early 1969. "The first day I got to L.A.," remarked Frey in a *Rolling Stone* interview, "I saw David Crosby sitting on the steps of the Country Store in Laurel Canyon, wearing the same hat and green leather bat-cape he had on for *Turn, Turn, Turn.* To me that was an omen. I met J. D. Souther, who was going with my girlfriend's sister, and we really hit it off. It was definitely me and him against whatever else was going on." Forming the duo Longbranch Pennywhistle, latter-day Everly Brothers, Frey and Souther appeared frequently at the Troubadour's open-mike Hoot Nights. Their vocal blend was easy on the ears, and both were already beginning to write. Souther was the more prolific of the two. The duo also had looks on their side. "Longbranch Pennywhistle were the cute boys," notes Ronstadt drummer John Ware.

Musing on Pennywhistle's influences, Souther told Eagles' biographer Marc Eliot, "I always thought that what I was trying to do at that time was modern country music. I'd been listening to the Flying Burrito Brothers, the Byrds, Poco, Dillard & Clark. Those guys had listened to Buck Owens and Merle Haggard, and those guys had listened to Hank Williams and George Jones, and *those* guys had listened to the Louvin Brothers, the Carter Family, and Jim and Jessie. It all went back to Celtic folk music. The line has always looked unbroken to me."

The duo's appealing sound soon drew label interest, with Pennywhistle signing with producer Jimmy Bowen's Amos Records, whose major asset at the time was Kenny Rogers and the First Edition. Bowen was a veteran of the L.A. music scene, having worked on sessions for Frank Sinatra and Dean Martin. He would go on to become a major kingmaker in Nashville's "new country" movement in the nineties, with discoveries like Garth Brooks, Reba McIntyre, and Patty Loveless. Always interested in country music, and with a keen ear for new trends, Bowen was acutely aware of the growing country rock movement in southern California when he found Frey and Souther and took them under his wing.

Bowen recruited the cream of L.A. sessions players, including James Burton, Buddy Emmons, Larry Knechtel, Joe Osborn, and Jim Gordon. To that list he added Doug Kershaw and the renowned Ry Cooder for Pennywhistle's eponymous debut. Featuring original material mostly from Souther, as well as a cover of James Taylor's "Don't Talk Now," the album is quite good, a light-rock with country touches best illustrated on tracks like "Rebecca" and the lovely "Kite Woman." Their style predates the southern California soft rock sound of the seventies, as championed by David Geffen's entire Asylum Records stable and spearheaded by Frey's Eagles. Had the duo been signed to one of the major labels and received adequate promotion, they might have had a shot at real stardom. But Amos Records was a small independent in an era where that status had little clout in the marketplace. Longbranch Pennywhistle withered from a lack of resources. After a stint sharing housing with budding songwriter Jackson Browne, Frey and Souther parted company by mid-1970. Frey drowned his sorrows at the Troubadour bar, biding his time and planning his next move. He had no trouble finding sympathetic listeners. "That's what the Troubadour was all about," offers John Ware. "Who was hanging out at the Troubadour, who was drinking with whom and when."

A&M Records released a single from the second Dillard & Clark album in November, pairing "Rocky Top" and "No Longer A Sweetheart Of Mine" to scant attention. With the group headed on a bluegrass course, Clark saw the writing on the wall and bowed out that month. The others soldiered on as Doug Dillard and the Expedition. "When they brought Byron in, it shifted more to bluegrass," offers Jon Corneal on Clark's departure. "Byron played fast fiddle, and in the right environment, Doug can play real fast banjo too. That's what happened, it ended up being a fast bluegrass group. Gene was not happy with that. They went from doing Gene's songs to doing Bill Monroe's. It was a shame. I didn't stay long after that. I went back east."

Berline cites several of Clark's personal demons as the reason for his exit. "We had this opportunity to play *Hee Haw*. *Hee Haw* had just started and they wanted us. We said okay, then Gene quit right before we were flying out. We all flew to Nashville, and he didn't want to do that. His fear of flying was a big hassle." Berline does acknowledge that the dynamic of the group had shifted significantly. "Gene got upset because he saw us going in another direction, and didn't think his songs fit. He was an *unbelievable* writer. But he had his ups and downs. Gene always seemed unhappy, like there was always a cloud over his head. He'd be happy one day, and you'd see him the next day and he would be a bucket of gloom. I was always getting on him about drinking too much." Clark retreated into semiretirement up in Mendicino, California.

Prior to Clark's departure, fiddle player Byron Berline was summoned for a guest appearance with rock & roll royalty. The Rolling Stones were in L.A. that October between stops on their first North American tour in more than three years, and were laying down tracks for *Let It Bleed*. At their heels was Gram Parsons, who had all but abandoned the Burrito Brothers to follow Keith Richards. Parsons had turned the Stones on to the pure country of George Jones, and now they wanted to tap his well for a number entitled "Country Honk," a laid-back version of "Honky Tonk Women." Parsons recommended Berline for an authentic fiddle sound. "I did the Rolling Stones' session and that really established my reputation," boasts Berline. "Gram was hanging out with Keith Richards, trying to get them to do more country stuff. Gram played acoustic guitar on it." Parsons would claim credit for the arrangement on 'Country Honk,' although the album credits don't acknowledge his contribution.

In November, the Great Speckled Bird arrived in Nashville to record their debut album for manager Albert Grossman's Bearsville Record Productions, with rock & roll studio wizard Todd Rundgren producing. "We made the album at Belmont Studios," recalls Ian Tyson. "Charlie Tallent was the engineer, and he was co-producer with Todd Rundgren. We had a big budget, which Albert financed from a Dylan deal. He was trying to take care of us, and Dylan was so big that Albert could say, 'If Dylan does this, I want an eighty thousand dollar budget for Ian and Sylvia.' And that's how we got it. But we were completely irresponsible. There was a lot of baseball playing with tennis balls in the studio, a lot of ladies in and out—and stuff like that, and it went on for two weeks. If you did that today the budget would be just astronomical. I wouldn't put up with that kind of shit now but we were young and stupid." Recalls Sylvia Tyson, "It was very strange sometimes. I don't think Nashville had ever seen anything like Todd Rundgren before, plus he had a couple of the GTOs with him, Miss something-or-other. They were sort of twin-like, with long hair. I think the Nashville police took one look at them and decided they were trouble."

With a charging country rock sound propelled by the twin leads of Amos Garrett and steel player Buddy Cage and driven by N. D. Smart's sledgehammer drumming, Ian and Sylvia's songs found a new attitude and the album took shape quickly. The band experience over the last few months had recharged their writing, and the group had a wealth of material. Bass player Ken Kalmusky had been dropped from the lineup prior to the recordings, and Nashville session star Norbert

Putnam played in his stead, with David Briggs contributing piano on the album. Smart, too, almost missed the sessions. "They weren't going to let me play drums on it," chuckled Smart. "Kenny Buttrey was going to play. Ian was of the opinion that they should go with experienced Nashville people. They had Kenny come in and play on one session, but it just didn't work out." Rather than let the Nashville cats shape their sound as Dylan and John Stewart had done, the Great Speckled Bird had already crafted their own approach before arriving in town, and merely let the tape machine capture it. "Ian and Sylvia's album was the first record of its kind cut in Nashville," maintains Smart. "They couldn't get used to the longhairs. They all figured that you had to have the hit done before lunch or there was something wrong with you. But we weren't in there for two or three hours watching the clock. We were in the studio for eighteen hours at a stretch. And David Briggs and Norbert Putnam were loving this, because they were getting *triple* scale."

Gram Parsons' interest in the group he had co-founded a year earlier was waning, and his involvement with the Stones only made matters worse. Recounts Chris Hillman: "Gram was hanging out with the Stones and almost being a pest. We had a gig one evening and I had to go find him. I finally found him at the Stones' session! I go in there to get him and he's going, 'Ah, I don't wanna go.' And Jagger got right in his face and told him, 'You've got a responsibility to Chris Hillman, the other band members, and the people who come to your show. You better go do your show *now*.' He was very matter of fact, I'll never forget that. So Gram got up and went to the show." Parsons managed to prevail on his heroes to grant the Burritos an opening slot on their upcoming free concert, the infamous Altamont Speedway show. Fortunately for the Burritos, their appearance was early and brief, ending before all hell broke loose. In the subsequent feature film of that dark event, *Gimme Shelter*, the Burritos have no more than a thirty-second appearance, doing "Six Days On The Road."

With Bernie Leadon in the group and Hillman back on bass, the Flying Burrito Brothers recorded a number of demos before Christmas, with an eye to releasing an album of country & western standards. For Parsons the idea worked for a couple of reasons. He had run dry of original ideas, and the collaboration between he and Hillman had foundered. Also, Parsons reveled in singing the material, fancying himself a longhaired George Jones on a mission to bring country purity to rock & roll. "We used to work the Palomino in 1969," recalls Hillman, speaking of his partner's obsession for bridging the gap between long-hairs and rednecks. "And, *man*, we used to hear it from the audience. 'Get off the stage, goddamn queers,' and every nasty name in the book. But we were playing Conway Twitty songs, Porter Wagoner songs, and we won people over." Tracks laid down in various stages of completion included songs by Buck Owens, Merle Haggard, Ray Price, Bob Dylan, the Rolling Stones, and even a Bee Gees number. The group offers laconic renditions of the country numbers, sounding as though they are merely going through the motions, and are completely out of their depth on the rock numbers, with Parsons croaking his way through the material.

Though the country standards album a la Flying Burrito Brothers never materialized, the bulk of the tracks surfaced years later on various Parsons' and Burritos' compilations. "We looked at recording those," admits Hillman. "Those were all practice rehearsal tapes from that period between the two albums. Those were songs we did on stage. We never knew that stuff would show up on a record years later. Those were just goofing around." Clearly, though, Parsons was running out of steam and wearing out his welcome.

# 7

# White Line Fever: 1970

*It was all new and I didn't have a clue. Amos Garrett didn't know how to put his instrument out there in front of electric instruments. Buddy Cage definitely didn't, N. D. Smart was a psychotic redneck drummer, and Jim Colegrove was stoned all the time. And that's who we were. It was just completely incompatible. But our karma was such that on the occasional night in the recording studio we made some music that's a little bit timeless and of that era.*

—Ian Tyson, on his move to an electric format with the Great Speckled Bird

Following up their groundbreaking *Wheatstraw Suite* album was no mean feat for the Dillards, but in January 1970 they released *Copperfields*. "*Copperfields* was the same kind of direction as *Wheatstraw*," notes Herb Pedersen, "but we used different players and had some different ideas. I think *Wheatstraw* had a little more of an edge to it. But I liked them both." Relying even less on their bluegrass roots this time out, *Copperfields* was more of a country rock effort, once again utilizing orchestration to great effect. Drummer Paul York had been added to the group between sessions, and his presence gave the music more country swing. Rodney Dillard deferred to John Boylan to handle production, though the singer continued to play a major role in shaping the sound. "That's when I learned that a producer could put his name on an album, stay on the phone making other business while you're recording, and never really have a hand in what's going on," smirks Dillard. "John Boylan 'produced' it. He was Linda Ronstadt's manager. Herb and I would be doing something, look up to see if John got the take—and he'd be on the phone. So we just did it ourselves."

*Copperfields* opens with Harry Nilsson and Bill Martin's whimsical "Rainmaker," and the track set the tone of the album. "In Our Time" features the group's unique harmonies, as does a remake of "Old Man At The Mill," from their debut album, which is a traditional bluegrass arrangement. The most overtly country track, "Woman Turn Around," is followed by a Beatles cover, a wonderful a cappella version of "Yesterday." "That was a spur-of-the-moment thing," acknowledges Dillard. "We were just warming up. We did it like 'I'll Fly Away.' That was our signature. All of a sudden we found ourselves having to put an a cappella song on each album. We were just goofing around, and it sounded *so* pretty, we just recorded it. To this day I just grin whenever I hear it." Side one closes with one of the most daring numbers in the Dillards' catalog, a Dave Brubeck–inspired jazz number, "Brother John," incorporating bluegrass instruments. The song works marvelously, with Dillard and Dean Webb (mandolin) taking solos. "'Brother John' was Herbie's thing," cites Dillard. "We just started playing it. For the first time I just picked up an electric guitar and put a guitar break in it. Dean put in a jazz mandolin solo. We were just having fun with it." A remake of their earlier single "Ebo Walker" enlivens the second side, which is dominated by mellower sounds, ending with the beautiful instrumental "Sundown" from Pedersen.

Though less adventurous than *Wheatstraw Suite*, *Copperfields* is nonetheless a very satisfying, consistently well-crafted album that would influence other country rock groups. "We knew about those other bands," acknowledges Webb. "We knew some of the guys in the Burritos. We'd known a lot of those musicians for years. I remember meeting Don Henley one time, we were playing some private club in Dallas. He came out to our little bus we had and talked with us for a long time. He was talking about going out to L.A. He knew all about our music and was a fan. I think we influenced a lot of people to some degree." Pedersen also recalls meeting Henley and his group Felicity. "I can remember playing in Fort Worth on Christmas Eve at this steak house. That's where Don Henley and the guys from Linden, Texas, drove all night to see us play. They were still in high school at the time. That's how I first met Don. He had a great love for that type of music and it was a big influence on him. And that's very flattering."

That same month saw the release of the Great Speckled Bird's debut album, with striking cover art that depicts a headless bird. Perhaps even more striking was the absence of Ian and Sylvia's name on the cover. "It was quite a gamble to *not* put Ian and Sylvia up front in the name of the group and just call it the Great Speckled Bird," admits Sylvia Tyson. "I can remember one of our very first concerts with the band, at Western University in Ontario. There were people in the audience who got up and walked out before the concert even started when they saw the steel guitar being set up on stage. We knew we had alienated the traditional Ian & Sylvia audience." Confirms Ian Tyson ruefully, "We thought it was the right idea, and it was, but we lost control of that once the word got out and all the morose Ian & Sylvia fans, with their long ironed hair, sat in front of us, denigrating what we were trying to do."

The tone of the album is established as soon as needle meets wax. On the opening track, "Love What You're Doing, Child," drummer N. D. Smart II pounds out a thunderous pattern, and is joined by the bass and Amos Garrett's screaming guitar before Ian and Sylvia's rich harmony kicks in. The Great Speckled Bird is in full flight right out of the nest. Forget "Four Strong Winds" and "Someday Soon"—this is country rock, with an emphasis on *rock*: thumping drums, pounding bass, and heavy guitar. Where *Nashville* and *Full Circle* had maintained an understated country backing, *Great Speckled Bird* left little doubt that a rock edge had insinuated itself into their sound. Ian wails like never before, and the interplay between Garrett's Stratocaster and Buddy Cage's pedal steel—a trademark of the Great Speckled Bird sound—is simply mesmerizing. In contrast to their contemporaries on the country rock frontier, the Great Speckled Bird place far greater emphasis on a rock-solid rhythm, largely due to Smart's expert stick work and rock experience. It's no wonder the Nashville establishment looked on the group with alarm during sessions for the album.

One of the standout tracks on a record filled with highlights is Ian's "Long Long Time To Get Old," propelled by Smart's thundering tom-toms and cowbell. "'Long Long Time' is one of the best songs I ever wrote and the band played it great," says Ian. "That became N. D. Smart's signature, the cowbell and the groove. It all came together on that song." Boasts Smart, "Ian wrote 'Long' around that beat. I was playing that beat in his basement, he liked it, and he wrote that song around it." The number would go on to become the theme song for Ian's television series *Nashville North*.

Possessing two gifted and experienced songwriters set the Speckled Bird apart. "What made us different from the other country rock groups, like the Burritos," asserts bass player Jim Colegrove, who joined the group following recording sessions, "was that Ian and Sylvia were singing the songs. To me it was a tremendous difference in style. Most of the material was theirs, too. They came at a lot of it from a different angle." Ian's cowboy roots emerge in tracks like "Calgary," "This Dream," and "Rio Grande." Sylvia holds her own in a country style on the wonderfully swinging, Buckaroo-flavored "Trucker's Café," "Smiling Wine," and "Disappearing Woman." "I never wrote for a particular situation or arrangement of musicians," she maintains, though she adapted to the country form easily. "I didn't specifically write for country music." Comments Colegrove, "Sylvia certainly had her say on how her songs were going to go, but I just always felt like the band represented Ian's vision. He thought he was forming a band akin to the Buckaroos, and it worked, arrangement-wise, like the Buckaroos." A novel choice is the country & western standard "Crazy Arms," which Sylvia sings in French, basing her delivery of the tune on an arrangement by the popular 1950s French-Canadienne chanteuse, Lucille Starr.

"With *Nashville, Full Circle,* and *Great Speckled Bird,* we found our direction," asserts Ian. To the band's misfortune, Bearsville Records' distributor Ampex put little energy into promoting or distributing the album, which came and went without much noise, a travesty for such a strong, innovative effort. "I think that album had an impact among musicians," claims Ian, who remains very proud of the *Great Speckled Bird* disk. "It was like a little rocket that went off, left some carbon sparks, and then died. I had to check out the remastering for the CD rerelease recently, and I was blown away. Stuff like 'Flies In The Bottle' stand up well. There's some good stuff there." If the record-buying public failed to notice, players did not. "*Great Speckled Bird* was considered a landmark," says Sylvia. "I've talked to people over the years in Nashville who recall that album as a signpost that things were changing, both in country and in folk. It had an influence."

Upon the record's release, the band undertook a hectic schedule of engagements throughout the spring, playing mainly for curious audiences on the East Coast college circuit, where the genre was still something of a mystery. "We played in the American Midwest, and the East Coast, from New England down to as far south as Washington, D.C." recalls Garrett. "That seemed to be Ian & Sylvia's turf in those days. We pounded the Northeast real hard." The group still found some audiences reluctant to accept their new direction. "We didn't go over real well with Ian & Sylvia's die-hard audience," states

Garrett. "When we played for audiences who didn't really know them, the band went over big time. It was just part of the period. Ever since Dylan took an electric guitar onstage at Newport, there were folk music fans who were *very* resentful about any kind of change. And Ian and Sylvia were victimized to a certain degree by their acoustic music audience." Confirms Ian, "It was the end of Ian & Sylvia; it put the nail in the coffin, and probably all for the good. They were insulted, outraged—whatever. I remember some pop festival we played in Florida and we just absolutely *died*. It was horrible. I remember some strange women coming up to us afterward telling us they liked it but that was two out of *twenty thousand*. Shortly thereafter our manager, Albert Grossman, handed us over to his partner John Court and washed his hands of us."

For Tyson, running a band was a whole new ballgame and he remains a bit cynical of that period in his career. "I was a very poor band leader," he admits. "I'd never done that, and never learned to do it. I could lead that band *now*. But it was one of those democratic sixties bands and that never works. It was a high-energy group, but we really didn't know what we were doing. Don't let Amos tell you any different. He didn't know any more than the rest of us. We weren't like those West Texas boys or Tennessee boys who'd been using amplifiers for the previous ten years."

*Rick Nelson In Concert*, recorded live at the Troubadour the previous October, was released in late January to generally favorable reviews. Critics praised Nelson's new sound and credited it for rejuvenating his flagging career. Those writers seemed to get great pleasure from the return of a former star who reinvented himself in a genre suited to his talents. *Rolling Stone* reviewer Lester Bangs gushed, "A brilliant collection of gutsy originals and exquisitely rendered favorites," and noted Nelson's early influence on latter-day country rockers the Buffalo Springfield and Byrds. It was an influence, Bangs went on, that cut both ways. "And the big, rich country sound of the guitars here show how thoroughly Rick has digested the lessons in rock ensemble sound of the Byrds and the Springfield." Nelson's efforts were backed by a tight, country rock unit updating his old hits ("Hello, Mary Lou" and "I'm Walkin'") with a country swing, while introducing several strong originals like the elegant "Easy To Be Free." The album is rounded off by credible covers of Dylan ("She Belongs To Me," "If You Gotta Go," and "I Shall Be Released"), Eric Andersen ("Violets Of Dawn"), Doug Kershaw ("Louisiana Man"), and Tim Hardin ("Red Balloon"). Listening to the record, it is clear Nelson approached country rock from the rock side, adding country textures with steel guitar and high harmonies much like Poco. Compared to his earlier country music recordings, *Rick Nelson in Concert* has a more solid rock base.

"Rick wanted out of that teen idol image so bad," remarks steel guitarist Tom Brumley. "He wanted to move on to other things. That's why he formed the Stone Canyon Band." Nelson gets solid backup from his band. Meisner's trademark high harmony blends well with Kemp and Nelson, while Brumley's steel playing is superb, proving his ability to integrate his style into a rock format. Brumley is the instrumental star of the group. "What got me back on steel guitar was hearing Tom Brumley playing with Rick," acknowledges Al Perkins. "He was the major steel guitarist that I liked. I didn't know at the time that he had come from Buck's band. That live album from the Troubadour turned everybody's head."

Nelson took to the road in support of the record, which enjoyed decent sales. "I didn't want to go out on the road when Rick called me," recalls Brumley. "I had a guitar company and couldn't do that. We worked out a situation where we worked seventy or eighty days a year, and I became a regular. With Buck it was working 250 to 300 days a year. I was just worn out. I didn't think I'd ever be on the road again until Rick called me." Brumley urged Nelson to take the act to the Palomino Club. "I didn't know there *was* a Troubadour until I got involved with Rick," he laughs. "It wasn't in the field of music I was involved in. But I knew where the Palomino was. Rick wouldn't play the Palomino for a long time, but when he did he made a lot more money there than he ever made at the Troub. The Troub acted as though it was a privilege just to play there, but you couldn't eat that, or pay your bills. At the Palomino Rick got the door, two shows a night sold out. He went over well at the Troubadour too, but it didn't hold more than a couple hundred people. Everybody at the Palomino knew him and had heard his records. They came to enjoy Rick, where the Troubadour crowd came to critique you."

That March, Nelson and the band undertook a grueling tour of American military bases in Europe, where his new sound and longer hair drew a hostile response from audiences expecting the teen idol. Returning to L.A., Meisner abruptly gave his notice. "When we got back," recounts Meisner, "I quit because I didn't feel I was getting a chance to express myself. It wasn't anyone's fault. Rick always consulted us and we all made suggestions, but even so I wasn't happy with the music. I wasn't making any money, and I had been away from my family a long time, so I told Rick I couldn't handle this anymore."

While the Stone Canyon Band carried on, picking up bass player Tim Cetera (brother of Chicago's Peter Cetera), Meisner returned to Nebraska to take a job at a John Deere dealership.

Out in East Texas, the group Felicity had been playing high school dances and college frat parties for several years. By 1969 the quartet was ready to move on to bigger and better things. Formed by the Bowden cousins, guitarist Richard and bass player Mike, they had recruited vocalist/keyboardist Jerry Dale Surratt and Don Henley on drums. The group's base of operation was the sleepy little town of Linden, where Henley lived with his parents. Henley's mother, unbeknownst to his father, had bought him his first set of drums, and before long he was playing and singing with a band called the Four Speeds, which would evolve into Felicity. The group had minor success, playing around and recording on a regional label. Henley had enrolled at North Texas State University while the group awaited their big break. Opportunity knocked the day Surratt ran into Kenny Rogers one afternoon in Dallas. Recalls Mike Bowden, "We were playing in Dallas at the Studio Club. The First Edition was in Dallas playing at that time. Jerry was a real outgoing guy, recognized Kenny, struck up a conversation, and told him about our band Felicity. Kenny had some time and wanted to come over and see us. We were doing a sound check that afternoon and he came by and liked what he heard a lot. From there he got us a deal fairly quickly after that, with Amos Records. Kenny ended up taking us to Memphis to record. We were there a couple of days and cut four sides. They released a single, "Jennifer," produced by Kenny and his brother Lelan, that got a little airplay regionally but didn't really do anything. That record came out under the name Shiloh. I think Don Henley came up with that name and we all liked it."

A veteran of the New Christy Minstrels, Kenny Rogers had formed the First Edition with ex-Minstrel members in 1967. He had enjoyed several pop hits by the time he crossed paths with the members of Felicity. Born and raised in Texas, Rogers had an early affinity for country music, expressed in tunes like "Ruben James" and "Ruby, Don't Take Your Love To Town." By 1969 he was already beginning to explore country music, and he appreciated Felicity's sound. Three years later the First Edition would record the ambitious, though largely ignored, concept album *The Ballad of Calico*, based on the work of Texas songwriter Michael Murphey. Rogers later enjoyed unprecedented success in the straight country market in the eighties. Shiloh (née Felicity) had fallen under the sway of country rock and were introducing country material into their repertoire. "We were huge fans of Ronstadt and Poco, the Byrds, Flying Burrito Brothers," notes Mike Bowden. "That was our vision at the time, country rock. We wanted to step into that genre of music and see what we had to offer. We were big fans of the Dillards, the *Wheatstraw Suite* album, when Herb Pedersen was with them."

But just as Shiloh's debut single was about to be released, tragedy struck. Mike Bowden recalls sadly, "Kenny and the First Edition were traveling through our little town on their tour bus. We had a little shack outside of town where we did our rehearsing. We had been into dirt bike riding for a couple of years; that was our hobby. They stopped by and Kenny brought the test pressing of our first single. Mickey Jones, their drummer, loved bikes and saw we had half a dozen bikes stored at the rehearsal hall. He wanted to go out and ride, so three or four of us were riding around. Jerry Surratt was sort of a hot dog and liked to show off. This rehearsal hall was set right alongside the highway, a little two lane, and cars would come by at highway speed. Jerry was on the other side of the highway climbing a little hill. He came down, was crossing the highway, wasn't looking, and there was a car barreling down on him. Unfortunately it was a friend of ours driving. There was this big group of people standing off to his right by the rehearsal hall, so he was looking over at that, and Jerry was crossing from the opposite side of the highway and got smacked head on at sixty miles-an-hour. He was killed instantly as everyone was standing there watching it, Kenny and his group and the rest of us, which was horrible. It just threw him like a rag doll. We were devastated. Jerry was the heart of the band. He didn't have the voice that Henley had, but he had great energy on stage and was a great performer."

The remaining members of Shiloh took several months to get over the accident but they tried to persevere. "Because of the way Jerry felt about the band," sighs Mike Bowden, "we decided for his sake to carry on. He just lived and breathed the band." Henley recruited a classmate from North Texas State, Jim Ed Norman, to play keyboards and guitar. The group also brought in pedal-steel guitarist Al Perkins. Perkins also doubled on regular lead guitar along with Richard Bowden. "At the time that Jerry was killed," notes Mike Bowden, "Al Perkins was a member of the band but he wasn't playing all the shows. He was in another band called Foxx, and was playing out his committed dates with them. But he had agreed to join us and didn't really become a full-fledged member until we decided to go out to L.A. He didn't record on 'Jennifer' though."

"Shiloh was my first successful venture," notes Perkins, who was raised in Bowie County, West Texas. "I had gone out to California two years earlier with a group called the Sparkles. I and my keyboard player joined up with them, and we were hooked up with this schmaltzy manager who changed the name to the Pearly Gates. I got fired from them because I just didn't fit the part, I didn't move right or do drugs. So I came back to Texas and got with another group named Foxx. We recorded in Nashville in 1969 and did a Decca album called *Revolt Of Emily Young*, released in 1970 on MCA, which was terrible. I was playing in Dallas with Foxx whenever Shiloh would come through. They had talked with Kenny Rogers and he promised that if they came out to California he would record an album for them on the Amos label."

In the summer of 1970, urged by both Rogers and Rodney Dillard, the reconstituted Shiloh headed to Los Angeles. Recalls Dillard, "We played a club in Dallas, and Don Henley came in with a girl he was seeing at the time. That's where we struck up a conversation. He was asking me about L.A. They'd been playing for seven years around Texas and I told him they owed it to themselves to go try it. So they came out and I got them an audition at the Troubadour on Hoot Night. Henley had such a style on the drums—it was simple but had a lot of feeling— and I really liked the songs he wrote. I still remember one called 'Jennifer.' He sang that song to me and I always liked it. I told him I thought they had something."

"On the way there," recalls Perkins, "Kenny's wife Margo booked us into some ski resorts up in Colorado just to give us some places to play and pick up some money." Upon arriving in L.A., the group headed straight to the Troubadour. "On Hoot Night at the Troubadour they had a cattle call to get up and play," chuckles Mike Bowden. "Maybe fifteen or twenty acts would get up, and see what the crowd reaction was. We went over really well. One of the songs we did was a cover version of Linda Ronstadt's "Silver Threads And Golden Needles." That was something that always went over great. Linda happened to be there and she really liked us and liked Henley, because he had such a strong voice."

Linda Ronstadt had released her second solo album for Capitol in March. Titled *Silk Purse*, the unflattering cover photo depicts the lovely Linda cozying up to a couple of rather large hogs in a pen. The record is a strong outing, although Ronstadt has continually disparaged the album over the years as more a product of her producers than her own. Still straddling the worlds of pop and country (from the aching "Long Long Time," to a cover of Goffin and King's "Will You Love Me Tomorrow"), *Silk Purse* was all over the map musically. It was recorded mostly in Nashville, using the top country session players. Alongside the other cover tunes, Ronstadt includes an excellent interpretation of Gene Clark and Bernie Leadon's "She Darked The Sun." The closing track, the traditional bluegrass "Life Is Like A Mountain Railway," features accompaniment by the Beechwood Rangers. "The Beechwood Rangers was me, Herb Pedersen, Bernie Leadon, and actor Harry Dean Stanton," explains Rodney Dillard. "I lived at Harry's house for several months. Linda Ronstadt was living in the apartment upstairs, and Bill Martin was living downstairs." The name derived from the Beechwood Canyon area of L.A. Though hardly an innovator on par with the Burritos or Poco, Ronstadt continued to pay homage to the country aesthetic.

Gram Parsons' erratic behavior, substance issues, and lack of commitment to the Burrito Brothers was beginning to wear on co-founder Chris Hillman. In January 1970, following futile sessions where the group covered a dozen or more of Parsons' favorite country & western standards, Hillman had felt it necessary to call in ex-Byrd mentor Jim Dickson to take charge and establish some direction for the new record. It was soon evident that the group lacked enough new material. More than a year had passed since they had cut *The Gilded Palace Of Sin*. During the *Sin* period Parsons and Hillman were working well together, creating and inspiring each other. But as time passed, disillusion set in: the two had drifted apart. The Burritos' reliance on cover material in their live shows stifled creativity. In the end they managed to cobble together eleven tracks, but the material could not stand alongside "Sin City," or "Hot Burrito # 1" or "Hot Burrito #2" in terms of quality. Guest appearances by Byron Berline and Leon Russell failed to help, and the album was a pedestrian effort.

Released in May, *Burrito Deluxe* shows a group caught in a sophomore slump, with few flashes of the brilliance and innovation they had shown on their debut. Worse, the sarcastic wit that permeated their previous lyrics was gone, replaced by earnest, threadbare lyrics. Overall, the group eschews country and leans more toward rock, with disappointing results. Sneaky Pete is underutilized, and the Everly Brothers harmonies that made the first album so exquisite were gone. Parsons resurrects the old and rather weak "Lazy Days" from his Submarine Band period, along with a few minor collaborations with

Hillman, including "Older Guys," "Cody Cody," and "High Fashion Queen," a leftover from the debut album. Leadon fills the void with "God's Own Singer" and the zydeco-flavored "Man In The Fog" (co-written with Parsons). One of the few highlights on the album is the bluegrass-gospel "Farther Along," a Hillman arrangement. Parsons deemed a cover of the Rolling Stones' "Wild Horses" the treasure of the album. He pleaded with Jagger and Richards to be allowed to put the stately ballad, not yet released by the Stones, on the record, and they allowed that. Parsons had boasted that the song was written about him, but Richards states flatly that the song stems from his reluctance to leave his infant son Marlon to tour. They originally sent the tape to Parsons to persuade Sneaky Pete to add steel guitar to the track.

"The second album was a mistake," Parsons told interviewer Chuck Casell. "It was a mistake to get Jim Dickson involved. We should have been more careful than that. He was trying to make it commercial. And he dictated to Chris Hillman. For some reason Chris was always listening to what Jim said. I think it's because of the success of the Byrds' cover of 'Mr. Tambourine Man.' The second album was a death blow to the Burritos." Suggests Hillman, "Jim Dickson, who did a lot of good stuff with the Byrds, just didn't understand what we were doing. And we were losing Gram by then. He had one foot in glam rock. It's a terrible record; I don't like it at all. 'Wild Horses' was horrible. *Burrito Deluxe* was written and recorded without any of the feeling or intensity of the first album. It seemed like we were walking on different roads. Gram was getting into a lot of drugs. He just went headlong in the direction of abuse, and it was an area where I just couldn't help him at all. There was nothing that any of us could do. I think his major failing, as far as being a member of the group was concerned, was that he lacked the sense of responsibility, which you *must* have if you work with others."

For Bernie Leadon, the feeling that he had joined a rapidly sinking ship was apparent. "I think the Burritos had used up their creative surge that had resulted in all the songs on that first album," he muses. "'Hot Burrito #1' and '#2' are brilliant songs. It was where Parsons united traditional country with traditional rhythm and blues. That first album was *brilliant*, even though it wasn't well recorded. But they had shot their wad. The record label had given them a lot of money to promote that album, and the band basically squandered it on wine, women, and song on that infamous train trip. So on the second album, A&M basically said, 'You can do another album, but there's very little money.' Gram was not being particularly creative and was not writing more of these kinds of songs. It was a fallow period."

To no one's surprise, the album failed to chart. As the band hit the road for increasingly lower-profile engagements, including high school dances in rural Minnesota, morale was at a nadir. "We played anywhere," moans Sneaky Pete. "High schools, grade schools, junior proms, even *prisons*. They really loved us at the prisons. But generally audiences didn't respond to us. We ended up in a black club that had just switched over and the clientele was not amused at us in our Nudie suits. They walked in, and said, 'Man, what is this shit?' then walked out."

For the trust fund baby Parsons, the humiliation of playing for chump change was too much to bear, and he began avoiding rehearsals *and* gigs. "I was starting to duck out about that time," he admitted. "I didn't want to go to Seattle for $800." For Hillman, the consummate professional, that was enough. At the end of May, Parsons was dismissed. He remarks, "We finally fired Gram. He would never show up for rehearsals. At that point he was just a nightmare. We'd kick off one song, and Gram would start singing something *else*, in a whole other time and groove. He'd be so drugged out we'd have to get a wheelchair to put him on the airplane." In an interview with Sid Griffin, Hillman placed Parsons' increasingly capricious attitude squarely on the shoulders of the Rolling Stones. "He worshipped the Stones. They could do no wrong. That's why we parted company: it was becoming more important to hang out with the Stones and play rock-star games than it was to do his own thing with the Burritos."

"I always got along great with Gram," notes Sneaky Pete. "He was a very sweet guy. But he could be like a naughty child, this big kid. He wasn't pushy, but he ran afoul of people because of his personality. He was very creative, a good songwriter. Gram was highly influential in the way the group developed. He was the leader, even though he was a soft-spoken person. On the rare times he was straight, he was a hell of a singer, very emotional. I don't know how the hell they got him to sing straight on 'Hot Burrito #1,' but it was one of the rare occasions where he had enough self-control to come into the studio and do the vocals right. That's probably my favorite song of the first Burritos configuration."

Parsons took the sacking in stride, having lost interest in the Burritos. "Things were always going wrong with the Burritos," he opined in a 1972 press release. "At first, we toured before our album was out, so audiences didn't know what to expect. And the group didn't evolve like I'd hoped it would. I was looking for some kind of total thing, almost like a revue, but it didn't grow that way. The Burritos were a group of good musicians, but collectively, they weren't what I was looking for in the long run." Parsons followed his Burrito stint by cutting a never-released record with Terry Melcher. Then Keith Richards remarked in passing that he might produce a Parsons album for the Stones' new record label, so Gram headed off to Europe, where he spent several months in a drug-induced lethargy with nothing to show for it in the end. Since Parsons could foot his own bills, he was allowed to stay on in the Stones' exclusive coterie indefinitely. The Stones tapped Parsons' extensive knowledge of country music to bolster their own country turns on their brilliant *Exile On Main Street* record.

Meanwhile, the Flying Burrito Brothers carried on through the summer as a quartet. Hillman and Leadon sang the vocals. "Bernie and I *had* to carry on," asserts Hillman. "We had to take over. We had to learn the songs really quick. Bernie was singing some and I was singing some, and it worked. We made it work." Adds Leadon, "We didn't do much gigging after Parsons was gone. I had a sinking feeling that, as erratic as Gram was, he was the resident boy-genius, where the rest of us were much more plodding and steady. There were gigs booked and Dickson was involved, so we were out there playing second bill on some big summer outdoor shows. We didn't have that many tunes. We had this one gig in a stadium before eight thousand people and we only had seven songs. It was ridiculous." The experience of stepping forward and leading the Burritos would serve Hillman well. "Chris, in the end, is a professional and knows how to organize and focus," adds Leadon. "It comes from his bluegrass training. He had the ability to make something actually happen. He had enough of an organizational frame of mind that he could see something through. He's proved that in his whole career and has a very consistent level of professionalism. So I have tremendous respect for Chris. He's a solid guy."

Despite decent sales for their debut album, Poco found their access to the studio to record their follow-up effort impeded by CBS. The last-minute crisis brought on by Randy Meisner's departure, and manager Dickie Davis' insistence that the cover art be redone, had caused some friction with the label. Furthermore, the failure of the group to make adequate headway in either the rock or country radio markets frustrated the promotional department. "CBS was not giving us the time to get into the studio and record," laments Furay. "We could not get studio time. Clive Davis was holding something against us. Radio never really picked up on us. The label didn't hear the commercial potential of the music we were doing, and backed away from us." Comments Messina, "At Atlantic, Ahmet Ertegun really loved the Buffalo Springfield, but when we got signed to CBS there was less personal attachment to what we were doing. They liked the band but there wasn't that personal appreciation." It took the intervention of an interested third party to break the log-jam. "Somehow, David Geffen got involved as an agent for us," continues Messina. "He appreciated the music we were trying to create and saw that we were floundering. He had a personal relationship with Clive, and told him, 'This is a great act. They need some help. Let's get them into the studio and get this record made.' That's when things started to move again."

Released in May 1970, the second album, titled simply *Poco* (but often referred to by fans as the "orange" album because of the prominent oranges on the cover), is more rock and less country. "That was us beginning to do something a little more rock & roll," acknowledges Furay, "especially with 'Hurry Up' and 'Don't Let It Pass By.' There were a lot of things happening musically—for example extended instrumental versions of songs, so we felt we had to get in on that. Again it was rock-meeting-country. We didn't want to deny the country aspect of our music, but we wanted to say, 'Hey, we can play rock & roll, too.'" In many ways *Poco*, like the Burrito Brothers and Dillard & Clark, suffered the second-album syndrome: they had their whole lives to prepare for their first album, and six months for their second. And Furay's ego was pricked by the notoriety of others. "Richie was really kind of disheartened by the fact that Stephen Stills and Neil Young were having such success with their music," acknowledges Messina. "We worked hard to write quality music, but they were getting a lot more attention and airplay."

For producer Messina, the second album holds far more positive memories than the first. "While I was working at Columbia, they denied me the privilege of running the board, even though I was a union member. That first album was a nightmare for me. I never liked anything that was cut on it in terms of the sound. It wasn't until we cut the second album that I was able to explain to Alex Kasanegras, our new engineer, things I *didn't* want, like all the drums on one track. I wanted separate bass drum, snare, and high hat, in stereo. If you listen to the difference between the two in terms of the sound, the second album comes *alive*. The sound is more in-your-face."

The lone country track is a cover of Dallas Frazier's "Honky Tonk Downstairs," an old George Jones hit. The remainder of the album rocks harder, capped by a funky "Nobody's Fool," which segues into an extended instrumental jam entitled "El Tonto de Nadie, Regresa." George Grantham explains the genesis of the track. "That long jam was a real step out from the first album. We always jammed at the Troubadour. We started experimenting with the arrangement and it turned into this jam. But our jams were different, more structured and arranged." Rusty Young feels the jam is a product of its era. "The second album is really hard to pull out of the context of time. It was 1970, and FM radio was such a force in selling albums and concert seats. Our goal was to have a song that would be a staple of FM radio and be artistically true. So that album was done from that viewpoint. I remember people were keen on the instrumental side of what we were doing, so it seemed like the perfect thing: to create a showcase for the album with the extended 'Nobody's Fool.' And FM radio played all eighteen minutes."

Despite reaching Number 58, the album lacks the freshness and accessibility of the debut release. Overall, the group sounds tired. "The weariness came from the fact we had a hard time getting airplay. It was the same story: too rock for country and too country for rock," assesses Messina. "There was an unspoken feeling that we needed to move in a different direction, more into rock. Richie had come to the conclusion that he needed to go more toward rock. If you look back at the Buffalo Springfield, Richie was usually the ballad singer and writer of love songs. His voice was more tender, whereas Neil's and Stephen's were edgier. There was a sense of 'Yes, let's make this feel more rock & roll.' I was digging that. I was missing the edge that I knew the band had. We needed something that had some energy so that when it hit radio, it would stand out."

Messina's lone writing and vocal contribution was a perfect slice of Poco: "You Better Think Twice." It would go on to become one of the band's best-known songs. Acknowledges Furay, "We put a lot into that song. It's very well crafted right from that beginning lick. It really showcased Jimmy. It had a different sound to it than just about anything else on that album." Notes Young, "On that track we all had the feeling Jimmy was ready to move out of the band. He was seeing what he could do by himself. It's a great song." Besides being a standout track, the song serves as an indicator of where Messina was headed in his later partnership with Kenny Loggins. Unfortunately, the track only went as high as Number 72 on the singles' chart.

The presence of Tim Schmit enhanced the vocals on the *Poco* record. "Tim added beautiful vocals that harmonized well with Richie," emphasizes Messina. But Young was not a fan of Schmit's musicianship. "Until Tim came into the band, Jimmy played bass, and he's a brilliant bass player, but Tim's not. He's adequate. As an instrumentalist, I really missed having that bottom. Everything came off of that and when it wasn't there anymore it really bothered me and I let him know it." Comments Messina, "It wasn't because Tim wasn't a good musician, he's a great player, but he just didn't have the hours or the time that I had being around the music and playing. As the arranger I would tell people how to play things and I tried to do it as sensitively as I possibly could but we were all young and had fairly sensitive egos, and that can be frustrating."

The popular Monkees' weekly television show was cancelled at the completion of its third season in June 1969. Due to contractual obligations the quartet continued to record and tour through the end of the year. At that point, Peter Tork bought out his contract and slipped into obscurity. The other three—Davy Jones, Mickey Dolenz, and Mike Nesmith—released a couple of lackluster albums and filmed a sharply criticized television special. At the same time, Nesmith issued his first solo album, an instrumental effort backed by the Nashville studio players who would subsequently become Area Code 615. Titled *The Wichita Train Whistle Sings*, it was financed by Nesmith and sold only to the curious. In March 1970, Nesmith quit the Monkees to launch a solo career. Recruiting John London and John Ware from Linda Ronstadt's Corvettes, and enlisting the services of pedal-steel ace Red Rhodes, Nesmith formed the First National Band. Their debut album *Magnetic South* was released that summer. "Red was the king-of-the-hill guy in L.A.," boasts Nesmith. "Everybody sat at his feet. Even respected musicians like Clarence White, Sneaky Pete, Bernie Leadon, Leon Russell, and Delaney and Bonnie would gather to watch him play."

Drummer John Ware says he inspired Nesmith to form the band. He recalls, "Mike knew the Monkees were history. I said, 'Let's do a band.' He replied, 'There isn't a band to do,' and I said, 'Yeah, I think there is.' We used to go to the Palomino, where Red led the house band, the Detours. He was fifteen years our senior, but I had played with him so I knew him. I told Mike I thought I could get Red to leave the house band. Mike thought I was nuts. So I challenged him, 'Do you have the nerve to form a band?' He said, 'Red won't do it.' I called Red and asked him and he said 'Yeah.' The next morning we had a band, the First National Band."

Nesmith acknowledges the country direction the band took was a subconscious decision. "If country music made it in through me, it made it through me as a songwriter. I wasn't attempting to generate a new category. It's always just been some form of artistic expression for me that gets the ideas across."

In early 1970, the band signed with RCA and recorded *Magnetic South*. Nesmith's First National Band would release three records, known as the red, white, and blue trilogy. *South* was the blue record in this grouping. "When I left the Monkees I had fifty songs, which I recorded over the next five years," claims Nesmith. "What I had was three albums' worth by then, and so I had to do at least one album. I was having a hard time getting a record deal; a lot of people thought of me as a television actor, not a musician. I put together a demo tape that Felton Jarvis heard. He was a good friend of Elvis, who was 'the Man' at RCA. Felton became my champion and told RCA to sign me." Jarvis was assigned to the project as producer, but Nesmith and the band did most of the production themselves. "Felton never showed up," explains Nesmith. "He told me, 'I don't know how to produce a band. Can you do it by yourself?'" Veteran country sideman Earl Ball guested on piano for the sessions.

Incorporating Rhodes' innovative pedal-steel guitar work with Nesmith's western influenced songs, *Magnetic South* was a solid debut, garnering positive reviews and healthy sales, though it stopped at Number 143. "Red played some stuff on our first album that just blows every other pedal-steel player right off the face of the planet," boasts Ware. Adds Nesmith, "Red loved all the sonic capabilities of the steel guitar. He just loved going out and doing all this stuff. The thing about Red's playing was that he basically played the same thing all the time. He had a very limited repertoire. What he would do was he would just convolute it. It would turn back on itself, it would go this way, it would go that way. That's one of the things that made it sound so interesting: it had this real familiar ring to it, but he had an ability to innovate around the same lick. The steel guitar has a very singular voice, it has a mellifluous voice. It has an ability to swim around, and smooth over the craggy surfaces of the drums and piano in a way no other instrument could, except maybe strings." Rather than simply playing licks around the music like other players did, Nesmith and Rhodes allowed the instrument to provide a lush sonic background for the songs.

Like Poco, the First National Band worked within a country rock frame. The pedal-steel guitar provided the country texture, creating a refreshingly upbeat sound on tracks like "Calico Girlfriend," "The Crippled Lion," and "Mama Nantucket." The record even features some beautiful, old-style yodeling by Nesmith on "One Rose," a country & western standard. One track, "Joanne," was released as a single and was a success, ascending to Number 21 on the charts. "The fact that it became a mild hit surprised everybody," says Nesmith, "but nobody more than me. I had been just as surprised when Linda had a hit with 'Different Drum.' The whole country influence at the time was not welcomed by radio or the industry. It was considered hokey." That AM radio should embrace a cut with yodeling on it was equally astonishing. "Yodeling was a staple of country music," maintains Nesmith. His western influences were rooted deep in the Texas soil. "If you were going to sing country music you had to know how to yodel. Jimmy Rodgers took us all down that road. Part of my early repertoire was Hank Williams and Jimmy Rodgers' songs: "The Yodeling Brakeman," traditional country music, that sort of thing." Recalls Ware, "Mike played me his version of 'Joanne' and told me, 'You're gonna hate this because it's got this stupid yodel on it. But tell me what you think of it.' I told him I loved it. It was fabulous. He didn't believe me. He asked if it should be the single and I said yeah. 'Joanne' was one of the biggest selling singles of that year. It was such a good record. The reason that song was so good was because of Mike. He was brilliant."

Following the album's release, the First National Band made its debut at the Troubadour, where they drew a cautious response from the self-consciously critical clientele. After that engagement the group headed to Europe for a series of club gigs booked before "Joanne" became a hit. "We really didn't come into our own until we got to England," laments Nesmith. "We played a lot smaller venues than the Monkees, mostly clubs, and joined with tours where we were packaged with other groups. I think management made an error in judgment in scheduling a big string of English dates. Given the fact that we had a hit record in America, going to England was a mistake. When we went to England, we were really just playing little casinos and clubs, little tiny places."

Back in America, his Monkees' past became a burden. "In England there was a lot of support from the power structure. But in America the First National Band was just a different animal, and there was a resistance to the country tinge of it. There was a curiosity about me as a television actor that brought some people to the concert hall. I mean, nobody came out to see the Eagles because they had been on television. And the Monkees' music was a very powerful part of the pop culture in a way nobody could have anticipated. So there was sort of a carry-over, but there was never the kind of Paul McCartney sense that 'I'll play Beatles songs and then these are mine.' It was more, 'Look, this is the music I've always been doing. And some of it has been on the *Monkees*, like "Listen to the Band," "Nine Times Blue," and "Papa Gene's Blues," and some of it hasn't. Some of it the Greenbriar Boys have sung and some of it I have sung. Here it is altogether and we're now playing it.' The fact that we were part of the new country rock thing was utterly lost on us. It was always just Nesmith tunes. But it worked because the band was good and the songs were good and gradually we eclipsed the confusion."

In June, the Great Speckled Bird made its Troubadour debut to a packed house of eager fans who had heard the album and the buzz surrounding the group. "Everybody associated with country rock in southern California was there to see us," boasts Jim Colegrove. "We got a great review in *Cashbox*." Sylvia Tyson recalls a humorous incident during their Troubadour stand. "I remember we were playing three sets a night and it was full every night. Amos kept getting louder and louder with each set. We couldn't figure it out. It was deafening; people in the first few rows had their fingers in their ears. Finally we said to him, 'Why are you playing so loud?' And he said, 'Well, my friend Fritz Richmond says he can't hear me.' So we said, 'Where is Fritz?' And he was sitting in the bar out in the *front*, not in the club."

Later that month the Speckled Bird went to Japan for two weeks, playing the Canadian Pavilion at Japan's "Expo 70." "The Japanese love country music," enthuses N. D. Smart. "It was encores and standing-room-only every night." On returning to Canada, the group joined the heavily hyped Festival Express tour, a rolling thunder revue of the hottest acts, traveling across Canada on a chartered train that had been specially equipped. With a lineup boasting The Band, Janis Joplin (and her Full Tilt Boogie Band), the Grateful Dead, Mountain, Delaney & Bonnie and Friends, and Eric Andersen, the partying never paused. "One lounge car was for blues and rock, and the other was country and folk," recalls Sylvia Tyson. "We all got along fine. There were jam sessions nonstop on the train. We did a jam onstage in Calgary with Delaney & Bonnie on 'Will The Circle Be Unbroken.'" The unending reverie had memorable moments. "The Grateful Dead ran out of other substances around Winnipeg and started drinking. It was not a pretty sight," laughs Sylvia. "I didn't really drink at that point, but I think Janis Joplin outdrank Amos, and *that* was quite an accomplishment." Recalls Ian Tyson with a smile, "I was drunk the whole time. I recall getting into a drinking contest with Janis Joplin and I was seriously overmatched. She drank me under the table. I remember me and somebody else, on the roof of one of these cars, howling like coyotes as the train hurtled across the prairies. At the end of the whole thing we had this wonderful concert in Calgary with a great jam session at the end. Then N. D. Smart with his big mouth got us into this brawl, a genuine street brawl. And I ended up breaking my hand on this guy's head and had to play two days later. But everyone acquitted himself/herself quite honorably on that trip. That's where Jerry Garcia spotted Buddy Cage. Jerry was a great person. He was perfect for that situation and just loved to play, a real California hippie the way they were supposed to be. A lot of seeds were sown on that trip." Adds Smart, "We were the darlings of that tour. We were the one everybody stood on the sidelines and watched. And they'd come out and jam with us."

Garcia and Cage engaged in a legendary steel guitar duel that was adjudged in Cage's favor. "The New Riders of the Purple Sage were a new group then," states Speckled Bird bass player Jim Colegrove, "and Jerry Garcia was playing steel guitar. One of the most memorable moments on that train was when Jerry and Buddy Cage jammed. Finally Jerry just stopped playing. He said, 'Sorry, I can't keep up with you.'" Garcia took to standing in the wings during the Speckled Bird's sets to watch Cage. A year later, when he left the New Riders, Garcia introduced the young Canadian as his replacement. "Jerry was just starting to fool around with the steel at that time," offers guitarist Amos Garrett, "but Buddy had been playing since he was a child, so he was very advanced." Earlier that year, Garcia had contributed some marvelously fluid pedal-steel work to Crosby, Stills, Nash & Young's "Teach Your Children." Amazingly, it was his first take of the song; he'd never heard it before and was still finding his way on the instrument. "I got one good note in on that tune!" claimed Garcia. "One good note makes it worthwhile!"

It was never Chris Hillman's intention for the Burritos to carry on as a quartet, so when manager Eddie Tickner suggested he give Rick Roberts a tryout, he agreed. Roberts had been attending college in South Carolina and playing clubs in Washington, D.C., before deciding to hitchhike out to California in the summer of 1969 to try his luck. "I did several auditions," recalls Roberts, "but nothing ever came of it. I was seriously considering going back to college." Columbia Records' collegiate rep Paul Rappaport heard Roberts playing at the Free Press Book Store near the UCLA campus in the summer of 1970. He brought the singer to the attention of his superiors, who contacted Eddie Tickner with the suggestion of having the Burrito Brothers back Roberts on some sessions. "I was astonished," Roberts continues. "I knew who they were because I was a huge Byrds fan. I had heard their first album and liked it. Frankly, as a kid I had never been a country music fan. It was the heyday of the formulaic Nashville sound and I hated it. Plus I had a nasally voice and everyone always told me I'd make a great country voice so I avoided it. When I first heard the Burritos I liked them, but I wasn't jolted by them. I was much more impressed with Poco's debut album."

Roberts joined the Burritos in a rehearsal room on the A&M lot that September, and the chemistry worked. "The very first night of rehearsals we went over to the Troubadour afterward, and they were going to introduce me around. Michael Clarke was saying, 'This is our new lead singer Rick Roberts.' They asked me to do a weekend with them opening for the Byrds at the Whisky-A-Go Go. During the course of the engagement Clarence White went up to Chris and said, 'Man, you better do something about getting him into the Burritos because if you don't, I'm going to see about getting him into the Byrds.' I heard this and couldn't believe it. And about thirty minutes later Chris came over to the other dressing room and asked if I'd like to be a Brother. And I joined as of that point."

Less country than Gram Parsons, Roberts brought a more commercial pop sound to the Burritos, and came on board with a back catalog of songs. He also began a creative partnership with Hillman, who was eager for another collaborator. "My background was more pop and the songs showed that," acknowledges Roberts. "The band was hungry for new material anyway, and looking for something that would click. That made it easier for me to ease in." Hillman felt that Roberts blunted the band's country edge. "We had this thing that was splintering apart and Bernie and I needed a tenor singer, another guy. Rick Roberts had a great tenor voice, and some of his songs were pretty good, but it pushed us back into the middle of the road."

Roberts faced the daunting task of replacing Gram Parsons, already a living legend in country rock circles. "My biggest challenge," notes

Roberts, "was taking the place of someone who was an icon and whose status increased after his passing. But I wasn't really *aware* I was replacing him. It would have been a tougher challenge had I been aware of what was going on."

With Roberts in the lineup, the Burrito Brothers went to Europe in October where they received a heroes' welcome in the Netherlands. "The Burritos are still beloved in the Netherlands," maintains Sneaky Pete. "It just took off there. We played the Concertgebouw in Amsterdam, and it was like the Beatles. The people there were just *nuts*. We were mobbed after the performance." Roberts was stunned by the response. "There was a sort of topsy-turvy nature to the Burritos," he remembers. "We never had a handle on where we stood. That was hard on Chris because he has a great sense of pride about being in the Byrds. So we go from playing junior proms to flying off to Amsterdam, get off the plane, and all these journalists are chasing us yelling, 'Mr. Hillman! Mr. Hillman!' They ushered us directly into this conference room where there were at *least* sixty journalists. We were totally shocked; we had no idea what this was all about. Turned out the Burritos had come in right behind the Beatles and Rolling Stones as one of the most popular bands in Holland. Then we'd come back to the States and couldn't get arrested."

When CTV, an independent Canadian television network, offered Ian Tyson his own weekly television show, he jumped at the opportunity. Titled *Nashville North*, Tyson hosted and performed while the Great Speckled Bird backed him, and a bevy of weekly guests passed through. The show offered the band members a steady paycheck and a chance at a normal existence. *Nashville North* was a hit right from its debut in September, drawing the top country performers as guests. "The most memorable guests I can recall," says Jim Colegrove with pride, "were Carl Perkins, Chet Atkins, and Mason Williams. We backed all of them. I had to play 'Classical Gas' with Williams. And Ronnie Hawkins being on the show was terrific, too. The only person who refused was Jerry Lee Lewis. Dolly Parton, Linda Ronstadt, Johnny Rodriquez all had guest spots." In deference to her husband, Sylvia Tyson was signed on to appear frequently throughout the first season. The following year the program's name was changed to *The Ian Tyson Show* and hovered at the top of the ratings until 1975, when Tyson walked out. Amos Garrett remembers his time on the show unhappily. "I think I did three or four episodes of *Nashville North*. My style was starting to cross other musical boundaries, and I didn't want to be stuck in a strictly country environment musically. I wanted to play a lot of different things. That's why I left. I loved what Ian and Sylvia were doing, but I just felt my guitar playing needed variety to grow at that point in time." His replacement was acoustic picker David Wilcox, who adapted to the electric country environment easily. "The David Wilcox version of the Great Speckled Bird was a helluva band," boasts Tyson. "We had Red Shea for two years after Wilcox. By then I knew how to do it."

Steel guitar ace Buddy Cage jumped ship for an offer from Anne Murray. Cage's replacement in the Speckled Bird was Ben Keith, who would also grace Neil Young's multiplatinum *Harvest* album. Colegrove recalls the time Linda Ronstadt appeared as a guest on Tyson's show. "I remember the guys who became the Eagles were backing her up when she came up and did the show. She did Patsy Cline's 'I Fall to Pieces.' When they found out that Ben Keith was the guy who played steel on the original recording, they just about shit."

"The reason that so many stars came up to do Ian's show," attests Smart, "was that they knew there was a good backup band. They wouldn't have to spend the money transporting their band, got paid a good taste, and sounded good. Ian got real insecure about us. Great musicians would come on and rave about the band, so he figured we were gonna split on him. He had us all sign a contract making a commitment to stay with him."

In late October, Jimmy Messina played his farewell performance with Poco at the Fillmore West in San Francisco. Since the release of their second album Messina had become increasingly estranged from Richie Furay. "I felt that we had lost our communication," offers Messina. "I think Richie was really unhappy. I don't think it was personal, he was just going through some changes, and my feelings were getting hurt too much during the conversations. I saw him upset and angry, and at the time I kind of personalized that, and thought it was me. So I felt the best thing to do was to get me out of the mix because there were certainly other things I could do." Responds Furay, "Jimmy probably felt he wasn't being able to express himself as fully as he wanted. He probably felt I was crowding him out of the band by writing as many of the songs as I did, singing the songs, and being the front man. He was feeling he had more to offer. There was really something special Jimmy and I had that never got fully developed, probably because of egos." According to Rusty Young, Messina wrote the song "Angry Eyes," later recorded with Kenny Loggins, following a

particularly unpleasant exchange with Furay onstage during that tur-
bulent period.

Messina gave his notice as the band was preparing to record a live
album, though he stayed on to see the album through as a producer. "I
was sad that I was leaving," admits Messina, "but professionally, I was
very straight ahead about getting the album done." The live album was
only part of the bigger picture. A suitable replacement had to be found
so that the group would be able to carry on. "Jimmy sprung it on us,"
states George Grantham. "We were set to do this live album, and
Jimmy called a meeting and said he was going to leave the band. We
were really caught off guard. But he still wanted to produce the album
and it was so close to doing it. He said that if we were willing to let him
produce it he would work his replacement in and all that stuff. We had
no choice but to accept his decision and persevere."

The band was fortunate to recruit Paul Cotton almost immediately.
Cotton had developed an early affinity for country music listening to
Johnny Cash and Marty Robbins records as a youngster growing up
near Chicago. By his teens he was playing guitar in local bands. As a
member of the Illinois Speed Press, Cotton crossed paths with Poco on
several occasions after witnessing their Troubadour debut. "I followed
their career as closely as I could," notes Cotton. "Then I saw them open
for the Who at the Hollywood Palladium, and they were as fresh as the
first time I saw them. They were down to a foursome by then. The
Speed Press opened for Poco once and I met them all in their dressing
room. I was hoping something might click. After that my friend Peter
Cetera from Chicago was taking a few steel guitar lessons from Rusty
and Rusty mentioned that Jimmy might be leaving Poco, so Peter mentioned my name, knowing what a fan I was of the band and country
rock in general. Richie called me in September 1970 and I went on tour
with them, not playing but rooming with Jimmy. This was just before
*Deliverin'* was released. We were on tour in the east along the seaboard,
and I was hanging with Jimmy; he was teaching me the songs and the
guitar licks. It was an odd situation easing another guy into a band. But
Jimmy wanted to carry on with other projects."

"Paul would watch me play the show," states Messina on the unusual arrangement that integrated Cotton into the lineup, "and afterward we would take out our guitars and I'd show him the parts, what
I was doing and how I approached it." Notes Cotton, "Jimmy has a
very distinctive guitar style. He could play two notes and you knew it
was him. He used metal finger picks, which is where that sound he got

came from. I could never get used to those picks, having been rockin' and rollin' for so long, so I adapted those songs without 'em, they were wanting my style and tone by then anyway. So it worked out. The guitar lick on 'You Better Think Twice' was the hardest thing I've ever learned to play. Of course he plays it like he's falling off a log. I didn't learn until years later that he used an open tuning on it."

The *Deliverin'* album was pieced together from dates played prior to Messina's exit. But Messina's farewell gig wasn't planned. The guitarist thought he would finish up a weekend Fillmore stand, but Richie coolly informed him that Cotton was ready to step in. Laments Messina, "I was supposed to play that night, but Richie wanted to go ahead and bring Paul on to perform. That was frustrating for me because I *really* wanted to play that night. Neil Young had shown up, and I wanted to play for him, but it didn't happen. It was over. Within a week or two Kenny Loggins came over to my house, and we recorded fourteen songs. So I began focusing on that almost right away." Messina would take his commercial sensibility, production and arranging savvy, and musicianship, to great success with Loggins over the next four years.

Cotton brought an edge to Poco that was welcomed by the others. "I played a Les Paul rather than a Telecaster, and used a pick so that contributed to a different sound," he asserts. "But that's what they wanted. And my voice is meatier than Jimmy's." Confirms Furay, "Paul took us in a more rock & roll direction. He had a different style. Paul brought us another songwriter, another lead vocalist, as well as a rock & roller's instinct. He expanded the band. The Poco that really stays in my heart as being most representative of what Poco was about was the lineup with Paul and Tim. We became more accessible during that period. Originally when we were playing the Troubadour, we were getting a lot of attention. But as far as spreading it out to a wider audience around the country, it was the lineup with Paul and Tim that helped us raise our profile around the nation."

Texas country rockers Shiloh had worked the slim country rock club scene around L.A. into the fall, while recording their debut album for Amos Records. "We played at a place called the Goose Creek Saloon out in Reseda for several weeks," recalls Mike Bowden. "We also played a beach club called Cisco's that the Smothers Brothers owned in Manhattan Beach. But mostly we played the Goose Creek Saloon. But the Troubadour was the hottest place to hang out and meet people. The Hollywood crowd hung out there, and you'd see Jack Nicholson in a corner at the bar. *That* was thrilling. I saw Ronstadt there, and Jackson Browne a year before he signed with Geffen."

In December Amos Records issued Shiloh's self-titled album, with Kenny Rogers listed as producer. Explains Mike Bowden, "Kenny wasn't around a lot. We wound up mixing a lot of it ourselves. He wasn't much of a hands-on producer." The album is a laid-back, Marshall Tucker–type of southern rock, with country textures courtesy of Perkins' pedal steel. "We were doing country rock, most definitely," asserts Perkins, "and original material. It was pretty basic, but we thought it was pretty good at the time. How country it was or how rock it was depended on who was singing. Don Henley always liked these heavier ballad things. He wrote a song called 'God Is Where You Find Him,' kind of long and slow. Another song, 'Swamp River Country,' was like Poco. They influenced the sound with the effects on the steel like a Leslie and all that. I was aware of Rusty Young. I had done some homework." Counters Mike Bowden, "We didn't use the steel guitar like Poco did. In general we used it in a more subdued form, more like a legitimate country instrument. Al played a lot of rhythm and lead guitar. But the steel wasn't a real focal point for us, like it was in Poco."

The album has its moments, chiefly provided by Henley. "We had worked up most of those songs and had been doing most of them playing at the Goose Creek Saloon," acknowledges Mike Bowden. "We wrote some of them while we were playing there. The club owner was nice enough to let us sneak in our originals in between all the cover tunes we had to do. So a lot of those songs were already forming when we entered the studio." The sound of the album is more removed from the Eagles than Glenn Frey and J. D. Souther's Longbranch Pennywhistle, a duo whose approach was lighter than Shiloh's. The traditional "Railroad Song" receives the heavy guitar treatment, with Perkins emulating Clapton where pedal steel might have served the tune better.

Henley's country influences resonate on "Same Old Song," where Perkins plays pedal steel. The introspective ballad "God Is Where You Find Him" gave listeners a taste of what was to come with the Eagles, and is probably the best cut on the record. "Don had been an English major and was listening to a lot of Neil Young," says Mike Bowden. "And he took elements of the way the songs were laid out, arrangement and production ideas, and adapted them to that song. I don't know if that's one of his prouder moments as a writer now, but you had to start somewhere." Jim Ed Norman shouldered much of the production and mixing duties in his role as the group's musical director. "Jim Ed had the musical credentials, read well, and could write out string music at the drop of a hat," marvels Mike Bowden. Norman would go on to arrange and orchestrate for the Eagles.

The opening track, "A Simple Little Down Home Rock & Roll Love Song For Rosie," was released as a single, where it was a surprise hit in Bakersfield, of all places. The thrill was short-lived, however. The album disappeared quickly. "I think Kenny found that song for us," recalls Mike Bowden. "Michael McGinnis wrote that song. He may have even done some writing for the First Edition. It turned into a huge hit, a Number One record, in Bakersfield. They had us come out to play there while it was peaking. We went and played one weekend there and on the way about fifteen miles out of Bakersfield we heard our song on the radio. They were playing it about every ten or fifteen minutes. That was the first time we heard our song on the radio. We were thrilled."

Henley offered his post mortem on the album years later: "It didn't sell, but then it wasn't that good. The songs weren't any good, and the production was terrible. We knew before we made it that it would turn out awful." Nevertheless Henley remains appreciative of the experience and of Rogers' involvement. "Kenny was certainly a mentor for me," he recently told writer Bill DeYoung in *Goldmine*, "and the fact that our paths crossed, even for a relatively brief span of time, has made an immeasurable difference in my life. Although I was not satisfied with the final product, it was a learning experience for me, as well as a stepping stone to bigger and better things. Had we not connected with Kenny, my buddies and I might never have worked up the nerve to pack up our little trailer and head west."

Comments Poco's Paul Cotton, "I heard that Shiloh album and there was no way Don Henley would have been overlooked. Don would have happened anyway, even if the Eagles had never come together."

# 8

# Will the Circle Be Unbroken: 1971

*I couldn't have asked for a better role model than Chris Hillman. Chris was an elegant businessman, very directed, very devoted, sometimes a little bit too stern about things but he had class about everything he did. He was absolutely the leader of the band. He's like an older brother to me, a mentor, and I've turned to him for advice many times over the years.*

—*Rick Roberts, on his experience in the Flying Burrito Brothers*

By the early seventies country rock pioneers who survived into the new decade were turning away from country and toward rock. Country rock's lack of commercial success had been a source of great frustration for groups like the Flying Burrito Brothers, Poco, the Dillards, the First National Band, and the Byrds, who all released more commercially oriented rock albums in 1971. Out of this shift in attitude emerged the most commercially successful and best known of the country rock exponents, the Eagles. As the second generation of country rockers, the Eagles were determined to avoid the mistakes of their predecessors. Gram Parsons and Emmylou Harris also teamed up to form a smoldering, albeit short-lived, country duo, and the pairing would have a profound impact on country rock's future.

Poco's third effort, *Deliverin'*, lived up to its name: issued in January 1971, it fulfilled the promise the group had posited two years earlier when it debuted its exciting new sound to enthusiastic crowds at the Troubadour. All the energy, exuberance, and good-natured fun of their music was captured on the album. Where most live recordings rely on rehashing hits to the screams of fans, Poco boldly chose to present five new songs from their repertoire, all crowd pleasers. "I think the album did a good job of capturing our live show," boasts George Grantham. "Our reputation was that we were better live than on vinyl. That's why we wanted to make the live album, to capture that on record."

Jimmy Messina, who by then had left Poco, puts *Deliverin'* in context: *"Pickin' Up The Pieces* was a nightmare in the studio; I see *Deliverin'* as showing the world what Poco was all about. For me it was a time full of excitement *and* heartache. The third album resolved everything for me. Once it was done, I let it go. When I heard it again, in 1989, I listened to Rusty and me playing and thought, 'My God, that is good! I don't think I could do that now!'"

The album kicks off with Furay's hard rocking "I Guess You Made It," which dates back to the final months of the Springfield. "The song was born out of the frustrations with the Springfield," admits Furay. In Poco's hands the song is well served. Two more new songs follow, "C'mon" and "Hear That Music," the first featuring Schmit and Furay's smooth vocal blend, the second a Schmit tune, a lyrical response to the song "Pickin' Up The Pieces." In the latter song one can hear the influence of Buck Owens. The Springfield's "A Child's Claim To Fame" and "Kind Woman" also get the empathetic Poco treatment, with Young's steel, filtered through a Leslie speaker, rounding out the tune. Messina shines on the rousing "You Better Think Twice," while two medleys revisit the band's better-known material from their debut album. The reliance on newer material, two Springfield favorites, and several numbers from their debut, point up the weaknesses of their second record, from which only "You Better Think Twice" makes the cut on the live effort.

*Deliverin'* was an attempt at a commercial breakthrough, the theory being "If their best showing was live, give 'em a live album of their best." The record would be the group's strongest chart entry, peaking at Number 26, quite impressive compared to their other efforts. The single from the album did not fare as well: "C'mon" (backed by "I Guess You Made It") limped to Number 69. *Deliverin'* also marked the end of Poco's first era. Following it, the group moved in a rock direction, led by Paul Cotton.

After recording the live disk, Poco reentered the studio under the aegis of rock producer Richard Podolor and engineer Bill Cooper to cut studio versions of two popular live numbers, which the executives at Epic/CBS flatly rejected. Says Furay, "Podolor had worked with Steppenwolf and Three Dog Night, and we were thinking, 'This is the guy who can do it.' We were searching for a producer because we didn't feel we had the capability to do it on our own. We were really happy with the result, but CBS was not. We were pretty well satisfied that we had what we wanted. It was a blow to me. It made me feel that if CBS was going to stand in our way we had to get off the label, or it just wasn't going to happen for us. Those were the beginnings of the seeds being planted for me to seriously think of getting out of there."

Recording with the notorious Podolor was a unique experience. "Richard was *something* to work with," marvels Grantham. "He was very different. He would record three or four vocal takes, take a word from this track and one from that track, and put it all together. It drove me crazy. But when I came back and heard what he did, it sounded cohesive." Because Podolor was not a CBS producer, the label refused to consider the tracks even though Furay, Grantham, and Young felt it was the best-recorded work Poco had ever done.

Following the success of "Joanne" and their *Magnetic South* album, the First National Band released *Loose Salute*, the red album of the trilogy. Nesmith and the group rocked harder on this outing, and all the material, save for a cover of Patsy Cline's "I Fall to Pieces," was written by Nesmith. "The second album was more of a collaboration," says drummer John Ware. Ware felt that the first record was all Nesmith. "We barely knew each other on that first album, but the follow-up was a band event. There was a storytelling nature to the songs on that first album, his response to the Monkees burning down, and about his relationship with his wife Phyllis."

In the context of a more experimental and eclectic approach, Nesmith introduces other elements into the First National Band's unique mix: the Mexicali and German music that he sees as part of the Texas musical landscape. "The underlying influence is Latin," he explains. "Much more Mexican, what was to become Tejano. Tejano music has the 'German meets the Mexican upper-influences.' That music played in the background of what I was doing. But culturally it was really in the forefront. So it was the Latin influence that was the most significant in my music, though the least noticeable because I didn't know *how* to play it. What I did know how to play was country & western, folk music, and other things I was playing. As I matured as an artist I began to recognize those Latin influences. There's a big Mexican-Latin influence in the band's sound." Tracks like the oom-pah bass of "Silver Moon," the infectious Latin rhythm of "Tengo Amore," and "Lady Of The Valley" illustrate those influences. Nesmith also reprised the Monkees' "Listen To The Band," revving it up to a more urgent pace. Though less country than their debut, "I Fall To Pieces," "Silver Moon" and "Thanx For The Ride" show that the band had not forsaken its country roots, and the tracks showcase Nesmith's Texas drawl and Rhodes' impeccable steel guitar.

*Loose Salute* is a solid effort, and remains Nesmith's favorite of the First National Band trilogy. "I think it's the best of the three," he maintains. "Sonically it's much more interesting, there's a lot of stuff going on that is very interesting. But I have to say I think all three are very close to each other in excellence. I'm very proud of all three of them." "Silver Moon" reached Number 42 as a single, but the album notched a less impressive Number 159.

Since parting company with Douglas Dillard, Gene Clark had been up in Mendicino in northern California, writing songs and considering his next move. In January the Burrito Brothers coaxed Clark out of seclusion to attend recording sessions. He was among friends with the Brothers. "There was sort of an on-again, off-again thing with Gene Clark and the Burritos," notes Rick Roberts. "He'd played with Chris and Michael in the Byrds, and with Bernie in Dillard & Clark, so they all wanted to help Gene get going again. We recorded two or three songs with him, and he came and sat in with us on a few shows from time to time. It was Chris Hillman's idea, and I thought it was damn nice of him. He's a good-hearted man." The Burritos recorded Clark's "Tried So Hard," as well as backing him on "Here Tonight," a lovely country number that had the elements of a hit single had it been released. "During that period there was a lot of back and forth among the bands," observed Clark. "People were doing sessions with each other. We were all signed to A&M at the time." "Here Tonight" is more commercial pop than previous Burritos' efforts. The pleasant experience motivated Clark to record a long overdue follow-up solo album to his 1967 effort with the Gosdin Brothers. Released in August 1971, *Gene Clark* (better known as the *White Light* album) was produced by ex–Taj Mahal sideman Jesse Ed Davis. It was a beautiful effort, an unparalleled powerhouse of acoustic folk rock. Despite limited sales, *White Light* stands as a masterpiece of contemporary folk music.

Between May 1970 and April 1971 the original five Byrds sat in on two tracks intended as Gene Clark singles. "She's The Kind Of Girl" and "One In A Hundred" feature that distinctive electric twelve-string sound, and the beautiful harmonies that only the Byrds could deliver. Acrimony among the five caused the tracks to be made piecemeal: each member laid down his part separately, rather than working with the others in the studio. Yet the results are still stunning. Perhaps due to Clark's "reputation" at various labels the songs remained in the can for several years before emerging on his *Roadmaster*, a record released in the Netherlands, where Clark's name was revered.

In May the third Flying Burrito Brothers album was released to a mixed response. Following the failure of *Burrito Deluxe* and the unceremonious departure of Gram Parsons, the group was in dire need of a shot in the arm. Further, the inability of country rock acts to break through commercially was inducement to retool the group's sound. Producer Jim Dickson's commercial instincts, in harmony with Hillman and Roberts' material, inform the record. The third effort presents an updated sound, more pleasant, less country, a slicker style that fit in well with the emerging soft rock sound of California. Often maligned by die-hard Burrito purists for what they perceived as a sellout, the album offers some strong original material. Much of that is due to Rick Roberts, who wrote or co-wrote seven of the ten tracks on the disk. In bringing in Roberts, the band was trying to find the right mix of country influences in rock and pop. Though they failed, the third album set the stage for the Eagles, who ran with the opportunity. Chris Hillman steps forward too, and although the outing is often cited as a product of Roberts' presence, Hillman's influence is strong and clear. That the young artist Roberts could add so much input is due to the fact Hillman allowed him the latitude. It was, after all, Hillman's band. "I wasn't trying to take over the band," says Roberts. "Chris was the leader. I was much more pop-oriented and we were going in that direction." It is clear that Hillman was looking to the future, not the past. The lyrics reveal a greater degree of sophistication when compared to the rather shallow writing that marked *Burrito Deluxe*.

The Burritos pay homage to their country influences on the opening track, Merle Haggard's "White Line Fever." Roberts' "Colorado" follows that track, and is arguably the finest song on the album, a sensitive ballad underscored by Sneaky Pete's subtle pedal steel. Roberts brought the song with him. "I wrote 'Colorado' in California. I hitchhiked from South Carolina, stopping off in Colorado. When I got to California and things weren't going well for me I really got lonely, and I started thinking about going back to Colorado. That's what motivated that song." Linda Ronstadt later covered the tune. Roberts' "Four Days Of Rain" is another polished pop gem, a song he crafted during a tour of Amsterdam.

Roberts and Hillman's four collaborations, all sung by Chris, are much less country and much more commercial, revealing a mellower side to the Burritos' sound. The exception is "Can't You Hear Me Calling," a cut dominated by Bernie Leadon's chugging Telecaster work. The presence of Pete's steel guitar lends the only country flavor to the tracks. Hillman also does an exquisite cover of Dylan's "Ramona," and he and Roberts cover Gene Clark's "Tried So Hard" adroitly. The album closer features Leadon on banjo on Roberts' "Why Are You Crying." Recalls Roberts, "I wrote 'Why Are You Crying' overnight just before the record was completed and the band liked it." It was a last-minute addition to the record.

The third Burritos album is a consistent and original effort from a group not content to rest on its laurels. It is an attempt to take country rock forward into a more mainstream pop sound, rather than carry on with endless George Jones retreads. Had the lineup stayed together for one more record the results may have been interesting. "The album we made with Rick wasn't bad," admits Hillman, "but it wasn't anything near the original concept. It strayed into a more middle-of-the-road, mellow rock sound." Diehards and critics disagreed, skewering the band for abandoning its original principles for the sake of a commercial breakthrough. The album was a disappointment anyway, peaking at Number 176 before disappearing entirely.

There was discord among band members about the new direction. Sneaky Pete saw the move as misguided. To his dismay, much of the steel playing is kept low in the mix throughout the album. "I think that was a mistake," notes Pete. "It changed the identity of the band considerably. Before, we had a distinct identity. Having a steel doing all the solos was really what gave the group a distinctive style. I was just honing my style to the point where I was more sophisticated and could bring more to the albums. And so I thought it was time to get out."

Sneaky Pete resigned that April, citing "irreconcilable musical differences." With his session schedule busy, he wasn't worried about money. "I was more and more dissatisfied with the material," states Pete, "and with the performances, which never seemed to get any better. I was already getting so many calls as a studio musician that I could live on that alone." The introduction of Rick Roberts' more commercial material held no appeal for Pete, who saw no future with the Burritos as pop makers. Pete chides Roberts gently, "I really appreciated Rick's style of singing, but his approach changed the whole complexion of the group, and I don't think the Burritos had the same appeal after the first album. It was going into a tailspin. Our original audience had loved the rough edge and the originality of the first album."

Although his misgivings are heartfelt, Pete remains positive about his time in the first incarnation of the Burrito Brothers. "It was a real opportunity for me to get out on the road and see what that lifestyle was like. I certainly don't regret the experience. Every steel player I knew went the Nashville route. I don't know many players who have taken off in my direction. That may have made me unique."

"Sneaky's leaving came as a surprise," recalls Roberts. "It was the night before we were to start a weekend engagement at a little beach club in L.A. Sneaky called and said, 'I'm out.' We thought we were through as a band, but Eddie Tickner still had a couple of tricks up his sleeve and told us about this kid named Al Perkins who had been bugging him about work. We brought Al in for a rehearsal and he was great. He was in. And we carried on." With Shiloh's prospects looking dim following the disappearance of their debut album, Perkins was the first to abandon ship. "We weren't making much money," Perkins notes. "We had done a few small gigs, and we played the Troubadour several times. Then I got a call to replace Sneaky Pete in the Burrito Brothers. I auditioned on a Saturday and was on the road with them the following Monday."

Don Henley was restless and disappointed by Shiloh's failure to break through, so when Perkins quit he began formulating his next move. "Our spirits just got lower and lower," states Henley, "until Al Perkins left to take up an offer to join the Burritos. That ended Shiloh. The record did nothing, and we were all flat broke. I was hanging out at the Troubadour getting drunk a lot, and getting ready to go back to Texas."

The sudden dissolution of Amos Records brought matters to a head. "Al was replaceable," suggests Mike Bowden. "There was no problem with that. What brought the band to a standstill was Amos Records folding. As soon as it did, Glenn Frey approached Don. Glenn and J. D. Souther immediately went to David Geffen when Amos folded. Asylum Records was just starting, and J. D. said he wanted a solo deal. Glenn pitched Geffen this band concept, which would become the Eagles. Geffen went for it."

With Longbranch Pennywhistle dead in the water and Souther keen to pursue solo interests, Frey had somehow finagled an introduction to David Geffen. Geffen was just coming into his own as a recording mogul, involved with Crosby, Stills, Nash, & Young, and Joni Mitchell.

Frey convinced Geffen to take him on if he could assemble a suitable band. "I had just played a couple of songs for Geffen," noted Frey. "Geffen told me point blank that I shouldn't make a record by myself, and that I should join a band. Then Linda Ronstadt hired·me." Ronstadt was to be the conduit to the formation of one of the seventies' most successful bands, the Eagles. She recruited Frey and Henley, and the nucleus formed over the next few months. "It was two days before rehearsal was supposed to start," continued Frey, "and they still hadn't found a drummer. Henley was just standing right there in the Troubadour. So I struck up a conversation with him. I told him I wanted to put together a band, but I was going on the road with Linda. We were both at impasses. So he joined Linda's group too. The first night of our tour, we decided to start a band." Added Henley, "Glenn kept telling me about David Geffen. I didn't even know who he was, but I decided I would stick my neck out to play with Glenn." They were joined by the Bowden cousins, Mike and Richard, who were also in Ronstadt's band.

Mike Bowden claims Linda had her eye on Shiloh from the first night they debuted at the Troubadour, playing "Silver Threads And Golden Needles," and was waiting to catch them when they fell. "As soon as Shiloh broke up, the thing with Ronstadt happened almost immediately. Don, Glenn, and I were all in her band at one time. The very first job I ever played with her, I'd never even rehearsed with her. I sort of auditioned to a tape of her music, and I got hired on the spot. The first show was at Terminal Island Prison, opening for Kris Kristofferson. We just stepped onstage cold, no rehearsing. Talk about a jolt of electricity. She looks timid when you see her onstage, because she's always been uncomfortable with that, but when she opens her mouth to sing, she really wails. She really kicks ass. That was me, Glenn, and Don. We went out on the road but by that time the Eagles thing was already in motion. Later they talked Linda into letting Randy and Bernie back her just to see how the band was gelling. So actually the Eagles backed her on a few dates." Bowden recalls a rivalry in the Geffen stable over the band. "Jackson Browne liked her band a lot and was trying to steal us away from Linda at one point. There was some friction going on, and so Linda went to Geffen and told him to tell Jackson to back off."

In early 1971 Randy Meisner returned to the Stone Canyon Band after his stint at a John Deere dealership. During his absence, Nelson had recorded the uneven *Rick Sings Nelson*, produced by Ronstadt's manager John Boylan, who had been instrumental in nudging Rick toward country rock. Nelson found he needed Meisner's high-harmony contributions. "Tim Cetera was a real good player," acknowledges Pat Shanahan. "When Randy decided to come back it was hard to let Tim go, but we *needed* that voice. He had that real high-end voice, so when you want a male singer who can do that, he's who you want." Explains Meisner, "Allen Kemp called me and told me the job was open again, so I went back to L.A. and rejoined Rick for another six months." With Meisner back in the fold, Nelson and the group recorded *Rudy The Fifth*, a logical successor to *Rick Nelson in Concert*. Offering a harder edged country rock sound on tracks like "This Train," as well as a cover of the Stones' "Honky Tonk Women," the record also demonstrates Nelson's admiration for Dylan on two tracks, "Just Like A Woman" and "Love Minus Zero/No Limit." *Rudy The Fifth* is a solid country rock effort. As a songwriter, Nelson's talent was growing, though many of his compositions were weak. Released in April, the album was a critical success but a commercial failure. And it wasn't long before Meisner once again became restless and quit. "I love Randy and he's probably one of the best people in the world," sighs Shanahan, "but he never knows what he's going to do next."

John Boylan suggested Meisner fill in for Mike Bowden at one of Ronstadt's gigs to see if Henley and Frey could work with him. Meisner failed to impress Ronstadt during the two-night stand, earning several steely glances from her during her sets, but his band mates were impressed. "I played with Linda Ronstadt up in San Jose at Chuck's Cellar," states Meisner. "That's where I met Glenn and Don. Linda was a little uncomfortable with my bass playing. I played a little busy, and liked to play a lot of notes. I learned from Henley to lay down with the bass drum, that's one good thing. That's where Glenn and I met and discovered that we got on pretty well playing together." Frey had already formulated his lineup with Henley on board. Meisner, who had won Glenn's admiration during his time in Poco, was the next piece.

Early in the recording process for their next album, *Roots And Branches*, Herb Pedersen bowed out of the Dillards over musical differences. "I quit for a number of reasons," states Pedersen. "I respected Rodney for his direction, but I wanted to try other things. I was more into a country-oriented thing and he wanted to get into really hard rock with the Dillards' kind of stuff." Rodney had turned to Richard Podolor to produce the new album, but Pedersen clashed with him. "Herb wasn't happy during the sessions for *Roots And Branches*," recalls Dean Webb. "Richie Podolor was famous for doing Steppenwolf, Three Dog Night, and all them." Podolor's production style was wreaking havoc on Pedersen's marriage. "We'd spend three or four days at a time in the studio," adds Webb, "and Herb was married to a woman who didn't appreciate that, so he left during the album sessions."

*Roots And Branches* was a departure for the Dillards, with Podolor bent on transforming the group by updating their approach. In so doing he lost much of the essence of what had been so endearing on their two previous albums: the group's simple, homespun charm. Recruiting ex–Kentucky Colonel Billy Ray Latham on banjo and guitar, the album suffers from the loss of Pedersen's vocal contributions and songwriting. Though their distinctive harmony remains intact, it is not as silky smooth as it had been on *Wheatstraw Suite* or *Copperfields*. Podolor's production is very aggressive, and the vocals are mixed high. It doesn't *sound* like the Dillards, which is a problem. Opening with Rodney's "Redbone Hound," the use of fuzz-toned banjo against harmony singing jars the ear, marring the track. "Forget Me Not," "One A.M.," and "Billy Jack" are fine examples of the Dillards' country rock, while "Sunny Day" highlights the group's superb harmony work. A cover of Gib Guilbeau's "Big Bayou" works well, as does the obligatory a cappella "Man Of Constant Sorrow," which introduces subtle mandolin play. "Get Out On The Road," punctuated by Paul York's heavy drumming, is the closest the Dillards ever got to rock & roll, though the banjo and mandolin provide a bluegrass foundation. Still, the Dillards fail as rockers. In the end, *Roots And Branches* is an uneven effort from a group that had temporarily lost its focus in a bid for commercial success. "That's my least favorite of our albums," states Dean Webb.

The Dillards' record label, Anthem, had high hopes for *Roots And Branches* after its parent company, United Artists, scored a major coup by placing the group on Elton John's *Honky Chateau* tour. "Elton John surprised me by how much he liked our music," marvels Dillard. "He came to see us at the Troubadour. The next thing I knew we were on tour with him. That brought us a whole other audience." The elevated profile resulted in mild success for *Roots And Branches*, and it sold faster than any of their previous releases. Yet critics seemed confused by the changes, and once the tour was over, and the album disappeared, the group returned to what they did best, acoustic bluegrass.

In June the First National Band issued *Nevada Fighter*, the last of Nesmith's trilogy. "I was intrigued with the whole notion of American music. So a lot of what I was doing was making kind of American folk songs without any real awareness that I was executing a concept. We ended up with red, white, and blue albums and it just sort of fell together; it didn't come together out of some long-ball vision. It just happened over eighteen months. I didn't realize it was a trilogy until it was done, then I thought, 'Well, far out, that's a trilogy.'"

The First National Band fragmented during the recording sessions for the third album. John London and John Ware exited, and Nesmith and Red Rhodes turned to Elvis Presley's band to finish the project. Notes Nesmith, "Because the *Magnetic South* album had done fairly well, Felton Jarvis and I had become friends. He was spending all his time with Elvis. Johnny Ware wanted to stay a little more country. And I said I didn't think those songs accommodated that, so I told him if he didn't want to do it I'd get Ron Tutt to come in and play. That seemed better to him so he left. So on that third album it was basically Elvis' band: Ron Tutt, James Burton, Glen D. Hardin, but Jerry Scheff didn't play. Joe Osborn and Max Bennett played bass."

Of the three albums, *Nevada Fighter* represents the most successful realization of Nesmith's musical concept. The material meshes perfectly. Much of the record is original compositions by Nesmith, but it included covers of Clapton, Harry Nilsson, Bill Martin, and Michael Murphey. The idea of segueing from "Texas Morning" into "Tumbling Tumbleweeds" is a masterstroke, and a high point on the record. Recalls Nesmith, "I had known Mike [Murphey] a long time. When I heard 'Texas Morning,' the connection between it and 'Tumbling Tumbleweeds' was immediately apparent. There is a place in West Texas called Van Horn, on the road from El Paso to Abilene. There's absolutely nothing out there. The first thing that greets you is a tumbleweed blowing across the highway. When I heard that song I thought of that imagery, a desolate stretch of road in Texas, and joining the two songs just made sense."

Nesmith does a credible version of Clapton's "I Looked Away," and a nice interpretation of "Rainmaker" from Nilsson and Martin. The original material, notably the beautiful "Propinquity" and the lilting "Here I Am," stand out on a strong record. Nesmith returns to the Texas two-step waltz time for "Only Bound" and ends with a breezy instrumental from Rhodes. "That album depends much more heavily on the material than the execution," he acknowledges, "though the playing is top-drawer. It didn't have the kind of lyrical sensibility that *Loose Salute* did, which is why I'd give *Salute* the edge. But there are some serious players doing some serious music on it." Even the usually flamboyant Rhodes lays back on the effort, allowing the songwriting to shine on its own. Despite the absence of a hit single, the album rose to a respectable Number 70 on the charts. "Every once in awhile I'll put all three on and after hearing them I feel I don't have any apologies to make," reflects Nesmith. "If anything, they improve with age." Nesmith retired the First National Band moniker and formed the Second National Band, a more eclectic aggregation allowing him to explore more than just country rock. He would remain committed to furthering the development of country rock, and form his own label to that end in the seventies. Countryside was a record company dedicated to recording unknown country artists and promoting their careers.

Like Sneaky Pete, Bernie Leadon was also disappointed with the Flying Burrito Brothers' new direction. Despite the fact the band would showcase him during a popular bluegrass interlude in their live performances, he found himself shut out of creative input on the third album. Rick Roberts' vocal gifts also meant Leadon had fewer singing parts. "The change in sound has everything to do with Rick Roberts' arrival," offers Leadon. "I had no writing credit on that third album, and as I had felt in Dillard & Clark, I resented being shunted aside. I understood why Chris was making the decisions he was making. I wasn't able to do the things that Rick could. It was Chris's call."

"Bernie told me he was becoming increasingly unhappy with his role in the band," states Roberts. "He was uncomfortable with the constantly shifting lineup and he was just getting used to that when I came in. There was a new rhythm guitar player and a new second lead singer behind Chris. He had been the second singer behind Chris and suddenly he was shuffled off to doing third harmonies. He and I talked about it at one point and he said, 'This is getting real difficult for me, Rick. If you're going to be permanently in the band I don't know what my role is anymore and I've got to think of my future.'" While the others had welcomed Roberts into the fold with open arms, Leadon had shown more reticence. "The other guys introduced me right away as their new member," notes Roberts, "while for the first six months Bernie would say, 'This is our friend Rick Roberts who's playing with us.'" Comments Chris Hillman, "Bernie and Rick didn't quite hit it off. That was pretty much the clash. It just didn't quite work out."

In July Leadon quit the group and took time off to sort out his options. "I was just fed up, I suppose," muses Leadon. "I felt that by staying, I was restricting my abilities. Sometimes we'd do awful shows; it used to get real embarrassing. We just couldn't be counted on to do a bang-up gig. In the Burritos everyone had just as much talent, but it was difficult to make the best possible use of it with that combination of people." Admits Roberts, "There was a growing distance at that point between all the guys in the band. That was the first step toward the band eventually breaking up. People were starting to look in other directions. The band hadn't achieved the success they had anticipated. There was no progress. We were selling the same number of records and playing to the faithful"

Meantime, Byron Berline saw no future with Doug Dillard & the Expedition, and by mid-1971 had turned in his notice. Following Gene Clark's departure, Jon Corneal, David Jackson, and Donna Washburn had left. They were replaced by Roger Bush (bass) and Billy Ray Latham (guitar and banjo). With the new lineup the group had transformed itself into a straight bluegrass outfit and found steady work in Las Vegas supporting Kay Starr in her cabaret act. When Latham left to replace Herb Pedersen in the Dillards, the Expedition ground to a halt. "It just got to the point where things started getting too weird," recounts Berline on the path he took to the Burritos. "Roger and I split with Doug, and got Kenny Wertz on guitar. Herb Pedersen had just quit the Dillards at that time and Billy Ray went off with them, so Herb came up and played a bit with us in Kay Starr's show. About that time Chris Hillman asked me if he could use Kenny Wertz to tour and record with the Burrito Brothers. He invited me too, so I went. We went out with Michael Clarke, Chris, Rick Roberts, Al Perkins, and Kenny. I talked Chris into taking Roger Bush along too. We were all in this big old bus while we did *Last Of The Red Hot Burritos*."

Donna Washburn left the Expedition to back Joe Cocker on his infamous *Mad Dogs And Englishmen* album and tour. Douglas Dillard embarked on a solo career, releasing a number of fine bluegrass albums, including several with Rodney. The two Dillards and Byron Berline appeared in the film and on the soundtrack of Bette Midler's *The Rose*. Douglas Dillard did more soundtrack work before reuniting with the Dillards for a 1989 tour. The Douglas Dillard Group received a Grammy nomination for *Heartbreak Hotel*. He continues to thrill audiences with his amazing banjo pickin'.

After several albums and years on the road fronting the Dillards, Rodney Dillard now manages Caravell Studios in Branson, Missouri. He is currently working on a Dillards box-set retrospective. In 1979, Herb Pedersen reunited with Rodney and Dean Webb for *Decade Waltz*, a Dillards disk released by Flying Fish Records featuring several songs by former Hearts And Flowers leader Larry Murray.

The reconstituted Burritos hit the road once again with Hillman, Roberts, Berline, Perkins, Clarke, Wertz, and Bush, doing well on the college circuit. "We developed a great live act after all those years of being sloppy," boasts Hillman. "The crowds would go crazy over that bluegrass set, and we'd do some hard rock and some country." Adds Roberts, "During our live shows we would do a flat bluegrass section in the middle. Chris would play mandolin, Bernie would play banjo, and I'd play acoustic guitar, doing bluegrass stuff like 'I Am A Pilgrim.' I'd do that flat-picking, and after about five minutes my right arm was ready to fall off. When Bernie left, we brought in some really good bluegrass players. Roger Bush had been with the Kentucky Colonels and Byron was three-time national fiddle champion. That lasted about six months."

Gram Parsons returned to the United States after an extended stay in Europe with the Stones in southern France. It had been said he had entered a detoxification program for heroin with the help of ex–Sub Band member Ian Dunlop. Gram liked what he saw of the new Burritos. "Byron Berline and Al Perkins added something that had been missing from the Burritos," he told interviewer Chuck Casell. "Which was real quick musicianship, and spontaneity." A&M Records, noticing the band's improvement, sent producer Jim Dickson and engineer Eddie Kramer to record several shows for a live Burritos album.

There is an Eagles legend that Bernie Leadon, fortified by alcohol, joined Linda Ronstadt onstage during a gig in Disneyland without invitation. Glenn Frey and Don Henley were in her backup band, and, far from being offended, fell into an instant rapport with the interloper, agreeing then and there to form a band. It's a nice story, but somewhat exaggerated. The reality is less romantic. Frey and Henley were aware that they needed players like Leadon and Meisner for a solid foundation. "Glenn told me about Randy Meisner and Bernie Leadon," remembers Henley, "and said we needed to get those guys because they could play the kind of country rock we were all interested in." Leadon relates what really happened: "I had already been a member of three different bands on major labels. I was twenty-four years old. Randy had been in The Poor, Poco, and Rick Nelson's Stone Canyon Band. We were well known among the players and producers. Glenn and Don had arrived more recently. Near the end of the Burritos, Sneaky Pete left. Chris came up with Al Perkins as a replacement. We went on the road that summer and I got to know Al pretty well. He was telling me about Don, that he was an amazing singer. I filed it away. I'd been on the lookout for people of exceptional talent. I could see the Burritos drying up. I had also seen some Longbranch Pennywhistle gigs and knew Glenn and J. D., but I didn't know Henley. Then a girl at Mc-Cabe's told me that Henley and Glenn Frey were looking to start a band and that John Boylan was helping them putting it together. I put out word I was interested. Within a few days Boylan called and invited me to a rehearsal at SIR." And what of the Disney story? "That was after that first rehearsal. Linda was playing, they were all playing and I came down. Both things happened right around the same time."

With Meisner already on board Leadon was the last piece of the puzzle. "Honestly, what made them invite me," say Leadon, "was the fact I was doing a pickup gig sitting in with David Grisman, Clarence White, and others down at the Ash Grove. They came by and saw me up onstage with guys of that level holding my own on banjo, and they were impressed." From the start the chemistry was perfect. "We were in this rehearsal space, and everybody played the songs they had. And I thought, 'Man, this sounds pretty good.' Mostly Glenn had the songs at the time, Henley wasn't really writing. He only shared a co-credit on that first album with me on 'Witchy Woman.'"

Each of the four members had been playing country rock for several years, with little success. They chose a broader approach, combining elements of country rock, rock & roll, bluegrass, hard rock, and rhythm & blues. What resulted was the Eagles sound, the sound of California soft rock, an explosively successful formula that other country rock ensembles only dreamed about, with multiplatinum success.* "I don't think there was a conscious decision to do country rock," stresses Leadon. "The Eagles combined all the influences from my early musical development: folk, country, and pop rock. I didn't have to pick one or the other any more, I could just do a bit of all of them. We were a synthesis of all the sixties music." Meisner explains, "Frey and I really liked rock & roll. Glenn had that Detroit, rhythm and blues thing. Henley had been into that—that's why he had that gravelly voice, from belting out behind the drums over the other instruments and lousy PA systems. And Bernie brought an acoustic element. He had the Burrito Brothers influence. He was a monster acoustic player. And I was blessed with this high voice."

Having been on the periphery of the country rock scene for a couple of years, Frey had seen the missteps of others. "We decided not to use steel guitar in the band. When we first were putting the band together we had our choice of steel players, but we decided to stay away from

*While this book was being written, the *Eagles' Greatest Hits* surpassed Michael Jackson's *Thriller* as the bestselling record ever.

that. And with just four guys there's a lot more air in the music. And Don Henley plays a different kind of drum, and Randy Meisner a different kind of bass, so our rhythm section was a little heavier than Poco or the Burritos had."

Meisner claims Frey wanted J. D. Souther in the new group, and that he had been against the idea. "I had a strong feeling that the Eagles wouldn't have been the same with J. D.," asserts Meisner. "But I stood up and said no because Glenn and J. D. had been partners before. The rest of us had all been with different groups. I felt strongly that it would be better if just the four of us formed the band because of all our backgrounds from different areas of the United States. Having one partner that we had worked with before could influence the decisions and dynamic." Even so, Souther became, in many respects, the "fifth" Eagle, contributing significantly to their songwriting and direction over the next few years.

With a lineup set, the new group needed a name and a manager. Recalls the Byrds' Gene Parsons, "Those guys were friends of ours. I remember them sitting Clarence White and me down in a little coffee shop in Laurel Canyon and telling us the name. Clarence and I went, 'That sounds pretty good.' And they did really well with it, obviously." Al Perkins remembers with a laugh first learning the group's name. "Tommy Nixon, a roadie who had played bass in a group from Texas called Friendship, came up to a rehearsal and said to me, 'Don and Glenn are rehearsing their new group and it's sounding really good.' And I said, 'Have they got a name?' I thought Tommy said, 'The Egos.' Thinking about those guys, I said, 'Well, I guess that fits.'" Leadon responds, "We were all reading books about the Hopis, and in Hopi mythology the eagle is the most sacred animal with the most spiritual meaning."

Frey's connections with David Geffen brought the future mogul on board. Recalls Meisner, "Glenn and J. D. had been trying to get a deal with Geffen. So when the Eagles thing came along, Glenn was instrumental in getting us with Geffen." Adds Henley, "Geffen had no idea what we sounded like, and here comes Bernie walking in saying, 'Okay, here we are. Do you want us or not?' It was a great moment. Geffen kinda said, 'Well . . . yeah!'" Geffen's first order of business was to give the band the space to develop as a unit, and to create their own style. He arranged for them to play a lengthy stand at a club in Colorado. "The Gallery in Aspen was a small dance bar where everybody just danced and drank until they fell down," recalls Meisner. "We did four sets a night for a month of songs we'd written and filled out the rest of the set with covers from the Beatles, Chuck Berry, and Neil Young. It tightened the group up, and then we went to play a club in Boulder, Colorado, a place called Tulagi's."

In the face of large-scale desertions from the country rock field, the Nitty Gritty Dirt Band took the opposite tack. Following the release of *All The Good Times* in 1971, which included Doug Kershaw's Cajun-flavored "Diggy Liggy Lo," Hank Williams' "Jambalaya," Richie Furay's "Do You Feel It Too?" and Jackson Browne's "Jamaica Say You Will," the group headed to Nashville to record with many of the pioneers of modern country and bluegrass music. The result of the band's traditionalist bent would be the legendary triple album *Will The Circle Be Unbroken*, a milestone in the integration of country and pop, and a seminal bridge between longhaired California country rock and Nashville. The sessions were the brainchild of Dirt Band banjo player John McEuen. His brother William, the group's manager and producer, was instrumental in making the dream a reality.

"It would not have happened without Earl Scruggs," maintains John McEuen. "I wanted to record with Earl. Nobody knew of him, and I wanted to let people know where I had learned banjo. A lot of this came from the college gigs we were doing as a result of our hit 'Mr. Bojangles.' These were inquisitive people who wanted to know the roots of this music. So I asked Earl Scruggs *and* Doc Watson if they'd record with my band. We went to the record company and got $22,000, to make *Circle*." The McEuens had to convince the remaining Dirt Band members. McEuen recalls, "They didn't want to go to Nashville. It was something I started that Bill put together. Though originally doubters, the others came to appreciate the importance of the project. Sure, it was a gamble but that's what makes any artist successful."

The three disks were recorded live in Woodlands Studios in Nashville, without the benefit of overdubs, during a ten-day stretch. The band also managed to recruit Merle Travis, Roy Acuff, and Mother Maybelle of the legendary Carter Family. Bass player Junior Husky, Dobro masters Norman Blake and Pete "Brother Oswald" Kirby, guitarist Jimmy Martin, and fiddling sensation Vassar Clements rounded out the backup band. Bill Monroe refused to participate in the project, citing his contempt for "hippies." Everyone received equal billing on the album sleeve. "Most of the songs were done in the first or second take and mixed live rather than remixed later," recalls McEuen. The song selection runs the gamut of traditional country and bluegrass standards like "Wildwood Flower," "I Am A Pilgrim," and "I Saw The Light" to a brief instrumental reprise of Joni Mitchell's "Both Sides Now," by Randy Scruggs. "The original idea was to select a double album's worth of the best stuff," recalls Dirt Band guitarist Jeff Hanna, "but we decided it was all best stuff and we ended up using just about all of it, so it is sort of like a portfolio of traditional country music."

Released in early 1972, *Will The Circle Be Unbroken* went platinum and earned the Dirt Band three Grammy Awards. "I think that album helped Nashville realize that we respected their music, and might take their music to a new audience," cites John McEuen. "We brought people who didn't listen to country and bluegrass to that music. The Nashville market accepted the album well, as did the younger, long-hair crowd. We got letters like, 'My father and I never understood each other for thirty years. I bought the *Circle* album because of you guys and I brought him in to listen to it and he was dazzled. From that day forward we've been the best of buddies.' I think it broke down some barriers." The *Circle's* success opened doors for the Dirt Band, who turned squarely in the direction of Nashville, notching an impressive string of hit singles on the country charts. "We found a comfort level in country music by the early eighties," offers McEuen. "Jeff felt more comfortable in Nashville. Rodney Crowell was writing songs there and gave us a couple. It was tough because it wasn't band-oriented music in Nashville at the time. It was primarily a male singer thing. Then in the eighties came a lot of the groups. Alabama helped open that up."

Greenwich Village singer/songwriter Paul Siebel released *Jack-Knife Gyspy* on Elektra in 1971. Crack mandolin player David Grisman, Clarence White, steel player Buddy Emmons, and young fiddle sensation Richard Greene (of Seatrain) backed his effort. Siebel's first record, *Woodsmoke And Oranges*, had contained a wealth of country material that Linda Ronstadt, Ian Matthews, Rick Roberts, and Bonnie Raitt would eventually cover. Siebel's plaintive "Louise" and the yodeled "She Made Me Lose My Blues" were already staples in country rock repertoires, though the songwriter was largely unknown outside the East Coast. The record company promoted *Gypsy* with more urgency than it had with *Woodsmoke*, yet commercial results were negligible. Nonetheless the album is a true gem of Dylanesque country rock. Siebel's nasal voice and his clever lyrics draw comparisons to *Nashville Skyline*. Siebel remained a folk circuit favorite over the next decade, but commercial success continued to elude him.

Having integrated guitarist Paul Cotton, Poco had entered Trans Maximus Studios with high hopes, only to be short-circuited by the severe limitations of the studio, and the indifference of producer Steve Cropper. The resulting album, *From The Inside*, issued in September 1971, was an uneven effort. "*Inside* was not a fun record to make," remarks Rusty Young. "Steve Cropper was drinking pretty heavily, and was more interested in jamming with the band. Clive Davis was pretty hot on us. But they lied to us about Steve's production experience and the quality of the studio facilities, which they told us had twenty-four tracks. And we really needed twenty-four tracks, because we had so many vocals and so many guitar parts. Clive Davis told us we had to do the record *now*, management was saying 'Can't you make it work on sixteen tracks?' The whole thing was a mess." Drummer George Grantham terms the atmosphere of the album "darkish." Even the photo of the group on the back cover reveals the prevailing somber mood of the album sessions.

Cotton injected a solid rock punch into Poco's sound. Enthuses Grantham, "What a great writer, singer, *and* player! He brought a rockier edge to the group." Ironically, Cotton contributed what many feel is Poco's quintessential country rock number, "Bad Weather." The combination of Cotton's husky voice, mellow steel guitar, and the group's gorgeous harmonies elevate the track. "I think 'Bad Weather' is probably one of the best songs I'd heard," acknowledges Richie Furay. "I *love* that song. It was a way of showing we could complement him as he enhanced us." Explains Cotton, "'Bad Weather' dates back to the Illinois Speed Press. It was about the demise of the first version of that band. And when Richie learned that beautiful guitar solo it just blew me away." It's Furay, never known as a lead guitarist, who plays the intricate acoustic solo in the middle of the number. Cotton's other contributions, "Railroad Days" and "Ol' Forgiver," are solid tracks featuring his heavier rock style. "I was trying to stay positive," notes Cotton on the problem-plagued sessions. "It was my first album with these guys. But the whole thing really forced us to hang out together, away from our families and friends."

For his part, Furay was suffering personal problems that colored his contributions to the album. "I was in a very dark place during the sessions," he confesses. "Nancy and I were going through a difficult time in our lives. And you write about those things in your life, too. 'Do You Feel It Too' was brought up again after we had tried it around the time of the first album sessions, and we redid it in a heavier rock & roll style.

That was just the mood I was in at the time. It was not a good song."
Indeed, a recording of their original attempt at the song has recently
been re-released on the *Pickin' Up The Pieces* CD and reveals a much
more engaging number than the heavy version on *Inside*. Cotton noticed Furay's anguish. "Scared the heck out of me. His mood was more
introspective at that point." The title track, from Schmit, shows his mat-
uration as a songwriter. Young's co-credit on the infectiously upbeat
"Hoedown" marks his move away from strictly instrumental compositions. Young's pedal-steel work is surprisingly subdued throughout
the album, quieted perhaps by the band's moves toward a harder rock
sound.

Despite the difficulties, *From The Inside* did fairly well on the charts,
reaching Number 52. Compared to *Deliverin'*, which entered the Top
30, it was a disappointment. Reviewing the album in *Rolling Stone*, Stu
Werbin termed it "pessimistic," noting the album lacked inspiration
and energy, for which he blamed Cropper.

Linda Ronstadt's next solo album, released in the fall, finally deliv-
ered on the promise only hinted at on her previous efforts. Everything
seems to come together for her on this album: the song selection, playing, and production. Titled simply *Linda Ronstadt*, the album has a con-
sistency and quality lacking from her two earlier albums. Her tastes in
bluegrass and country are well represented too. Gone are the Goffin and
King pop covers and Nashville country standards, replaced by material
more reflective of Ronstadt's personal tastes, including covers of Jackson Browne ("Rock Me On The Water"), Neil Young ("Birds"), and Liv-
ingston Taylor ("In My Reply"). The record also features an outstanding
cover of Patsy Cline's "I Fall to Pieces," as well as covers of Johnny
Cash, Eric Andersen, Ray Price, and Woody Guthrie. The future Eagles
show up on much of the album in various groupings, while Sneaky
Pete, Herb Pedersen, Gib Guilbeau, Buddy Emmons, and the Bowdens
can be heard on various tracks. Ronstadt was held in such esteem that
she was always able to pull in the country rock elite to support her.

Mike Bowden recalls the making of the record. "It's got a rawness
about it that's real charming; I guess it captured an era. About half of it
was recorded live at the Troubadour. There are a lot of musicians who
have said they'd wished they'd been a part of that album." For Frey,
Henley, Meisner, and Leadon, it was a fitting farewell to the lady who
had played a key role in bringing the Eagles together. The album set the
stage for her phenomenal success in the late seventies. Following this
album, Ronstadt signed with David Geffen's Asylum Records.

The Burritos were booked for a four-night stand at Washington, D.C.'s, Cellar Door club in early October. It would be their last tour in preparation for a final album. Despite setting audiences afire since expanding their bluegrass set, founder Chris Hillman was frustrated at the group's lack of momentum and looking elsewhere. Following the Burritos last set Rick Roberts and Kenny Wertz went out and chanced to wander into a tiny folk coffeehouse. The singer providing the entertainment for the handful of disinterested patrons that night was a waif-like young singer, Emmylou Harris. That encounter would have a profound impact on the course of both country rock and country music. Aware that they were in the presence of a rare talent, Roberts immediately called Hillman to hear Harris for himself.

As Roberts tells it, "Chris and I had talked about adding a female singer to the group. I went to this club and listened to this woman sing and she knocked my socks off. I called Chris and said, 'Get down here!' He was furious that I had bothered him. He said, 'Yeah, I'll come down there but you're not gonna like it.' Chris comes in the door looking all around and by the time he got to our table he wasn't even looking at us, he was looking over his shoulder at Emmylou, smiling. We had Emmylou sit in with us the final three nights at the Cellar Door." At the time, Harris' repertoire leaned more toward folk than country. As Roberts recalls, "Emmylou wasn't doing country then. She was doing a lot of Joni Mitchell, Judy Collins, the kind of catalog that most folk singers in clubs did. The closest country she was doing was Canadian folk country, from Ian & Sylvia, and Gordon Lightfoot."

Born in Birmingham, Alabama, Harris at first considered a career in acting while attending college in North Carolina. Working as a waitress and sometimes singing to support her young daughter, she began playing clubs along the eastern seaboard. By the time she met the Burrito Brothers in Washington, D.C., Harris had already recorded an album of folk standards on the tiny Jubilee label in 1969. She needed a break, being at loose ends with her career. Harris began integrating the odd country number into her sets to broaden her appeal, and found she possessed the kind of voice and phrasing that could be adapted to country with ease.

"I was playing down the street at a bar called Clyde's, which was sort of a singles' hangout place," recalled Harris to writer Sid Griffin, "but they had this room that didn't draw a crowd so someone got the idea to hire musicians to play. Rick Roberts came in with Kenny Wertz who was playing with them then. I got up and sang 'It Wasn't God

Who Made Honky Tonk Angels.' Chris asked me to come sit in with them. There was real strong talk about me joining the Burritos." Clarifies Hillman, "We talked and we got to know her. She sat in with us and sang. I was impressed. I said, 'You really should sing more country songs, they're great, they're really magical.' We parted company and I told her it would be great to do something with her someday."

Roberts says he met Harris briefly years before their Clyde's encounter. "My friends Bill Danoff and Kathy Nivert of the Starland Vocal Band had brought Emmylou up to the Philadelphia folk festival where I met her, but didn't hear her sing. She was a beautiful woman. She had made a record prior to that with a company out of Alabama and had given up music in favor of a family but had gone back to it."

Whether the Burritos considered Harris for their group is uncertain. Hillman, Perkins, and Roberts were already recording with Stephen Stills' new project, Manassas, on off days. In any case, the young singer left an indelible impression on the members of the Burrito Brothers. As they headed out to their next engagement they were happy to learn that Gram Parsons, back in Florida to visit family, was going to visit them to catch up on old times. Recalls Roberts, "Gram joined us at the airport and rode with us over and sat in that night. He didn't look anything like I'd expected him to, not the thin country rocker. He was healthier and beefier than before. We were telling him all about this incredible singer we had heard. Gram had such a good time sitting in with us that he decided to come up to Baltimore with us. The whole time Chris and I kept talking about this woman we had seen. After the gig Gram made a beeline right to D.C. He looked up Emmylou, saw her, was knocked out like we were, and asked her to join him right there." Parsons was considering a return to recording, and was on the lookout for a female voice to harmonize with. Hillman had urged him to check out Harris. Parsons' attempt to convince Harris to come pick him up in Baltimore was a request she refused. Perhaps familiar with Parsons' reputation, the young singer turned him down flat. In the end, Parsons took the train down to Washington to take in one of her sets.

"He was a vague name in my mind," acknowledged Harris. "I was not really up on what was happening in the music world. I was completely out of the scene for a long time. I was struggling to make a living. I liked country music, but not on a very deep level. It was like day and night, the time before and the time after I met Gram. He hadn't sung for a long time at that point, and I wasn't aware of what he had inside of him as an artist. Yet the first time we sang together our voices seemed to blend well, even though I hadn't done a lot of duet singing." Impressed with Harris' talent, Parsons proposed they team up. She put him off until he convinced her to come out to California in the summer of 1972 to help him record his first solo album. It was a match made in honky-tonk heaven. "We had been talking about asking Linda Ronstadt to join," suggests Roberts. "I told her about that much later and she replied, 'I'd have done that in a minute.' But things take their own courses. I don't think we ever actually officially asked Emmylou to join the Burritos, but I think she made the right decision because she and Gram made a great duo."

During that same tour, Stephen Stills had called Hillman to assist him with a double album set encompassing a number of genres, from rock to bluegrass, country, and Latin rhythms. "We were doing the live album *Last Of The Red Hot Burritos* and playing weekend gigs," recounts Roberts "Chris, Al Perkins, and I would fly down to Miami on Sunday night and stay there until Thursday, recording the first *Manassas* album with Stephen." Adds Al Perkins, "About the third trip down there they had a little impromptu meeting and Stephen said he'd like to start a band with us. Chris and I were both offered the job in Stephen's band." That band would become Manassas.

"It was time to leave," Hillman remarks on the Burritos' demise. "It was the right thing for me. I couldn't see going on. We couldn't get on either country radio or rock radio. I had a good time working with that Manassas band. It was a whole other level of musicianship, and made me learn a lot. I like being kept on my toes, and I was getting complacent in the Burritos. Those guys in Manassas were great players. At that point in his life Stephen was peaking. There were times of brilliance with him. I learned a lot about leadership from him, too."

Roberts wasn't asked, but Berline turned down an offer to join. "Stephen contacted all of us to come down to Miami to record. Afterward he asked me, Chris, and Al Perkins to join his band. I already had a deal with United Artists. Then Stephen Stills called me and asked me to go to Europe with him and Manassas. I told him I was committed, but he offered to pay my bandmates to sit and wait. And I said no thanks. I didn't like his lifestyle much. I'd seen what was going on in the studio staying up for days doing drugs. I played on the second Manassas album with Roger Bush and we could hardly play to it. It was the most god-awful stuff. He sent it to Ahmet Ertegun at Atlantic, who sent it back and told him to do it again."

Perkins was disappointed with the Burrito Brothers' dissolution, but without Hillman he saw no future for the group. "I was having a ball because it was the first touring band I was in. We had some problems with tempos and things like that, but the other guys were sort of acting like they were whipping a dead horse. They wanted more success. But that was, in my opinion, a real country rock group. I think the Flying Burrito Brothers with the right lineup and given more time could have been a strong influence, the Rick Roberts lineup. He was a very good singer and songwriter and Chris had songs to contribute. It might have been pretty interesting."

"We were at a point in our career that we would take whatever work was there," admits Roberts. "So it made for some odd couplings sometimes. We were opening for Sha Na Na in upstate New York. Needless to say we didn't go down well. By the same token, we were too rock to be billed with true country artists. One of the weirdest bills we did was at the Fillmore East with the New York Rock & Roll Ensemble and Albert King. Talk about *eclectic*. But I have nothing but good feelings about the Burritos. It was my initiation into the recording business, and a chance to get to play with the big boys."

But the Burritos weren't done. With a series of December dates in the Netherlands, where the group was still revered, it fell to Roberts to cobble together a group to fulfill outstanding commitments. "I got stuck leading the band," confesses Roberts. "When the Burritos finally did disintegrate, Chris and Al went off to Manassas, Michael went off to Hawaii, and the other three guys we had in the band became Country Gazette. I was going to take a little time off and then work as a solo artist. I had a solo offer from A&M. Nonetheless we had a tour booked with deposits in that had been spent to cover outstanding bills. I agreed to do the dates. So the promoter said, 'As long as you've got some of the guys who were there last year, come back.' The guys in Country Gazette said they'd do it, and we came up with some other people; it wasn't a bad band, but it was understood it was just to fill obligations." Recruiting Berline, Bush, Wertz, and Alan Munde from Country Gazette, and adding drummer Eric Dalton and Don Beck on pedal steel, the pseudo-Burritos were embraced by Dutch audiences obsessed with country rock. "I'd never been to Europe," admits Berline. "The crowds would come unglued when we played bluegrass. They just went wild. I got to experience what being a superstar was like over there."

The only downside for Roberts was the surreptitious recording made of the performances. Entitled *Live In Amsterdam* on the obscure Bumble label, it was unauthorized. Promises that the record was for the Dutch audience proved to be lies. The album later showed up in America and Canada. The members saw no money from the project.

Country Gazette cashed in on the Dutch hunger for American country, scoring a surprise hit single with a cover of Gene Clark's "Keep On Pushin'" from their wonderful debut album *A Traitor In Our Midst*, produced by Jim Dickson. The album, a lively mix of traditional and contemporary bluegrass, also includes Clark's "Tried So Hard" and Bill Martin's "Forget Me Not," previously recorded by the Dillards.

In the mid-seventies Sneaky Pete resurrected the Flying Burrito Brothers with a lineup including Chris Ethridge, Gib Guilbeau, Gene Parsons, Skip Battin, and Joel Scott Hill. They recorded albums for Epic Records and other independent labels. The current lineup, led by Guilbeau and ex–Rick Nelson sideman John Beland, doesn't even include Pete. "They've tried to keep the Burritos name going in various different lineups, to Chris Hillman's dismay," notes Al Perkins. "He thought he'd put it to bed once and for all back in '72."

In December Johnny Cash introduced Rick Nelson and his group at the fabled Ryman Auditorium in Nashville when the Stone Canyon Band performed for the Grand Ole Opry. Unlike the chilly reception given the Byrds three years earlier, the welcome was warm. Rick's standing as a member of television's first family, and his reputation as a pioneer of rockabilly, might have made the audience more receptive. It was a breakthrough event for the country rock genre, despite the fact that no other acts of the type followed his lead.

# 9

# Take It Easy: 1972

*It's funny, I never realized how good Gene was until about two years ago. I knew he was good, but I didn't know how good. He was a monster. Everybody's going on about Gram, but you should listen to Gene. Here was a guy who was not well read, but he could write lyrics that would make your hair stand on end. He was the best songwriter in the Byrds.*

—Chris Hillman, on the late Gene Clark

The Flying Burrito Brothers could not have picked a finer way to go out than with *Last Of The Red Hot Burritos*, released in March 1972. Solid evidence of what the group was capable of on a good night, it is no-holds-barred, energetic country rock, with an emphasis on rock. Clearly, it's Chris Hillman's turn to shine, and he does so admirably in the honky-tonkin' "My Uncle," the bluegrass mandolin of "Dixie Breakdown," and the thumping bass lines of the group's rocking rhythm & blues cover tunes. It is Hillman's finest hour in a long and illustrious career, and it finds him front and center, the lead singer on eight of the nine vocals. "We had a really good live show," notes Hillman of the live album. "It's ragged, but it's good because it has excitement and energy." On *Last Of*, the Burrito Brothers ride off in a blaze of glory, a fitting epitaph to a gifted and unique group of musicians.

Recorded during several dates in their final touring days, the album boasts the expanded seven-man lineup, including the Country Gazette additions Byron Berline, Kenny Wertz, and Roger Bush. The inclusion of a bluegrass interlude energized their shows. From there, through a number of well-chosen rhythm & blues tunes, the Burritos transform into a pure rock group, with Hillman's thunderous bass driving the rhythm, and Al Perkins' electric lead guitar work icing the cake. The album shows Perkins at his best. Between his scintillating steel and lead guitar, it's apparent what a major addition he was for the group. His steel work on "Devil In Disguise" (a tribute to the late Girl Together Outrageously, Miss Christine) and "Hot Burrito #2" is inspired, and his (uncredited) lead guitar on "Ain't That A Lot of Love" and the funky Pickett/Cropper number "Don't Fight It" is electrifying. "I had been drawn to the Clapton and Hendrix style of lead guitar, as much as you could use that style in country rock," acknowledges Perkins. "I'm uncredited on the live album, but it's a matter of deduction. Whenever you hear the steel, there's no lead guitar and whenever there's lead guitar there's no steel. But I was dismayed that they forgot the credit."

The latter-day Burritos choose to present their version of rhythm & blues in a rock context, unlike *Gilded Palace Of Sin*, where pedal steel dominated the record. Hillman's "Gimme-Some-Lovin"–style bass on "Ain't That A Lot Of Love" serves notice that it's Memphis, not Nashville, he's emulating. Stax singer James Carr's "Losing Game" opens with a Beatles *Get Back* riff, and adds some uncredited piano to the track. Hillman thrives in the rhythm & blues sound, and might have enjoyed success as a soul stirrer had he chosen that direction. The three bluegrass numbers that round out the live effort demonstrate the depth and versatility of the final Burritos lineup. "If you listen to the live album there's no overdubs on the audience responses for the bluegrass segment," boast Perkins. "They just went crazy for it. It was like football touchdowns." Byron Berline's fiddlin' leads those numbers, and a hyperactive take on the fiddler's showcase "Orange Blossom Special" caps his addition to that part of the record. Berline expresses some reservations over that rendition, preferring the cut he did with the Dillards on *Pickin' And Fiddlin'*. Groused Berline, "That 'Orange Blossom' is *the* most terrible job that I've ever done. They released it because of the crowd reaction, they just went wild. The performance wasn't all that good."

After playing a pivotal role in reshaping the Burritos on the previous record, Rick Roberts respectfully steps back on *Last Of*, allowing Hillman the spotlight. The absence of new original material was no coincidence. "We wanted to save our new material for a new album," says Roberts. "That album never materialized because the band broke up. While we were making the live album and down in Miami during the week working on that Manassas album, I told Chris, 'It's obvious

Stephen wants you in his band. I think you'd be happier doing that, so if you do I'll have no hard feelings.'"

Reviews were glowing, both the album's high energy level and Hillman's performance as leader drawing kudos. Bud Scoppa, in *Rolling Stone*, dubbed the album "Fast, pounding rock & roll from start to finish, as if the group wanted to go out with a bang instead of a twang." Unfortunately the record stalled at Number 171 on the charts: the Burritos just couldn't get any respect.

Gene Clark returned to the studio in the spring of 1972 to follow up *White Light* with a new effort for A&M. Eschewing a stripped-down folk approach, Clark enlisted session stars from the country rock community to provide support on the new outing. Boasting the talents of Clarence White, Sneaky Pete, Michael Clarke, Chris Ethridge, Byron Berline, and pianist Spooner Oldham, and produced by Terry Melcher's right-hand man Chris Hinshaw, the record fell into limbo for a year.

"The sessions were a lot of fun," recalled Clark, "but the record company didn't like it when I was finished." Clark went back to another dormant project for several months, re-mixing and in some cases re-recording vocals on his 1967 solo album with the Gosdin Brothers. That effort was re-released later that year as *Early L.A. Sessions* on Columbia Records. The results were somewhat disappointing, though the album did bring Clark's woefully neglected work to the attention of many who had never heard the original album. Commented Clark, "We were all just a little bit ahead of our time, I think. No country rock sold well until after 1969."

Following a year of sitting in the can, the sessions were gathered together and released in the Netherlands as *Roadmaster*. *White Light* had been voted by Dutch critics the top album of 1971, and Clark was still a star in that country. It's a melancholy record, with the title track the only up-tempo cut. Nine Clark originals, most slow and somber, are an intriguing insight into the songwriter's heart, and the supporting playing is sympathetic and tasteful. Though never intended as a complete album, *Roadmaster* holds together as a cohesive effort. The Byrds' tracks that round out the effort are strong, notably "One In A Hundred," which Clark had cut as an acoustic track on *White Light*. This time McGuinn's twelve string transforms the song from folk to folk rock. "Here Tonight" should have been a hit: it's a potent combination of Clark, Burritos' harmonies, and Sneaky Pete's flowing pedal steel. One of the cuts, the remarkable "Full Circle Song," would be re-recorded a year later on the Byrds' reunion album for Geffen's Asylum label. The title cut of *Roadmaster* is a bluesy Freddy Weller number featuring White's lead guitar. Sneaky Pete contributes lonesome train whistle sounds to a mournful "I Remember The Railroad." Clark transforms the Byrds' "She Don't Care About Time" into a somber slice of lyricism a la Dylan. The album closes with "Shooting Star," a rock number with what sounds like a synthesizer but is in fact Pete's steel guitar filtered through a fuzz-tone and mixed high in the fade-out.

*Roadmaster* is a stellar country rock effort from an artist often better remembered for his contributions as a Byrd. The vaunted Byrds reunion of late 1972, which yielded the disappointing self-titled album the following year, did return Clark to critical attention due to his contributions on the record, which are considerable. His reworked "Full Circle" opens the album on a high note, but the record falls short from there. Clark would go on in the next decade, releasing brilliant albums like *No Other*, to scant notice beyond the faithful. His work with the Silverados in the seventies marked a return to country rock. Teaming with Hillman and McGuinn in the late seventies produced a couple of albums, but when Clark's performance and behavior become increasingly erratic, the two dropped him. An evening at the Palomino in late 1982 reunited Clark with Hillman, Herb Pedersen, Al Perkins, and Emmylou Harris for a rousing performance. Talk of a possible album remained just that, though Perkins and Pedersen did join Clark in some country rock sessions, the trio calling themselves Flyte. Clark would also tour in a Byrds tribute group, which included The Band's Rick Danko and ex-Burrito Rick Roberts. While work with Carla Olson and the Textones revived his sagging career in the mid-eighties, alcohol problems plagued Clark until his death on May 24, 1991.

John York feels Clark's contributions are neglected in evaluating the evolution of country rock. He points out, "The music that Gene Clark created was very innovative. I don't think even Gram did anything that was as innovative. If you analyze Gene's music in terms of chord structure and imagery, it was *very* different from what other people were doing." Because his contributions to country rock are considerable, the fact that Clark's legacy remains largely overlooked is unfortunate.

June saw the release of the Eagles' eponymous debut and a new era in country rock. "Take It Easy," a Frey/Jackson Browne collaboration, rose to Number 12, heady territory for a country rock single. Recorded in London with Glyn Johns producing, *Eagles* was a harbinger of things to come. Boasting solid songwriting, tight harmonies, uncluttered playing, and a freshness not heard since Poco's *Pickin' Up The Pieces*, *Eagles* is the total package, and aimed directly at the mainstream market, which the group would dominate over the next few years. The record is the culmination of what had begun with the Dillards in 1965.

"Glyn Johns had a lot of influence on the sound of the Eagles," acknowledges Randy Meisner. "He wanted that country sound. He brought us to what it *should* be. All he wanted to hear were those great harmonies. He sparked the whole Eagles sound." Despite his previous experience with hard rock, Johns had an affinity for country music, which is what attracted him to the Eagles. Bernie Leadon relates how Johns came to work with the group. "Glenn Frey wanted the best producer in the world. Glyn Johns had done the Stones and the Who. Glyn came to see us in Colorado and he didn't much like what he heard. We saw ourselves as a rock & roll band with other abilities, trying to pretend we were the Stones without the weight to pull it off. *He* knew it. He's produced them. He thought we were second rate. Only our connection to Geffen brought him back for a second look, which he *still* didn't like. It wasn't until one or two of us picked up acoustic guitars during a break and we began doing what we had been doing in vocal rehearsals that he sat up and took notice. It was like how Dillard & Clark was originally created: we sat, singing harmonies with acoustic instruments, and we were singing four-part harmony. He flipped out. 'That's it! You guys are out of your freakin' minds doing this other shit. That's it. If you want me to work with you I will, but I'm going to make the *vocals* happen.'"

Following engagements in Colorado, the group had returned to L.A. to record some demos. "That's when things like 'Witchy Woman' started happening, and Jackson Browne was involved. We started writing songs and looking for a producer," recalls Meisner. "We did some demos with Bill Halverson, who had worked with the Stones. He had a real nice bass and drum sound, but that didn't work for us." It took Johns to define the group's sound, building on their vocal strength and not their instrumental prowess. At Geffen's insistence the group went to London to record. "Geffen wanted us out of town because we partied too much," laughs Meisner. "If we were isolated, he reasoned, we'd be focused—and it worked." Johns' no-nonsense studio ethic proved difficult for the band. Marijuana breaks were taken clandestinely, outside the studio door like school kids getting high on the sly.

*Eagles* boasts seven original numbers and three covers. Gene Clark and Bernie Leadon contributed "Train Leaves Here This Morning."

"Nightingale" was written by Jackson Browne, and songwriter Jack Tempchin wrote "Peaceful Easy Feeling." Henley's lone co-credit on the debut is "Witchy Woman." Meisner contributes three numbers. States Randy, "I never wrote for Poco. The Eagles convinced me to try and write. But still to this day writing is real hard for me. I needed co-writers and I wasn't fast enough, like Henley and Frey became." Leadon's songwriting experience with Dillard & Clark and the Burritos serves him well. But it's Frey who contributes most of the original material. Lead vocal chores are shared by all, leaving the impression the group was an equal partnership.

"Take It Easy" starts the record, leaving no doubt the album is *country rock*. The number is a smooth country rocker, graced with Leadon's terrific guitar break and gorgeous harmonies from the band. It is the Eagles' signature tune. Remarked Henley a few years later, "We got put into that country rock category. No matter how much our music would change, we would never escape that category." "Witchy Woman" is more rock and less country, with Henley's gritty voice leavened by the pristine harmony vocals. "The Eagles had four competent singers," explains Leadon, "and because I had a lot of arrangement expertise from being in choirs when I was a kid, I understood the concept of divergent parts. We constructed things where you could have a lead and a third above doing one part, and there could be some background doing oooh's or aaah's coming in with two or three parts. So we had people jumping from singing a harmony behind a lead on one verse to being a voice in a three-part blend behind. Where most bands had maybe one, two, or three good singers, we had four—and we knew how to use them."

Frey's "Chug All Night" rocks hard, while the softer, more introspective side of his writing comes through in the plaintive "Most Of Us Are Sad," a neglected gem from Frey that Meisner sings. Randy's high voice is well suited to the number. Though Henley and Frey would come to dominate the sound and direction of the Eagles on later albums, Meisner and Leadon contribute a lot to the debut. Side two belongs to Randy and Bernie, although "Peaceful Easy Feeling" is sung by Frey and features Leadon using a Clarence White stringbender. Meisner recalls that he was so excited about the group's potential his energy was boundless. "I used to go in two hours early, I was so enthusiastic about the project." Meisner sings both "Take The Devil" and "Tryin'," the closing number, where his high vocals soar. "Earlybird" lets Leadon shine on banjo *and* vocals, which he shares with Meisner.

The debut illustrates both the strengths and weaknesses of the country rock genre. The Eagles avoided the pitfalls that befell other contenders by choosing to add country rock to a rock & roll base. While their harmonies, instrumental work, and feel draw from country rock, the group broadens their appeal by playing solid rock & roll. The proof is in the pudding: the album rose all the way to Number 22, while three singles also scored on the charts ("Take It Easy" at Number 12; "Witchy Woman" at 9; and "Peaceful Easy Feeling" at 22). The Eagles were the first country rock band embraced by AM radio. They were, for all intents and purposes, the best of both worlds. But the question most often raised by pundits remains: Are the Eagles country rock? On the basis of their debut release, the group shows solid country rock influences without being exclusively a country rock outfit.

Members of the country rock fraternity applauded the Eagles' debut. "I have respect for them," notes Chris Hillman. "I think they are great. But they are really an extension of what preceded them: the Burrito Brothers, the Byrds, and the Buffalo Springfield. It's a real heavy family tree."

Adds Rick Roberts, "I thought the Eagles were excellent from the get-go. Those guys knew what they wanted to play. They were very directed. I was really happy to see it happen for guys who played and sang as well as they did."

Paul Cotton sees the Eagles sound integrating the various facets of the genre into a commercially viable sound. "The Eagles fine-tuned the whole machine. They didn't take long to figure out what was missing. They knew what to put in and what to leave out." Notes Rusty Young, "The difference between *Pickin' Up The Pieces* and *Eagles* is huge. They could be played on AM *and* country radio, and we couldn't. They made *commercial* music, and we never did."

Though acknowledging their talents, Mike Nesmith feels that Geffen deserves a lot of the credit. "The Eagles' success was due to David. It was his management, his record label, and his money. He was really the architect of the Eagles, in the same way he was architect to Linda Ronstadt's later career. But it was Glenn and Don who did it. The songs were well-crafted, and the group was very focused and went after it with a vengeance. That was really the lightning in a box. It's way too easy and probably mean-spirited to say they crassly commercialized country rock. Everybody was trying to make a hit out of country rock. It was their hard work that made it happen. We all owe them a debt of gratitude. And at the end of the day they're really, really good."

The previous October, Rick Nelson agreed to perform at an oldies concert at Madison Square Garden. Though he had resisted such overtures in the past, Nelson reluctantly took the booking in order to promote *Rudy The Fifth*. It was a decision he would regret. Sharing the roster with Chuck Berry, Bo Diddley, Bobby Rydell, and the Coasters, Nelson was billed as "the Special Added Attraction." The mistake became evident when the band took the stage: longhaired, and clad in their denim bell-bottoms, they faced a sea of ducktails and bobby socks. Nelson wisely opened with his early hits, which the crowd responded to well. But when he began to introduce his new material the audience turned on him. Dylan's "She Belongs To Me" and the Stones' "Honky Tonk Woman" were met with boos. Nelson was shaken by the experience, sitting in his dressing room in stunned silence in the aftermath of a disastrous reception brought on by the colossal blunder of accepting the gig. "Considering where I was musically I had no business doing a nostalgia concert," remarked Nelson. "When I have a hunch deep down that something is wrong for me, and I go against that judgment, I always regret it." Musing further, he remarked, "My hair was a lot longer. The physical appearance, combined with the new band—I had a steel guitar player at the time—made the decision to take the gig an error in judgment. But I figured as long as I was there and I was singing the songs, it wouldn't make much of a difference."

"Rick went over really well, a lot better than he thought he did," maintains Tom Brumley. "*Somebody* booed up in the audience. I actually never heard it, but he did. Somebody told us later that the cops were taking somebody out for smoking pot and that's what they were booing, not Rick. But back in the dressing room Rick was sitting there so dejected and said, 'Oh Tom, why'd I do this? I wish I'd never done it.' But the reaction *was* a positive one. I think he was prepared to misread it because he didn't want to do it."

But Nelson's cloud had a gold lining. Continues Brumley, "About three weeks later he sang me 'Garden Party.' I thought it was a little strong but that song said so much. When he sings, 'But if memories were all I sang, I'd rather drive a truck,' he was just saying what he felt. He felt very satisfied when it became a hit."

"Garden Party," released as a single in early summer, climbed slowly, peaking at Number 6 by late September. With sparse backing, Nelson avoided obscuring the message with the instrumentation. And that message was pointed: This is who I am now, I'm not what I used to be. Following the success of the Eagles' "Take It Easy," "Garden

Party" was a clear indication that country rock was growing in popularity. The *Garden Party* album, an effort with more emphasis on rock, boasted a rare Kemp-Meisner collaboration, "I Wanna Be With You." It sold well, earning a Number 32 on the charts. Rick Nelson was back, and on his own terms.

Unfortunately, the success of the record sparked discord in the band. Shanahan, Kemp, and bass player Steve Love walked out just prior to Nelson's gold record presentation for *Garden Party*, in March 1973. The players were angry that their pay stayed the same while their boss's appearance fee had swelled. Concedes Shanahan, "We were young and stupid. We were pulling good money for then, but Rick had his cousin managing, and we felt he was trying to keep us down. We figured, 'Here's this big star and we're not getting much money.' We were told we'd get a raise once we hit the college circuit, but management reneged. But we didn't go to Rick and tell him his manager wouldn't give us the raise he promised. We decided to teach Rick a lesson and go out on our own. We asked Tom if he wanted to go with us and he thought it was a bad time to leave. We announced to Rick that we were leaving. I look back at it now as some stupid kid move. I regret it. I should have stayed with Rick. But that's what happened." Shanahan, Kemp, and Love attempted, unsuccessfully, to launch themselves as Canyon before going their separate ways.

Nelson recruited replacement players, including guitarist Dennis Larden (from Every Mother's Son), but the magic was gone. *Windfall*, a follow-up released in early 1974, failed to chart like *Garden Party*, and the Stone Canyon Band folded. Nelson made the road his home for the next decade doing as many as 250 dates a year. Unable to sustain *Garden Party*'s success, he turned more and more to the loathsome nostalgia circuit, billing himself once again as Ricky Nelson. Brumley left in 1979, finding the pace too grueling. Financial woes plagued Nelson in later years. In an ironic twist, Randy Meisner purchased his former boss's Canyon home after the Eagles rose to prominence. Rick Nelson died tragically, in a plane crash shrouded in rumor and innuendo, on New Year's eve 1985. At the memorial service his twin sons sang an a cappella version of Rick's ballad "Easy To Be Free." The assembled wept.

"Rick is passed right over when people talk about country rock," laments Brumley. "Rick was around doing that stuff in the fifties, when he had that rockabilly sound with James Burton. Musicians and artists recognize his role, but the media never has." Unfortunately, Nelson is given scant mention in reference books for his contributions to either rockabilly *or* country rock.

The Great Speckled Bird had lost much of their fire by 1972 after Buddy Cage and Amos Garrett left and the group turned to television work. Signed to Columbia Records, Ian and Sylvia had released a well-received album, *Ian & Sylvia*, recorded in Nashville. It featured two of Ian Tyson's most enduring country songs, "Summer Wages" and "Some Kind Of Fool." "Fool" was written during the Great Speckled Bird's 1970 visit to Japan, and sung at the close of his television show each week. With the continuing popularity of *The Ian Tyson Show*, the label was anxious for another Great Speckled Bird effort. Released in mid-1972, *You Were On My Mind*, billed as "Ian & Sylvia with The Great Speckled Bird," has a far more mainstream country sound than the Buckaroo-influenced debut two years earlier. Retained from the former lineup were drummer N. D. Smart II and bass player Jim Colegrove, with newcomers David Wilcox on lead guitar and former Nashville session man Ben Keith on steel. Keith also assisted in production, a position he served for Neil Young whenever the enigmatic artist took a country turn.

Notes Colegrove, "We recorded that album at Toronto Sound. Ben Keith ended up being the producer. John Hill was the producer, but Ian didn't like his work. Ian was a *very* tough guy to work for, but I got along with him pretty well." Smart, on the other hand, did not. "Ian almost fired me one night," laughs the outspoken drummer. "The movie *Little Big Man* was out and I had the makeup people do me up like I was ninety-five years old. Ian went *ballistic*. They had to stop taping the show so I could get the makeup off." Recalls Tyson, "N. D. Smart was a troublemaker, a real redneck jerk. He played drums fine, but I wouldn't put up with that kind of nonsense now."

The album includes songs by the Tysons together and individually, as well as a cover of Robbie Robertson's "Get Up Jake," an obscure B side from The Band. The sound is pure country. "The Speckled Bird only did seven tracks on *You Were On My Mind*," explains Colegrove. "The others included only David Wilcox and Bob Walker. There were great internal changes going on. The former lineup was more Buckaroos, while the latter was more mainstream country, although there is still some rock there." A remake of Sylvia's "You Were On My Mind" works well in a country arrangement, but much of the material is low-key and melancholy. By then Ian and Sylvia were spending more time apart, Ian with his television show and ranch, Sylvia in Toronto raising their son Clay. The couple would divorce in the mid-seventies.

For Ian Tyson, memories of the Bird are bittersweet. "It was an off-shoot of Ian and Sylvia," he muses philosophically. "A fork in the road that we explored, like Lewis and Clark— a tributary that we traveled up with sincerity, until mutinous forces within our group and rejection by our recording company brought it to an end."

In 1974 Ian released a solo country album, *Ol' Eon*, on A&M Canada. He was backed by the last vestiges of the Great Speckled Bird, many of whom were serving double duty, backing Gordon Lightfoot as well. The album shows Tyson well equipped to compete in the pure country market, and it remains a personal favorite of his. Disappointed at his failure to make inroads in Nashville, Tyson would turn his back on music for several years. He produced Sylvia's solo debut around that time, before packing up his guitar and heading out west to Alberta, much like the character in his "Someday Soon," which Judy Collins would bring to prominence.

On the changes and tumult of the time, Sylvia Tyson reflects, "I think it was a gradual thing. Members changed and the nature of the band changed. Bands tend to be transitory. Musicians come and go. And Albert Grossman showed less inclination to be a manager and more interest in being at his restaurant." Adds Smart, "The band became more generic, less distinctive. Due to the TV show, we became a professional studio band. Ian was settling down and didn't want to go on the road anymore. It's real boring to do TV: hours of boredom punctuated by a few minutes of sheer terror." Smart headed to California to work with Hello People, later hooking up with Gram Parsons. Ian Tyson quit the show abruptly at the end of the 1974–75 season, eventually buying a ranch in the foothills of Alberta to raise cutting horses. The ranch was partly financed by a healthy check from Neil Young after he recorded Tyson's "Four Strong Winds" on his hugely successful *Comes A Time*. Tyson returned to music in the eighties with a series of critically acclaimed albums of western music for Stony Plains Records. Sylvia released a number of solo albums, became a popular Canadian radio personality, and formed the singing group Quartette.

Fueled by a renewed sense of purpose, Gram Parsons returned to the studio to make his first solo record. Signed to Reprise Records, Parsons had an album's worth of new material. With Emmylou Harris supporting him on vocals, and backed by the talents of a number of the country rock fraternity (including Al Perkins, Byron Berline, and members of Elvis Presley's band, James Burton, Glen D. Hardin, and Ron Tutt) Gram was sky high on the project. It was partially funded by Parsons himself after Reprise balked at the costs. Hugh Davies, who worked with Merle Haggard, engineered the project, while Parsons and Rik Grech (formerly of the British supergroup Blind Faith) assumed production duties after Merle backed off. "I began getting ready for a solo album in earnest about eight months before I went in the studio," claimed Parsons in a 1972 interview. "It took a lot of mental preparation. When the time came, I was lucky enough to get good people to help." He mentions Emmylou in the interview, crediting Chris Hillman with discovering her.

Barry Tashian, a friend from the International Submarine Band days, joined the effort. Recounts Tashian, "Gram called me and told me he had this girl singer he admired. I hadn't been doing too much music at that time so I welcomed the invitation. I was out there for six weeks for that album." Tashian recalls Parsons' mood during that period. "Gram was really *up* for the sessions. It seemed like an historic moment. He seemed to have a good sense of direction, but he still had his weaknesses—he would drink too much and be a little shaky in the studio. There was a lot of pot smoking and drinking going on. And his rehearsal habits were anything but disciplined. He had his human frailties and temptations." Tashian has no reservations about the direction Parsons was taking. "It was a country album, not rock. Gram never liked that term country rock. He was playing country music." Confirms Perkins, "Gram was doing country but when you would look at him you'd see a young guy with long hair."

Rehearsals were held at Byron Berline's house. "I taped all those rehearsals," recalls Berline, "and erased them later. Man, I wish I still had those! Gram needed a place to rehearse and Eddie Tickner wanted him to get his mind on the music. We were working through the tunes. That stuff was country. He loved country. But Gram had a lot of soul and put a lot into it. Gram was in pretty good shape until we got into the studio that first night and he got pretty whacked out. Everybody told him, 'Look, you've got another chance now. Straighten up.' And he straightened up for the next few days."

Once Parsons rolled into the studio, the album took shape quickly. Openly contemptuous of the Eagles' sound as "soulless bubble gum," Parsons poured his heart and soul into the record, determined to create a strong country statement. Despite Parsons' clear vision there were problems beyond his control. Grech bowed out early, though his name remains on the album credits, due to illness. "Rik Grech had been involved prior to the sessions," recalls Tashian. "It says on the back of the album that he co-produced it, but he wasn't there for most of it. He had a gall blander attack the day before the sessions and went to the hospital." Parsons stepped up, taking the helm by himself. And others stepped up as well. "Glen D. Hardin played a big role in those sessions," notes Tashian. "I wrote out some of the basic charts that showed the chord changes, but Glen D. elaborated on those. He was a seasoned studio pro. I was kind of the outsider at the sessions even though I had known Gram the longest." Nevertheless, Tashian too played a significant role in shaping the material for the resulting album. "I recommended 'The Streets Of Baltimore,' and 'I Can't Dance,' which ended up on the second album. I also suggested 'Cry One More Time,' and 'Burn The Candle,' which didn't make the cut, but was later recorded by Emmylou."

"Emmylou was in awe of the whole scene and very nervous," notes Berline. "She was not as refined as she would be later, but she did a really good job. I think she and Gram knew they had something special going when they started singing for the first time." Adds Tashian, "'That's All It Took' was a song that was really done well. I think Emmylou saw her future with Gram and was delighted by it." In an interview with Sid Griffin, she reflected on her chemistry with Parsons: "We wanted to sing together like George Jones and Tammy Wynette, and it wasn't a thing like anything else. He enjoyed it and he loved singing with me. We were a natural duo. I think he got a great deal of joy from that and it was a mutual feeling." Harris saw more to Gram's music than a sincere appreciation for the country form. "I think he had a way of incorporating culture into his songs," she noted. "Country has always been a traditional form, and he was always injecting incredibly poetic images that were so down to earth. It's like taking Hank Williams' stuff forward. Hank Williams is wonderful, but at the same time, things progress."

Released in January 1973, the *GP* album was a breath of pure country air from a master of the new idiom. *GP* is contemporary country music, a statement of where country music had been, and where it could be going. Incorporating every nuance of the country music form, from George and Tammy duets and country shuffle rhythms to Buckaroo guitar interplay, Parsons shows his profound understanding, and appreciation, of country music. Opening with his own "Still Feeling Blue," Parsons sets the pace with an uptempo honky-tonk shuffle highlighted by Berline's fiddling, Burton's fine Dobro picking, and Perkins' marvelous steel work. "James and I did twin parts, like were heard on country records of the late fifties and early sixties," notes Perkins. "We'll Sweep Out The Ashes In The Morning," another country shuffle, features a magical Parsons-Harris duet, and introduces Harris' solo voice in one verse. "A Song For You" is another new Parsons tune, a gorgeous country ballad made even more appealing by Harris' subtle harmony. Parsons offers solid covers of "Streets Of Baltimore" and "That's All It Took," the latter among the finest examples of their superb vocal blend. "She," a song dating back to Parsons' time working with Chris Ethridge, is the standout track on the album, a plaintive ballad that stretches Parsons' vocal talents to their limit, injecting a raw quality of sincerity and emotion into the song. "The New Soft Shoe," "Kiss The Children," and "How Much I've Lied" offer further evidence that Parsons' gift for writing had returned. The original material on *GP* stands head and shoulders above the contributions on his last effort, *Burrito Deluxe*. "Cry One More Time," a J. Geils Band number, and "Big Mouth Blues" are the only examples of rock on the album. "'Cry One More Time,'—I don't know why but I just took the melody and started singing it," recalls Tashian, "and Emmylou and Gram were singing harmony. So I just sang this song. When the album came out, it didn't have any credits on who was singing on that song. Everybody thought it was Gram."

Despite dismal sales, *GP* was a triumph for Parsons. The album served notice that there was no one operating in the young contemporary country milieu who presented the music better, and no finer blending of voices than Parsons and Harris. It represented the future of country music.

By the time Poco was preparing to record their fifth album, the group had relocated to Colorado, taking up residence in and around Boulder. The new rural setting encouraged greater camaraderie among the five. Notes George Grantham, "We were really close. It was like a family. We'd go out to dinner together and hang out." But the convivial mood could not change the fact that, creatively, the group was in a rut. The five hoped their next studio effort would take them to a higher level of success. They poured their hearts into recording *A Good Feeling To Know* during late summer and early autumn, enlisting the aid of Canadian producer Jack Richardson, fresh from a string of top chart hit singles. Acknowledges Richie Furay, "Our efforts with Steve Cropper had failed. We went with Jack because of his track record with the Guess Who. We desperately wanted to tap into commercial radio."

The success of the Eagles' debut, spawning three hit singles, was in the forefront of Poco's mind-set. "We all had that feeling of, 'Why not us?'" notes Grantham. "They used to watch *us*." Adds Rusty Young, "The record label was telling us we needed commercial product, because the Eagles were happening and everybody saw what it could be." For Furay, watching his buddies (Stills and Young with Crosby, Still, Nash and Young, Meisner with the Eagles, and Messina teamed with Kenny Loggins) scale the heights only deepened his resolve to make the next album the success he yearned for. "I thought for sure that *A Good Feeling* was going to happen," states Grantham. "It was a lot of fun to record. For six weeks we were in the studio every day." In marked contrast to their previous studio experience, a general mood of optimism ran high.

Epic released the title track, Furay's infectious "A Good Feeling To Know," aimed squarely at AM radio. The song was the most commercial track the group had recorded. Audiences loved it, and everyone close to the group felt it was destined to be a hit. "We pinned a lot of hopes on 'Good Feeling'" confirms Paul Cotton. "I'm still not sure why it didn't chart better. We were very disappointed." Issued a month before the album's release in late 1972, the single failed to dent the Top 100, a bitter disappointment for the band. Recalls Young, "We used to have radio program directors come up to us and say, 'Gee, that song is an absolute smash. Why haven't you recorded it?' So we did. I really can't understand what happened. It never really broke through like we expected it to."

Epic issued the album in January 1973 to positive critical response and high hopes. *A Good Feeling To Know* is a return to the optimism and exuberance of *Deliverin'*. The group's intentions are posited immediately with the opening cut, "And Settlin' Down," as Furay shouts out, "Boogie!" and the band follows his lead over the next nine tracks. Furay's three contributions meet his high standards, not encumbered by the introspective musings that weighed down the previous album. The title track and "Settlin' Down" demonstrate that Furay could rock out with the best of them. The powerful "Sweet Lovin'" is almost gospel flavored with its heavenly harmonies. Cotton and Schmit had become first-rate songwriters, and both have several credits on the album. Cotton's "Ride The Country" is a worthy follow-up to "Bad Weather." The heavy guitar riffing of "Keeper Of The Fire," and what he terms his "fat" guitar sound on the slower paced "Early Days," are noteworthy contributions. Schmit's two tunes, the pleasant "I Can See Everything" and the grinding guitar of "Restrain" are strong tracks.

Perhaps the low point of the record is the ill-considered decision to include a cover of the Springfield's "Go And Say Goodbye," which does nothing to improve on the original. The number fails to rise beyond average on an album of high-caliber tracks.

Having so much invested in the album, Poco was disheartened when it rose only as high as Number 69, a poorer showing than even the troubled *From The Inside* album. The group, though still selling to the faithful, were failing to build a larger audience. "Richie had his doubts after that album," notes Cotton, "but we carried on."

Two members of the country rock fraternity issued solo efforts late in 1972. J. D. Souther released his self-produced solo debut on the Asylum label. Given his mystique among the country rock *cognoscenti*, Souther could have recruited the A-list of players to back him, but instead enlisted Glenn Frey and fellow Troubadour habitués Ned Doheny, Bryan Garofalo, and Gary Mallaber. The album cover features the perpetually sullen Souther staring blankly from the cover. Much of the music fits that mood; Souther's well-crafted songs are set in sparse arrangements that hark back to Longbranch Pennywhistle with Eagles-style harmonies. Even on the uptempo numbers like "The Fast One" he sounds depressed. Souther's strength was his writing, with songs like "How Long," "Kite Woman," and "Jesus In 3/4 Time." Listening to his record, his influence on Frey and Henley becomes clear. Linda Ronstadt once remarked that she would get up each morning to make breakfast, while Souther would get up and write a new song. The album is country rock, like the early Eagles' sound, but without the same commercial appeal. As a songwriter Souther had few peers; as a commercial recording artist he still had much to learn.

Rick Roberts' first solo effort stands in stark contrast to Souther's. It was obvious Roberts ached to succeed. Entitled *Windmills*, Roberts' supporting musician credits read like a "Who's Who" of southern California country rock. Three Eagles, three Burritos (Chris Hillman, Al Perkins, Byron Berline), two from Crosby, Stills & Nash (David Crosby and drummer Dallas Taylor), and session stalwart Joe Lala join Jackson Browne and (Leon Russell's Asylum Choir's) Marc Benno on a star-studded effort. Laughs Roberts, "I called in a lot of markers, and used guys that I knew and played with. Don Henley played drums on nine cuts and sang backup. Randy Meisner was on five cuts." The result is a finely crafted set of nine songs, eight of which are Roberts' originals, with the Harlan Howard–penned country classic "Pick Me Up On Your Way Down" the lone cover. In many respects *Windmills* is the logical successor to the third Burritos album, presenting Roberts' confident pop-country-rock style. Roberts' songs are more accessible and appealing than Souther's darker offerings. The elegant "In A Dream," "Jenny's Blues," and the stirring "Deliver Me" reveal his growing maturity as a songwriter. Roberts would follow up *Windmills* with 1973's *She Is A Song*. *Song* is a less satisfying effort, with Roberts trying too hard to cover a wider range on more rock-oriented material. One highlight is a rousing cover of Paul Siebel's "She Made Me Lose My Blues." Roberts pays tribute to his friend Stephen Stills when he does a nice job on the Springfield's "Four Days Gone." Once again, the record features a fine supporting cast, including Joe Walsh and his Barnstorm crew, and several Poco members.

Roberts cashed in on the Dutch's continued fascination with the Burritos when, in February 1973, he led a group dubbed the Hot Burrito Revue on a trip to the Netherlands. Boasting the members of Country Gazette, Eric Dalton and Sneaky Pete, the reception was warm. The tour was a resounding success, with both Roberts and the Gazette performing material from their respective albums and Pete along for the fun. Ironically, while country rock had chosen a mainstream path to success in America, it continued to thrive in its purer form overseas.

# 10

# Farther Along: 1973

*Like everybody else, I fell in love with Emmylou the first time I heard her sing. When I first joined the band I kind of thought of Gram, "God, who is this guy?" He was totally wasted, he could hardly play the guitar, and his voice was cracking. I didn't know his whole story, but I thought, "He's the star of the show, and he's the weakest guy in the band." But I was amazed at Emmylou. She was with a band that was really starting to cook. She was the star of the band.*

—*Jock Bartley, on the saving grace of the Fallen Angels tour*

The country rock community was rocked by two tragic deaths in 1973, and a defection that stalled the momentum of the movement. That same year, the Eagles would release one of their finest efforts only to see it ignored. The failure of *Desperado* to garner the sales figures it deserved would ignite a shift in their attitude, a mind-set less country and more rock, that would ultimately take them out of small halls and put them into stadiums around the world. *Desperado*, despite a weak commercial showing, would set the tone for all the later soft country rock sounds, and impact what would become the foundation of "new country," in both image *and* music. By the end of the year, the first phase of country rock ended. The marketing of a less adventurous, more mainstream country rock would follow, most notably on David Geffen's Asylum label. Unable to sustain a significant commercial breakthrough, pioneers of the genre would either move in a more mainstream rock orientation, or turn squarely in the direction of country music.

It would be left to the next generation of country rockers, Nashville-based artists like Marty Stuart, Travis Tritt, Clint Black, and others to pick up the torch. As spiritual guru to the nineties' alternative country rock movement, known as "no depression," Gram Parsons would inspire a future generation to explore country music's virtues.

Gram Parsons loved to perform. On a good night, if sufficiently lucid, Parsons could be spellbinding. His charm, as well as his heartfelt love of country music, won over the toughest crowds. And he was fearless, baiting hostile "redneck" audiences with his long hair and his hippie attitude. But he hated the grind of rehearsals. Time and again he undermined the quality of his craft with a lack of discipline. His first solo tour in early 1973 was no exception. With the marvelous *GP* released in February, Parsons scheduled a road tour in support of it, a cross-country odyssey in a refurbished Greyhound bus playing clubs and small halls. This was Parsons' version of Dylan's "rolling thunder revue." The cast of characters he assembled for his journey only added to the mayhem: country pickers, rockers, hippies, a mother and child, a jealous spouse, and an ex-con who counted Charles Manson among his friends. This was Gram Parsons and the notorious "Fallen Angels Tour," the story of which has passed into legend.

N. D. Smart II, the wild man of Speckled Bird infamy, was at loose ends when he received a call from Eddie Tickner to join Parsons' touring group. Road manager Phil Kaufman, the self-styled Road Mangler, newly released from Terminal Island Prison, was another unstable element of the explosive traveling party. He had taken Parsons under his wing with the dubious idea that he would look after the southern lad. Recalls Smart, "Eddie Tickner is the straightest shooter in the music business. He said, 'Norman, you gotta do something.' Gram didn't know how to run a band and was too drunk to do it. The first gig was a disaster. We didn't have beginnings, endings, we didn't have shit." Confirms Emmylou Harris, a novice to the road experience, in a later interview, "It was pretty hectic. We worked on *all* his stuff, but Gram knew so many songs we never finished anything. We must have gone over fifty songs, but we didn't finish one. Everyone sat around and played and there was no structure." Rehearsals at Kaufman's house devolved into jam sessions, with an increasingly loaded Parsons calling out his favorite country classics. They never worked out a song completely. Parsons would simply wave them on to another number, declaring the previous attempt satisfactory.

Parsons' reputation as a minor deity from his stints as a Byrd and Burrito Brother may have been undercut by his reputation as a flake, yet it's surprising that he failed to attract the caliber of musicians who had graced the *GP* album. Perhaps his penchant for excess, coupled with his limited budget, restricted his choices. Neil Flanz was a competent enough steel player, but he lacked the virtuosity and imagination of Sneaky Pete or Al Perkins. Newcomer Kyle Tullis was a decent bass player who, working with Smart's solid drumming, kept a consistent rhythm. The odd man out was guitarist Gerry Mule, whose acoustic folk credentials hardly qualified him for Parsons' team. Recommended by his friend Harris, Mule had flown in from the East Coast at Harris' suggestion, but his inexperience as an electric country guitarist was soon glaringly evident. His tenure as a Fallen Angel would be brief. Smart was the only band member with any significant pedigree and experience. Following what, in Parsons terms, was a suitable period of rehearsal, the group set out in early February for their first stop, a three-night stand at the Edison Electric Company club in Boulder, Colorado.

It would prove to be an ignominious debut. Mule's lack of confidence resulted in a lengthy stop at the bar that affected his already limited ability on electric guitar. Parsons drank too much, and, in combination with various chemical substances he was taking, was in no condition to perform at a professional level. "Gram played this little club in Boulder and he was so out of it," recalls Rusty Young, who witnessed the performance. "He was drinking shots of whisky and popping these pills every few minutes that his driver kept handing him. It was sad." Richie Furay termed Parsons' performance "one of the most pitiful things I ever saw." Another witness to the fiasco was a young lead guitar player, Jock Bartley.

Classically trained, Bartley had also studied under jazz great Johnny Smith before turning to rock in his teens. He was a Byrds fan, though unaware of Parsons' brief time with the group. Already a local legend in Boulder after replacing Tommy Bolin in the hard rock group Zephyr, Bartley received a panicked phone call from the club manager after the Fallen Angels' first desultory set. Remembers Bartley, " He told me 'You get down here right *now*! There's a band in town, Gram Parsons from the Byrds.' Thinking he meant Gene of the current Byrds I hurried down and heard their show. The band was really cool, but the guitar player was *terrible*. I realized who Gram was from the Burrito Brothers. After their set, Gram, Emmylou and the Fallen Angels were putting feelers out because they were worried that they'd have to cancel the whole tour." The ill-starred booking was cancelled due to complaints over noise ordinance violations. With time on their hands and a lead guitar dilemma to solve, the Fallen Angels decided to use the layoff to sort out their lineup before moving on to gigs in Texas.

Continues Bartley, "There was a place called the Pioneer Inn in Colorado, about twenty miles up in the mountains, notorious for all the fights that the mountain guys got into, a really raucous place. Phil Kaufman and Eddie Tickner told me to bring my guitar. I set up on the floor right next to Gerry Mule, and he knew *exactly* what was happening. I didn't know the songs, didn't know country, and I was not impressive. But it was my good fortune that the other act that night was a local group who I knew and had sat in with. After Gram's set I stayed there and played and I was *smoking*. So Gram and the others were watching and thinking, 'Yeah, this guy really can play.' They hired me on the spot. I was at the right place at the right time. It was a window of opportunity and I jumped through it. You don't get too many of those, so you've got to take them."

Confirms Smart, "Neil Flanz wasn't happy. 'He ain't country, he's a boogie player.' We were looking for the best guitar player in town. Jock provided the missing piece to get the tour finished." Despite his reservations, Flanz took Bartley under his wing to teach him the set. Admits Bartley, "I was probably the weakest link in that band because I wasn't really country. I didn't have that James Burton feel. What we were doing in Gram Parsons and the Fallen Angels was straight country music." Yet Bartley managed to keep the tour from falling apart.

With Bartley on board, the next order of business was tightening up the group's sloppy play. "After that we decided we had better *really* rehearse," notes Harris. "We went back to the hall and picked about twelve songs and we decided on beginnings and endings and breaks." At that point Smart took over the reins of the group. Surprisingly, he rose to the occasion. "Gram was really in rough shape. I just became like a drill sergeant. I didn't tell anybody what to play, but I made up the sets, counted in the songs, introduced a lot of the songs, and arranged the beginnings and endings so we'd sound like a professional band. I *had* to; Gram was so drunk he couldn't do it. I got a lot of criticism for doing that when it was Gram's show, but I was just keeping things rolling, otherwise it'd be twenty minutes between songs. And I had the most professional experience of anyone in the group. After that they loved us everywhere we went."

Next stop was Austin, Texas, where the newly rehearsed Fallen Angels went down a storm. "We blew the roof off the top of the Armadillo World Headquarters in Austin, Texas," boasts Harris. "In fact, we had to go back and re-do a song for an encore—we had been called back so many times we didn't have anything left." From there, the group headed on to Houston for a four-night stand at the Liberty Hall. During that stand Parsons, Harris, and the Fallen Angels hit their stride and never looked back. With each performance, Harris grew stronger, threatening to surpass Parsons as the tour's star. Bartley recalls, "In later gigs they actually had to start supplying bodyguards for her, to and from the stage, because these guys in the crowd wanted Emmylou real bad. And Emmylou was very shy, frail. And all these guys would be reaching for her."

Though not romantic in nature, the incandescent aura surrounding Parsons and Harris was apparent to all. "Everybody knew there was something special there," attests Smart. "Emmylou was the real McCoy. And she idolized Gram. There was never any funny business going on, but it was damn sure a mutual admiration society. To sing with those two on a couple of songs, man, what an *honor*. That was one of the coolest things I ever did." Adds Bartley, "Gram and Emmylou had their mikes facing each other, staring into each others' eyes singing 'Love Hurts.' The singing was so emotional. 'Love Hurts' was the most amazing one. It still makes me cry to listen to it today. Gram's frail voice cracked a lot and was not always in control, but what they created together was unbelievable. They made love with their voices." Bartley acknowledges that Parsons possessed a unique gift. "Emmylou had this beautiful voice, but I have to say it was Gram's voice that was the real emotional character to the shows, cracking and on the edge of breaking down, forgetting lyrics and mouthing words. Part of that was the fact that Gram had decided to bring his wife Gretchen on the road with us. That was a volatile relationship. She was *so* jealous of Emmylou."

Despite the reverie and copious substance abuse, Parsons and Smart took it upon themselves to shield Harris and her young daughter from the tour antics. "Gram really protected Emmylou," notes Smart. "He wouldn't let her get Kaufmanized. Phil's got a heart of gold, but he's as X-rated as you can get. There was a lot of shit going on during that tour that even I didn't know about. Emmylou and I used to do a window patrol on the bus. We'd run through the bus and open up all the windows and get all the smoke out. I'd always look out for Emmylou and her kid." Among the cargo of band gear and suitcases was an extensive collection of pornographic movies. During the group's radio concert in New York, Parsons made an innuendo-laden reference to a sixteen-millimeter projector on the bus.

During the group's stay in Houston, Neil Young came through town on his Time Fades Away tour. Opening for Young on his mammoth stadium trek was Linda Ronstadt. In Ronstadt's band was Mike Bowden. "We went to this club in Houston after our gig," Bowden recounts on the first time Ronstadt and Harris met. "We knew Gram was in town and had this band put together. There was a buzz around about Emmylou, so we thought we'd go see what it was all about. Emmy had great stage presence and energy. Most of the show she was singing background, though he gave her a couple of songs at the end of the set. One of the songs was 'Jambalaya'—that was just great. We went backstage and met them and wound up coming back to the hotel. Emmylou, Linda, Gram, N. D., and a couple of other members of the band ended up staying up all night singing country songs. It was just one of those great evenings." Years later Bowden wound up in Harris' sensational backing outfit, the Hot Band.

Jock Bartley was overawed by the presence of rock royalty. "During our show, onstage walked *Neil Young* and *Linda Ronstadt*. I couldn't believe that just a few days earlier I had been painting apartments and here I was on stage with Neil Young! After the gig Neil invited us over to their hotel. They had the top two floors of the swankiest hotel in Houston, and we were at the Travelodge. Everybody got totally wasted and played all night. That was the first time Linda and Emmylou sang together. It was an amazing moment. Emmylou's voice was angelic, fragile, and high, while Linda's was bigger, deeper, and more forceful. When they put those voices together it was *magical*. And you could see it in their faces. They were as blown away as everyone else." For Bartley the all-night session gave him a deeper appreciation for Parsons. "That night in Houston I sat and listened to Gram play about fifty country songs, just pull them out of the hat—old Louvin Brothers songs, George Jones, all that stuff—and Emmylou and Linda would jump in and it was unbelievable. My estimation of Gram went way up that night."

The tour eventually arrived in New York, where the Fallen Angels played Max's Kansas City with guitarist Dave Mason sitting in for a set. "At Max's Kansas City, I couldn't believe all these stars would come to see Gram," marvels Bartley, "and he was drunk every night. Here I was, a naive kid from Colorado, what did I know? Most audiences were very receptive to what we were doing, and the band had so much fun that people enjoyed the show. But in New York some people weren't sure what we were about."

Following the engagement at Max's, the group played a live radio concert on WLIR in Hempstead, Long Island. Recorded and released some years later, the performance is a testament to the remarkable chemistry created by Parsons and Harris. Their heartbreaking duet "Love Hurts" was nominated for a Grammy in 1983 for best country duo or group. "We showed up late for that job," laughs Smart. "We were across the street at a Chinese restaurant eating, and we're just about done when somebody comes running in from the radio show and says, 'The radio show's *started*. Would you *please* come over?' And it was *live*. So we ran over and I made a skit out of tuning up. It was near the end of the tour. We didn't know at the time that it was being recorded and would someday be released."

The Fallen Angels tour wrapped up its three-week run at Oliver's in Boston, where Barry Tashian joined the group onstage. "I was originally asked to go on the Fallen Angels tour but I declined," said Tashian. "But when Gram came to Boston I sat in and played some songs. Phil Kaufman told me he had searched Gram's room and flushed some drugs down the toilet. It was unusual to hear a band like that in Boston. After the final set at the club, in the parking lot of the motel, Gram had a whole grocery bag full of fireworks. There was a construction site next door and Gram set the whole bag off in the ditch. I left at that point, I didn't want to be around for that." What had begun on a ragged note ended with a bang. With the tour dates completed, everyone returned to their various homes while Parsons set about preparing to record a follow-up album.

Former Sub Band member John Nuese ran into Parsons during his Boston stopover. "I was staying with Barry and Holly Tashian," Nuese recalls, "and Gram came through. We got together constantly. Gram told me he was doing another solo album that summer, and he asked me to put together a new band for him after the album. I did that. We had some fantastic players lined up: Gram, Emmylou, Barry Tashian, and Mickey Gauvin (the original drummer from the Submarine Band). I would play lead guitar. The only position not solidified was the bass, but it probably would have been Emmylou's boyfriend at the time, Tom Guidera. That band would have been terrific."

Rick Roberts was in New York performing solo during the Fallen Angels engagement at Max's Kansas City where he renewed acquaintances with Parsons and Harris, and met guitarist Bartley. Following completion of the Angels tour, Bartley returned to Colorado. A year later he hooked up with Roberts, first to back Chris Hillman's solo tour, then to join Michael Clarke, along with (former Spirit bass player) Mark Andes, to form the highly successful Firefall. Roberts' knack for crafting commercial AOR* songs like "You Are The Woman," "Just Remember I Love You," and "Strange Way" made for financial success. Firefall scored a half dozen gold records during the seventies. Roberts later left to briefly join Randy Meisner and drummer Dewey Martin in the Meisner-Roberts Band before becoming involved in Gene Clark's Byrds tribute project. Michael Clarke's stint in Firefall gave him the opportunity to stretch his drumming chops to rhythms beyond the 4/4 tempo of the Burritos and Byrds. Two years later he played behind singer Jerry Jeff Walker. Clarke's attempts to tour with his own Byrds tribute group brought legal action when Crosby, McGuinn, and Hillman served papers on Clarke for copyright infringement of the Byrds' name, though in the end, the drummer prevailed. An amiable character always content to remain behind the scenes, Clarke had a serious drinking problem that would cost him his life: on December 19, 1993, he passed away at the age of forty-seven.

Roger McGuinn had carried on the franchise with Gene Parsons, Clarence White, and Skip Battin prior to the ill-fated Byrds reunion project and 1973 album. Though a solid concert draw, their creative output had bottomed out. The dismal *Byrdmaniax* and *Farther Along* records failed as country rock or straight rock, falling somewhere in between. McGuinn had allowed the employees too much input. With the reunion project already in the works, Crosby insisted that McGuinn put the current incarnation to rest. This he did in February 1973. The final engagement, in Passaic, New Jersey, was helped by Chris Hillman. By then, Gene Parsons and Skip Battin had already left due to conflicts over money. McGuinn fleetingly considered carrying on with White, bringing Michael Clarke and Hillman in as replacements, but then thought better of the idea. Gene Parsons immediately began recording his own solo debut, *Kindling*, relying on Clarence White, (Country Gazette's) Roger Bush, perennial sideman Gib Guilbeau, and (Little Feat's) Bill Payne. The multitalented Parsons plays guitar, banjo, harmonica, pedal steel, bass, and drums. *Kindling* offers a fresh bluegrass sound, and includes Guilbeau's Cajun-flavored "Take A City Bride," as well as a wonderful rendition of Lowell George's poignant "Willin'."

A Byrds reunion tour slated for the spring of 1973 (on a package rumored to include a reunited Buffalo Springfield and Hollies) fizzled

---

*Album Oriented Radio, so called because it featured albums rather than singles.

after critics savaged the *Byrds* album, killing sales. Although the five went their separate ways, they would continue to reunite in various combinations over the next twenty years.

Following the market explosion led by the Eagles and Rick Nelson, a plethora of country-influenced contenders emerged from obscurity to sign with major labels. The majors hadn't failed to notice big money was available, and were pushing country rock enthusiastically. From Michigan's Commander Cody and His Lost Planet Airmen to San Francisco's New Riders of the Purple Sage, bands previously ignored were getting more label support. The New Riders released a number of low-key country-flavored albums with a revolving door of personnel, including Buddy Cage, Skip Battin, Pat Shanahan, and Steve Love. Country Joe McDonald, leader of the dormant Fish, recorded a strange album of country standards at the legendary Bradley's Barn in Nashville. Even the Beau Brummels, American contenders in the British Invasion genre, had given country rock a go back in 1969.

Creedence Clearwater Revival's (CCR) John Fogerty entered the country rock sweepstakes with *Blue Ridge Rangers* in early 1973. That record yielded a hit single, a cover of Hank Williams' "Jambalaya." No strangers to country influences in songs like "Lodi," "Bad Moon Rising," and "Looking Out My Back Door," CCR often fell back on country music in their off hours, notes bass player Stu Cook. "We were into country music. We even had a country band, the Shit-Kicker Three, with John on pedal steel, Doug Clifford on a practice drum set, and me on guitar. Lots of Merle Haggard, Buck Owens, Jimmie Rodgers, and so on. We'd come back to the hotel after the show and play country music and drink all night." *Pop Music And Society* magazine went as far as to boldly declare the Blue Ridge Rangers, "the finest country rock band, even outstripping the Flying Burrito Brothers," although there was no such band. Fogerty played all the instruments himself. "I'd been wanting to play steel guitar, and I've been afraid of it all these years, because of those pedals and wires and everything," he remarked regarding the *Blue Ridge* record. "I bought one and played it. I caught on really fast." Fogerty took the same hands-on approach to the banjo and fiddle, quickly gaining competence and overdubbing the instruments in the studio. The album notched an impressive Number 47. In the early eighties Cook formed Southern Pacific, a country rock outfit that enjoyed several country hits on the Nashville charts.

Pure Prairie League (PPL), an Ohio-based band featuring the talented Craig Fuller, released a number of fine country rock albums and enjoyed a smash hit with Fuller's "Amie." The band originally formed in Columbus in 1969. "We started playing a mix of country and original material," recalls Fuller. The band took its name from an old Errol Flynn movie. Fuller had grown up listening to country music until the British Invasion caught his ear. He cites the Byrds' move into country music as a turning point in PPL's development. "The Byrds were our biggest influence," continues Fuller, "they had Clarence White in the band. When we started, we said, 'If the Byrds are doing this, it's good enough for us.'" The band also drew inspiration from Poco, the Burrito Brothers, and the Great Speckled Bird. "We loved the Bird," says Fuller. "Amos Garrett and Buddy Cage were incredible." Soon after forming, the group added pedal-steel player John Call and signed with RCA in 1971. Their eponymous debut followed in 1972. Their second album, *Bustin' Out*, issued in late 1972, included the single "Amie" but by the time the record charted Fuller had left the group. "The band was dropped from RCA after I left," acknowledges Fuller. "I was a conscientious objector during the Vietnam War. That's why I had to leave. They sort of scrambled to get something going when the single became a hit." "Amie," with its lilting harmonies and subtle acoustic playing, remains a classic of the country rock genre.

Plagued by constant personnel changes, Pure Prairie League carried on throughout the seventies, releasing albums for RCA and Casablanca, a disco label. Their third album, *Two Lane Highway*, featured a credible cover of Gene Clark's "Kansas City Southern." Current Nashville favorite Vince Gill got his first big break with the band in the late seventies before going on to fame and fortune in Music City.

Other purveyors of country rock included the Goose Creek Symphony; Indiana-based Mason Proffit (led by the Talbot brothers); Redwing (who released a couple of excellent albums on Fantasy Records); Fool's Gold (Dan Fogelberg's backing band); and the Cooper Brothers (who scored a hit with "Rock and Roll Cowboys"). Canadian guitar hero Randy Bachman, late of the Guess Who, released a country rock album under the banner Brave Belt. Another Capricorn act, Cowboy, featuring Tommy Talton and Scott Boyer, played a southern fried version of country rock. Even some of the southern blues-based rock groups, like the Allman Brothers and the Marshall Tucker Band, dabbled in country rock.

Mike Nesmith's Countryside label was formed with the idea of giving bands a chance to create with autonomy. With the Los Angeles country rock community growing exponentially, Nesmith had few problems finding the talent to stock his fiercely independent label.

"L.A. was the center of country rock," states Nesmith. "In southern California all this country-influenced music was beginning to emerge. Countryside was a label devoted to giving this music a home. The music needed a home. Most of the record companies here didn't understand it, their efforts ended up in that never-never land someplace between rock & roll and country & western: it didn't work." With Jac Holzman of Elektra Records behind him, Nesmith built Countryside Studio and stocked it with a hot band of players, including Red Rhodes, stringbender guitar ace Bob Warford, Jay Lacy on guitar, drummer Danny Lane, and Billy Graham on bass. Over the next year this band provided able backing on country-flavored albums by Nesmith, including his marvelous *Pretty Much Your Standard Ranch Stash*. Other Countryside artists included Garland Frady, Steve Fromholz, ex–Our Gang leader Spanky MacFarlane, and Ian Matthews (whose arrangement of Steve Young's "Seven Bridges Road" would become the model for the Eagles' version). Red Rhodes released his own curious steel guitar instrumental album.

When David Geffen took over Elektra, absorbing it into Asylum, he viewed Countryside as a distraction and closed it down.

"Just as we were opening our doors," notes Nesmith, "he closed them. He started Asylum. Countryside didn't last long. David was a typical businessman: his agenda was to make money. Asylum was already devoted to country rock. His business skills were far more aggressive and better than mine. I wanted to create an artistic home."

Nesmith moved on to other artistic endeavors, continuing to record and release albums into the eighties. In 1977 he reunited with Johnny Ware for an Australian tour, accompanied by Al Perkins, which yielded *Live At The Palais* the following year. Nesmith produced feature films like *Repo Man* and *Time Bandits*. He also wrote a novel and pioneered the rock video format, inspiring the creation of MTV. These were things he did without the need the rest of us had to earn money: his mother's invention of liquid paper had left him with a $25 million legacy.

Following the success of their debut album the Eagles released *Desperado*. Recorded in London with Glyn Johns it was a gamble, an album conceived in the spirit of adventure of the era they championed in the song. Artistically, the gamble paid off: *Desperado* offers a cohesive, consistent collection of songs tied together by a common theme. Commercially it did not: it bewildered the public and was seen as a colossal misstep by the label. In the evolution of the genre it stands as a high water mark, the culmination of the vision of four musicians raised on cowboy lore and western movies. *Desperado* was as much a product of image as substance, though the substance was worthy. "We saw ourselves as living outside the law," notes Glenn Frey, "just like the guys we were writing about." Adds art director Gary Burden, who laid out the elaborate Wild West cover art, "The group saw a parallel between the gunslinger of the 1870s and the guitar player of the 1970s." That image played out in the writing of the songs and the construction of the concept album. "We grew up wanting to be the cowboys," smiles Bernie Leadon. "So much so that we actually wanted to act that out. The album was our chance to do that: a dream come true."

Randy Meisner is proud of the record, "I think it's one of the best albums we ever made, along with *Hotel California*. It was focused because we had the concept from start to finish. But Geffen and Elliot Roberts thought it was the biggest mistake we ever made." Laughs Frey, "There were some people who weren't too happy with it. All they could think was, 'They made a goddamn *cowboy* record! Where's "Witchy Woman"? Where's "Take It Easy" for chrissakes?'" The seed of the outlaw concept was planted by Eagles' associates J. D. Souther and Jackson Browne. They first saw the parallels between the western outlaw gunslinger and the country rock musician. Glenn Frey and Don Henley realized the concept. "J. D. and Jackson were a big influence on Don and Glenn," continues Meisner. "Don and Glenn were living together, they were the two principal writers, and they focused right in on that concept." Framing the theme around the infamous Doolin-Dalton gang of western lore, the two wrote songs to fit the story line. The title song was the centerpiece, a metaphor for the outlaw musicians on the fringe, as well as the perils of aging and forsaking the dreams of youth. The "Desperado" reprise, coming at the end of the album, tied the pieces together neatly. "We had a gunfighter's photo album," noted Frey in a later interview, "and one night we just started writing a song about the Doolin-Dalton gang. We were going to do an album about outlaws that didn't have a time reference. We also started writing a song about James Dean that same night, the one that ended up on *On The Border*. Halfway through, we realized it was holding together. The whole outlaw and rock star idea that we were trying to get across was working."

Following the haunting harmonica strains that introduce "Doolin-Dalton," Henley's voice sets the theme. Sighs Henley, "It's sad when you learn what the rock & roll business is all about. That's basically what the album deals with. With learning there are certain compromises and sacrifices you have to make. The idea was a reaction to our success. We would have these conversations about whether we were just banging our heads against the wall. People seemed to want things that take them away from their everyday lives." As the utility man of the group, Leadon's talents lend the album its country flair, whether his contribution was acoustic flat-picking, banjo, Dobro, or mandolin. His own song "Twenty-One" uses all the instruments he plays. The number went on to become his showcase in their live shows. In "Out Of Control" the duel lead guitar harmony, rocking tempo, and frenetic ending simulates a shootout. During the cover shoot, the band actually filmed a gunfight sequence that their record label deemed far too violent for public consumption. "Tequila Sunrise," with its similarity to "Peaceful Easy Feeling," is the only tune that sounds like it could have come from their debut. Despite the fact that it would become one of their best-loved hits, the track failed to dent the Top Fifty. The title track is unquestionably the finest bit of writing on the album, an early example of the developing power of the Henley-Frey team.

"A Certain Kind Of Fool" is Meisner's lone lead vocal. "I just got in at the last minute of that album with that one," admits Meisner. "With Don and Glenn living together it was kind of hard to be heard. I had a riff, and they helped me finish it." Songwriter David Blue's composition "Outlaw Man" fit the concept and was included. The band gives the song a tougher guitar-oriented arrangement. The melancholy "Saturday Night" is an example of the Eagles' lovely harmonizing. The album closes with a slowed-down reprise of "Doolin-Dalton," opening with a solitary voice that ultimately segues into a powerful reprise of "Desperado," after which it fades out over voices and banjo.

The record shows the maturity and the stronger sense of lyricism the four songwriters had developed since their first release. It's unfortunate that the album, perhaps the finest expression of the genre, resulted in poor sales. It peaked at Number 41, although it eventually turned gold. "David Geffen wasn't too happy with that album," notes Meisner, "and the record label didn't want it at all." The failure of the disk to bring the Eagles recognition as country rock's premier band pushed them toward rock.

*On The Border*, released in 1974, was the Eagles' response: it straddled the lines between softer country rock and a harder-edged rhythm and blues sound. Rock guitar ace Don Felder was recruited to bring a heavier guitar sound to the band. It was a transitional album, and the group was poised to take the leap into a heavier rock sound, though they still hedged their bets with numbers like "Already Gone," and

"My Man," Leadon's heartfelt ode to Gram Parsons. "The Best Of My Love" was another country-influenced track, lushly backed by Leadon's pedal steel, and was their first Number One single. *One Of These Nights* (featuring the disco-influenced title track) became their breakthrough album, followed by *Hotel California*, which shot them to superstardom. By then Leadon was gone, with Meisner soon to follow. With their departures went much of the Eagles' country rock direction.

"Bernie is an amazing acoustic player," remarks Meisner, "and Felder came in with all that Clapton kind of stuff. That's what Frey and I were into. I think Bernie felt left out. I remember the night that he said he was going to quit. Bernie went down to the bar and poured a glass of beer over Glenn's head." With the Eagles' change of direction, Leadon found his position diminishing and left angry. Joe Walsh took his place. Leadon went on to release a solo album with Michael Georgiades, and later lent his talents to a number of country projects. These included the ambitious Civil War concept album *White Mansions*, several Christian recordings with Chris Hillman and Al Perkins, and a tongue-in-cheek bluegrass project, Run C&W. He also sat in with the Dirt Band, replacing John McEuen in the late eighties. A resident of Nashville, Leadon now works in music production.

Meisner walked out after *Hotel California*. He bridled at the absolute authority of the Henley-Frey team, and following a confrontation with them quit the band. "I was married and had three kids, and I hadn't seen much of them," states Meisner. "My family was in Nebraska, and the band was in Miami recording *Hotel California*, or on the road doing gigs. I was frustrated. Things were rocky with my marriage. Don and Glenn became a little more powerful. It finally came to a head in Knoxville, Tennessee. We did the gig and I had the flu or something. We did two encores and came off stage, and I said, 'Man, that's about all I can do.' Glenn called me a pussy. I snapped and took a swing at him." Meisner was fired from the band. His replacement, Timothy B. Schmit, had originally taken Meisner's place in Poco. By then the Eagles were arena rockers. Meisner went solo, scoring a hit with "Hearts On Fire," off his *One More Song* record. Further solo albums followed, plus a short-lived union with ex-Burrito Rick Roberts. The 1989 Poco reunion resuscitated Meisner's career, and he continues to record, perform (currently with World Classic Rockers), and lend his production experience to several country rock projects.

The packaging of Linda Ronstadt as a pop star began with her next release, *Don't Cry Now*. Her first for Geffen's Asylum label, Ronstadt receives the full Asylum treatment: songs tailored for her by beau J. D. Souther, covers of the Eagles and Neil Young, and slick production by Peter Asher (formerly of British Invasion duo Peter and Gordon), the Svengali behind her chart-topping success. The backing of the country rock fraternity was toned down by Asher to prevent *too* much country flavoring to cloud the mix. While her previous effort found her working in several genres—country, rock, folk, and pop—this record was pure country rock. Even Randy Newman's quirky "Sail Away" is set in a country rock arrangement awash in steel guitar. Rick Roberts' gorgeous "Colorado" is a disappointment, and the Eagles' "Desperado" also fails to ignite. A much-improved remake of "Silver Threads" is one of the few high points on the album. Though the material is carefully selected, the backing tasteful, Ronstadt's singing excellent, and the pacing well thought out, the results are bland. It lacks the elements that had made her previous effort worthy: her love of acoustic country music and bluegrass, a full-hearted delivery where subtlety may have been more appropriate, and an innocent exuberance. Though Asher's calculated approach would vault her to greater stardom and much more money, it came at the expense of her early charm. One has the impression that the album was crafted in the studio without her artistic input. Ronstadt's transformation into an AM radio star would come to fruition with 1974's *Heart Like A Wheel*, the album that launched her into the pop stratosphere, where she remains today.

Ronstadt's success across a wide range of styles—new wave, Broadway musicals, big band, and Mexicali music—was followed recently by a return to country rock on an album recorded with, among others, Bernie Leadon.

With several charter members of the country rock community at loose ends, and with the increasing mass appeal of country rock, an enterprising promoter saw the opportunity to package the genre as a traveling country rock festival on the college circuit. With the support of Warner Brothers Records, the concept was test-marketed in June with shows in Annapolis and Philadelphia. The success of the concept begat an entire tour, and the possibility of a European leg as well. As Byron Berline tells the story, "It was Gram and Emmylou, Gene Parsons and Clarence White from the Byrds, Sneaky Pete, Chris Ethridge, the Kentucky Colonels with Roland, Clarence and Eric White, and Country Gazette. Boy, that was exciting. It was a three-hour show and we'd all get together at the end with Gram and Emmylou on stage. It was the best thing I'd ever been a part of." Despite minor problems, like a backstage confrontation between

White and Parsons over issues of ego, the concerts were a great success. The players were looking forward to the fall tour.

But tragedy struck. Clarence White, age twenty-nine, died on the evening of July 14 after being hit by a drunk driver while loading his gear into his car. The news stunned the country rock community. Respected and loved, White's senseless demise was a staggering blow to the musicians he planned to tour with. "The night Clarence got killed we were supposed to jam at the Nashville West club down in El Monte," recounts Byron Berline. "But I never heard from him. Clarence went up to Palmdale to see one of his houses. He went over to his mother's house, and he and Roland had dinner with his mother. They decided they'd go over to Palmdale and jam with Gib Guilbeau. That's the night he got killed. Chris Ethridge called me the next day. I thought he was drunk—he sounded *real* out of it. He told me Clarence was dead. I didn't believe him. After he said it again I knew he wasn't kidding."

White had been working on tracks for a solo album, released under the title *Silver Meteor*. He had recently brought the revamped Kentucky Colonels to Europe. He had also contributed to a project entitled *Muleskinner*, an innovative bluegrass rock fusion. That group included Richard Greene and Peter Rowan of Seatrain; ex–Speckled Bird Bill Keith; as well as Dave Grisman. After White's death they would go on to form Old and In The Way, with Jerry Garcia. "Clarence's star was on the rise until the day he died," opines ex-Byrd John York. "He always served the music. We used to joke about all the guitar players at every gig watching his hands."

The memorial service for White was emotion-choked and heavily attended, with tributes pouring in from around the globe. Following the service, Bernie Leadon and Gram Parsons broke into an impromptu rendition of the gospel standard "Farther Along." As others joined in, tears flowed freely for a fallen comrade. Mourners noted that Gram Parsons seemed particularly distraught, and for Gene Parsons, the loss was almost beyond comprehension. "Clarence was my best friend. I quit playing for two years after his death. He was such an inspiration."

Sessions convened in August for Gram Parsons' second solo album under the working title *Sleepless Nights*. The project had many of the same supporting musicians that backed *GP*. "Gram was very congenial," recalls Al Perkins. "He was very appreciative of the guys, and allowed them the freedom to do what they wanted to." Elvis Presley's band was involved. Bernie Leadon, Herb Pedersen, Barry Tashian, Linda Ronstadt, and N. D. Smart also contributed to the sessions. "I remember being knocked cold by the whole band," gushes Smart. "I kept thinking, 'Hell, I'm with the *Elvis Presley band!*'" Though in the end it remained a Parsons-only project, noted Perkins, "He really wanted Emmy to be an equal partner with equal billing. But there were internal pressures from the label, and I think his wife Gretchen had some problems with Emmylou as a full partner."

Many of the songs selected for the album were already familiar to Parsons and Harris from the Fallen Angels tour. "Most of those songs were written and sung in the back of the bus," noted Harris. Parsons drew on his extensive back catalog for "Brass Buttons" and his Byrds' classic "Hickory Wind," and "$1000 Wedding" came from his Burrito days. The Everly Brothers' "Love Hurts," a show-stopper on tour, was a natural for inclusion. "Hearts On Fire" was a new tune from Tom Guidera and Walter Egan. Parsons wrote "In My Hour Of Darkness" during the sessions, a tribute to Brandon De Wilde, Clarence White, and mentor Sid Kaiser, all of whom had died. The passings had made him keenly aware of his own mortality. Harris receives co-credit for contributing to the song. The title track, "Return Of The Grievous Angel," was inspired by a poem given to him by Boston poet Tom Brown and ultimately became not only the album title but synonymous with Parsons himself.

The energized 'Las Vegas' had been written around the time of *GP*, but, like "I Can't Dance," was held over. "I wrote one of the verses in "Las Vegas," maintains Tashian, "but was never credited for it after Gram died. I went to Las Vegas with Gram the night he went to talk to the guys in Elvis' band. Gram said, 'Come on guys, we gotta finish up this song.' We were standing around singing it and snapping our fingers and I sang, 'First time I lose I drink whiskey, the second time I lose I drink gin.' I wrote a letter to get Gretchen to sign over a form to get me credit as one of the writers, but nothing happened." What many have assumed to be a live recording of the Louvin Brothers' "Cash On The Barrelhead," with a segue into "Hickory Wind," was concocted in the studio. "They wanted to record a live session with an audience," recalls Perkins, "but it could not be worked out. So after we laid down the music tracks and some vocals in the studio, engineer Hugh Davies dug up some audience tapes, and added additional sounds provided by Gram and friends." Parsons' re-read of "Hickory Wind" pales by comparison to the Byrds' version.

Recalling those sessions, Harris told Ben Fong-Torres, "Our singing came together on two songs, 'Love Hurts' and 'The Angels Rejoiced.' I finally learned what I was supposed to do. Each night we'd get the mixes of what we'd done and we'd take them back and listen to them over and over again. We'd get so excited, dancing around. His singing was so much better after a year on the road. I felt like Gram was on his way to getting himself under control." The two weeks of sessions completed, Parsons took time off to relax and get in shape for the next leg of the Country Rock Festival, soldiering on despite the absence of Clarence White.

Never one to remain too far from music, Sneaky Pete recorded what purports to be a solo album entitled *Cold Steel* in the summer of 1973, following his stint in Europe with the Hot Burrito Revue. When no American label showed interest, the album ended up being released the following year on the Dutch label Ariola. The album was, in fact, a group effort: Cold Steel was the name attached to Pete, Mike and Richard Bowden, Gib Guilbeau, and newcomers Greg Attaway and David Lovelace. The group was short-lived and the album, boasting one Pete original, "Wings That Make Birds Fly," was quickly forgotten. Recalls Mike Bowden, "Why it didn't stay together I can't remember, but I don't think we went into it seriously. I never saw it as a long-term deal."

Richard Bowden, Attaway, Lovelace, and Steve Love backed McGuinn on *Roger McGuinn And Band*, produced by former Ronstadt manager John Boylan. Pete returned to the stage two years later with his revamped Flying Burrito Brothers, which was more satisfying for him. "I got the chance to do what *I* really wanted to do, and more of a chance to design the arrangements," offers Pete. "I have better feelings about the later albums because I had more input. The *Gilded Palace* was a significant, trendsetting album. Yet to my taste, the reformed band with Gene Parsons, Chris Ethridge, Gib Gilbeau, and Joel Scott Hill was better."

Recorded over a marathon set of sessions in the spring, Poco's *Crazy Eyes* was released in September. Richie Furay was gone from the group soon after it was issued. Following the poor showing of *A Good Feeling To Know*, Furay's frustration had reached a crisis point. He laments, "We weren't able to make the records cross that line. Even though we had another commercial song in 'Let's Dance Tonight,' I was feeling like I could write commercial songs all day now and if CBS wasn't going to help us, I was outta there. I wanted to be a rock & roll star. I was blinded by it."

To their credit, the members of Poco did not let the disappointment of the previous album limit their effort on *Crazy Eyes*. With Jack

Richardson once again producing, the group brought another slate of strong songs to the sessions, including what would be an unintended tribute to Gram Parsons, a sympathetic cover of "Brass Buttons," and the title cut, Furay's impression of young Parsons. With Parsons' reemergence that year the timing seemed right to release it.

"Gram hadn't recorded 'Brass Buttons' yet," acknowledges Furay. "He taught me that one when we lived across the street from each other in Greenwich Village back in 1964." Poco's version of the song predates the commencement of Parsons' *Grievous Angel* sessions. "'Crazy Eyes' was about the mystique of Gram Parsons. If you looked in his eyes, he was the kind of guy you could never really read. I wrote it earlier back in 1969, and I was toying with the idea for the song, but it never had the expansion that it needed until Jack brought in his friend Bob Ezrin to orchestrate it. We cut it raw in the studio and Bob and Jack took it back and put this orchestra on it. And then we added our instrumentation to it, which was certainly an experiment for us." Furay brought in several other numbers, including "Believe Me," "Nothin's Still The Same," and "So You've Got A Lover," a demo number from Stephen Stills dating from Buffalo Springfield days. None of these made the cut.

Opening with Paul Cotton's thumping "Blue Water," the group segues into Rusty Young's showpiece "Fool's Gold," which features his lightning-quick Dobro, banjo, and steel playing. Chris Hillman contributes mandolin on the track. Tim Schmit weighs in with the slower-paced "Here We Go Again," revealing his growing strength as a writer. Cotton's "A Right Along," a fine country rocker, follows. "Crazy Eyes" opens side two, followed by Cotton's beautiful rendition of J. J. Cale's "Magnolia." The album ends with Furay's polished pop gem, "Let's Dance Tonight." *Crazy Eyes* fared much better than *Good Feelin'*, reaching Number 38 on the charts, and reviews were glowing. For Furay it was too little, too late.

David Geffen had a scheme in mind for Furay. He assembled a supergroup—Furay, Chris Hillman, and J. D. Souther—designed to emulate the phenomenal success of Crosby, Stills & Nash. Hillman's presence on *Crazy Eyes* was the result of the covert discussions he'd had with Furay.

Leaving Poco was something Furay would come to view with mixed feelings. He regretted the damage. "I hurt people. I'm sure Rusty, George, Tim, and Paul were devastated that I could make that decision. It was like abandoning ship, leaving them out there. But I was so focused, my mind was made up, and I was getting encouragement from

David. So it was Souther, Hillman, Furay. 'This is the formula that worked for these guys so let's just do it.' He was a big fan of J. D. Souther, so we just all got together." But while Crosby, Stills & Nash had formed of their own volition, Souther, Hillman & Furay (SHF) was manufactured by David Geffen.

For the other members of Poco, the news was a jolt. "We weren't aware until near the end of those sessions," avers George Grantham. "The sound of the supergroup deal was very appealing. That was a *big* blow when Richie announced that. We sat with it for a few days then had a meeting and everybody indicated they wanted to go on." Indeed, Furay's abrupt departure spurred the quartet onward, providing incentive to show they were more than his backing group. "We had built up a solid fan base," asserts Cotton, "and could get booked anywhere any day of the week and our records were steady sellers. And Rusty was starting to turn into quite a writer. Boy, did *he* turn around."

Furay's departure opened a door for Young. Recalls Young, "David Geffen and Elliot Roberts were interested in giving us advice, they called the four of us in to a meeting. Geffen pointed to Paul and said, 'You write and sing; you'll be okay.' He looked at Tim and pointed, 'You write and sing; you'll be okay.' Then he turned to George and me and said, 'You guys don't write and sing; you're in trouble.' That moment really helped push me to start writing for the group."

A further incident galvanized the group's resolve. Chuckles Young, "Around the time that Richie left for Souther, Hillman & Furay, there was this article with a picture of Chris and J. D. Souther throwing a rose on a coffin that said, 'Poco, 1969–1973. Rest in Peace.' And Chris was quoted saying 'Richie Furay *is* Poco, Poco is over.' They were writing us off without ever giving us a chance. But that was the best thing for us, because it motivated us to show we could still do it." The quartet came back strong with the driving *Seven*, a potent antidote to their softer country rock sound. "It was certainly heavier," admits Cotton, who was largely responsible for the shift. "I was into English rock then. I was miking my amps the way The Who's Peter Townshend did." The group's volume went up several decibels, and bewildered longtime fans. Subsequent albums found the group returning to a sound that highlighted their gorgeous harmony singing. And along with his other emerging talents, Young proved to be a competent singer as well.

Despite Geffen's encouraging words, the powerful manager tried to undo them. As Young remembers it, "David did call the head of our booking agency and say, 'If you don't drop this act, I'm pulling

Joni Mitchell and Neil Young.' He did everything he could to make sure that when Richie left he took the Poco audience with him. He wanted Poco to be over. But he couldn't do it. And John Hartmann left *him* and helped *us*." Former Geffen associate Hartmann assumed co-management of the group for the next decade.

Toiling away year after year, releasing a series of consistently high-quality albums to a loyal clientele, Poco was once again rocked when Schmit departed for a spot in Geffen's Eagles vacated by Meisner. The announcement came following the release of Poco's sterling *Rose Of Cimarron*. The band's perseverance was finally rewarded in 1979 when "Crazy Love" became a Top Twenty hit, earning Poco's first gold record. By then, Young's innovative steel guitar work had given way to acoustic guitars and a mellower AOR rock sound. In 1989 the original five-member Troubadour-era lineup reunited for the successful *Legacy* album and tour. Young and Cotton continue to tour sporadically as Poco, and as he entered his thirtieth year as a member of the band, Young's optimism remains undaunted. He has also lent his support to several "new country" artists, including Vince Gill and Bryan White. While touring behind Gill, Young met Bill Lloyd of the country duo Foster & Lloyd, and the two later teamed up with New Grass Revival member John Cowan to form the Sky Kings, Young's attempt to crack the new country market.

Furay opines, "I think Poco gets overlooked. Poco innovated, it didn't copy, and that's what made us special. The ones who really *did* get it were Glenn and Don, and Pure Prairie League, whom we definitely influenced. There couldn't have been the Eagles without us. Poco was the launching pad for the more commercial aspect of country rock music. I know the country rock label hurt us. Gram and the Flying Burrito Brothers got underground acceptance, where we were someplace else. So people look to the Burrito Brothers more than to us. Look at the country groups today. They'll acknowledge the Eagles, of course, because they were the popular band. We have to be satisfied in our hearts with what we did in the early days." Suggests Young, "I wonder how many things would have been different without Poco? Would there have even been a country rock era?" During the Eagles' hugely successful 1994 Hell Freezes Over reunion tour, Glenn Frey pointed out Richie Furay to the audience and stated openly, "We wouldn't be here without you."

The supergroup of Souther, Hillman & Furay was a bust, despite the hand of Geffen. Even the contributions of Al Perkins (on guitar and steel), Paul Harris (on keyboards), and session drummer extraordinaire Jim Gordon couldn't get the effort off the ground. A clash of personalities and musical directions didn't help either, and the group ultimately imploded. A scathing piece in *Crawdaddy* revealed the mistrust and conflicts undermining the group. Hillman and Furay were pitted against Souther, a loner who chafed at the group concept. "The idea looked great on paper, but we never gelled," admits Hillman. "It was three *individuals*. Richie was going through some tough times in his personal life. I don't think Richie ever really understood J. D., and I don't think J. D. was a team player. There was always a little bit of tension between them. But it wasn't just them, the idea didn't work." Adds Al Perkins, "J. D. had been a loner all the time, still is. We'd all be ready to go and J. D.'d be off somewhere, keeping us all waiting. He was a gentleman about it, but it really ran up Chris's and Richie's blood."

"We got a gold album for that first record," notes Furay ruefully, "but I'm not sure about all those sales."

Furay and Souther locked horns at the rehearsal stages even before the album was recorded. The two managed to hold things together through a tour, and a second album, appropriately titled *Trouble In Paradise*, before going their separate ways. Opines Furay, "One thing that was not in our favor was that the band was started by outside people. When musicians get together voluntarily and start a band it has a much better chance. When outside people start a band there's something artificial about the whole situation. It was understood there was going to be no more group after the tour. I was fed up with music, and my family life was all screwed up. For the first six months after the group broke up I didn't even touch a guitar. I took this time to get close to my family again." Furay also converted to Christianity. "I really didn't want to have anything to do with devout Christian Al Perkins because, to me, we were on the road to success and anything that had to do with Jesus Christ was going to get in the way. As it turned out, the Lord used Al to lead me to Him." For the last fifteen years Furay has served as pastor at the Calvary Chapel of Boulder. He recently released *In My Father's House*, a country-rock-gospel album, and has resumed performing, mixing devotional numbers with songs from both the Buffalo Springfield and Poco.

Following the dissolution of SHF, Chris Hillman embarked on a solo career, releasing a number of excellent albums before teaming up with McGuinn and Clark. His next move was to the highly successful Desert

Rose Band, with old friends Herb Pedersen and Jay Dee Maness. With Hillman front and center, Desert Rose enjoyed several hits on the country charts in the eighties. Former Stone Canyon Band member Tom Brumley eventually replaced Maness, before Hillman folded the group to resume a solo career that was geared to a slower pace. Hillman and Pedersen recorded a tribute to the Buck Owens–Merle Haggard sound on *Bakersfield Bound*. Both have released their own bluegrass albums or joined notable pickers on contemporary bluegrass releases. Hillman's most recent album, *Like A Hurricane*, was produced by Richard Podolor. Souther resumed his solo career. He scored a chart hit with the ironically titled "You're Only Lonely." Al Perkins moved to Nashville, where he remains in demand as a session player, working with artists like Emmylou Harris and Garth Brooks.

With the *Grievous Angel* sessions completed and the Country Rock Festival engagements looming ahead, Gram Parsons took some time at his favorite retreat, Joshua Tree National Park. On the night of September 18, during a chemical misadventure, Parsons fell into unconsciousness in a room at the Joshua Tree Inn. He was pronounced dead at 12:15 A.M., September 19. Parsons was twenty-six years old. Attempts by companion Margaret Fisher and hotel staff to resuscitate him were in vain. The news was conveyed to his friends and contemporaries the next day. Parsons' penchant for overindulgence had finally caught up with him. With his career on the upswing following a two-year absence and a new album in the can, suicide was not a possibility. In a rather bizarre twist, Phil Kaufman stole the body before it could be transported to family members in New Orleans. Kaufman and a friend spirited the coffin to the town of Joshua Tree, where Parsons was crudely cremated. Arrested soon after, the two claimed it was Parsons' own wish, expressed at Clarence White's graveside. A shattered Emmylou Harris received the news at her parents' home in Maryland.

"I don't think he meant to die, it was an accident," maintains close friend Barry Tashian. "But I kind of expected it. When I was out there for the album sessions, I feared for Gram's health. I remember talking to him one night and saying something like, 'Gram, this could be the turning point,' and I tried to encourage him to get outside and get some fresh air, encouraging some health." But Parsons would have none of it, preferring to live life on the edge. "When it comes to Gram Parsons, those who remember him remember him strong," suggests N. D. Smart. "The average fan may not know who he is, but the people making the music certainly do. Gram and I got real close. He just always wanted me around socially, which I was grateful for, but it was difficult for me because I really couldn't relate to those kind of excesses. I looked at this guy and thought, 'You're talented, things are breaking for you, you've got a beautiful wife and you're doing this to yourself?' I mean, a rough day for him was going into the office and picking up a check. I always thought *Desperado* was written about Gram. Doesn't it sound like it? If Gram could have cleaned himself up he'd be a huge star today. He and Emmylou." Concurs Chris Hillman, "If Gram had stayed on the straight and narrow, he and Emmylou would have been huge." Notes Keith Richards, "He redefined the possibilities of country for me. If he had lived he probably would have redefined it for everybody."

Some view Parsons' demise as a product of the persona he had worked to create, and part of a grand scheme to achieve immortality. "Gram was just a romantic," asserts Bernie Leadon. "He set out to become legendary by dying young. He saw that it worked well for James Dean and Hank Williams. I think he thought that was a great idea, to live a tragically excessive life, die a tragic hero, and become immortal. And he pulled it off."

The following February, Reprise released *Grievous Angel* posthumously. It garnered critical superlatives but slim sales. Gone was a controversial photograph of Parsons and Harris together astride a motorcycle, replaced instead by a somewhat ethereal head-shot of Parsons. Harris' name is relegated to the back cover. Though not as consistently strong as *GP*, the album is a fitting epitaph to Parsons: a vision of contemporary country music that bridged generations and social classes, appealing to long- and shorthair alike, Cosmic American Music. With much of the energy of the original country rock movement dissipated either through commercial dictates or public indifference, *Angel* marked the end of an era.

One can only speculate what Parsons might have achieved had he not left us so quickly. He had yet to hit his stride, and *GP* and *Grievous Angel* both evinced a renewed creative spark. With the phenomenal financial success of the Eagles, Parsons may have reacted bitterly, retreating deeper into traditional country in his disgust. Since he had soldiered on in the face of Nashville's indifference, and his failure to achieve commercial pop success, it's more likely he could have toughed it out long enough to accrue the influence and attention he so richly deserved. Today, the Nashville elite and the music business com-

munity know his name and legacy only in passing: he has slipped into
esoteric legend. Emmylou Harris mentioned Parsons' name during a
Nashville television interview a few years ago, only to have her host in-
quire, "Where is old Gram these days?" A stunned Harris replied quietly that he had been dead for years. "A lot of people don't know who
he is," she recently told *Billboard* on the release of Almo Records' Parsons' tribute album. "They've heard his name; they haven't really
heard his music. Let's face it: Gram had never torn up the charts."

Harris launched her own solo career with *Pieces Of The Sky* in early
1975. Dedicated to preserving Parsons' legacy, she has recorded several of his songs over the years, as well as carrying the banner for
country music's traditional roots. Her own composition "Boulder To
Birmingham" reflects her experiences with him, as does *The Ballad Of
Sally Rose* concept album. Throughout her career Harris has success-
fully straddled both traditional country and country rock. Her recent
albums *Wrecking Ball* (produced by rock music wizard Daniel Lanois)
and *Spyboy* boast a young-guns backing band. She remains willing to
take risks and shake up the Nashville community. In 1987, she, Linda
Ronstadt, and Dolly Parton teamed to produce the critically acclaimed
*Trio* album. Harris' live work in the early eighties with the Hot Band
(at various times featuring Ricky Scaggs, Rodney Crowell, James Burton, Mike Bowden, Johnny Ware, and Albert Lee) offered one of the
most electrifying country shows on the circuit. A return to a simpler,
acoustic bluegrass country format with the Nash Ramblers (featuring
Al Perkins on Dobro) won her even more accolades. In the early eighties Harris moved to Nashville, where she has served as president of
the Country Music Association and is a member of the Grand Ole
Opry. Never catering to trends, Harris maintains a strong sense of integrity and dedication to her craft. She recently spearheaded the tribute album to Gram Parsons' legacy entitled *Return Of The Grievous
Angel* on Almo Records.

As the ill-starred Hank Williams of country rock, Gram Parsons is
often given a lion's share of credit by critics for founding the genre of
country rock. But has the myth surpassed the achievements of the
man? Some view his coronation as a legend cynically. Poco's Rusty
Young feels history has distorted Parsons' role. "A friend of mine
showed me a magazine from London that gave Gram Parsons credit
for *inventing* country rock. I was there: Gram Parsons didn't have a *clue*
about country rock. He played stone country. He came over and sat in
with Poco before forming the Burritos and we showed him what *we*

were doing. Gram saw what was going on and he took those things he saw with him. But people say he invented country rock. Gram is given *way* too much credit. That really bothers me. He was stoned out of his brain. But he knew a good idea when he heard it."

"I loved Gram's stuff but death creates myth beyond our understanding sometimes," emphasizes his former partner Chris Hillman. "Yes, Gram was influential, he had a great impact, but not to the extent of becoming a cult figure leading us all through the wilderness. It just wasn't that way. It's like Jim Morrison, God rest his soul. The Doors made a couple of great records but he *wasn't* a great poet or a good singer. Some of that stuff was embarrassing. We're all guilty of that. Because he's gone he's become a saint, an icon. I think Ben Fong-Torres' biography of Gram was pretty accurate. He kept the fine line there between the myth and reality of Gram Parsons. The funniest thing is this Gramfest they have every year out in the desert. It's like the necrophiliac society. Emmylou doesn't go out there, and I don't want to go out there. What makes me mad is that the guy did have some talent, and he didn't use it because he lacked discipline. There are a few things that Gram got on record that are magnificent, one is 'Hot Burrito #1' and the other is 'Hot Burrito #2.' They're the most beautiful singing I've ever heard. But there's a lot of stuff he just couldn't get because he wasn't hungry. When you've got that in the back of your mind—that you'll never have to suffer because you've got $50,000 a year—it takes that edge off."

As band mate, friend, and confidante, Chris Hillman has lived under the shadow of Gram Parsons' legacy, and it has not been easy. Regarding the deification of Parsons in recent years, Hillman is unequivocal. "People forget things. With all due respect to Gram, he and I started the Burrito Brothers together. It wasn't his idea alone. I was doing country things with the Byrds *before* we met Gram Parsons, on *Younger Than Yesterday*. It was a year before we met him. But I read 'Gram did this' and 'Gram did that.' But to this day, I've got to be honest here, he'll get credit for 'Sin City!' 'Gram Parsons' "Sin City."' It bothers me. I wrote half that song while he was *asleep*. But it's okay. My wife says, 'You wanna trade places with him right now? Don't worry about it.'"

Parsons was an innovator, and for that he deserves credit; but he was not operating in a vacuum, nor was he the first to consider the possibilities inherent in the merger of country with rock. He was one of several young visionaries to see the redeeming qualities in country music, and there were others: Hillman, Gene Clark, Rodney Dillard, Larry

Murray, Richie Furay, and Mike Nesmith to name a few. Parsons' tortured life of indulgence, excess, and early death by overdose have cast him in a romantic light that makes it easy to the hang the title "legend" on him. But the country rock movement that went on to influence a whole new generation of country artists in the nineties was the product of a large number of like-minded musicians willing to break down the barriers that had grown between rock and country.

"We were all there, we played this kind of music," offers Hillman on the burgeoning country rock fraternity of the late sixties. "We all strayed from rock & roll. And many people contributed, whether it was Rusty Young, Sneaky Pete, Bernie Leadon, or whoever." These were risk-takers motivated by a genuine love for country music's simplicity, and its honesty as an authentic American music form.

"I think that you really have to look very carefully at these kinds of things," muses Mike Nesmith. "The roots tend to be very broad and very wide, and there are many of them. There is no real taproot. What it spawned was the phenomenal success of the Eagles. That's what everybody sees. What's underneath—I'm sure Gram was a part of that, and I think the First National Band was a part of that too. And if Poco wants to be the first, they can be the first. It doesn't make any difference, because everybody was there at the same time. Everybody contributed something."

# 11

# Return of the Grievous Angel

*The first times I went out there to Joshua Tree was because I knew the history of Gram dying there. It was simply for soul medicine. I was going through a hard time, and I'd just go out with my dog and camp out for a weekend. That led to me renting a little cabin out in the high desert. For three years I rented this room in a hotel up there. My first time there, I stayed in that same hotel where he died. I loved Gram. There's some good soul medicine up there.*

*—Victoria Williams*

The impact of the early country rock founders prevails even though they failed to earn sufficient recognition and success in their own time. "Do I hear our influence in the new country artists today?" muses Poco's Rusty Young. "You bet! What they're calling country music today is what we called country rock in the seventies. That's why you hear so many remakes of seventies' songs on country radio. And the same writers and producers and musicians who made those records in the seventies are here in Nashville doing it in country music today." Fellow Poco member Paul Cotton concurs. "Tim Dubois, head of Arista Records in Nashville, told Rusty and me a while ago that every time he went into the studio to produce a Restless Heart album he went in with the thought of making a Poco album. And out came Restless Heart." Ex-Shiloh member and Eagles arranger Jim Ed Norman is now a major mover in the Nashville music community, as a producer and record label executive. Rusty Young, Doug Dillard, and ex-Burrito Al Perkins are in demand as session players, while the Nitty Gritty Dirt Band is ranked among the Nashville establishment. Their *Will The Circle Be Unbroken II* album brought many of country music's youthful elite together to celebrate the rich heritage of country music.

With a new generation of country artists proclaiming their love of country rock openly, awareness of the pioneers is increasing. "Guys like Vince Gill and Ricky Scaggs are aware of the influence of Gram Parsons and Gene Clark," affirms Byron Berline, "because they were out on the West Coast for awhile." In his bio for RCA Records in the mid-eighties, Nashville's current favorite Gill remarked, "There's a whole bunch of people my age out there who like a brand of music they can't get that much of anymore. Music like Poco, the Eagles, Jackson Browne, and James Taylor used to make. A lot of those people can't really relate that well to things like the Grand Ole Opry. That's the gap I wouldn't mind helping to fill. I know there's a lot of those people who don't mind hearing a good country song with a little bit of rock and roll edge to it." Country king Marty Stuart is playing Clarence White's original stringbender Telecaster, his way of keeping White's legacy alive. One of the most successful and important country music albums of the mid-1990s is *Common Thread: The Songs Of The Eagles*, a loving tribute by Nashville's country hit-makers, including Gill, Travis Tritt, Trisha Yearwood, Diamond Rio, Lorrie Morgan, and others. Tritt's video for his remake of "Take It Easy" reunited the band after years of acrimony, and was the catalyst for their lucrative Hell Freezes Over tour.

No longer viewed as "carpetbaggers because we were from rock & roll," country rock's practitioners have become mainstream. Nashville has come to embrace the California country rock sound. Boasts ex-Poco member and founding Eagle Randy Meisner, "That whole 'new country' scene is inspired by the Eagles, the Burrito Brothers, Poco— all those groups. The young record executives in Nashville grew up on the Eagles and Poco music. They are looking for the 'new' Eagles, but they won't find them." Recent tribute albums have celebrated the legacy of both Gram Parsons (featuring Elvis Costello, the Mavericks, Sheryl Crow, the Pretenders, Steve Earle, and Beck), and Gene Clark (on Not Lame Records with covers by the Continental Drifters, Ghost Rockets, Bill Lloyd, and Steve Wynn, among others). In doing these records, these artists have introduced Parsons and Clark to a whole new audience.

"I do feel like the spirit of those country rock bands was carried through to country radio," says Bill Lloyd, former member of the country duo Foster & Lloyd, and a noted songwriter. "You could hear a lot of Desert Rose Band, Dirt Band, Rodney Crowell, Steve Earle, and Lyle

Lovett on the radio in the eighties. We all had a certain autonomy that most acts just don't have these days. That freedom isn't around in country any more, I'm sad to say."

Raised in Kentucky, Lloyd grew up a dedicated Beatles fan who paid little attention to country music. "Hillbilly wasn't considered cool," he recalls. "The Beatles' *Rubber Soul* had lots of acoustic instruments, and more of a country feel, but I wasn't even conscious of it at the time." For him, the turning point came with the Byrds' *Sweetheart Of The Rodeo*. Lloyd developed an interest in the music of groups like Poco, the Burrito Brothers, the Dillards, Nitty Gritty Dirt Band, and the Eagles. "*Desperado* is one of my favorite albums. All those bands made it okay for me to go search out Hank Williams, George Jones, Bill Monroe, and other giants."

Antipathy toward Nashville's cookie-cutter approach has spawned a new generation of "desperados" working under the flag of "rebel roots" music, a media phrase for a variety of styles that includes alternative country, "No Depression,"[*] "Americana," and "insurgent country." "Nashville has always been ten years behind the music," opines Buddy Woodward, formerly of the Ghost Rockets. "That whole thing in Nashville now sounds like eighties pop to me."

"What Nashville is turning out today," Nan Warshaw[**] told *Discoveries* magazine, "has little to do with country music. It's more to do with soft pop, and it's mall music." For some of these musicians, the line begins at Gram Parsons, who has assumed the role of spiritual godfather and a mentor to country pickers more likely to have grown up on Nirvana and REM than George Jones. Indeed, rebel roots draws its inspiration from a mid-eighties phenomenon known as "cowpunk," a blend of traditional country filtered through an energized punk sensibility. One cowpunk act described their sound as "Hank Williams chained to a Marshall stack." The Long Ryders emerged from the short-lived cowpunk scene, evolving from sixties revivalists to performers following in the footsteps of Gram Parsons and Gene Clark. The group recruited Clark to record a track with them, and would have done the same with Parsons had he not died. Ex-Ryder Sid Griffin, now a member of the Coal Porters, has become the custodian of both Parsons' and Clark's legacies, spearheading reissues of both artists' works.

"We were very aware of those records, the Burritos and others," acknowledges Mark Olson, founding member of the Jayhawks, a leading

---

*Named for both a 1930s-era Carter Family song and the title of the debut album by "alternative country" founders Uncle Tupelo.
**Founder of Chicago's Bloodshot Records, and home of "insurgent country music."

alternative country band and a personal favorite of David Letterman. "They meant something to us. We'd play those songs late at night in bars. I always liked the take the Burritos had on country, the hippie kid getting lost in town. It was cool. Gram wasn't the only mentor but he was one of the guys doing it. His singing with Emmylou Harris, though, was definitely one of the best things that happened. I read that biography of Parsons and was sickened. Basically, he couldn't take care of himself. That kind of soured me holding him up as a role model. But he could sure sing well with Emmylou."

Roots country artist Gillian Welch concurs that the Parsons and Burritos influences remain vital. "You put a certain kind of band together," notes Welch, "and you play a certain attitude, and you kind of sound like the Flying Burrito Brothers. I don't think that's going away anytime soon. Those records influenced a ton of people. That influence is gonna stick around."

"Gram Parsons is fortunate he died *before* he got to make a bad album," muses Buddy Woodward on Parsons' mystique. "And the media latched onto the myth: the young, tortured guy who burned out early, your classic Hollywood drama. I'm not saying Gram wasn't good, he was, but he wasn't the only guy. I was listening to the Byrds, the Dillards, and the Springfield. I heard 'Go And Say Goodbye' and thought, 'I *know* that lick. That's "Salt Creek!"' I'm not saying Gram doesn't deserve the accolades. But he co-wrote a lot of that stuff with Chris Hillman."

In the mid-eighties Nashville paid grudging respect to Parsons with an annual Gram Parsons/Clarence White tribute show. Foster & Lloyd performed, as did Chris Hillman's Desert Rose Band. Roland White has guested with the Nashville Bluegrass Band, while the Dirt Band and Rodney Crowell also appeared regularly. "To have Roland, Hillman, and some of the folks who knew and worked with Clarence and Gram was cool," recalls Bill Lloyd, "but they weren't so into the deification of Gram." Lloyd acknowledges Parsons' pivotal role in the development of country rock. "Gram spoke the loudest about the mix of country, rock, southern soul, and bluegrass and making it into his own cosmic formula."

Gene Clark remains a seminal artist. *"The Fantastic Expedition of Dillard & Clark* was a *great* record!" effuses Victoria Williams, a solo singer/songwriter in her own right and a member of the Original Harmony Ridge Creek Dippers with husband Mark Olson. "I think we learned every song on that album. When I started playing music in

Louisiana we'd go out to this bar where Hank Williams, Elvis, Jerry Jeff Walker, and others would play. Afterward, we'd go back to the house and play until the sun came up. We did Dillard & Clark songs, and Gene Clark's songs, and, of course, Gram Parsons'. They sort of gave me that inspiration to think, 'Well, I'll write songs too, then.' I got to meet Gene Clark when I first moved to California. He was so wonderful. He was one of these people whose music I loved back in Louisiana. I met him at the Whisky. I was in awe of him." Adds Mark Olson, "When you listened to Gene Clark, you realized you were listening to someone who could really sing and write well. For me, listening to that first Dillard & Clark album shoved me more in the folk direction." Olson and Williams duet on Parsons' "In My Hour Of Darkness" on the tribute CD *The Return Of The Grievous Angel*.

"Gene Clark is probably a bigger influence for me than Gram Parsons," states Buddy Woodward. "Gene was a great songwriter and had a better voice than Gram. He was doing it *before* Gram, with 'Keep On Pushin',' and that electric banjo on his first solo album."

Alternative country artists are bringing a renewed vitality to country music. Groups like the Original Harmony Ridge Creek Dippers, Waco Brothers, Continental Drifters, Grievous Angels, Old 97's, Ghost Rockets, Coal Porters, and artists like Lucinda Williams and Gillian Welch, to name but a few, have led the charge. Their new efforts in traditional country, bluegrass, and country rock offer an appealing diversion from the slick country pop of Garth Brooks and Shania Twain. There is a reverence among them for the traditional roots of folk country music—like the Carter Family, Jimmie Rodgers, and Hank Williams—and a desire to bring it to younger audiences. In that sense they share similar goals with the musicians in the late sixties who pioneered country rock. "Those country rockers of the sixties were trying to take an old form and renew it," muses Buddy Woodward. "What *we're* trying to do, the alternative country artists today, is to take it back to the early days, the roots. We'll go back and do a Bill Monroe tune straight, the right way, the way Bill did it. Putting a funk beat on *Blue Moon Of Kentucky* has been done. Putting elements of the old style into something new makes it new again. I guess there's an irony in that somewhere."

For Woodward, his own epiphany as a young country rocker came, strangely enough, via the Monkees. "When I heard the Monkees on TV doing 'What Am I Doing Hangin' Round' it freaked me out. There was that Earl Scruggs banjo style, I didn't know at that time it was actually Doug Dillard, and there's that rock beat, and they all looked cool and were having a helluva good time. They had harmonies, Mike Nesmith singing, and that twang with a rock beat. I just said, 'That's it!' It was like in the *Wizard of Oz* when Dorothy walks out of the house after the tornado, all of a sudden everything's in Technicolor. I'd been bringing Buck Owens records to school, and they'd laugh at me because the other kids were bringing in rock & roll records. I just figured here's something my friends can dig too."

Despite his status in the media as country rock guru, for most alternative country musicians Gram Parsons is the middleman between the old and the new: Buck, George, Hank, and the Louvin Brothers were the sounds he introduced into the mix. "I followed it back from the Burritos and Byrds to Willie, Waylon, Buck Owens—all that stuff," enthuses Mark Olson. "I was into Waylon Jennings' folk records. He made a bunch of folk records before he made those honky-tonk albums. And I liked the Glaser Brothers. Anytime there was a lead I could investigate I got into it. We had record stores that carried all that stuff, and you could find all sorts of country records: Buck Owens, Tommy Collins, and Merle Haggard. Those three guys had a great sound, that Bakersfield sound. They wrote real meaningful songs. It was good music."

Young groups like the Texas-based Derailers are taking fans back to Parsons' influences by championing Buck Owens and the Buckaroos, and Merle Haggard and the Strangers. "Where some people stop their search at Gram Parsons or the Burrito Brothers," muses Derailers' leader Tony Villanueva, "I'd much rather listen to Buck Owens or George Jones. You've got to keep going back. The Buckaroos had a mystique about them; they were just the coolest thing going. That twangy Telecaster, dual vocal sound. Very stripped down and in your face. That's probably our primary influence."

The Derailers offer a unique twist on the West Coast sound with "California Angel" on their *Reverb Deluxe* album, blending the Beach Boys with the Buckaroos. "It kind of has that California groove to it, that 'go go twist' beat, and those guitars loud and wild," laughs Villanueva.

"Gram Parsons' music really played a part in my finding old-time country and then further on," offers Gillian Welch. "Through him, I got into Buck Owens and Merle Haggard, and then after that I got into Lefty Frizzell."

Dwight Yoakam set out to revive the legacy of Buck Owens in the early nineties, before shifting gears to a more hard rockin' country sound with his *This Time* record. Yoakam also spearheaded Nashville's reassessment of Elvis Presley as a country music pioneer, covering his "Little Sister" and "Suspicious Minds." Nevertheless, like his early mentor, Yoakam remains an outsider in Nashville, a true rebel. He has even recorded a version of the Parsons-Hillman Burritos-era classic "Sin City."

Tony Villanueva rejects labeling the Derailers' music. He finds it difficult to define his sound. "I like to call it American music, that's what we play. It's country music. Back in 1966, Buck Owens called his music American music, because at that time they were dealing with being called hillbilly music. He didn't like that. American music works good for me." Adds Woodward, "I'm not sure where the Ghost Rockets fit in, but I know we're similar to the California country rock pioneers. We've got so many different influences that we're utilizing it's hard to put us into any one particular bag."

"Labels have never been important to me," maintains Victoria Williams. "As with all things, it depends on the person speaking and what their definition of country may be. I think what I'm doing is more like soul/country/folk or country/folk soul. The people who have influenced my life have done so because they're honest in their music. I think people now are going back to a sound where you can hear the story again. And magazines like *No Depression* really seem to get in-depth with the music."

Rebel roots music has much in common with early country rock. Both are imbued with an appreciation for the integrity and authenticity of traditional American roots music, coupled with a sincere desire to integrate country music into a more contemporary setting that will appeal to younger audiences alienated from mainstream country. This is where the Parsons influence comes into play, his dedication to a Cosmic American Music: uniting the hippie and redneck, traditional and modern. Both movements began as fringe musical forms, perceived as too left-of-center to garner commercial acceptance. "It's a struggle when you're doing something different," concedes Villanueva. "We have a community that is struggling, playing honky-tonks—and no one knows who we are."

Record sales for rebel roots music, as well as support from radio, has been weak. There are exceptions. Lucinda Williams' recent album sold a quarter of a million copies. Enfant terrible Steve Earle, the epitome of a country music rebel, continues to toil away in relative obscurity, content to release independently produced albums sold to the faithful. Major label interest remains illusive. "If it wasn't for magazines like *No*

*Depression*," emphasizes Olson, "there'd be nobody out there to hear it. Websites, too. They keep people interested. When the Jayhawks started touring, we were playing to fifteen people at a time. You have to reach more if you want to make a living at it."

"The current scene is full of excitement right now," says Bill Lloyd, whose most recent album draws more from the Beatles than Buck and Merle. "Like the early days of punk, it has become a movement. Like punk, there's an 'anyone can do it' spirit. The courage to just fly with it is what country radio lacks. That's where the term 'alternative country' really *means* something."

Mark Olson rejects the notion that there is a united alternative scene. "There are what I'd consider a number of like-minded individuals who I've run across over the years who enjoy listening to country records and playing some of those great songs. I certainly did that. Really good themes and ideas. And for the most part, people who take it from that angle they don't give a hoot about success, otherwise they wouldn't be doing it. They're doing it because they feel drawn to that kind of music."

Rebel roots, or alternative country, remains a subculture of country music that has yet to gain mainstream acceptance. But it appears to be garnering increasing attention. "So many people only know what's on television, CMT and TNN," offers Villanueva. "But we've been getting a good reception in Nashville. We have a lot of support there."

Much like the sixties country rock pioneers, alternative country is carrying the torch for a purer form of American country music. "People are looking for something that makes them *feel* good," insists Mark Olson, "and that music will make you feel good. It just seems like there are a number of groups out there where that kind of spirit lives on."

# A Selected Country Rock Discography

All listings are CD releases unless otherwise noted (*) as vinyl records.

Buffalo Springfield:
Last Time Around—Atco 90393-2
Retrospective—Atco 38105-2

The Byrds:
Younger than Yesterday—Columbia CK 64848
Notorious Byrd Brothers—Columbia CK 65151
Sweetheart of the Rodeo—Columbia CK 65150
Ballad of Easy Rider—Columbia CK 65114
Live at the Fillmore—Columbia/Legacy CK 65910
Dr. Byrds & Mr. Hyde—Columbia CK 65113

Gene Clark:
Echoes—Columbia/Legacy CK 48523
Gene Clark with the Gosdin Brothers—Edsel ED CD 529; Columbia
Special Products 75016
Roadmaster—Edsel ED CD 198
American Dreamer 1964–1974—Raven RV CD 21 (Australia)
Flying High—A&M 540 725-2

Country Gazette:
A Traitor in Our Midst*—United Artists UAS 5596

Dillard & Clark:
Fantastic Expedition of Dillard and Clark—Edsel ED CD192
Through the Morning, Through the Night—Edsel ED CD 195

The Dillards:
Wheatstraw Suite*—Elektra EKS 74035
Copperfields*—Elektra EKS 74054
There Is a Time 1963–1970/Best Of—Vanguard VSD VCD 131/32
Roots and Branches/Tribute to the American Duck—Beat Goes On 306

Bob Dylan:
Nashville Skyline—Columbia CK 9825

The Eagles:
Eagles—Asylum SD 5054
Desperado—Asylum SD 5068

The First National Band:
Loose Salute*—RCA Victor LSP 4415
Magnetic South*—RCA Victor LSP 4371
Nevada Fighter*—RCA Victor LSP 4497
Listen to the Band—Camden 523772 (UK)
Complete—Pacific Arts Audio Inc. PAAD 5066

The Flying Burrito Brothers:
The Gilded Palace of Sin—Edsel ED CD 191
Burrito Deluxe—Edsel ED CD 194
Flying Burrito Brothers—Mobile Fidelity MFCD 772
Last of the Red Hot Burritos—A&M SP 4343
Close Up the Honky Tonks*—A&M SP 3631
Hot Burrito—A&M 294343-2 (Netherlands)
Live in Amsterdam*—Bumble 301 (Netherlands)
Dim Lights, Thick Smoke & Loud, Loud Music—Edsel ED CD 197
Farther Along—A&M SP 5216
Out of the Blue—A&M SP 540408
Hot Burritos—Anthology 1969–1972—A&M Universal 069 490 610-2

The Great Speckled Bird:
Great Speckled Bird—Stony Plain SP CD 1200

Emmylou Harris:
Pieces of the Sky—Reprise 1202284
Elite Hotel—Reprise 1202286
Luxury Liner—Reprise 1203115

Hearts And Flowers:
Now Is the Time for Hearts and Flowers/Of Horses, Kids and Forgotten Women—Edsel ED CD 428

Chris Hillman and Herb Pedersen:
Bakersfield Bound—Sugar Hill SH 3850

Ian and Sylvia:
Nashville—Vanguard VSD 79284
Long Long Time —Vanguard VSD 79478
Movin' On 1967–1968—Mercury 314-538-563-2

The International Submarine Band:
Safe at Home—Sierra SCD 4088

Longbranch Pennywhistle:
Longbranch Pennywhistle*—Amos 7007

Ian Mathews:
Valley Hi*—Elektra EKS 75061

Nashville West:
Nashville West—Sierra SCD 6016

Rick Nelson (& The Stone Canyon Band):
Bright Lights and Country Music*—Decca DL 74779
Country Fever*—Decca DL 74827
Rick Nelson in Concert*—Decca DL 75162
Rudy the Fifth*—Decca DL 75297
Garden Party*—Decca DL 75391
Rick Nelson & The Stone Canyon Band, 1969–1976—Edsel ED CD 417
Rick Nelson & The Stone Canyon Band, Vol. 2—Edsel ED CD 521

The Nitty Gritty Dirt Band:
Uncle Charlie and His Dog Teddy—Liberty CDP 0 777-7-90430-2-6
All the Good Times—Beat Goes On 93

Will the Circle Be Unbroken—EMI E2-46589
Will the Circle Be Unbroken, Vol. 2—Universal UVLD 12500

Buck Owens:
I've Got a Tiger by the Tail*—Capitol ST 2283
Best*—Capitol ST 2105
Carnegie Hall Concert*—Capitol ST 2556
Very Best Of—Warner R2 71816
The Buck Owens Collection (1959–1990)—Rhino R2 71016

Gene Parsons:
Kindling—Sierra SCD 6007

Gram Parsons:
GP/Grievous Angel—Reprise 9 26108-2
Sleepless Nights*—A&M SP 4578
Gram Parsons and the Fallen Angels: Live 1973—Sierra SCD 6002
Warm Evenings, Pale Mornings—Raven RV CD 24 (Australia)

Poco:
Pickin' Up the Pieces—Epic/Legacy EK 66227
Poco (2nd album)—Epic EK 26522
From the Inside—Epic EK 30753
Deliverin'—Epic EK 30209
Good Feelin' to Know—Epic EK 31601
Crazy Eyes—Epic EK 66968
Rose of Cimarron—MCA MCAD 22076
The Forgotten Trail—Epic/Legacy E2K 46162

Pure Prairie League:
Best of Pure Prairie League—Mercury 314-528-236-2

Rick Roberts:
Windmills*—A&M SP 4372
She Is a Song*—A&M SP 4404

Linda Ronstadt:
Hand Sown . . . Home Grown*—Capitol ST 208
Silk Purse*—Capitol ST 407
Linda Ronstadt*—Capitol SMAS 635
Don't Cry Now*—Asylum SD 5064

Shiloh:
Shiloh*—Amos AAS 7015

Paul Siebel:
Paul Siebel—Philo CD PH 1161

Sneaky Pete:
Cold Steel*—Ariola 87 736 ET (Netherlands)

J. D. Souther:
John David Souther*—Asylum SD 5055

John Stewart:
California Bloodlines—See For Miles SEE CD 87

Steve Young:
Rock Salt and Nails—Edsel ED CD 193

Various Artists:
Heroes of Country Music, Vol. 5: Legends of Country Rock—Rhino R2 72444

# Acknowledgments

I would like to extend my sincere thanks to all those whose names appear throughout the book for their willingness to share their time and recollections in interviews with me. As well, special acknowledgment is due to the following, who were invaluable to me in the research and preparation of this book: Chris Hillman for all his support and assistance with contacts; Richie Furay for his continuing friendship and encouragement; Holger Petersen at Stony Plain Records (Box 861, Edmonton, Alberta, Canada, T5J 2L8); Al Perkins for his many contacts and support; Jim Colegrove; Tim Connors (ByrdWatcher website: http://ebni.com/byrds) for being an early sounding board for me; James McKelvey for graciously providing his Steve Young interview; Poco archivist extraordinaire Jerry Fuentes (thanks once again for helping me get another one out); Buddy Woodward (founder and leader of the fabulous Ghost Rockets: "maximum rhythm and bluegrass"—http://www.hudsonet.com/~undertow /ghostrockets—currently fronting the Nitro Express) for valuable advice, expertise, and contacts; Cheryl "Pinkie" Jennings for all her contributions, tapes, and support; Nicholas Jennings; Nurit Wilde and Jason Nesmith; Victoria Foreman at the Videoranch (http://www.videoranch.com); Sierra Records and Books (PO Box 5853, Pasadena, California, 91117-0853); Johnny Rogan; Dave Zimmer (el supremo CSN historian and friend); Kenton Adler (Byrds website: http://www.uark.edu/~kadler /rmcguinn/); Traci Thomas at Grass Roots; Peter van Leeuwen down in Curaçao for providing the introduction to Mr. Cotton; Jim Ciborski; Jeffery Dunn in Nashville for the southern hospitality, tapes, and contacts; Dillards fan par excellence Randy Dawson (Dillards website:

http://home1.gte.net/padlock/dillards/index.htm); the real Rick
Roberts; Lisa and Melissa on the Eagles list; Gib Guilbeau; and Re-
bekah Radisch at Sugar Hill Records (PO Box 55300, Durham, North
Carolina, 27717).

Thanks also to Rob Matthews in New Zealand for the CDs that originally helped to inspire this book; Colorado music historian Michael
Stelk (for all the articles and tapes); Tom Robinson (http://members
@aol.com/byrdsonlne/byrdsstuff/byrds.htm); Greg Tonn and John
Neal at Into The Music, Winnipeg, Manitoba (http://www.intomusic
.mb.ca); Chris Hollow way down in the land of Oz for the Gene Clark
tape;   Ken Varga; Ralf Narfeldt (Gene Clark homepage http:
//ps.ket.kth.se/gc/); Mike Ward; Carny Corbett; Stuart Rosenberg for
his relentless research; Michelle Stevens (John Stewart website:
http://stevens.cnchost.com); Tom Ordon; Billy Gerstein; Torbjorn Or-
rgard (Poco website: http://www.geocities.com/SunsetStrip/8385
/continue.html); Danny Casavant; Mark Gould; Johnny Black at *Mojo*;
my friend Paul Nicholas over in Wales; John McEuen (http:
//www.johnmceuen.com). Special thanks go to Mark Fladeland, Dave
Tikes, Richie Unterberger (author of *Unknown Legends of Rock 'n' Roll*),
David Marsteller, Steve Cafarelli, Johnny Norris, Don Loiacano, Steve
Rowe, Kevin Dockrell, Brandon Rose, Dennis Richards, and
Jeremy R. Bierlein for sharing their thoughts on country rock with me.

The following served as invaluable resources: various articles and
chronologies on country rock artists by Pete Frame, Brian Hogg, and
John Tobler in *ZigZag* magazine; *Timeless Flight: The Definitive Biogra-
phy of the Byrds* by Johnny Rogan (Square One Books); *Hickory Wind:
The Life and Times of Gram Parsons* by Ben Fong-Torres (Pocket Books);
*Gram Parsons: A Musical Biography* by Sid Griffin (Sierra Books); *Pete
Frame's Rock Family Trees* (Omnibus); *Everybody on the Truck: The Story
of the Dillards* by Lee Grant (Eggman Publishing); *The Long Run: The
Story of the Eagles* by Marc Shapiro (Omnibus); *I Never Sold My Sad-
dle* by Ian Tyson with Colin Escott (Douglas and McIntyre); *Ricky
Nelson: Idol for a Generation* by Joel Selvin (Contemporary); *Teenage
Idol, Travellin' Man: Rick Nelson* by Philip Bashe (Hyperion); "Rebel
Roots," an article by Alex Green in the April 1999 issue of *Discoveries*
magazine; and *The Legends of Country Rock, Volume 5*, from Rhino
Records.

A special thanks to Ron Ade (Fillmore, Riley, Barristers & Solicitors)
for helping me pick up the pieces and make a fresh start. Thanks to
Dave Zimmer for introducing me to Michael Dorr.

And extra special thanks, as always, to my wonderful family—my wife Harriett, son Matt, and daughter Lynsey—for all their love, support, and understanding.

John Einarson

# About the Author

John Einarson is a respected rock music historian and writer based in Winnipeg, Canada. He has written feature articles for *Goldmine, Record Collector, Mojo,* and *Rock Express,* among others, and has written for television and radio. He has published a number of music history books, including *Shakin' All Over: The Winnipeg Sixties Rock Scene* as well as biographies of Neil Young, John Kay and Steppenwolf, the Guess Who, Buffalo Springfield, and Randy Bachman. In addition, he has contributed to several recent CD compilation projects.

John lives in Winnipeg with his wife Harriett, son Matthew, and daughter Lynsey, where he teaches history at St. John's-Ravenscourt School. He has written or contributed to several textbooks, teaching manuals, and educational kits. Each year he organizes a popular rock & roll revue at his school, involving close to one hundred students.

# OTHER COOPER SQUARE PRESS TITLES OF INTEREST

**LENNON IN AMERICA**
**1971–1980, Based in Part on the Lost Lennon Diaries**
Geoffrey Giuliano
300 pp., 50 b/w photos
0-8154-1073-5
$27.95

**DREAMGIRL & SUPREME FAITH**
**My Life as a Supreme**
Updated Edition
Mary Wilson
732 pp., 15 color photos, 150 b/w photos
0-8154-1000-X
$19.95

**MICK JAGGER**
**Primitive Cool**
Updated Edition
Christopher Sandford
354 pp., 56 b/w photos
0-8154-1002-6
$16.95

**ROCK 100**
**The Greatest Stars of Rock's Golden Age**
David Dalton and Lenny Kaye
288 pp., 195 photos
0-8154-1017-4
$19.95

**ROCK SHE WROTE**
**Women Write About Rock, Pop, and Rap**
Edited by Evelyn McDonnell and Ann Powers
496 pp.
0-8154-1018-2
$16.95

## SUMMER OF LOVE
The Inside Story of LSD, Rock & Roll,
Free Love and High Times in the Wild West
Joel Selvin
392 pp., 23 b/w photos
0-8154-1019-0
$23.95

## FAITHFULL
An Autobiography
David Dalton
320 pp., 32 b/w photos
0-8154-1046-8
$16.95

## ANY OLD WAY YOU CHOOSE IT
Rock and Other Pop Music, 1967–1973
Expanded Edition
Robert Christgau
360 pp.
0-8154-1041-7
$16.95

## HE'S A REBEL
Phil Spector—Rock and Roll's Legendary Producer
Mark Ribowsky
368 pp., 35 b/w photos
0-8154-1044-1
$17.95

## THE BLUES
In Images and Interviews
Robert Neff and Anthony Connor
152 pp., 84 b/w photos
0-8154-1003-4
$17.95

## TURNED ON
A Biography of Henry Rollins
James Parker
280 pp., 10 b/w photos
0-8154-1050-6
$17.95

**MADONNA**
**Blonde Ambition**
Updated Edition
Mark Bego
368 pp., 57 b/w photos
0-8154-1051-4
$18.95

**GOIN' BACK TO MEMPHIS**
**A Century of Blues, Rock 'n' Roll and Glorious Soul**
James Dickerson
284 pp., 58 b/w photos
0-8154-1049-2
$16.95

**HARMONICAS, HARPS, AND HEAVY BREATHERS**
**The Evolution of the People's Instrument**
**Updated Edition**
Kim Field
368 pp., 32 b/w photos
0-8154-1020-4
$18.95

Available at bookstores; or call 1-800-462-6420

 **Cooper Square Press**

150 Fifth Avenue
Suite 911
New York, NY 10011